19-

# Unnatural Doubts

# Unnatural Doubts

*Epistemological Realism and the Basis of
Scepticism*

MICHAEL WILLIAMS

PRINCETON UNIVERSITY PRESS
PRINCETON, NEW JERSEY

Copyright © 1996 by Princeton University Press
Published by Princeton University Press, 41 William Street,
Princeton, New Jersey 08540
In the United Kingdom: Princeton University Press, Chichester,
West Sussex

First published by Blackwell Publishers, Inc.,
3 Cambridge Center, Cambridge, Massachusetts 02142

*Library of Congress Cataloging-in-Publication Data*

Williams, Michael, 1947 July 6
    Unnatural doubts : epistemological realism and the basis of
scepticism / Michael Williams.
        p.   cm.
    Includes bibliographical references and index.
    ISBN 0-691-01115-X (pbk. : alk. paper)
    1. Knowledge, Theory of.   2. Realism.   3. Skepticism.   I. Title.
[BD161.W49    1995]
121'.2—dc20                                                      95-40064

This book has been composed in Baskerville

Princeton University Press books are printed on acid-free paper
and meet the guidelines for permanence and durability of the
Committee on Production Guidelines for Book Longevity of the
Council on Library Resources

Printed in the United States of America by Princeton Academic Press

1   3   5   7   9   10   8   6   4   2

*For Meredith*

*This sceptical doubt, both with respect to reason and the senses, is a malady, which can never be radically cur'd, but must return upon us every moment, however we may chace it away, and sometimes may seem entirely free from it. 'Tis impossible upon any system to defend either our understanding or senses; and we expose them farther when we endeavour to justify them in that manner. As the sceptical doubt arises naturally from a profound and intense reflection on those subjects, it always encreases, the farther we carry our reflection, whether in opposition or conformity to it. (Hume.)*

*We need to realise that what presents itself to us as the first expression of a difficulty, or of its solution, may not yet be correctly expressed at all. Just as one who has a just censure of a picture to make will often at first offer the censure where it does not belong, and an* investigation *is needed in order to find the right point of attack for the critic. (Wittgenstein.)*

# Contents

# Preface

My claim is this: there is no such thing as knowledge of the external world. The same goes for knowledge of other minds, knowledge of the past, and other such familiar objects of epistemological investigation. Whether or not I convince anyone of this, I hope at least to open up a line of inquiry.

How does this differ from scepticism? Isn't scepticism the view that there is no such thing as knowledge? In a sense. However, intended sceptically, the claim that there is no such thing as knowledge of the external world would be meant to imply that it is never correct to credit someone with knowing something about ordinary physical objects. By contrast, I want to suggest that though we correctly credit people with such knowledge all the time, even so there is no such thing as knowledge of the external world. My objection is not to what would generally be taken to be *examples* of such knowledge but to the idea of knowledge of the external world as a *kind* of knowledge, which we might assess or explain as a whole. More generally, I am concerned with the very idea of knowledge as an object of theory. I think that asking how we have to conceive knowledge, for knowledge to be an object of theory, is the key to understanding scepticism.

As I hope to show, all this bears on what I believe to be a deep and important issue: the relation of philosophical reflection, at least as it has often been conceived, to everyday epistemological practices. To bring this issue into focus, I take as my point of departure Hume's vision of an irremediable conflict between our everyday attitude towards our beliefs about the world around us and the attitude to which (he thought) we are inevitably led by sustained, reflective philosophical inquiry into their grounds and status. Everyday life is characterized by a kind of natural certainty, expressed in our willingness to claim not just to believe but actually to know all sorts of things about the world we live in. Of course, there are many things that we don't know, and many that we will never know. But for all that, there are many things that we do know; and some are so simple that, in the ordinary course of events, we are incapable of doubting them, even to the slightest extent. However, when we step back from our immediate, everyday concerns and ask whether those beliefs amount to knowledge, we experience a disturbing transformation. We find ourselves driven inexorably to the conclusion that none of our ordinary beliefs really do amount to knowledge or that, even if by some standards they do, we will never understand how. If, at least with respect to our simplest factual beliefs, certainty is the natural condition of ordinary life, scepticism is the natural outcome of philosophical reflection. Thus we are left with two ways of looking at the world, which we can never reconcile. But one cuts deeper than the other: scepticism points to a profound, albeit normally incredible, truth about the human condition.

Recent years have seen a remarkable revival of this Humean attitude. Not all the philosophers who have contributed to this revival accept the entire Humean package, but the central Humean themes – scepticism as the apparently inevitable outcome of the quest for philosophical understanding, and the consequent clash between philosophy and ordinary life – play a decisive role in shaping their philosophical conclusions. Thus the burden of Barry Stroud's meticulous analysis of anti-sceptical strategies in *The Significance of Philosophical Scepticism* is that scepticism is at least conditionally correct, in the sense that it is the inevitable result of the sort of assessment of human knowledge that philosophy has traditionally undertaken. Like Hume, Stroud thinks that we set foot on the road to scepticism *as soon as we ask distinctively philosophical questions* about human knowledge. Thomas Nagel's *The View from Nowhere* comes to a very similar conclusion: as philosophers, we try to understand our place in the world from a fully objective standpoint; and scepticism is inherent in any such attempt at objective understanding of our capacity for knowledge. Taking up an objective standpoint, Nagel Tells us, "produces a split in the self which will not go away." In a similarly pessimistic vein, P. F. Strawson explicitly advocates a return to Hume: we have no reason to expect a decisive theoretical response to sceptical problems, and so we should content ourselves with Hume's "naturalistic" solution to scepticism. This is that there are convictions so fundamental that they can be neither undermined nor usefully supported by argument: and this is *all* that can be said by way of reply to the sceptic.[1]

It is particularly striking that similar attitudes can be detected even in philosophers who are either untroubled by traditional sceptical concerns or who think that the sceptic's objections can be turned aside. Thus Quine's suggestion that we let psychology *replace* traditional epistemology takes off from the thought that "the Humean condition is the human condition." And Stanley Cavell, though he finds the sceptic's procedure ultimately incoherent, remains drawn to the thought that there is a residual and deeply significant "truth of scepticism": that "the human creature's basis in the world as a whole, its relation to the world as such, is not that of knowing, anyway not what we think of as knowing." The sceptic may be wrong to claim that we don't know the simplest things, but this is not exactly because we *do* know them after all.[2]

I think that this "New Scepticism" is one of the most important movements in contemporary philosophy. It represents a powerful reaction to post-Wittgensteinian (or "ordinary language") and neo-pragmatist tendencies to *dismiss* traditional philosophical problems, particularly sceptical problems, as not real problems at all.

The first kind of dismissal finds that the sceptic's characteristic claims and arguments rest on distortions or misunderstandings of ordinary epistemic concepts. Or perhaps they are based on violations or misunderstandings of the general conditions for meaningful discourse. Either way, if the distortions are sufficiently severe, the sceptic will be found to lapse into serious conceptual incoherence, hence not to advance any significant claims. So either way, there will be no clash between ordinary claims to knowledge and the results of philosophical inquiry.

The New Sceptics, or New Humeans, are unconvinced. The fact is that we seem to understand the sceptic very well, certainly well enough to understand how to argue against him or why so many popular antisceptical arguments fail. It is therefore difficult for us to convince ourselves that we do not understand the sceptic at all: so difficult in fact that the intuitive intelligibility of scepticism creates a severe problem for views about meaning that entail its incoherence. And as for the charge that the sceptic distorts the meaning of ordinary epistemic terms, this is not easy to show either. Rather it seems, as Bernard Williams puts it, that there is something in our ordinary concept of knowledge that "contains a standing invitation to scepticism."[3] True, it may be that this sceptical potential in our ordinary concept of knowledge is ordinarily and even in a way justifiably ignored; it may be that only in the course of philosophical reflection, when ordinary practical concerns have been set aside, that we can hold it clearly in view; but this does nothing to show that scepticism results from a distortion or misunderstanding or ordinary epistemic concepts, rather than, say, from a peculiarly sustained and uncompromising scrutiny of them.

The second kind of dismissal of scepticism comes from seeing it as tied to an outmoded and artificial philosophical project, typically the Cartesian "quest for certainty." This project encourages, perhaps even demands, a strongly foundationalist conception of knowledge and justification, and, given such a view of knowledge, we will never understand how we have knowledge of the world around us. But if we abandon the Cartesian project and the epistemological preconceptions associated with it, the threat of scepticism will recede.

Here too the New Sceptics are dubious. They do not doubt that sceptical problems *can* be generated by certain theoretical preconceptions about human knowledge, but they deny that such preconceptions constitute the deep source of sceptical concerns. For them, scepticism is an *intuitive* problem, a problem that can be posed and understood without prior indoctrination in contentious theoretical ideas. Indeed, they are inclined to think that this neo-pragmatist dismissal of scepticism gets things backwards. Theoretical views, such as foundationalism, are *reactions to* the threat of scepticism, not the *sources from which* the threat arises.

In thinking of scepticism as an intuitive problem, the New Sceptics are rightly impressed by the simplicity, brevity and seeming transparency of typical sceptical arguments, compared with the difficulty and frequent obscurity of the positive theories of knowledge advanced to combat them. Sceptical arguments, they tend to think, appeal to something deep in our nature, and so sceptical conclusions, if correct, reveal something profound and disturbing about the human condition. Scepticism is the inevitable outcome of questions that, to creatures like us, come naturally. Thus although some philosophers treat "the sceptic" as a mere literary invention, complaining that their colleagues who take scepticism seriously spend their time refuting an adversary that has never existed, if the New Sceptic's are right, this too is badly wrong. If scepticism is inherent in the quest for a philosophical understanding of human knowledge, and if the urge to ask philosophical questions is rooted in something deep in our nature, then the figure of the sceptic is no invention: he is all of us in our philosophical moments.

I believe, then, that what I have been calling the New Scepticism forces us to confront a vital question, one that has never been adequately considered. This question is: "Is scepticism really a natural or intuitive problem?" If it is, then Hume is right, and we will never reconcile everyday attitudes with the results of philosophical reflection. The best we will be able to do, as Nagel argues, is to "live in light of the truth" that no reconciliation will ever be accomplished. I believe also that we must admit that the New Sceptics make a powerful case for the inadequacy of the standard ways of dismissing scepticism. To avoid their pessimistic conclusions, then, we will have to do better.

What are the different ways in which we might respond to scepticism? In first approximation, we can distinguish two main approaches, the "constructive" and the "diagnostic." They are represented, respectively, by Kant's famous remark that "it remains a scandal to philosophy . . . that the existence of things outside us . . . must be accepted merely on faith and that if anyone thinks good to doubt their existence, we are unable to counter his doubts by any satisfactory proof," and by Heidegger's ironic reply that "The 'scandal of philosophy' is not that this proof is yet to be

given, but that such proofs are expected and attempted again and again."
The constructive epistemologist hopes to meet the sceptic by arguing for
a positive theory of knowledge, a theory that will enable him to explain
how and to what extent knowledge, especially knowledge of the world, is
possible. He therefore takes the sceptic's questions more or less at face
value. By contrast, the diagnostically inclined philosopher suspects that
there is something drastically wrong with the way the questions are posed.
Accordingly, he thinks that the appropriate response to scepticism is not
a proof of what the sceptic doubts but further investigation of his claims
to doubt it.

Though far from completely clear cut, the constructive/diagnostic distinction is useful enough as a rough guide. On the whole, the New Sceptics
are certain that no adequate constructive response to scepticism has ever
been given, and most doubt that any ever will be. Stroud even thinks that
there is a pervasive element of bad faith or self-deception in the way that
we so often pursue questions in the theory of knowledge. We are aware,
Stroud thinks, that asking distinctively philosophical questions about
knowledge pushes us inexorably in the direction of scepticism. At the same
time, we cannot regard scepticism as a satisfactory outcome of philosophical inquiry. The result is that we "continue to acquiesce in the traditional
problem and do not acknowledge that there is no satisfactory solution. We
proceed as if it must be possible to find an answer, so we deny the force,
and even the interest, of scepticism."[4] Perhaps this is further evidence of
the difficulty of coming to terms with the irreconcilable conflict between
our everyday attitudes and the lessons of philosophy.

As to the prospects of our coming up with a satisfactory constructive
response to scepticism, my sympathies are very much with the New Sceptics. So I think that if we are ever to come to terms with philosophical
scepticism, it will have to be by way of a deep diagnosis of its sources.
But here too, as we have seen, the New Sceptics are pessimistic about
our chances.

We must, however, distinguish two forms of diagnosis, corresponding
to the two strategies for "dismissing" sceptical problems discussed above.
As we saw, some philosophers who think that sceptical problems need to
be "dissolved" rather than "solved" argue that sceptical claims and arguments are defective in point of meaning. They think that the sceptic does
not mean what he seems to mean, or even that he fails to mean anything
at all. Clearly, we do not need to "answer" the sceptic if he fails to ask
a coherent question. I call this approach "therapeutic diagnosis."

Here I agree once more with the New Sceptics: we will never find it
easy to convince ourselves that we do not understand the sceptic at all.
Rather, our sense that we *do* understand him — well enough at least to

appreciate why certain anti-sceptical strategies are doomed to fail – works against the credibility of views about meaning that suggest we don't. For this reason, I prefer what I call "theoretical diagnosis." The aim of theoretical diagnosis is to show that sceptical arguments derive their force, not from commonsensical intuitions about knowledge, but from theoretical ideas that we are by no means bound to accept.

The distinction between therapeutic and theoretical diagnosis is no more clear-cut than that between constructive and diagnostic strategies, and perhaps less so. In particular, if we think that the sceptic's deep theoretical presuppositions have to do with meaning, and that these presuppositions encourage an illusory sense of his having presented coherent problems, the distinction threatens to vanish. So to sharpen the distinction, I think of theoretical diagnosis as the project of investigating the sceptic's distinctively epistemological ideas: his ideas about knowledge and justification. Even this need not yield a knife-edged distinction: it will not do so if we include among the sceptic's epistemological ideas his ideas about truth, for it is not clear to everyone that questions about truth should or even can be cleanly separated from questions about meaning. But in practice, the distinction is useful enough, especially since I do not think that ideas about truth really have much to do with scepticism. Accordingly, my kind of theoretical diagnosis stays well clear of controversial issues in the philosophy of language. In any case, the main point of distinguishing theoretical from therapeutic diagnosis is to underline the fact that my diagnostic strategy nowhere depends on accusing the sceptic of incoherence. Indeed, as we shall see, the kind of theoretical diagnosis I propose is not just distinct from all versions of therapeutic diagnosis but incompatible with them.

The immediate aim of theoretical diagnosis, as I understand it, is to redistribute the burden of theory, thereby depriving the sceptic of what would otherwise be an overwhelming dialectical advantage. If, as the New Sceptics tend to think, scepticism presents an "intuitive" problem, a problem arising out of tensions in our most ordinary ideas about knowledge and justification, the burden of theory falls squarely on the critic, and theoretical responses fare badly against intuitive problems. I think that this inequality in the burden of theory is what dooms therapeutic diagnosis too. Although arguing that the sceptic's claims are incoherent may obviate the need for a constructive response at the level of epistemology, it will require shouldering a considerable burden of theory with respect to the character of linguistic meaning: far more than the sceptic seems to shoulder in posing what seem to many people to be perfectly intelligible questions. To make headway against the sceptic, then, the critic needs first to level the playing field. It may not be necessary to shift the burden of theory entirely to the sceptic's shoulders. but it is crucial that the sceptic be forced to acknowledge his share. In fact, however, I think that in the end we shall find that the sceptic's share is larger than his critic's.

Many theoretical diagnoses have been put forward. Scepticism has been traced to a misguided "spectator theory" of knowledge, to the dualism of subject and object, to the quest for certainty, to thinking of "experience" as a kind of impenetrable veil between ourselves and "reality," and to the correspondence theory of truth. Here too I agree with the New Sceptics: these familiar diagnoses, in their usual forms, are all inadequate, when not simply mistaken. This said, however, I continue to believe that the threat of scepticism is indissolubly linked to a foundational conception of knowledge, which I distinguish from all the suggestions just alluded to. I therefore continue to believe that to understand scepticism we need to understand how foundationalist ideas inform sceptical arguments and how foundationalism itself goes wrong. But my understanding of foundationalism is such that this diagnosis should prove to be much less familiar than it sounds. My understanding of foundationalism is intimately connected to my thought that there may be no such thing as our knowledge of the external world.

I expect the very idea of theoretical diagnosis to encounter intuitive resistance. To feel to the full the force of sceptical arguments is to undergo a powerful, perhaps formative, intellectual experience. Accordingly, if ideas that have often been connected with scepticism come under a cloud, as has surely happened to one degree or another with all those alluded to above, it is only natural that some philosophers should want to detach the problem of scepticism from all such ideas. But more than that, it may seem to many that the project of theoretical diagnosis wears its hopelessness on its sleeve. Isn't it just obvious that scepticism is an intuitive problem? Or if it isn't just obvious, isn't it established conclusively by the fact that sceptical problems can easily be made intelligible to people with no prior acquaintance with recondite philosophical theories of knowledge? Compare sceptical problems with, say, the apparent paradoxes of relativity theory. These are paradigmatic of problems that arise within a definite theoretical framework and so can only be explained to those who have been schooled in the relevant theory. Surely sceptical problems are nothing like that.

In fact, I do not think that apparent immediate intelligibility indicates independence of problematic theoretical preconceptions. Think of Zeno's paradoxes of motion. They too can be explained fairly readily to the scientifically unschooled. Nevertheless, the attempt to understand how they really arise soon involves us with difficult and arcane questions about infinity. This said, however, I take my critic's point and so I agree that, before arguing about which ideas are the essential theoretical presuppositions of scepticism, we need to be convinced that any are. In my first book on these subjects,[5] I was inclined to take scepticism's dependence on foundationalism more or less for granted. In this book, by contrast, the question of scepticism's status as a problem guides my whole discussion.

Since I concede that the problem of scepticism can easily come to seem far more intuitive and far more compelling than any positive, theoretical ideas about knowledge, to defend my project of theoretical diagnosis, I must show how the apparent simplicity and transparency of sceptical arguments is a kind of illusion. I must show how seeming platitudes or truisms become vehicles for problematic and highly theoretical ideas. This will involve going very deeply into the theoretical background of sceptical problems. And because we will have to clarify the way we think about the whole range of epistemic concepts, the results of this inquiry should be far from entirely negative. Theoretical diagnosis is not to be equated with hasty dismissal.

In consequence of this, my argument is long and complex. It may, therefore, be useful for me to give a brief guide to its general direction. In chapter 1, then, I explore some of the consequences of thinking of scepticism as an intuitive problem. I connect this conception of scepticism with Hume's sense of a fundamental clash between philosophy and common life; and though I do not accept this view, which I call "biperspectivalism," as the final verdict on our epistemic situation, I do suggest that Hume grasped something of great significance: the extreme context sensitivity of sceptics' doubts. As Hume saw, although sceptical arguments can often strike us as irrefutable, the conviction they command is not easily detached from the special context of philosophical reflection. This feature of scepticism, I suggest, is something that any worthwhile account should explain.

My next step is to explore further why it is that, if we think of scepticism as an intuitive problem, we will never be able to deal with it in a satisfying way. The reason for this, I argue, is that we will find ourselves caught in what I call "the epistemologist's dilemma": either we admit at once that the sceptic is right or, in order to be able to continue to lay claim to knowledge of the world, we modify our pretheoretical thinking about knowledge in ways that make our final position difficult to distinguish from the scepticism we claim to have refuted. This is why theoretical diagnosis is indispensable: the only way out of the dilemma is to show that scepticism is not an intuitive problem, so that what we abandon in responding to the sceptic are not everyday platitudes but contentious theoretical ideas.

In chapter 2, I make a preliminary case for the dependence of scepticism on foundationalism, say why it is inadequate, and then go on to argue that foundationalist ideas are less easily dispensed with than critics of my kind of diagnosis are apt to suppose. Scepticism with respect to our knowledge of the external world, I argue, proves difficult to detach from the doctrine of the priority of experience over knowledge of the world. But though some progress has been made, my argument is far from complete. In particular, it has not yet paid sufficient attention to the fact that the sceptic wants to know why we think we have *any* knowledge of the external world. Does the need to answer this question force us to recognize the ultimate epistemic priority of experience? Isn't the sceptic right, that in the end experience is all we have to go on?

I address this question in chapters 3 and 4, where the question of knowledge as an object of theory comes to the fore. The sceptic tries to assess all our knowledge of the world, all at once. But is there really anything to assess? This is how the question arises: is there such a thing as "our knowledge of the world"? I argue that, in one very clear sense, there doesn't have to be. I explain my position by introducing the notion of "epistemological realism." This is not realism as a position within epistemology but realism with respect to the objects of epistemological reflection. My claim is that, in attempting to assess our knowledge of the world as a whole, the sceptic must assimilate terms like "our knowledge of the world" to natural kind terms like "heat" or "electricity." So in denying that there is such a thing as knowledge of the world, I am not agreeing with the sceptic but questioning the theoretical integrity of the kinds of knowledge he tries to assess.

Introducing the notion of epistemological realism leads me to what I hope is a novel and deeper understanding of foundationalism and its essential role in the generation of sceptical problems. Virtually all critics of foundationalist ideas – Sellars, Rorty, Davidson, Putnam, Bonjour, and myself at one time – have assumed that abandoning foundationalism means adopting some kind of coherence theory. I think that this is a mistake. The only alternative to epistemological realism, hence to foundationalism, is a contextualist view of justification. This is because contextualism alone takes issue with foundationalism's deepest theoretical commitment, which is to the idea that beliefs possess an intrinsic epistemological status. But a contextualist epistemology brings with it a partly "externalist" conception of knowledge. However, I do not suppose that an appeal to externalism can provide a direct or constructive response to the sceptic. Externalism in the theory of knowledge is acceptable only in the aftermath of a successful theoretical diagnosis of sceptical problems.

My contexualist view of knowledge explains the context sensitivity of the sceptic's results and threatens to convict him of a fallacy: confusing the discovery that knowledge is impossible under the conditions of philosophical reflection with the discovery, under the conditions of philosophical reflection, that knowledge is generally impossible. But the sceptic has a powerful defence, in the form of his own account of the nature of philosophical reflection and its relation to everyday life. There is also the question of whether diagnostic responses to scepticism are inevitably just as unsatisfying as constructive responses that tinker with our pretheoretical, epistemological ideas, ideas about objectivity for example. If we cannot understand our knowledge of the world in the general way that epistemology has traditionally aspired to, but if the sceptic's questions still make sense, aren't we left permanently unable to respond to a perfectly intelligible request for an explanation? In other words, does a diagnostic approach to scepticism simply force us to recognize an irremediable intellectual lack? My answer is: not if that diagnosis casts doubt on the very existence of the traditional objects of epistemological inquiry. These are the topics of chapter 5.

Serious problems remain to be dealt with. The first, taken up in chapter 6, has to do with metaphysical realism and its relation to scepticism. Philosophers who think of scepticism as an intuitive problem often do so because they think there is sceptical potential in the very aspiration to knowledge of an objective world. I do not agree. Realism, whether as an ontological thesis or a doctrine about truth, has no particular connection with scepticism. It follows from this that philosophers such as Rorty and Putnam are wrong to argue that we must reject "realistic" conceptions of truth, if we are to avoid sceptical entanglements. If we abandon epistemological realism then, at least so far as scepticism is concerned, we can say what we like on the metaphysical and semantic issues.

A further objection to tracing scepticism to foundationalism is that it seems perfectly possible to pose sceptical problems within the context of a coherence theory of knowledge and justification. I answer this objection in a preliminary way in chapter 6. But in chapter 7 I tackle head-on the question of whether the coherence theory is *any* alternative to foundationalism, let alone the only one. I argue that there is no stable position that deserves to be called "the coherence theory." Coherence theories either collapse into contextualism or turn out to be foundationalism in disguise. The way that sceptical problems arise for coherence theorists turns out to confirm my diagnosis, not to refute it.

The final chapter begins with what appears to be a change of direction. I look into the question, recently much discussed, of whether knowledge is "closed under known logical entailment." In part, I look into this issue because my own views might be thought to commit me to denying closure, and I argue that they do not. Nevertheless, although I think that arguments against closure are, to say the least, less than compelling, I also think that philosophers who have denied closure may have been responding to something real, which I call "the instability of knowledge." This somewhat speculative addition to my main diagnosis brings my argument full circle, for I see the instability of knowledge as the obverse of Hume's discovery, the instability of scepticism. The sceptic, I argue, identifies the instability of knowledge with its impossibility. But this is not a straightforward mistake: it is another consequence of his commitment to epistemological realism.

This book is the result of many years of thinking about scepticism and I am sure I have learned things from more people than I can now remember. But of those who have affected my thinking primarily through their writings, special mention must go to Barry Stroud. As much as anything, his penetrating discussions of the significance of scepticism made me see my erstwhile approach to the problem as facile, and so forced me to rethink my position from the ground up. Others whose writings have exerted a special influence and whom I must thank accordingly include Myles Burnyeat for making me think about the distinctiveness of modern scepticism; Thompson Clarke for his challenging account of scepticism's deep sources; Laurence Bonjour and Donald Davidson for helping me understand why I am not a coherence theorist; Stanley Cavell and Marie McGinn for forcing me to think hard about what I could and could not appropriate from Wittgenstein and ordinary language philosophy; Fred Dretske for his development of the "relevant alternatives" account of knowledge; Bernard Williams for his account of philosophy as pure inquiry; and Hilary Putnam for his subtle explorations of realism. As the reader will soon see, I have generally learned most from those with whom I disagree most sharply.

I have presented versions of several chapters, or parts of chapters, at numerous institutions in Britain, America, and Germany, and though I cannot thank members of my audiences individually, I am grateful for the sympathetic criticism I received and hope that it led to improvements in what follows. Certainly, it led to changes. I must, however, offer particular thanks to Edward Craig who commented on the paper I gave to a conference on realism at the University of St Andrews and who forced me to think hard about the way in which a contextual theory of justification is hostile to demands for global legitimations of belief; to Huw Rice, whose response to a paper I gave to the Oxford Philosophical Society made me clarify my position on knowledge and deductive closure; to Alvin Goldman who, at a conference on epistemology at Rice, pressed me on my claims about the unreality of knowledge; and to the members of Ralph Walker's Oxford discussion group for their reactions to drafts of several chapters.

Others have helped me in more personal ways, though often they have influenced me through their writings too. Special thanks go to Crispin Wright, who got me to start on this book in the first place; to Stephan Chambers for being an unfailing source of encouragement; to Arthur Fine and Paul Horwich for a continuing conversation on realism and truth; to Robert Fogelin, for many discussions of Hume; and to Richard Rorty and

Meredith Williams who both read the manuscript in draft and whose criticisms led to major surgery.

Three further debts of gratitude. First to the National Endowment for the Humanities and to Northwestern University. Their generous support, which gave me a year away from teaching, enabled me virtually to complete the manuscript in draft. Second to the Principal and Fellows of Brasenose College, Oxford, and especially to Michael Woods, who by welcoming me back after many years of expatriation helped my year's leave pass so enjoyably. And finally to all my colleagues in the Philosophy Department at Northwestern for the congenial and supportive environment they have created. To all and to anyone I may have overlooked, once more my thanks.

Michael Williams
Evanston, Illinois

# 1

## Pessimism in Epistemology

### 1.1 UNNATURAL DOUBTS?

My theme is scepticism. More precisely, it is scepticism in its modern or "Cartesian" form, for which our claim to knowledge of the external world sets the original and paradigmatic problem. So in what follows, unless I indicate otherwise, "scepticism" may be taken to mean "scepticism with respect to our knowledge of the external world." Nevertheless, as I hope will become clear, my discussion is meant to have wide implications.

I think that the absolutely crucial question to ask about scepticism is this: to what extent are sceptical doubts "natural" or "intuitive" and to what extent are they the product of contentious and possibly dispensable theoretical preconceptions?[1] Or as Thompson Clarke puts it, "What is the sceptic examining: our most fundamental convictions, or the product of a large piece of philosophising about empirical knowledge done before he comes on stage?" I believe that our response to this question affects decisively how we think the sceptic should be answered, or whether we think he can be answered at all. But what our response should be is far from obvious.

A problem's sudden appearance at a definite point in time is suggestive of its dependence on a particular, newly emergent theoretical outlook. It is therefore an intriguing fact that the problem of our knowledge of the external world is, comparatively speaking, a philosophical novelty. In classical antiquity, there was a sceptical tradition that lasted the best part of seven hundred years; this tradition underwent a notable revival in the sixteenth century, particularly in the works of Montaigne; yet what has become for us the paradigm of a sceptical problem cannot be identified with any certainty in sceptical writings prior to those of Descartes. Still, such evidence is hardly decisive. Perhaps the materials for constructing the problem were always at hand, buried in the most basic and universal epistemological ideas, but unnoticed until a philosopher came along with sufficient clarity of mind to see their true significance. Perhaps, too, a

changed conception of the point of sceptical argumentation played a role.
It is a commonplace that ancient scepticism had a moral point, that scepticism was a way of life, life without the false comfort of dogma or theoretical conviction; and it is not likely that philosophers intent on putting
forward a way of living in the world would push their arguments to the
point where the very existence of the world became a problem. Thus, it
is sometimes said, the intentions of the ancient sceptics contrast sharply
with those of Descartes who, for the first time, embeds his sceptical reflections in a project of starkly theoretical purity and, as a result, is able
to follow them to a far more radical conclusion.[2]

Though I think that this view seriously underestimates the difference
between modern scepticism and its ancient forebears, I shall not pursue
historical questions here. For the fact is that, whatever their novelty or
antiquity, the sceptical problems I am concerned with can be presented
in ways that make them seem dramatically simple and compelling, far
simpler and far more compelling than the theories of knowledge invoked
to rebut them. If sceptical doubts really are unnatural doubts, this will
take some showing. But first I want to say more about why I think the
question is so important.

## 1.2  PHILOSOPHY VERSUS COMMON LIFE

No philosopher of the modern period has thought more deeply about
scepticism than Hume, and Hume was led to the pessimistic conclusion
that no satisfactory theoretical response to scepticism is possible. No doubt
certain of the ideas that go to make up Hume's outlook can be found in
Descartes: for example, there is thought that the sort of reflection on our
knowledge of the world that leads to scepticism demands a withdrawal
from the concerns of common life, and there is the connection of scepticism
with the urge to trace our knowledge to its ultimate source or foundation.
But Hume brings these ideas into a new and disturbing alignment.

As is familiar, Descartes feels free to traffic in scepticism because he
believes he has an ace up his sleeve: an account of the true nature of
human knowledge that will place various fundamental truths beyond the
sceptic's reach. For Descartes, sceptical reflections are important because
they loosen our attachment to both out prephilosophical beliefs and the
epistemological ideas that underwrite them. More positively, by finding
truths that resist sceptical undermining, we will get invaluable clues to
the true metaphysics and the proper epistemology. But the significance
of scepticism, though great, remains exclusively methodological. There
is never a serious worry that scepticism might simply be true.

By contrast, Hume's account of human understanding is haunted by
the thought that scepticism is the final, inescapable verdict on our pre-

tensions to knowledge of the world, or indeed of anything beyond the pale of current experience. Like many philosophers today, Hume sees the case for scepticism as far more intuitive, and so far more compelling than the elaborate theoretical structures raised against it, the hidden truths about human knowledge that we supposedly "discover" by seeing where the sceptic goes wrong. In Hume's eyes, there is simply no hope of our reaching a reflective understanding of human knowledge that will explain to us how we come by the knowledge we are ordinarily so ready to claim. To try for such a philosophical understanding is to engage the sceptic on his own terms and, thus engaged, the sceptic always triumphs.

Of course, Hume's pessimism in the area of theory is more than offset by optimism in the area of practice, or so it first seems. The sceptic may be invulnerable, Hume says, but only so long as he confines himself to making "philosophical" – that is *purely* theoretical – points. He cannot draw the conclusion, which initially seems to be the lesson of scepticism, that we ought to repudiate our ordinary outlook. There is no question of our forgoing inductive expectations or suspending belief in the external world, for we are simply not made that way. We are "determined to judge as well as to breathe and feel." In matters of practical importance, "Nature," which is "always too strong for principle," blocks the move from theoretical insight to practical prescription.[3]

So can we say that optimism triumphs over pessimism: that the bad news – that scepticism is irrefutable – is overwhelmed by the good that there is no danger of our ever taking sceptical lessons to heart? Not really. Hume's theoretical pessimism goes very deep and even his practical optimism is more qualified than it first appears.

For a start, on the theoretical front this "naturalist" response to scepticism heightens rather than alleviates the sense of paradox that surrounds the sceptic's conclusions. Indeed, Hume's reply to the sceptic puts a finger on what might be seen as one of scepticism's most paradoxical aspects, which is that a thoroughly sceptical outlook is quite unsustainable, even if we are persuaded that the case for scepticism is irrefutable. The hallmark of sceptical arguments is that they "admit of no answer and produce no conviction."[4] Scepticism seems to show something important about human knowledge, but something we cannot believe: *le plus c'est profond, le moins c'est croyable.*

Now we might think that the incredibility of the sceptic's conclusions shows that his arguments are *mere* puzzles, *jeux d'esprits* that are amusing enough for those who like that sort of thing but with no serious claim on our attention. There is a strain of this in Hume, as when he writes that:

the chief and most confounding objection to *excessive* scepticism [is] that no durable good can ever result from it; while it retains its full force and vigour. We need only ask such a sceptic, *What his meaning is? And what he proposes by all these curious researches?* He is immediately at a loss, and knows not what to answer.[5]

However, it is hard to believe that anyone seriously interested in scepticism would be that tongue-tied. If nothing else, in theoretical pursuits paradox can be its own reward, so why suppose, as Hume's question apparently does, that the sceptical philosopher needs an ulterior motive? The sceptic might reveal something deeply disturbing about the human condition, even if the lesson he teaches is one that we do not, and perhaps in some sense cannot, really live with. Indeed, this strange conjunction of irrefutability and unliveability might itself tell us something important about the human condition. And, in fact, this is Hume's own view. His excuse for displaying "the arguments of that fantastic sect" is "to make the reader sensible of the truth of [the] hypothesis that . . . *belief is more properly an act of the sensitive, than of the cogitative part of our natures.*"[6] The lesson of scepticism is that belief is natural, even though finally groundless. More than that, we have to see how it is groundless in order to appreciate its naturalness.

If scepticism points to a deep and troubling truth about the human condition, it is hard to believe that it can be utterly devoid of practical significance. Even if we cannot live with the full implications of scepticism, this hardly shows that a serious encounter with it will leave us completely unaffected. Nor does Hume suppose so. On the contrary, he is convinced that such an encounter can have a permanent, chastening effect. Nothing dampens dogmatic enthusiasm quite so effectively as having once made oneself aware of the weakness and frailty of human understanding. To curb a penchant for flights of metaphysical or religious fancy, we need only peer into the abyss and acknowledge what Wittgenstein, in a Humean moment, calls "the groundlessness of our believing."[7] The "mitigated scepticism" Hume is at pains to inculcate is less a reasoned position that the vector sum of our sceptical and dogmatic tendencies, the natural result of the permanent tension between the Pyrrhonism of philosophy and the credulity of common life.

We should not, then, let Hume's officially optimistic naturalism lead us to underestimate the intellectual hold that he thinks acepticim has on us. There is an important nuance to his view that the sceptic's conclusions are utterly incredible. Even to allow scepticism to be a tendency inherent in the philosopher's sifting humour is, if nothing more is said, to do less than justice to its power. For Hume does not claim that sceptical arguments *never* carry *any* conviction, but rather that no one was ever a sceptic "sincerely and constantly."[8] Though sceptical arguments induce no *stable* breakdown of belief, they do produce the striking, if transient, effects memorably captured in the conclusion to book 1 of the *Treatise*. There Hume describes the state of one "affrighted and confounded with that forelorn solitude, in which [he is] plac'd [in his] philosophy." With the progress of his arguments, his thoughts have taken an increasingly sceptical turn, leading to a state of mind in which:

> The intense view of these manifold contradictions and imperfections in human reason has so wrought upon me, and heated my brain, that I am ready to reject all belief and reasoning, and can look upon no opinion as even more probable or likely than any other.

The attempt to philosophize leaves him "in the most deplorable condition imaginable, inviron'd with the deepest darkness, and utterly depriv'd of the use of every member and faculty."[9] Like the still sad music of humanity, scepticism has the power to chasten and subdue; and small wonder.

This theme recurs in the conclusion to the first *Enquiry*, though in more muted tones. Fright and despair give way to "momentary amazement," and the human condition is not so much dark as "whimsical." But the underlying philosophical view has not changed, only its affective coloration. The condition of mankind is whimsical in that they must:

> act and reason and believe; though they are not able, by their most diligent enquiry, to satisfy themselves concerning the foundation of these operations, or to remove the objections, which may be raised against them.[10]

Our whimsical condition is our paradoxical condition. Hume may have made his peace with the groundlessness of our believing: he has not changed his mind about it.

It is striking that Hume does not see the sceptical outcome of his philosophical reflections as at all idiosyncratic. He takes the progress of his thought to be exemplary of a tendency deeply embedded in human nature itself. Scepticism is implicit in ways of thinking that come naturally to anyone with a reflective turn of mind. That is why scepticism tells us something about the condition of mankind, not just about the consequences of some particular philosophical ideas. A certain permanent tendency to extreme scepticism is what makes mitigated scepticism a sustainable outlook. We are not stable extreme sceptics only because we are incapable of sustaining the reflective stance. Hume writes:

> the understanding, when it acts alone, and according to its most general principles, entirely subverts itself, and leaves not the lowest degree of evidence in any proposition, either in philosophy or common life.[11]

And he tells us that we are saved from total scepticism only by the fact that "we enter with difficulty into remote views of things, and are not able to accompany them with so sensible an impression, as we do those, which are more easy and natural."[12] Everyday belief is more easily sustained than philosophical doubt.

The reason given for this is worth remarking. When we take up a reflective stance, reason acts "alone." This echoes Descartes's thought that we come face to face with the possibility of scepticism, not in the course of everyday practical affairs, but in the context of an extraordinary form of inquiry in which we have no aim beyond knowing the truth: scepticism arises when we set aside all particular interests and attachments and attempt to command an objective view of the world and our place in it.

Hume sees this as explaining the quotidian incredibility of the sceptic's conclusion. When reason acts alone, it is not restrained by particular perceptions and passions. So everyday existence masks the potential for a sceptical breakdown of belief because, in common life, our attention is gripped by particular objects and narrow interests. By contrast, when we philosophize we forget particulars. We try to get a grip on the "foundation" of our beliefs and inferences, to understand in some highly general way how they can have the status we ordinarily, and unthinkingly, grant them. But when we make the attempt, we find only contradictions. Though knowledge is supposedly the product of reason, the senses, or both, neither reason nor the senses is properly intelligible, and the two sources of knowledge are anyway in conflict with each other. Whether we reflect on either or on both, we are led inevitably to scepticism. But this urge to command a reflective understanding of our deepest epistemological and metaphysical commitments is as natural to some people as complacent certainty is to others.

The sceptic's theoretical invulnerability means that we can expect no relief from philosophical theories of knowledge. Attempts to rescue the certainties of common life from the sceptic's paradoxes lead, not to solid insights, but to a "confusion of groundless and extraordinary opinions."[13] No doubt Hume's sense of the devasting simplicity of sceptical argument, in contrast to the baroque edifices of philosophical theory, does as much as anything to convince him that the sceptic is theoretically unassailable. In fact, it matters not at all whether our intention is to buttress or subvert the sources of knowledge for, as Hume sees it:

> 'Tis impossible upon any system to defend either our understanding or senses; and we but expose them farther when we endeavour to justify them after that manner.[14]

Theoretical defences of human knowledge encourage scepticism as much as sceptical attacks on it, rather as proofs of the existence of God encourage atheism. Defending something implies that there are legitimate questions about its status. As Wittgenstein remarks, "When one hears Moore say 'I *know* that's a tree,' one suddenly understands those who think that has by no means been settled."[15] The first fatal step on the road to scepticism is taken *as soon as we ask the basic epistemological questions*, and the urge to ask them belongs to human nature itself. Like Kant, Hume sees human reason as fated to ask questions it cannot answer. Unlike Kant, he sees no hope of a cure in elaborate epistemological or metaphysical speculations. The power and simplicity of the arguments for scepticism will always overcome the "extraordinary opinions" advanced to rebut them.

One important consequence of this is that, in its own way, sceptical doubt is as natural as ordinary belief. Hume's talk of "natural" belief might seem to suggest otherwise, and he does sometimes represent sceptical doubts as "strained."[16] When we try to focus on a certain kind of sceptical reasoning, our spirits are "diverted from their natural course" and "the same principles have not the same effect as in a more natural conception of ideas."[17] But there are trains of thought which, once set in motion, have scepticism as their natural outcome. Thus:

> As the sceptical doubt arises *naturally* [my emphasis] from a profound and intense reflection on those subjects, it always encreases, the farther we carry our reflections, whether in opposition or conformity to it.[18]

So although the reflective stance is not easily sustained, and is to that extent unnatural, scepticism comes as "naturally" to the philosopher as belief to the man in the street. If we say that the sceptic is irrefutable on his own terms, we must add that his terms are also ours.

This aspect of the Humean position cannot be stressed too much. In pointing to the "unnaturalness" of the sceptical outlook, Hume is *not* suggesting that scepticism is in any way *artificial*. Scepticism is not, for example, an artifact of a misreading of our epistemic situation. If it were, there would be a "philosophical" response to the sceptic, whereas the burden of Hume's naturalism is that no such response is available. The sceptical outlook is "unnatural" only in the sense that it is not easy to sustain. To put the point a slightly different way, sceptical doubts may appear "cold, strained and ridiculous," *but only from the standpoint of common life.* This is why, for anyone inclined to philosophical reflection, scepticism is "a malady, which can never be radically cured, however we may chace it away, and sometimes may seem entirely free from it." If "carelessness and inattention alone can afford us any remedy," the concerns of common life are a palliative, not a cure.[19] The potential for a sceptical breakdown of belief is always there, even though our eyes are for the most part drawn away from it.

Actually, it is not quite right to say that sceptical doubts are unnatural only in the sense of being *difficult* to sustain. Hume's view is rather that outside "the study," that is to say, outside the peculiar context of philosophical reflection, they cannot be sustained *at all*, though some residual effect may be felt. Descartes, too, notes the difficulty of sustaining the extraordinary doubts he had propounded but Hume, I think, sees even more deeply into the phenomenology of scepticism; and what he finds is that the sceptic's conclusion is experienced as a deep yet curiously evanescent insight: deep because in violent conflict with our everday – and in that sense "natural" attitude – but evanescent because strikingly context-bound. Among recent philosophers, Stanley Cavell follows Hume in his own, most perceptive, account of the experience of scepticism. As Cavell puts it, scepticism has the air of a shocking *discovery*: philosophical reflection *reveals* something completely unexpected about our ordinary outlook, something "deeper than our everyday, average ideas." Yet, at the same time, it is a revelation whose convincingness "will not detach from the context of investigation itself."[20] The sceptic's conclusion is peculiar in more than what it says.

Still, we must remember that, if the force of scepticism dissipates outside the study, everyday certainty dissipates in it. The central *motif* in Hume's vision remains that of an irreconcilable clash between two outlooks or perspectives: the outlook we naturally assume in common life, which involves no deep systematic doubts about the reliability of our data, the reasonableness of our inferences, or the objectivity of our judgments, and the outlook to which we are inevitably led when we step back and reflect on everyday practices and procedures, which is total scepticism, a complete inability to see everyday certainties, inferences and judgments as deserving anything remotely like the status we otherwise effortlessly attribute to them. The view of the true philosopher, the sceptic, is that there are fewer things in heaven and earth than are dreamt of in everyday life. His positive task is to explain why we systematically project more into the world than is (or at least can be known to be) there. Hume's "projectivist" accounts of our beliefs in causal necessity, the continued and distinct existence of body and objective moral differences are all reactions to the truth of scepticism.[21]

This clash of outlooks means that, in the end, even on the practical front Hume's optimism is far from unqualified. We have one outlook in the study and another in the street, and since they can be neither integrated nor reconciled, if we are born with a sifting humour we will oscillate between them, as our appetite for philosophical reflection waxes and wanes – *croyants d'habitude, sceptiques à nos heures* – yet always with an underlying uneasiness that we can never entirely "chace away." It may be difficult to realize the groundlessness of our believing, but after we have been made to realize it, things are never quite the same. The true philosopher has no truck with abstruse metaphysical speculations and in this way "*approaches nearer* to the sentiments of the vulgar."[22] But he cannot recover them completely. Innocence once lost is never regained.

We must not suppose, however, that this oscillation between the commonsense and philosophical outlooks puts them on an equal footing; still less that the greater time spent seeing the world through the lenses of common sense accords our everyday views some kind of epistemic privilege. True, our everyday outlook comes easier, and so is in that way more compelling, but scepticism cuts deeper. The most fundamental reason why scepticism is not just a puzzle, which we can take or leave alone, is that the sceptic's conclusions are *true*. In moments of clarity, we are forcibly struck by their truth; and though at other times philosophical doubt recedes into the background, the force of the sceptic's insights, though attenuated, is never entirely extinguished. The asymmetry thus favours the sceptic: though in philosophy, commonsense certainty is powerless against sceptical doubt, in everyday life sceptical doubt plays faint, discordant descant to the dominant themes.

We have here a strikingly original and deeply seductive constellation of ideas.[23] To summarize:

- Scepticism expresses a profound, though in normal circumstances incredible, truth about the human condition. The sceptic has made a catastrophic, though peculiarly unstable, discovery.
- This means that there is a conflict between the epistemic attitudes typical of common life and the results of philosophical reflection.
- Everyday certainty is connected with our absorption in highly particular projects. Scepticism, by contrast, arises out of a quest for understanding that is in some distinctive way unconstrained.
- But scepticism is not underwritten by arcane theoretical ideas. As soon as certain questions are raised, we are on the way to scepticism. Scepticism is the legacy of the attempt to philosophize.
- There is therefore nothing artificial about sceptical doubts, which are the inevitable outcome of pursuing questions that occur naturally to reflective human beings. If scepticism cannot survive in full vigour outside the study, commonsense certainty evaporates inside it. Sceptical doubts and everyday certainties are equally context-bound.
- Since scepticism is the natural outcome of philosophical reflection, there is no hope of theoretical relief. To defend human knowledge, as much as to attack it, is to put the question of its "foundation" on the table – hence in the end to encourage scepticism. In any case, natural sceptical doubts will always overcome artificial theoretical responses.

- Thus to make ourselves immune to scepticism, we should have to persuade ourselves not to ask philosophical questions in the first place. But there is no hope of this. The tendency to raise them belongs to human nature.
- This means that, in the end, it is just a fact of human psychology that we are not crippled by sceptical doubts.
- But it also means that the clash between philosophy and common life is irreconcilable. The result is *biperspectivalism*: we have two incompatible outlooks and can only oscillate between them. Scepticism is a disease that goes into remission, but which can never be cured.

## 1.3  THE NEW HUMEANS

Whether or not we finally accept Hume's account of scepticism, there is no denying that scepticism can easily seem to be all that Hume says it is. His account of the experience of scepticism remains valuable even to those disinclined to take it at face value. Hume brings to light things that any worthwhile account of scepticism must come to terms with. Why are sceptical doubts and everyday certainties so strikingly context-bound? How *can* the conclusion of a philosophical argument seem to embody an extraordinary and undeniable discovery and yet be incapable of commanding stable assent? Of course, there is always Hume's own answer: scepticism *seems* irrefutable because it *is* irrefutable; and if we do not generally acknowledge its truth, this is only because (psychologically) we can't. But we should like to do better than this. Still, doing better will require coming up with more satisfying answers to the questions Hume suggests than either Hume himself or any other philosopher who thinks of scepticism as an intuitive problem. An adequacy condition on an account of the basis of scepticism is that it provide a satisfying explanation of the context-sensitivity and consequent instability of the sceptic's doubts and discoveries.

Wishes aside, however, the history of attempts to refute scepticism is not encouraging. In our own times, though the problems that confronted Hume have been attacked with a degree of sophistication and technical ingenuity that he could scarcely have imagined, the problems have proved hardier than the solutions. Scepticism, it begins to seem, has been refuted *too often*. Ingenuity has only multiplied the "confusion of groundless and extraordinary opinions."

Of course, not everyone takes this view. The Cartesian view of scepticism as being of primarily heuristic significance remains influential, so that there are plenty of philosophers still willing to use an encounter with scepticism as a way of testing their positive theories of knowledge. At the same time, and not surprisingly, there is in contemporary epistemology an influential and perhaps growing strain of Humean pessimism. But that it is hard to be finally satisfied with Hume's position is suggested by the fact that even those most strongly drawn to it betray hints of unease.

Evidence of pessimism is not hard to find. Strawson, for example, in his most recently published thoughts on scepticism, is an open advocate of a return to Humean naturalism.[24] As he presents it, the naturalist response to scepticism is to insist that, since belief in the external world, or the uniformity of nature, is a matter of natural inclination, not reasoned conviction, the sceptic's doubts *and* the theoretical responses they provoke are equally pointless. Beliefs that are not founded on reasoning can *neither* be undermined *nor* usefully defended by it.

Admittedly, Strawson's defence of naturalism is not infused with a pessimistic tone. But it is pessimistic for all that. The point that sceptical arguments fail to permanently undermine ordinary beliefs is common property. What makes the naturalist's position distinctive is his insistence that there is nothing to say to a sceptic *beyond* underlining the everyday ineffectiveness of his arguments, which is to concede scepticism's theoretical invulnerability. This is a considerable retreat for someone who once thought that scepticism results from denying some commonsense views while quietly helping oneself to others that tacitly presuppose what one explicitly rejects.[25]

I am inclined to trace Strawson's tendency to strike a more optimistic note than Hume to a reluctance finally to embrace a fully Humean response to scepticism, or to face up completely to the consequences of so doing. In other words, Strawson is an uneasy Humean. For a start, he does not claim that a philosophical defence of belief in the external world is *absolutely* impossible, since he sees one strategy whose resources may not have been completely exhausted. We might be able to ground our belief on some kind of quasi-scientific inference: the existence of the external world as the best explanation of the coherence of experience.[26] He objects to this strategy, not because it is demonstrably theoretically inadequate, but because he is certain that no such inference provides anyone's actual reason for believing in an external reality.

This is not all: Strawson is also inclined to think that the point that sceptical doubts and philosophical rejoinders are *equally* ineffective allows us to shrug off the sceptic's conclusions. But when we remember that naturalism concedes the sceptic's theoretical invulnerability, it is hard to see why this should be so. For then, as we noted before, naturalism seems less a response to scepticism than a forceful reminder of its paradoxical character. True, in daily life philosophical scruples have no impact on commonsense convictions. Equally, however, in the course of an attempt to gain a reflective understanding of ordinary practices, commonsense

*Moore* *

certainties have no impact on philosophical scruples. Though everyone shares Moore's certainty, when he holds up his hand in good light, that "Here is one hand," no one thinks that this performance refutes philosophical scepticism. So we must avoid the slide from noting the apparent clash between common sense and philosophical reflection to thinking that we can resolve the conflict by appealing to the one against the other.[27] As we have seen – and this fact will be crucial to the argument of this book – commonsense certainty and philosophical doubt seem both to be context-bound: given the right frame of mind, either can seem entirely appropriate. Hume is responding to this when he depicts the condition of the reflective portion of humankind as involving a ceaseless oscillation between outlooks that can never be reconciled.

It is tempting, as we noted, to turn the Humean, "naturalist" response to scepticism into a kind of bluff pragmatism: we don't *have* to respond to scepticism because it makes no difference whether we do or not. Hence Hume's remark that asking the sceptic for his "meaning" is "the chief and most confounding objection" to his position. The trouble with this, as we now know, is that by Hume's own account the sceptic is not some external adversary, who needs to be confounded. The enemy, as they say, is us. Scepticism is the position to which we are *all* led if we have a sifting humour and the nerve to follow it to the bitter end. We do not argue for scepticism out of some ulterior motive, so that inability to say what it is takes the steam out of sceptical reasoning. Rather, out of natural curiosity, we try to satisfy ourselves concerning the foundation of certain operations. Only we fail.[28]

It is important, therefore, not to confuse two quite distinct ways in which we do (or might) not "have" to respond to scepticism. There are all kinds of theoretical problems that we do not have to solve *for immediate practical purposes* (or at all, if we either lack or have trained ourselves out of the sifting humour). We can treat scepticism as one of those. We can learn to live with our whimsical situation. Indeed, if Hume is right, we have no choice. But if we can trace the sceptical outcome of traditional epistemology to theoretical ideas that are less than compelling, there will be a quite different and much more satisfactory sense in which we do not have to respond. We will not have to respond to scepticism, in any of the usual ways at least, because we will be able to see scepticism, not as belonging to the human condition, but as a problem internal to a set of theoretical ideas that we are not bound to accept. If this is what is meant by saying that we do not have to respond to the sceptic, we have moved a long way from Humean pessimism. We can afford to concede that sceptical arguments cannot be answered on the sceptic's own terms, if we can show, *pace* Hume, that the sceptic's terms are not forced on us by human nature.

I think, then, that another factor in Strawson's failure to come to terms with the pessimistic character of naturalism may well be a tendency to run together the two ways in which responding to scepticism might be optional. Although he starts from the point that life will go on in the absence of a theoretical reply to the sceptic, he sometimes infers from the naturalist's claim that our most basic beliefs are neither to be undermined nor supported by arguments that there is *no such thing as the reasons for which we hold them*, so that attempts to show that our reasons are inadequate must misfire.[29] The sceptic's doubts are thus not *merely* idle but also misconceived, reflecting his profound misunderstanding of the epistemological status of the beliefs he examines. Something goes badly wrong *before* familiar sceptical arguments even get started.

This is a far cry from pure, Humean naturalism, for it reveals a tendency, on Strawson's part, to let his naturalism modulate into the very thing it is supposed *not* to be: a form of theoretical criticism of the sceptic's arguments. As we shall see in due course, this tendency does not result from a slip: it is intrinsic to the Humean naturalist position. For now, however, let me just note that it is significant that Strawson is inclined to trace affinities between Hume's natural beliefs and Wittgenstein's propositions that stand fast. This temptation is quite understandable. Consider the following, entirely typical, remarks from *On Certainty*:

> I did not get my picture of the world by satisfying myself of its correctness; nor do I have it because I am satisfied of its correctness. No: it is the inherited background against which I distinguish between the true and the false. . . . if I were to say "It is my unshakeable conviction that etc.," this means in the present case too that I have not consciously arrived at the conviction by following a particular line of thought, but that it is anchored in all my *questions and answers*, so anchored that I cannot touch it.[30]

How can this fail to remind us of such Humean claims as:

> We may well ask, *What causes induce us to believe in the existence of body?* but 'tis vain to ask, *Whether there be body or not?* That is a point, which we must take for granted in all our reasonings.[31]

Or again, Hume teaches that inductive inference is not rationally defensible because it presupposes, what we cannot justify without circularity, that there is a certain uniformity in the course of nature. Nevertheless, the principle of the association of ideas, the psychological basis of inductive inference, is one of the most fundamental factors in human thought. And if to form expectations for the future in the light of past experience is just *how we think*, there can be no serious question as to whether we *ought* to think this way. This is a lesson Wittgenstein seems to echo when he writes:

> But do we not simply follow the principle that what has always happened will happen again (or something like it)? What does it mean to follow this principle? Do we really introduce it into our reasoning? Or is it merely the natural law which our inferring apparently follows? This latter it may be. It is not an item in our considerations.[32]

If there is a difference between Hume and Wittgenstein, we might suppose, it is that Hume is concerned only with the most abstract and fundamental features of our way of understanding the world – our irrepressible tendency to identify and reidentify "bodies," form expectations about the future, and find value in a world of fact – whereas Wittgenstein ("Back to the rough ground!") is also interested in what must stand fast in more particular investigative and judgmental practices – doing history, calculating, conducting an experiment. For Wittgenstein, the list of propositions which "we must take for granted in all our reasonings," is much more varied and diverse than it is for Hume and includes many claims that might easily seem to be straightforwardly empirical, hence to need justification.

It would be foolish to deny all affinities. Perhaps, at certain points, Wittgenstein is drawn to the Humean outlook (though whether he *ever* adopts it without qualification is another question). Even so, I think that in the end Hume and Wittgenstein are opposed on fundamentals. That certain propositions stand fast is not a *psychological* fact. Rather it reflects their special logical status, which arguments for scepticism consistently ignore, obscure or distort. At any rate, this I am certain of: nothing Wittgenstein says is meant to imply that what the sceptic claims is in some fundamental yet entirely straightforward way *true*. If Wittgenstein is right, Hume is wrong: arguments for scepticism are deeply defective, however hypnotic.

Strawson, then, is an equivocal pessimist. Less so Barry Stroud who, in a recent and deservedly influential book, concludes on the basis of a painstaking examination of the most significant anti-sceptical strategies available that scepticism is at least *conditionally* correct, in the sense that, if the sceptic is allowed to ask his questions about the possibility of knowledge in the way he wants, the case for returning a negative answer is overwhelming.[33] No form of inference will ground our belief in the external world to the sceptic's (which is to say our own) satisfaction. Our best (perhaps only) hope for coming to terms with scepticism, therefore, is to find something wrong with the questions themselves, to see how, initial appearances to the contrary, they are less than fully intelligible. The trouble is, they do not seem defective in point of intelligibility and no one has so far succeeded in showing that they are. So even the most promising anti-sceptical strategy is not very promising. This is reminiscent of Hume's idea that the simplicity and naturalness of his reasoning give the sceptic a formidable advantage over his theoretically minded critic.

Stroud's most recent writings reveal an even deeper strain of pessimism. The lesson of scepticism, he now argues, is that a certain kind of general, reflective understanding of human knowledge, and how it comes to be – the kind of understanding that traditional epistemology tries to provide – is forever beyond us. But even if we manage to convince ourselves that there is something misconceived in the traditional epistemological enterprise, we will still lack the kind of understanding we crave. The choice is between forgoing the quest for epistemological understanding and seeing it end in scepticism. What we will never get is a satisfying philosophical understanding of our right to our everyday certainties.[34] So either way, we will be dissatisfied. This is an important argument, which we shall need to examine in depth. But for now let us simply note that the echoes of Hume's two outlooks are clear.

Clear but perhaps not completely unqualified. However, if there are qualifications, they are different from Strawson's. Whereas Strawson wavers on whether the sceptic is as theoretically invulnerable as he looks, Stroud is willing to ask whether the conflict between philosophy and everyday life is as stark as it first appears. Can the two be reconciled, to a limited extent? Is it even possible that they do not conflict at all? These are important questions, to which we shall return.

The most thoroughgoing Humean pessimist among contemporary philosophers may well be Thomas Nagel.[35] However incredible in ordinary circumstances, from the objective standpoint scepticism is the only possible verdict on our supposed knowledge of the world. Nagel sees no way at all of reconciling our everyday, engaged, "subjective" attitudes with how things appear from the philosophical, detached, "objective" standpoint, and so he does not share even the residual hope that a sufficiently deep "diagnosis" might reveal either the sceptic's questions or his conclusions as less than fully intelligible. In Nagel's view, the argument will always go the other way: the evident intelligibility of what the sceptic says will invariably call in question whatever arcane theory of language underwrites the charge of incoherence. Again we come to a variation on a central Humean theme: the artificiality of philosophical theories contrasts unfavorably with the naturalness of the case for scepticism.

Still, perhaps not even Nagel is completely happy with the Humean view. I do not want to read too much into a single phrase, but his way of

putting his conclusion threatens to take the edge off his epistemological
pessimism. Nagel tells us that if the philosophical problem of scepticism
is to effect a reconciliation between our two outlooks, "Our problem ...
has no solution, but to recognise that is to come as near as we can to
living in light of the truth."[36] And the question is: what truth are we to
live in light of? Simply that we have two outlooks that we cannot inte-
grate, each valid in its own way? If this were Nagel's view, it would be
pluralism rather than scepticism.[37] But there is surely nothing eirenic
about Nagel's final position. Living in light of the truth requires more
than recognizing the impossibility of integrating our everyday outlook
with the results of philosophical reflection: it requires acknowledging the
final truth of scepticism. If this were not so, there would be no point in
calling the philosophical standpoint "objective": how things look from
the "objective" standpoint is how they are. Equally, to call our everyday
outlook "subjective' is to imply that it is partial, limited, or even distorted,
in a way that its philosophical competitor is not, that it represents not how
things are but how we hope or would like them to be. Life's dome of many
coloured glass stains the white – hence featureless – radiance of eternity.
This is the disquieting truth in the light of which anyone who reflects is
condemned to live.[38]

Hume's vision of an irreconcilable conflict between the shallow certainties of everyday life and the deep truth of scepticism has an undeniable fascination, so much so that even those who are officially optimistic
about our chances of giving a theoretical response to the sceptic can find
themselves drawn to it. Take Stanley Cavell, who thinks that the sceptic
can be convicted of only seeming to make sense. Cavell argues that though
the sceptic speaks in grammatically correct sentences, he uses them in a
peculiar, indeed finally unintelligible, way. This result is a kind of illusion
of sense. The sceptic deploys familiar words and phrases. But in a way
that makes it impossible to see what *he* means *by* them.[39] However, because we know what *they* mean, it seems that his pronouncements must
mean something, even if we can't quite grasp what it is.

If all this is so, we have a refutation as definitive as we ever see in
philosophy. Nevertheless, Cavell finds himself drawn to the idea that there
is a kind of truth in scepticism. He writes of "the human disappointment
with human knowledge"; and he notes that the lesson of Wittgenstein's
reaction to scepticism, which he sees himself as elaborating, is that "Our
relation to the world as a whole . . . is not one of knowing, where knowing
construes itself as being certain."[40] The sceptic is wrong when he claims
that we do not know that the external world exists, but not wrong because
we *do* know it after all. So in a way he is right too: his sense of discovery is
far from entirely illusory. Even if he fails to mean what he wants to mean,
he may manage to mean something else, something true and profound.

However, in spite of the magnetic attraction of Hume's vision, I remain unconvinced that there is a *human* disappointment with human knowledge. More likely, once in the grip of certain ideas about knowledge, a philosopher is fated to be disappointed with all responses to scepticism, his own included. Having begun to trace the character of pessimism in epistemology, we must identify its source.

## 1.4  THE EPISTEMOLOGIST'S DILEMMA

Though the history of attempts to refute the sceptic strikes pessimists as a chronicle of failure, the basis of pessimism is not really inductive. We have already encountered its wellspring: the conviction that scepticism is a "natural" or "intuitive" problem.

To see scepticism as an intuitive problem is to hold that arguments for scepticism are minimally dependent on contentious theoretical ideas. This is not to say that arguments for scepticism must be completely presuppositionless. But it does mean that everything the sceptic needs has to be already present in our most ordinary ways of thinking about knowledge. It may be that scepticism only appears as a serious possibility in the context of philosophical reflection, but this cannot be because, in the attempt to gain a philosophical understanding of human knowledge, we distort our ordinary epistemic position. If anything involves distortion, it must be our ordinary outlook: our everyday engagements must somehow occlude the real truth of the matter. Philosophical reflection is a searchlight that brings into view what was always hidden in the darker recesses of our conceptual landscape.

This view of scepticism has a powerful immediate appeal. What speaks most strongly for it is the apparent simplicity and brevity of sceptical arguments. Standard arguments for scepticism can be very compactly stated and, at least in a preliminary way, readily understood. As we have seen, our prototypical pessimist, Hume, is struck forcefully by this. Though tempted to treat sceptical arguments as strained and unnatural, he is well aware that this is not always how they seem. The naive realism that is the "primary and universal opinion of all mankind" is undermined, not by elaborate theories, but by "the slightest philosophy." Sceptical doubts are "unnatural" only in the sense that it is a strain to keep one's attention firmly focussed on philosophical subjects. In another, more important sense, they are entirely natural: there is nothing *artifical* about them; they are not the artifacts of any peculiar theoretical ideas; their roots lie in human nature itself.

The new Humeans share this perception. Thus Stroud claims that "when we first encounter . . . sceptical reasoning . . . we find it immediately gripping," which he takes to indicate that such reasoning "appeals to something deep in our nature."[41] I take it that arguments that appeal to something deep in our nature contrast with arguments that turn on special theoretical presuppositions. Stroud's thought is that if arguments for scepticism turned on such presuppositions, they would not be so immediately gripping.

As I just noted, to appeal to something deep in our nature, an argument for scepticism need not be completely presuppositionless. It must, however, exploit only the most deeply embedded features of our ordinary conception of knowledge. So we find, for example, that while Stroud concedes that scepticism depends crucially on a certain conception of the objectivity of the world, he holds that this conception can be expressed in terms of "platitudes we would all accept."[42] Scepticism arises from ideas about ourselves and the world that it is very difficult to imagine ourselves abandoning, once we bear the consequences of abandoning them clearly in mind. This is what someone struck by the naturalness or intuitiveness of sceptical arguments has to say. If the case for scepticism depended on special theoretical ideas which we might abandon without strain, there would be no reason to fear a "human" disappointment with human knowledge.

It is obvious right away that conceding the naturalness of the case for scepticism places the critic under a crippling dialectical disadvantage. It is no accident that Hume finds in the theory of knowledge only "a confusion of groundless and extraordinary opinions." As Nagel sees, no recondite philosophical theory can undermine scepticism, *if the sceptic's arguments are genuinely intuitive.* The very fact that a theory contradicts something much more intuitively appealing than itself will always, in the long run, prevent it from carrying conviction. This is particularly clear when theories of meaning are invoked to deny intelligibility to sceptical claims. Our sense that we *do* understand the sceptic – well enough, for example, to understand how we might argue *against* him – will eventually wear down the credibility of theories that imply that we don't. The result will be that we end up arguing for conclusions that have as much an air of paradox as scepticism itself: for example, that "the sceptic 'must' and 'cannot' mean what he says."[43] This suggests that the sceptic cannot mean what he wants to mean: but how can I even *want* to mean what I can't mean *at all*? Or we may try claiming, with John Skorupski, that the conception of meaning we use to combat the intelligibility of scepticism must itself "be seen to shrink into insignificance as a mere truism about what understanding consists in."[44] It is not easy to imagine any philosophical conception of meaning, least of all the verificationist conception Skorupski has in mind, managing to do this.

In fact, the situation is even worse. Conceding the naturalness of sceptical arguments does more than work against the long-term credibility of theoretical responses: it makes any theoretical response visibly incapable of accomplishing what is demanded of it, which is rescuing ordinary claims to knowledge from the sceptic's negative assessment. Barry Stroud shows sensitivity to this problem when he alludes to:

a familiar pattern in the theory of knowledge. We find ourselves with questions about knowledge that lead either to an unsatisfactory sceptical conclusion or to this or that 'theory' of knowledge which on reflection turns out to offer no more genuine satisfaction than the original sceptical conclusion it was meant to avoid.[45]

The widespread sense that sceptical arguments are natural or intuitive explains why this happens. To see how, consider this account of sceptical arguments, recently offered by Crispin Wright:

the best philosophical paradoxes ... signal genuine collisions between features of our thinking that go deep. Their solution has therefore to consist in fundamental change, in taking up conceptual options which may have been overlooked. ... [T]he traditional sceptical arguments, in their strongest forms, are such paradoxes.[46]

Wright brings out very clearly the basis of the pattern Stroud detects. If sceptical paradoxes do indeed signal collisions between deeply entrenched features of our thinking about knowledge, Wright is correct: their solution must involve "fundamental change." But effecting fundamental change, taking up new conceptual options, will involve uprooting some deeply entrenched feature of our thinking: in other words, denying one of Stroud's "platitudes we all accept." Accordingly, no such "solution" to scepticism will amount to a defence of our pre-theoretical claims to knowledge *as we have always intended them to be understood*. How could it, once the basis of such claims has been admitted to be irremediably paradoxical? Rather, such a solution will inevitably appear as signalling our willingness to settle for less than we originally wanted. Put it this way: why isn't making fundamental changes in our ordinary thinking about knowledge *just another way of agreeing with the sceptic*? Recall Cavell who, though he thinks that the sceptic cannot mean what he says, still finds a deep truth in scepticism: that "the human creature's basis in the world as a whole, its relation to the world as such, is not one of knowing, *anyway not what we think of as knowing*."[47] To follow Wright and respond to scepticism with "fundamental changes" is precisely to give up "what we think of as knowing," just as the sceptic demands.

Stroud's examples of unsatisfactory theoretical responses to scepticism are Kant's transcendental idealism and Carnap's verificationism. Both are unsatisfactory because they let go the intuitive conception of objectivity – the sense that the world is what it is, independently of how we take it to be. The sceptic denies that we can have knowledge of the real world (if there even is one), cutting us off from what Cavell calls "the world as such." Kant replies that such knowledge is visibly in our grasp, once we admit that, transcendentally speaking, the real world is ideal. So whereas the sceptic tells us that we cannot have knowledge of real things, but only of appearances, the transcendental idealist, like his descendant the phenomenalist, tells us that we *can* have such knowledge, since talk about real things *is* just elaborate appearance-talk. Not only is this an extraordinary opinion, it is not obvious why it should not be counted a form of scepticism.

Carnap ends up in a similar trap. He tells us that the proposition that there are material things is not a genuine fact-stating proposition at all. Within the appropriate "linguistic framework," that which involves concepts and lays down rules for verifying material-thing propositions, it is analytic that there are material things. But the sceptic wants to raise a question about the empirical adequacy of the framework as a whole, and this is what cannot meaningfully be done. Since there are empirical questions only where there are procedures for answering them, empirical questions can be asked within frameworks, but not about them. Speaking the language of material things thus reflects a decision or convention, not a cognitive achievement. At this point, however, we must feel the force of Nagel's objection: the sceptic seems to have argued, quite intelligibly,  that certain facts may obtain but can never be known. Aren't we more certain that we understand the case for scepticism than that Carnap's theoretical distinctions hold water? And in any case, didn't we think, pre-theoretically, that speaking of objects reflected more than a convention? Didn't we think that there really is a material world and that it is not meaningless to claim that there is? If so, Carnap's theory involves a considerable retrenchment from our pre-theoretical position, for it shrinks the domain of factual knowledge. Again, we have a way of agreeing with the sceptic that our ordinary thinking about knowledge is beyond repair.

Still, this broad anti-sceptical strategy continues to attract adherents. Wright, for example, having put his finger on the source of the problem, favors a solution along these lines, though he draws his inspiration more from Wittgenstein than from Carnap. He suggests various principles that might govern the concept of fact-stating discourse: for example, that no member of a given class of statements is factual unless "it is possible to explain what would constitute cognitive abilities commensurate to the task of acquiring knowledge of, or sufficient reason for believing, statements in that class."[48] He then argues that, with such a convention in place, the case for scepticism undercuts itself. To the extent that the sceptic succeeds in showing that certain statements are beyond evidence, he removes them from the realm of factual discourse, even though it is essential to him to represent them as factual propositions whose truth can never be known.

As Wright is well aware, to philosophers like Stroud and Nagel, this verificationist account of fact-stating discourse will appear simply to beg the question against the sceptic, who seems to have argued with perfect intelligibility that most facts are unknowable. This impression of begging the question is, if anything, strengthened by Wright's intention, meant no doubt to buttress its plausibility, that his principle should have "no controversial consequences but its manner of classification of [the sceptic's target-] propositions."[49] This response to scepticism begins to look less like an all out counter-attack than an exercise in damage control. The sceptic has hopelessly compromised our pre-theoretical thinking about knowledge. All that remains is to keep the necessary "fundamental changes" to a minimum: to let the domain of factual knowledge shrink far enough to deny the sceptic his conclusion, but no further. However, shrink it must. Again, to admit this is to make a very large concession to scepticism. Significantly, Wright himself shows signs of uneasiness here. He writes:

> if any of the principles is indeed representative of our actual concept of factuality, ought it not to be possible to recognise that it is? . . . It is no good just telling a story . . . about any . . . of the sceptic's presuppositions . . . which, if it were true, would short-circuit the sceptical argument. We have to know that it is true, otherwise the case is not proven, and scepticism triumphs at second order.[50]

This is not an argument Wright finally accepts, for he thinks we can shift the burden of proof to the sceptic's shoulders, requiring him to prove that the proposed principle "misrepresents the concept of fact which we actually have." But even to raise the worry in this way is to retreat from the account of sceptical paradoxes as exploiting "collisions between aspects of our thinking that go deep." If *that* is how scepticism works, any response to scepticism is *inevitably revisionary*, requiring, as Wright himself says, "fundamental changes." And if this is true, there can be no question of showing that a principle adopted to deny the sceptic his conclusion is "representative of our actual concept" of anything. In effect, we agree to sacrifice what the sceptic proves we cannot have. As for shifting the burden of proof, why should the sceptic have to *argue* that his conclusions derive from features of the epistemic concepts we actually have when we have agreed from the outset that they do?[51]

Wright's own solution to the problem – that we do not need to prove any such principle since we can adopt it as a convention – does not speak to the objection that we have not only made fundamental changes in our concept of factual knowledge, but have made them in the direction demanded by the sceptic. How could it? There is no avoiding this consequence, once the naturalness of the case for scepticism has been conceded. Conceding its naturalness lands us in the *epistemologist's dilemma*: we can either accept scepticism, or make changes in our pre-theoretical thinking about knowledge that shrink the domain, or alter the status, of what we previously thought of as knowledge of objective fact. In making such changes, however, we inevitably appear to be making very large concessions to the sceptic. Unkindly put, the epistemologist's dilemma is that we can either agree with the sceptic directly, or in a roundabout, grudging way – Hobson's choice.


## 1.5   UNUSUAL QUESTIONS

Should we conclude from this that Hume was right, that the fatal first step on the road to scepticism is taken as soon as we agree to subject our knowledge of the world to a "philosophical" examination? Perhaps. But what is a "philosophical" examination of our knowledge of the world?

According to Stroud, the traditional philosophical examination of knowledge "aims at an assessment of all our knowledge of the world at once, and it takes the form of a judgment on that knowledge from what looks like a detached 'external' position."[52] Furthermore, the world, our putative knowledge of which we intend to assess, is conceived to be an objective world, a world in which the facts are what they are "independently of their being known or believed or said to be that way by anyone."[53] This perceptive analysis points to four central ideas: an *assessment* of the *totality* of our knowledge of the world, issuing in a judgment delivered from a distinctively *detached* standpoint, and amounting to a verdict on our claim to have knowledge of an *objective* world. Assessment, totality, detachment, objectivity: all four elements in the traditional epistemological project will be recognizable to anyone who has been concerned with scepticism. Evidently, all are present in the matrix of Humean pessimism and each will need eventually to be examined in detail. But some preliminary remarks are in order now.

That the traditional project is evaluative in intent is implicit in the fact that it aims at an examination of our *knowledge* of the world. The aim is not, or not just, to trace the origins or explain the causes of our beliefs, but to discover their bases or grounds, with a view to assessing their adequacy. The threat of scepticism arises when we become aware of some barrier or obstacle to our beliefs ever having the kind of justification they need to amount to knowledge. Humean naturalism is a pessimistic or sceptical response to the sceptical problem precisely because it offers causal accounts of the origins of our beliefs while conceding that these do nothing to overcome the barriers to justification that sceptical arguments exploit.

The evaluative project undertaken by traditional epistemology is unusual in various ways. However, being out of the way is not the same as being illegitimate. The traditional epistemologist may ask unfamiliar questions, or familiar questions in an unfamiliar context. But to show that his procedure is misguided, or that his results do not have the significance he thinks they have, we will have to do more than highlight his project's unusual character.

Perhaps the most striking feature of the epistemological project is its uncommon generality. We are all familiar with inquiries into the grounds for particular beliefs, or even for quite large classes of beliefs. But when we embark on the sort of inquiry that threatens to end in scepticism, we do so in the hope of understanding something about human knowledge *per se* or, if not that, all knowledge belonging to some *very* broad category. Thus Descartes sets out to examine *all* his former beliefs, not just those he has some *specific* reason for distrusting; and Hume turns his sceptical gaze on "reasonings concerning cause and effect" and our belief in "the existence of body," not on beliefs about particular causal relationships or the existence of particular things (or kinds of things). This is not to say that it is easy to explain precisely what the distinctive generality of the traditional epistemologist's questions consists in. But it is clearly crucial that we attempt not only to assess all our knowledge, or all knowledge in some broad category, but all of it at once. This is why I say that distinctive generality of the sceptic's (or traditional epistemologist's) questions imposes a *totality condition* on a properly philosophical understanding of our knowledge of the world. This is certainly an unusual requirement. But, as yet, we have seen no reason to think that it is intrinsically misguided, still less that it is unintelligible.

We can see right away that the thought that the sceptical implications of our ordinary ways of thinking about knowledge emerge only when we ask questions that are distinctively and unusually general does a lot to explain why those implications are ordinarily ignored. The pursuits of common life exclude the sceptic's systematic doubts in virtue of their narrow focus. So although Hume sometimes suggests that only "carelessness and inattention" protects us from a paralyzing awareness of the truth of scepticism, his judgment is too harsh and anyway misleading. It is not that our involvement in ordinary pursuits so absorbs our attention that we are led to overlook sceptical problems. Rather, in virtue of their particular focus or direction, ordinary pursuits logically exclude sceptical doubts. To get on with any specific, directed activity, various things have to be taken for granted. If they are not, the particular activity lapses. It is not carried on in a more careful, though more laborious, less convenient way. It cannot be carried on *at all*. For example: "When I am trying to mate someone in chess, I cannot have doubts about the pieces perhaps changing places of themselves and my memory simultaneously playing tricks on me so that I don't notice."[54] If I were to take such a possibility seriously, I simply could not play chess. My excluding it, for the purpose of getting on with a game of chess, has nothing to do with my being careless.

What goes for chess goes for forms of inquiry. As Wittgenstein puts it, certain propositions are like "hinges" on which our doubts and questions turn. Thus when doing history, "We check the story of Napoleon, but not whether all the reports about him are based on sense-deception, forgery and the like. For whenever we test anything, we are already presupposing something that is not tested."

Or in chemistry:

> Lavoisier makes experiments with substances in his laboratory and now he concludes that this and that take place when there is burning. He does not say that it might happen otherwise another time. He has got hold of a definite world-picture.... I say world-picture and not hypothesis, because it is the matter-of-course foundation for his research and as such also goes unmentioned.[55]

We cannot entertain Hume's sceptical worry about whether the course of nature is subject to unpredictable changes and get on with the kind of experimental research that interested Lavoisier. This doesn't mean that Lavoisier is careless or inattentive, only that his interests are different from those of the epistemologist. Similarly, entertaining radical doubts about the very existence of the earth one hundred and fifty years ago does not amount to a more rigorous way of doing history. Once these doubts come to the fore, history gives way to another subject entirely, sceptical epistemology perhaps.

The aim of the traditional examination of knowledge, then, is to bring to the fore precisely those propositions that normally go unmentioned. But though these considerations bring the unusual character of epistemological inquiry into clearer focus, do they amount to a criticism of the sceptic's (or traditional epistemologist's) questions? Some philosophers – perhaps Strawson when he moves from pure Humean naturalism to some form of theoretical objection to scepticism – are inclined to think so. The sceptic is accused of misrepresenting the logical structure of our ordinary system of beliefs, treating all beliefs as if they were on a par. His mistake is to

framework judgements

treat "hinge" or "framework" propositions as if they were empirical, hence needing to be backed up by evidence. But they are not like that. Rather, they give structure to our whole way of making judgments. As Wittgenstein himself puts it:

> All testing . . . takes place already within a system. And this system is not a more or less arbitrary point of departure for all our arguments: no, it belongs to the essence of what we call an argument. The system is not so much the point of departure, as the element in which arguments have their life.[56]

But what exactly is the objection here? According to Marie McGinn, the sceptic's (and the traditional epistemologist's) cardinal error, which Wittgenstein has put his finger on, is to treat "judgments of the frame" as if they were particular items of empirical knowledge. What we must recognize is that our true relation to them is "non-epistemic." Taking them for granted is built into the very structure of anything we could recognize as a judgmental practice. Accepting is thus, in the end, less a matter of assenting to propositions, hence of knowing *that*, than of acting in the only way we know *how*.[57] Or as Meredith Williams has put it:

> the truth of this methodological proposition (that the Earth has existed long before my birth) is a causal condition for doing history and is logically assumed by historical inquiry. It is not, however, an epistemic condition. In other words, in order to do history and to be justified in one's findings, it is not necessary to establish or determine the truth of that proposition. It simply doesn't figure in the justification of an historical claim.[58]

This is an explicit statement of the sort of view Strawson seems to lean towards when he remarks that, according to naturalism, the sceptic goes wrong in trying to undermine the reasons for our belief in the existence of body and the reliability of inductive inferences since there are *no such things* as the reasons for these alleged beliefs.[59]

I do not say that there is nothing to this line of attack. In fact, I think that there is a lot of truth in it; or perhaps I should say, fragments of several truths. But the difficulty is to make it clear why these Wittgensteinian observations show that the traditional epistemologist's questions are illegitimate, rather than just unusual. It is all very well to claim that our relation to framework judgments is non-epistemic: the problem is to show that this amounts to more than the claim that our relation to them is not *ordinarily* epistemic, or (an even weaker conclusion) not ordinarily *treated as* epistemic, neither of which the sceptic is obviously committed to denying.

What needs to be ruled out, if this response to scepticism is to work, is the suggestion that our relation to such judgments *becomes* epistemic in the context of the traditional project of assessing our knowledge of the world as a whole. The sceptic agrees that his project is unusual but denies that this alone reveals it as incoherent.

We might note that Wittgenstein himself is struck by the fact that, when their unusual generality is kept in mind, sceptical doubts are far from being evidently senseless. Thus:

> It would strike me as ridiculous to want to doubt the existence of Napoleon; but if someone doubted the existence of the earth 150 years ago, perhaps I should be more willing to listen, for now he is doubting our whole system of evidence. It does not strike me as if this system were more certain than a certainty within it.[60]

Perhaps if our aim is to assess "our whole system of evidence," we *can* treat as putative items of empirical knowledge propositions which ordinarily are not, and perhaps in some sense could not, be so treated. If we can't, this needs to be shown. This will require more than calling attention to the unusual generality of the traditional epistemologist's questions.

Williams too concedes that "an historian in a reflective mood might indulge in certain metahistorical speculations in which he might come to think that all the while he was doing his researches, he has presupposed that the Earth had existed for some time."[61] Again, this suggests that propositions that are not ordinarily treated as empirical hypotheses may become such *in the special context of philosophical reflection*. But surely, when they do, we will be forced to return a negative verdict on them. It seems, then, that the Wittgensteinian way with the sceptic tends in the direction of Humean biperspectivalism. As an answer to the sceptic, it is at the very least incomplete. But it does point towards what we need: a deeper understanding of the context of philosophical reflection and of the relation of the results of such reflection to everyday epistemic practices.

If this is right, everything depends on what ordinarily stands in the way of treating our most basic commitments as empirical. The sceptic has a ready answer: practical necessity. So this is the point at which the third element in the traditional examination of knowledge makes its presence felt. The "detached" standpoint from which that examination is conducted, whatever else it is, is one where ordinary practical concerns have been set aside. Thus Descartes encounters scepticism in the course of "meditating" on his previous beliefs; and Hume finds that scepticism surfaces in the study, not the street. We have already seen why this must be so. Acting towards a specific end is impossible without taking all sorts

*practically*

of things for granted. Hume's thought that Nature has determined us to judge would be better put as Nature has determined us to act, for acting will require us not to doubt. Perhaps this is what he glimpsed when he noted that scepticism arises when Reason acts alone. Without the influence of the passions, we lack particular interests to move us to action. In this frame of mind, nothing has to stand fast for us. Everything can be brought before the tribunal of reason, and the result is scepticism.

Earlier, I criticized Strawson for being too ready to assimilate Hume's naturalist response to scepticism to Wittgenstein's more theoretical criticism. There I had in mind the dominant strain in Hume's thinking: that belief is a matter of psychological necessity. But, as just noted, we can find in Hume at least a hint that action is the antidote to sceptical doubt. On this view, belief is not directly a matter of psychological compulsion. Rather, Nature constrains us to act, and action, because directed to a specific end, requires excluding various logical possibilities from current consideration. If this is how Hume sees Nature's remedy for the sceptical malady, there is some convergence between his views and those of Wittgenstein. Wittgenstein is quite sure that: "Giving grounds . . . comes to an end; but the end is not certain propositions' striking us as immediately true . . . ; it is our acting which lies at the bottom of the language game."[62]

But even supposing this to be so, it is still not clear why or even whether it shows that there is something flawed about the traditional examination of knowledge, which takes place in a context in which all requirements of action have been set aside. In this context, we can ask whether the hinges of our ordinary system of judgments are held in place by anything more than practical necessity. We can ask whether our putative knowledge is more than knowledge-for-all-practical-purposes.

I am not saying that Wittgenstein was unaware of this. On the contrary, he knew full well that the "idealist" will say that he is not dealing with "the practical doubt which is being dismissed" but with "a further doubt *behind* that one," and "that this is an *illusion* has to be shown in a different way."[63] This is just the point I want to underline: that if Wittgenstein's observations on ordinary doubting are to amount to a criticism of scepticism, or of traditional epistemology, they must do more than establish that, sceptical arguments notwithstanding, we have knowledge-for-all-practical-purposes, as much certainty, in Locke's familiar phrase, "as our frame can attain to or our condition needs." For this is not something that the sceptic denies, at least if knowledge-for-all-practical purposes is taken to involve making do with presuppositions which, though completely unjustifiable in a theoretical way, we are *practically* constrained to accept. But I think Wittgenstein means to establish more than this.

Certainly, this is how some critics of scepticism take his remarks. In their eyes, Wittgenstein shows that the concept of knowledge cannot meaningfully be applied to "hinge" or "framework" propositions. This is what is meant by the claim that our relation to them is "non-epistemic."

As we saw, the thought that our relation to various basic certainties is non-epistemic has to be understood this way. Otherwise, the sceptic will say that, though our relation to such judgments is ordinarily non-epistemic, things change in the context of epistemological investigation. But he wants to force the critic to argue not just that our relation to them *is* not epistemic but that it *cannot* be, because it is hard to see what the basis for such an argument could be, other than the fact, which he readily concedes, that attempts to treat them "epistemically," hence to support them by evidence, are doomed to failure. The anti-sceptical strategy in question begins to look less like a satisfactory diagnosis of scepticism than a simple reassertion of ordinary certainties against the unsettling results of philosophical reflection.

The problems with this "Wittgensteinian" response to scepticism do not end here. The thought that we have a special non-epistemic relation to certain "framework judgments" suggests that these judgments, while genuinely factual, have a privileged place in the scheme of things, and we can now see why such a view will be hard to sustain. No matter what account we try to give of this privileged place, it will be difficult to deny the sceptic his triumph if we admit that these judgments are ultimately groundless, while continuing to insist that they are genuinely factual. In consequence, anyone who goes down the path of claiming that we enjoy a special "non-epistemic" relation to our basic commonsense certainties will come under strong pressure to deny that these judgments are straightforwardly factual, which brings us back to the question of whether the envisaged reply to the sceptic offers more than verbal camouflage for a large concession. Once more, the epistemologist's dilemma.

This tension is evident in Wittgenstein's own notes on scepticism. Wittgenstein is tempted by the thought that the concept of knowledge is at home only where there is a possibility of giving grounds, so that the propositions that underwrite "our entire system of evidence" cannot sensibly be thought of as either known or not known. At the same time, he is aware of – for he seems himself to feel – an instinctive resistance to thinking this way about what seem to be factual commitments, hence his allusion to the *difficulty* of recognizing "the groundlessness of our believing." However, a critic might respond that the difficulty is not so much to recognize the groundlessness of our believing as to grasp the difference between being willing to recognize it and falling in with scepticism. The claim that our relation to our basic commitments is non-epistemic sounds more than a little reminiscent of Cavell's thought that "our relation to the world as a whole is not one of knowing," which was Cavell's candidate for the *truth* of scepticism.

The thought that scepticism results from abandoning the standpoint of the "actor" for that of the "spectator" is by no means the exclusive property of Hume and Wittgenstein. The point figures largely in pragmatist diagnoses of scepticism, for example in the writings of Dewey and latterly Rorty. Thus Dewey decries "the separation of knowledge from practical activity", noting that: "Theories which assume that the knowing subject, that mind or consciousness, have an inherent capacity to disclose reality, a capacity operating apart from any overt interactions of the organism with surrounding conditions, are invitations to general philosophical doubt."[64]

But for pragmatists too, the problem remains to explain why this is a criticism of the traditional epistemological project, rather than just a description. For not merely does the sceptic not deny that he conducts his "curious researches" from an unusual standpoint, he appeals to the difference between the reflective stance of the philosopher and the engaged attitudes of common life to explain why the truth of scepticism is ordinarily ignored.

This brings us to the final element in the traditional examination of knowledge. The idea of detachment from everyday practical concerns explains the sense in which the traditional knowledge is supposed to involve an objective assessment. We are not concerned with the practical consequences of doubting certain propositions but only with whether there is any reason whatever to suppose that they are true. But traditional epistemology does not only aim at an objective examination of knowledge: the knowledge it examines is also supposed to be knowledge of an objective world.

Reflection on the demands of this requirement is what really makes us wonder whether the thought that our relation to the fundamental certainties of everyday life is non-epistemic will ever amount to a satisfactory response to scepticism. As we just saw, responses to scepticism that stress the primacy of the "engaged" attitude, typical of everyday life, are under pressure to evolve into doubts about the factuality of the presuppositions the sceptic calls in question. Pragmatists like Dewey eagerly embrace this aspect of their diagnosis of scepticism. The deep source of the fatal separation of knowledge from practical activity is "the assumption that the true and valid object of knowledge is that which has being prior to and independent of the operations of knowing."[65] Now, if stressing the primacy of action forces us to modify our conception of objectivity, we can see why it is supposed to lead to a criticism of scepticism. But then the question is one of distinguishing this criticism from roundabout agreement. This is why other critics, though tempted to travel a similar road, are more cir-

cumspect than Dewey. They realize how difficult it is really to abandon
the conception of objectivity that pragmatists blithely toss aside.

Although the Wittgensteinian reaction to scepticism stresses the primacy
of action, it also has obvious affinities with Carnap's theory of "internal"
and "external" questions. According to Carnap, within a given "linguistic
framework," constituted by its characeristic "meaning-postulates," there
will be procedures for verifying propositions expressible within the system.
It follows that questions about the entire system are not meaningful, empirical questions at all. At best, they are calls for decisions as to whether
to adopt a given framework and are therefore to be decided on pragmatic
rather than factual grounds. Thus, in the case of the external world:

> To accept the thing world means nothing more than to accept a
> certain form of language, in other words to accept rules for forming
> statements and for testing, accepting or rejecting them. The accept-
> ance of the thing language leads, on the basis of observations made,
> also to the acceptance, belief and assertion of certain statements. But
> the thesis of the reality of the thing world cannot be among these
> statements, because it cannot be formulated in the thing language
> or, it seems, in any other theoretical language.

The sceptic's attempt to undermine our belief in the reality of the world
thus misfires, for "there is no such belief or assertion or assumption, because it is not a theoretical question."[66]

In important ways Wittgenstein differs from Carnap. For example,
he does not suppose that we *decide* to talk about physical objects. This is
surely correct: our way of looking at the world is the "inherited background" against which we distinguish between the true and the false, not
something we picked out of a range of alternatives. Indeed, Carnap's view
borders on paradox: for what "framework" are we thinking in when we
decide between competing frameworks, pragmatically or otherwise?[67]
Wittgenstein's does not: if the framework totters, our ability to think goes
with it.[68]

Still, it is arguable that the differences are outweighed by a major point
of convergence. One of Carnap's most fundamental ideas is that truth is
an intra-theoretic notion. Propositions are true-in-a-framework, but the
framework itself is not meaningfully thought of as either true or false.
Wittgenstein too is taken with this thought: not doubting certain things
belongs to our system of, say, historical evidence and we "cannot say of
this . . . that it is definitely *correct*."[69] What this reveals is that, like Carnap,
Wittgenstein is inclined to tie the concept of truth to that of verification:
"Really '[a] proposition is true or false' only means that it must be possible to decide for or against it," a thought which leads naturally to "If the

true is what is grounded, then the ground is not *true*, nor yet false."[70] And that Wittgenstein should move in this direction is not surprising since, as we saw, if we try to meet scepticism with the claim that the sceptic has misrepresented our relation to our basic certainties by treating it as "epistemic," we will be under pressure to claim that they are not really factual.

So we return to what is by now a familiar impasse. To those who see scepticism as an intuitive problem, all such claims will seem to beg the question against the sceptic, who appears to argue, quite intelligibly, that ordinary life involves factual commitments that we cannot justify. In fact, don't we acknowledge the sceptic's success if we start to talk about realizing the groundlessness of our believing? For if the ground is not true, nor yet false, what is it that we *believe*? Again, it seems, our sense that we understand the sceptic's conclusion is stronger than our sense, if we have it at all, that it is meaningless to speak of our belief in an external world or the reality of the past as true. And if we become convinced, as a result of our encounter with scepticism, that certain propositions need to be removed from the realm of factual discourse, doesn't this involve us in a modification of our pre-theoretical conception of empirical knowledge so substantial as to amount to a roundabout way of agreeing with the sceptic? That even Wittgenstein feels the force of the epistemologist's dilemma is indicated, as I said, by the tension between wanting to acknowledge the ultimate groundlessness of our beliefs (thus apparently conceding that there is something we believe, even at the bedrock level) and being tempted to remove our most basic commitments from the realm of the factual.

What all this shows is that we cannot afford *simply* to concede that the sceptic shows that our most basic commitments are beyond justification and then hope to turn this into the conclusion that they do not need justification, whether by removing them from the arena of fact-stating discourse or some other way. What we need to do is examine the sceptic's barriers to knowledge with a view to seeing how we have to think about knowledge for them to be barriers at all. The peculiarity of the sceptic's questions is certainly relevant to a theoretical diagnosis of scepticism. But pointing to their peculiarity does not, by itself, give us the diagnosis we are looking for.

## 1.6 DEFINITIVE REFUTATION

How do we avoid the epistemologist's dilemma? I want to argue that there is only one way: we must not concede the naturalness of the sceptic's doubts. As I see it, the pre-condition for the success of any response to scepticism is *a shifting of the burden of theory*. We must show that sceptical

arguments depend essentially on theoretical commitments that are *not*
forced on us by our ordinary ways of thinking about knowledge, justification and truth. We must attempt what I shall call a *theoretical diagnosis* of
the case for scepticism.

Obviously, a philosopher convinced that sceptical doubts *are* natural
will not see this as an option. To hold that sceptical doubts are natural
is to deny that the sceptic depends essentially on distinctive theoretical
commitment not clearly implicit in our ordinary handling of epistemic
concepts. Supposing he still entertains hopes of responding theoretically
to scepticism, this leaves him only one resource: he must try to deprive
the sceptic of the ability to ask his questions or express his conclusions.
He must attempt a *therapeutic* diagnosis of scepticism. The problem of
scepticism must be *dissolved* by showing that the sceptic doesn't or can't
mean what he seems to mean, perhaps even that he does not succeed in
meaning anything at all. It is not enough to show that the case for scepticism is less than compelling: he has to show that no coherent problem
was ever presented.

The idea that sceptical doubts are natural doubts thus leads to a demand for *definitive refutation*. Consider, for example, Stroud's idea of what
an adequate response to scepticism would achieve. Stroud, like Hume,
thinks that scepticism arises when we try to step back from our everyday
engagements so as to understand in some very general way how it is possible for us to have knowledge of the world. To turn scepticism aside, then,
we would have to show that this "'philosophical' conception of our relation to the world is an illusion, and not a way we can coherently think of
ourselves at all." To accomplish this, we will have to "reveal the incoherence" of the sceptic's conception of objectivity.[71] Or, as he has put it more
recently, "We need to see how the almost effortlessly natural ways of
thinking embodied in [the traditional epistemological] enterprise nevertheless distort or misrepresent our position, if they do." This way we may
hope to "come to see how and why the epistemological enterprise is not
fully valid, or perhaps not even fully coherent."[72] Not less than compelling;
not misguided: *incoherent*.

Or take Strawson. Strawson contrasts direct refutations of scepticism,
which try to provide rational justifications for the beliefs the sceptic questions, with indirect refutations, which try to show that the sceptic's doubts
are self-defeating, thus not finally intelligible.[73] This is an odd dichotomy.
It seems not to occur to Strawson that the sceptic's doubts might be less
than compelling, even though not exactly unintelligible.

Cavell, too, is under the spell of the idea of confronting the sceptic with
a definitive refutation. He hopes to show that sceptical doubts are "less
than fully natural." But this turns out to mean not "essentially dependent
on tendentious theoretical ideas" but "less than fully intelligible." The

sceptic's claims "cannot be made fully natural (= projected with a clear sense) without destroying their point."[74] So they are not proper claims at all. For all these philosophers, the sceptic enjoys an absolute triumph or suffers an absolute defeat. To end the war we must impose a Carthaginian peace: *scepticus delendus est.*

Exactly the same thought underlies Wright's dichotomy: either we prove the correctness of some verificationist restriction on the domain of fact-stating discourse or we adopt it as a convention. That is to say, either we show that the sceptic's claims are already incoherent or we revise our concepts to make them so. Combat with the sceptic is always *à l'outrance*. There is no room for a response that is less than definitive.

But why should we have to prove the correctness of an anti-sceptical account of fact-stating discourse, or of anything else? Why isn't it enough to show that it fits in with our ordinary epistemic practices as well as do the sceptic's ideas? The answer must be that the sceptic has no ideas of his own. Sceptical arguments are wholly natural, trading only on features of our ordinary ways of thinking that are obvious, however deep. This leads inevitably to the thought that a successful response to the sceptic should have the same status: it should appeal only to principles that are provably correct and so potentially obvious.

If we once concede the naturalness of sceptical doubts there is no escaping the demand for definitive refutation. To see sceptical doubts as natural is to agree that the sceptic has no distinctive theoretical commitments. His ideas about knowledge, so far as he has any, are our ideas. Not only do his arguments seem valid, they exploit only our ordinary, familiar epistemic concepts, bringing to light their unwanted consequences. We might try modifying our concepts but – the epistemologist's dilemma again – the result of doing so seems hardly more appealing than, if indeed distinguishable from, scepticism itself. So if the sceptic goes wrong, it can only be because he subtly mishandles the ordinary concepts his arguments exploit. This means that, for all their surface plausibility, his questions or conclusions must involve some kind of conceptual mistake and so must be, in the end, somehow "incoherent" or "unintelligible." If a philosopher who concedes the naturalness of sceptical doubts is unhappy with both pessimism and the prospect of radical conceptual change, he commits himself to arguing for the incoherence of scepticism. The trouble is, it is not easy for anyone to convince himself that he does not understand the sceptic at all: hence the attraction of phrases like "not *fully* coherent", "natural but not *fully* natural," "less than *fully* intelligible."

This problem does not have to be left on an intuitive level. There are reasons why attempts to convince oneself that the sceptic's claims are unintelligible are unlikely to succeed. But these same reasons suggest that the sceptic's doubts are less natural than he thinks.

intelligible,
but not natural

First we have to see why, however convinced a philosopher might be of the "almost effortlessly natural" character of the line of thought that leads to scepticism, it is difficult to make the case for the sceptic's apparent theoretical invulnerability without taking on substantial theoretical commitments. To begin with, even if we agree that the sceptic exploits only the demands of our ordinary epistemic concepts, and not theoretical ideas of his own, we have not conceded that it is obvious what the demands of those concepts are. But if the demands of our ordinary concepts cannot simply be read off the surface features of everyday epistemic practices, even the advocate of the naturalness of sceptical doubts is committed to a theory: that is, *a theory of our ordinary concept of knowledge*.

Recall Wright's thought that sceptical paradoxes are compelling and require fundamental conceptual change because they exploit "features of our thinking that go deep." There is a hidden tension here. The features of our thinking the sceptic exploits have to go deep if his paradoxes are to demand fundamental change. But this conflicts with their being evidently compelling, for only surface features of our thinking are obvious. If sceptical arguments turn on deep features of our thinking, the sceptic's starting point is not ordinary epistemic practice but *a theory of the systematic demands on knowledge that ordinary practice implicitly imposes*. This means that his arguments can neither be obviously correct nor demand changes in anything that belongs uncontroversially to our ordinary ways of thinking. In fact, as Wright himself insists, the fundamental changes he proposes are meant to have no controversial consequences outside our attitude towards the sceptic's target propositions.

However, it is not just that we have been given no reason to think that the systematic demands imposed by our ordinary concepts can simply be read off the surface features of everyday epistemic practices: we know that they can't. For even the most determined sceptic admits that what he takes to be clear consequences of our ordinary epistemic concepts are ordinarily ignored. There are various ways that the apparent conflict between everyday epistemic attitudes and the results of philosophical reflection might be explained: but it is always at least *possible* that our ordinary concepts are not what the sceptic takes them to be. This reinforces the conclusion that even the advocate of the naturalness of sceptical doubts has at least a theory of the systematic demands of the ordinary concept of knowledge.

This is not all. To admit to disparities between his discoveries and ordinary attitudes, while denying that they signal a distortion of ordinary concepts, the sceptic must hold that his extraordinary questions bring out surprising consequences of ordinary ways of thinking. This leads to another way of assuming theoretical commitments. In addition to a theory of the systematic demands imposed by our ordinary epistemic concepts, he will need an explanation of why those demands are not ordinarily enforced. One way or another, he will be forced to argue that the deep demands of our ordinary ways of thinking only come to the surface in the context of his extraordinary investigation into the status of human knowledge in general. There are various accounts of this project that might explain how this is so: traditional epistemological inquiry is detached, pure, fully objective, hence unlike more ordinary investigations, which are engaged, practical, subjective, etc. All these explanations have their merits. But all promise to be rich in theoretical commitment.

This point requires special emphasis, since it will be central to the argument of this book. Not merely are the general prospects for theoretical diagnosis encouraging, I think that Hume provides us with an invaluable clue to where a correct theoretical diagnosis of scepticism should be sought. The clue lies in the context-sensitivity of both sceptical doubts and everyday certainties. Something we must never lose sight of is that although those who see scepticism as a deep and disturbing truth about the human condition may recognize that the power and convincingness of sceptical arguments are fully felt only under conditions of philosophical inquiry and do not persist under conditions of everyday life, they still *must* hold that the sceptic discovers, in his study, something about human knowledge in general. The contextual restrictions on the effectivness of the sceptic's arguments cannot be allowed to reflect any kind of theoretical insulation of everyday belief from sceptical evaluation. For example, it cannot be that the *epistemic* aims of philosophy and everyday life are so different that the sceptic's results leave knowledge, as we ordinarily understand it, untouched. Or it cannot be that when the sceptic says that he does not know whether he is dreaming right now, he means by those words something quite different from what would ordinarily be meant by them, so that his claims do not really conflict with anything we ordinarily claim. Whatever his other commitments, then, the sceptic must have an implicit theory of the relation of philosophical reflection to everyday life; and that theory must acknowledge the contextual sensitivity of sceptical doubt while, at the same time, preserving his sense that the results of philosophical reflection clash with our ordinary outlook.

With these remarks in hand, we can explain why attempts to convict the sceptic of making unintelligible claims or asking unintelligible questions are unlikely to succeed. If there is no way to develop the case for scepticism while avoiding all theoretical commitments, any worked-out argument for scepticism will be open to theoretical diagnosis. But this is not a bonus: we cannot put forward a theoretical diagnosis and still hold out hopes for a definitive refutation, for theoretical and therapeutic diagnosis exclude each other. The reason is this: to try to place the sceptic's claims and questions in a broader theoretical context is to try to *make sense of them*. There is a holistic aspect to meaning, particularly to the meaning of theoretical propositions. The full meaning of sceptical claims and questions cannot be divined simply through familiarity with English grammar and the ordinary employment of the words they contain. To this extent Cavell is right to distinguish between what the sceptic's words mean and what he means by them. To determine what the sceptic means, we must place his claims in their proper philosophical context: we must connect them with the right kind of epistemological project and identify the ideas about knowledge, justification and truth that make that project seem a plausible or even a necessary undertaking. If those ideas can be shown to be less than compelling, we will have a theoretical disgnosis of scepticism and an answer to those who see scepticism as revealing an unpalatable, if incredible, truth about the human condition. But we will also have gone a long way towards making sense of what the sceptic is up to. So we will have made it difficult, if not impossible, to turn round and claim that what the sceptic says is utterly unintelligible.

These latest remarks point to the need to guard against a possible misunderstanding of my notion of theoretical diagnosis. I have said that theoretical and therapeutic diagnosis exclude each other. But surely, someone might think, they need do no such thing. In particular, they will not do so if we locate the source of the sceptic's appeal, not in the mishandling of particular concepts, but in certain general ideas about meaning, so that by criticizing those ideas we are led to feel less certain of the intelligibility of some of the sceptic's characteristic claims. This way, we might try to defuse the threat to an anti-sceptical theory of meaning that comes from the intuitive intelligibility of what the sceptic says by arguing that the sense of intelligibility is not really intuitive, but rather an artifact of unacknowledged theoretical influences. We might even try to weaken the sense of intuitive intelligibility by explaining how the sceptic manages to generate a kind of illusion or hallucination of meaning: and in fact, this is just what Cavell tries to do. We see, then, that a certain kind of theoretical diagnosis might issue in a therepeutic dissolution of sceptical problems.

Obviously, this is a possible strategy, and I never meant to suggest that it isn't. But it is not the sort of strategy that I shall be following. For one thing, such "theoretical" approaches to therapeutic diagnosis turn out, in practice, to rely heavily on intuitions about meaningfulness and so are apt, even if correct, to be dialectically ineffective against philosophers who have different intuitions or are less sure of what intuitions they have. More than that, because the sceptic does not make any obvious mistakes, and certainly appears to speak coherently enough, the misconceptions about meaning that have to be attributed to the sceptic tend to be highly controversial, hence far more open to question, as Nagel and other intuitive sceptics insist, than our pre-theoretical sense that we understand the sceptic very well. Accordingly, I shall use "theoretical diagnosis" to refer to the strategy of attempting to uncover the sceptic's essential *epistemological* presuppositions. I shall never accuse the sceptic of incoherence. I shall not argue that his problems are pseudo-problems. On the contrary, I think that they are fully genuine, *but only given certain theoretical ideas about knowledge and justification.* It is in this sense of "theoretical diagnosis" that theoretical and therapeutic diagnosis work at cross purposes.

Since pressures to take on theoretical commitments are inherent in concessions that even die-hard defenders of the naturalness of sceptical doubts are compelled to make, we should expect philosophers who hold out hopes for a definitive refutation to betray occasional signs of uncertainty. If, in spite of themselves, they are under pressure to assume theoretical commitments, they should also be under pressure to advocate a theoretical rather than therapeutic response. This is what we find.

One example we have encountered already. We saw earlier that Strawson's antithoretical naturalism shows signs of instability, tending to modulate from an initial pessimism into a form of theoretical criticism. This is not an accident: the naturalist position is intrinsically unstable. The instability comes from the fact that the naturalistic outlook has two dimensions – substantive and methodological – which come into conflict. According to substantive naturalism, which tends to dominate in Hume, the truth of scepticism is that the staying power of certain fundamental beliefs cannot be explained in terms of their logical or epistemological status and so can only be explained by appeal to the (causal) workings of human nature. By contrast, methodological naturalism, which comes to the fore in Wittgenstein, insists that the demands imposed by the concept of knowledge are to be recovered from an examination of ordinary practices, not assumed as antecedently given. Such a naturalistic approach to recovering the claims of reason is not apt to reveal the conditions on, say, knowledge of the external world that the sceptic is committed to imposing. How could it? After all, the sceptic himself admits that, ordinarily, knowledge claims are entered and withdrawn in ways that betray no sensitivity to what he regards as the most fundamental constraints on knowledge of the world: this is why the results of philosophical reflection clash with our natural attitude. So by admitting that the lesson of scepticism clashes with everyday attitudes and procedures, the naturalist automatically opens up the possibility that sceptical arguments misread, distort, or at least supplement ordinary epistemological conceptions.

To illustrate, consider how Strawson, following Stroud, characterizes the sceptic's central point. The sceptic is said to argue that the fulfillment of the "experiential conditions" which we take to warrant "the application of physical object concepts" is "consistent with the falsity of all the propositions we then affirm," so that "we cannot be said really to *know* that any such propositions are true."[75] This simply assumes that knowledge of the physical world must be derived from more "basic" experiential knowledge: otherwise, the difficulty of effecting such a derivation will pose no obstacle to knowledge of the physical world. But an examination of ordinary practice suggests that this is a distortion of real-life justification. We do not ordinarily treat *any* experiential judgment as if it were firmer or more certain than *any* judgment about an object in the external world. Examining our ordinary attitude towards certainty, Wittgenstein finds that:

> My having two hands is, in normal circumstances, as certain as anything I could produce in evidence for it. That is why I am not in a position to take the sight of my hand as evidence for it.[76]

This is a claim that will bear looking into and I shall return to it on more than one occasion. But this much is clear from the start: Wittgenstein is right if his remark is taken as a description of our ordinary attitude towards the epistemic status of certain judgments about physical objects. Our ordinary attitude does not appear to involve acceptance of the general epistemological priority of experiential knowledge over knowledge of the world. Yet Strawson's account makes scepticism turn on just this doctrine of epistemological priority. No wonder, then, that Strawson oscillates between agreeing that the sceptic has undermined or excluded any reasons we might have for believing in the existence of physical objects, and hinting that the sceptic has misread our ordinary epistemic concepts by looking for reasons where none are required.

It is not obvious that there are specifiable "experiential conditions" which we take to "warrant the application of physical concepts." Nor is it obvious that a proposition must either be derived from experience or else clung to irrationally, by dogmatic assumption or through psychological compulsion. Perhaps, as Wittgenstein suggests, propositions "stand fast" in virtue of the different ways they are built into the structure of various particular practices, which is more a matter of logic than psychology. Strawson recognizes that ordinary practice lends itself to more than one interpretation when he argues, as we have already seen, that the sceptic goes wrong when he tries to attack our reasons for holding certain fundamental beliefs, because there are no such things as the reasons for which we hold them. But the main point here is that the instability in Strawson's position results from his tacit acknowledgment of the point argued for above: that sceptical arguments start from definite theoretical interpretations of our ordinary epistemic concepts, not from uncontroversial claims about their employment in familiar cases. So though we begin with a naturalist dismissal of all theoretical responese to scepticism, we end up with one account of our ordinary epistemic concepts confronting another.

This same ambivalence is present in Wright's views about how to deal with the sceptic. As we have seen, Wright starts from the thought that, since the sceptic exploits what are clearly "features of our thinking" about fact, knowledge, etc., his paradoxes demand fundamental change. But when he comes to defend the convention he proposes, a convention implicitly definitional of "fact" and "fact-stating discourse," he seems to change his mind. There he argues that the sceptic cannot object to the idea of such a convention because the concepts at issue are concepts the sceptic himself relies on and which, therefore, he must "allow to be encoded, somehow or other, in our linguistic practices." The sceptic's objection can only be to the specific content of the proposed convention, which he must show "misrepresents the concept of fact which we actually have or, by criteria we acknowledge, ought to have."[77] If he can't do this, then presumably we have reason to think that we have turned his argument aside, not by fundamental conceptual change, but by a better understanding of the concepts we had all along. Perhaps the epistemologist's dilemma is making itself felt here: if we fail to hang on to our ordinary concepts, we concede too much to scepticism. But we should also note that this attempt to shift the burden of argument to the sceptic implies that the question of what concepts we actually have is itself theoretical, hence that the sceptic is less of a plain man than he likes to appear. So Wright should never have claimed, without qualification, that the sceptic exploits "features of our thinking that go deep." His view should have been that this is what the sceptic claims to be doing but that we should suspend judgment on the merits of this claim, pending arguments over which articulation of the concept of fact best fits in with the evidence of "our linguistic practices." The sceptic's implicit theory of our epistemic concepts is to be met with an alternative which fits in equally well with the uncontroversial data, while failing to generate sceptical consequences.

Finally, recall Stroud's account of what an adequate response to scepticism needs to do. Although, we may recall, Stroud concedes that the sceptic depends crucially on a certain conception of the objectivity of the world, he insists that this conception can be expressed in terms of "platitudes we would all accept."[78] However, his eventual assessment of our prospects for coming to terms with scepticism suggests a change of heart. There he returns to the sceptic's reliance on the "traditional conception" of objectivity, arguing that the challenge of scepticism is:

> to reveal the incoherence of the traditional conception, and perhaps even to supply an alternative we can understand, without falling once again into a form of idealism that conflicts with what we already know about the independence of the world or denies the intelligibility of the kind of objectivity we already make very good sense of.[79]

But if the sceptic appeals only to "platitudes we would all accept," there
is no room for such an alternative. An alternative to the "traditional conception," will *have* to violate one or more of our cherished platitudes.
Anyone committed to the naturalness of the traditional conception *must*
endorse Wright's original strategy and advocate conventions that are explicitly revisionary of our pre-theoretical understanding of epistemic concepts. Of course, Stroud does not want to do anything of the sort, because
he thinks that giving up on our platitudes will involve too large a concession to the sceptic, perhaps by committing us to an "idealist" account
of objectivity: again, the epistemologist's dilemma. But the point here is
that the prospect that attracts Stroud is open only if the traditional conception of objectivity goes beyond "what we already know about the independence of the world" and "the kind of objectivity we already make very
good sense of": in other words, if one of the sceptic's key ideas involves
more than is implied by the platitudes we would all accept. Only if that is
so can we hope to tinker with the traditional conception while leaving the
platitudes untouched. So what we need to see is what the sceptic adds to
the platitudes and why he is constrained to add it. Stroud is driven, that
is, to hope for a theoretical diagnosis of scepticism, even though his requiring us to show the "incoherence" of the traditional conception of
objectivity reveals his continued attachment to the ideal of definitive refutation and hence to therapeutic diagnosis. However, if we can show that
we are under no compulsion to add what the sceptic adds, we are not bound
to argue that what he adds is "incoherent."


## 1.7  THE BURDEN OF THEORY


If scepticism really could be derived from platitudes, there would be a
strong case for pessimism. But, as I have said, I hope to show that it can't
be. We have already seen that the view that sceptical doubts are natural
doubts is hard to sustain. It is time to stop trying to sustain it. We should
aim at a theoretical rather than a therapeutic diagnosis of scepticism.
    The prospects for this are not hopeless. We saw in the previous section
that it may not be so easy for the sceptic to avoid all theoretical commitments. But in any case, though it often *seems* that sceptical arguments are
strikingly brief, simple and compelling in comparison with theoretical rejoinders, which are long-winded, complicated and hard to assess, perhaps
this is an illusion. After all, as is evident from the fact that philosophers
still disagree radically over the interpretation of the *First Meditation*, even
if standard sceptical arguments can be very compactly stated, explaining
how they really work is apt to be a long and involved affair A sceptical

argument in canonical form may be a distillate from a complex infusion of theoretical ideas.

This is what I hope to show: that no matter how natural or intuitive sceptical arguments appear, or can be made to appear, they cannot be divorced from epistemological foundationalism. But I agree with those struck by the apparent intuitiveness of sceptical arguments that this takes some showing. I cannot take it for granted, in the way I was once inclined to.[80] Those who see sceptical doubts as natural doubts need not deny that foundationalist ideas emerge readily in the course of traditional epistemological inquiry. But they will hold that they emerge as response to deeper and more intuitive questions. They will deny that they are the basis for asking such questions in the first place.

I agree too that if we hand the sceptic his foundationalist presuppositions, there is no refuting him: this is what the conditional correctness of scepticism consists in. And, if we miss the way seeming platitudes, or apparently innocent methodological proposals, can be used to smuggle in the crucial epistemological ideas, the conditional correctness of scepticism will take on the air of absolute correctness. But if we keep these ideas clearly in view, the situation is changed: there is no danger in conceding that the sceptic cannot be refuted on his own terms if those terms are not ones we are bound to accept. Similarly, if it turns out that the very notion of epistemological inquiry that the traditional epistemologist takes for granted proves to be shot through with foundationalist preconceptions, then scepticism may well be the inevitable outcome of epistemological inquiry – as Hume and others have said it is – but only of epistemological inquiry so understood.

If this is right, pessimism about our chances for responding theoretically to scepticism stems from a failure to find the right point of attack. Though this will not be apparent to those who think of his arguments as intuitive or natural, the proper strategy against the sceptic is to deny him the foundationalist presuppositions he relies on. So, the way to undermine pessimism is not to question the intelligibility of sceptical claims and arguments but to question their intuitiveness, by way of exposing (and criticizing) their implicit foundationalism. Foundationalist ideas, I shall argue, are both more pervasive and more peculiar than is generally realized. And though, as we saw in the previous section, theoretical diagnosis precludes the possibility of definitive refutation, which might be thought a drawback, it has the advantage of not being hopeless from the start. This is because its task is not so onerous. Its aim is not to deprive the sceptic of the power of speech but to destroy scepticism's aura of inevitability.

To shift the burden of theory, then, is not necessarily to shift it entirely to the sceptic's shoulders but, at least initially, to get him to acknowledge his share. To take away the sceptic's inbuilt advantage, it is enough to show that the case for scepticism is at least as dependent on less-than-compelling theoretical ideas as any anti-sceptical accounts of knowledge. Thus the critic of scepticism need not suppose that the evidence of ordinary epistemic practice settles the case in his favor. Rather, it is enough for his purposes that ordinary practice underdetermine its theoretical interpretation. If this is so – and what sceptic can deny the underdetermination of theory by evidence? – the case for scepticism, once shown to be theoretically loaded, will cease to be compelling.

I hope this makes it clear, if I have not made it clear enough already, that nothing I have said is meant to suggest that the issue of scepticism can be resolved through a simple confrontation between tendentious philosophical theory and "ordinary language," as if pointing up disparities between the traditional epistemologist's investigation of knowledge and more familiar epistemological questioning settled matters in favor of the anti-sceptic. I agree that this cannot be done. Once we have felt the power of sceptical arguments, and so experienced the apparent clash between our natural attitude and the results of philosophical reflection, we are no longer in a position simply to back one against the other. Indeed, in pointing up the clash we are emphasizing rather than dispelling the paradox of scepticism. In my view, the temptation to put all the weight on ordinary language is another instance of the hankering after a definitive refutation. (Recall Skorupski's thought that any views brought to bear against the sceptic ought to themselves shrink into platitudes.) Of course, this is not to say that the evidence of ordinary language is irrelevant. Though the disparity between ordinary attitudes and the results of sceptical reflection does not by itself settle any issues, it is still crucially important because it offers ways of arguing that scepticism does not spring from everyday platitudes alone but from a particular theoretical interpretation of them.

This is relevant to the question of whether the critic of scepticism has to be able to prove that his account of our epistemic concepts is correct. Because of the (apparent) naturalness of his arguments, the sceptic is allowed to occupy the default position, all the burden of proof falling on the other side. But if ordinary practice underdetermines its theoretical interpretation, there is no question of proving any such principles. Equally, however, there is no need to. For once the sceptic is revealed as a fellow-theorist, there is no question of proving scepticism either.

These remarks bear on the puzzling character of Moore's "Defence of Common Sense" and "Proof of an External World." In his "Defence," Moore lists various propositions he knows to be true: that he lives on the Earth which has existed for many years past, that he has never been far from it, that there are many other people in the same situation, and so on. In his "Proof," he holds up his hands to show that at least two external objects – objects to be met with in space – exist. Moore confronts the sceptic with definite pieces of knowledge: things that he knows and knows that he knows. Philosophers have found (and continue to find) these performances fascinating. For one thing, Moore's responses to scepticism are almost unique in being as short and to the point as the sceptic's own arguments. For another, although we are all certain that the sceptic cannot be dismissed in this way, it is not entirely easy to say why not.

I think that Moore's performances highlight the need for a theoretical diagnosis of scepticism. If I am right that, appearances perhaps to the contrary, scepticism is not an intuitive problem but arises only in the context of an acceptance, perhaps implicit, of epistemological foundationalism, it is clear why Moore's arguments must fail, even though nothing that he says is false. To get as far as seeing scepticism as a problem, we must already be susceptible to ideas that block Moore's response. In particular, we must acquiesce in what Stroud calls "the doctrine of the epistemic priority of sensory experiences over independently existing objects." Accepting this doctrine, we cannot possibly see the knowledge claims Moore advances as in any way primitive. Rather, we will see his conviction that there is a hand in front of him, when he apparently holds it up in good light etc., as the conclusion of an inference from his current experiences, and so will want to know how, in the face of such sceptical possibilities as that Moore may simply be dreaming, those experiences provide the kind of conclusive evidence his certainty demands. Having thus become questionable, Moore's paradigm knowledge claims can no longer be invoked to rule out the sceptic's counter-possibilities: Moore's attempt to confront the sceptic with undeniable examples of knowledge inevitably fails.

The problem is that Moore offers his examples of knowledge as a direct response to the sceptic's *conclusions.* They cannot be put forward like that because, once we have conceded that the sceptic has raised a problem that demands this kind of a direct answer, we have implicitly acquiesced in epistemological views that make such an answer inevitably ineffective. Everything Moore says may be true, but none of it can be entered at *this* stage of the argument. But the situation would be quite different if Moore offered his examples as a challenge to the sceptic's essential theoretical presuppositions and not as a direct response to his conclusions. This possibility crossed Wittgenstein's mind, for he writes that: "one might grant that Moore was right, if he is interpreted like this: that a proposition saying that here is a physical object may have the same logical status as one saying that here is a red patch."[81] Moore's remarks do not disprove the sceptic's conclusions: they challenge the ideas about epistemic priority on which those conclusions are based.

Of course, if Moore had really intended his remarks to be taken this way, he could not have offered them as a "proof" of the external world or "defense" of common sense. To offer them like that is to concede that the sceptic has raised a reasonable question, which demands a straightforward response; whereas to offer them in the spirit of theoretical diagnosis is to argue that, as an artifact of less than compelling theoretical presuppositions, sceptical doubts do not need to be answered on their own terms. So I think that Moore's remarks are all true, and all relevant to the problem in hand, but even so cannot be put forward in Moore's way. This is why his performance is so puzzling.

I am aware that all this will seem unsatisfactory to many: the urge to confront the sceptic with a definitive refutation is very strong. It is connected with the nagging worry expressed by Wright: that unless the antisceptic can prove his principles to be correct, scepticism will triumph at second order. The thought is this: that if one view of knowledge is correct, we will know all sorts of things about the world whereas, if another is the true one, we won't. This means that, unless we can prove the correctness of the view with the benign consequences then, though we may in fact know all sorts of things, we shall never know that we do. If this is right, a theoretical diagnosis, which pits one philosophical view against another, with neither being provably correct, plays right into the sceptic's hands. The sceptic always wins ties.

At this juncture, I think we *can* look to Moore for an important suggestion. Moore does not always advance his commonsense certainties in direct opposition to the sceptic's conclusions: he sometimes opposes them to what he sees as the "principles" underlying sceptical arguments. Thus he says in opposition to Hume: "I *do* know that this pencil exists; but I could not know this, if Hume's principles were true; theorefore, Hume's principles . . . are false. . . . [T]he fact that, if Hume's principles were true, I could not know of the existence of this principle, is a *reductio ad absurdum* of those principles."[82]

This argument is not inconsiderable, though it moves rather too quickly. What it misses is Hume's thought that, though it takes philosophical reflection to bring this home to us, the sceptic's principles are ours too. Moore sees Hume as attacking ordinary claims to knowledge on the basis of some gratuitous philosophical assumptions. But if sceptical arguments really are natural or intuitive, the sceptic will not be trying to undermine our claims to knowledge of the world from without but, in a sense, from within. It is true that, since he wants to raise questions about our right to claim any knowledge of the world, he must conduct his investigation from a standpoint "external" to that knowledge. But his grounds for his negative conclusion cannot be "external" in the sense of based on assumptions about knowledge that have nothing to do with our ordinary epistemic views. If they were, Moore would indeed be entitled to back his commonsense convictions against the sceptic's "assumptions." But the sceptic does not see himself as making assumptions: rather he takes himself to be exploiting features of our everyday epistemic concepts that we are all bound to recognize. This is what we need to show is not the case.

Stroud is right here: if the sceptic's "assumptions" are "nothing more than truths inevitably involved in any general assessment of our knowledge of the world, Moore does not successfully refute them."[83] Even so, Moore's argument underlines something of crucial importance: that it is *essential* to scepticism that sceptical doubts appear to be natural doubts. That scepticism seems to arise out of only the most platitudinous features of our epistemic concepts is what makes it a paradox rather than a mere puzzle. If scepticism can be shown not to arise this way, its character and significance are transformed. Scepticism will no longer appear as a deep truth about or paradox intrinsic to the human condition but simply as the unwanted consequence of a particular set of epistemological ideas. And once scepticism has been cast in this light, it is no longer so clear that the sceptic wins ties, or that a tie on the theoretical level leaves us not knowing whether we know anything about the world. For if we can show that sceptical criticism of our ordinary claims to know is criticism from *without*, so that the sceptic's principles are not necessarily our own, then perhaps we *can* follow Moore and regard those claims as more certain than any arcane theoretical account of knowledge, even one with benign consequences. In effect, we will be able to reverse Hume's thought that the intuitive force of the case for scepticism will always overcome any credibility attaching to obscure philosophical theories: the unnaturalness of sceptical doubts will make them powerless against ordinary epistemological convictions. And not just powerless in the way that Hume recognizes but powerless because, even on reflection, they seem no more, indeed less, compelling than our ordinary views.

Perhaps this will still seem unsatisfactory. It now seems that, even if we are left knowing *that* we know all sorts of things, we will still not know *how* we know them. However, the argument I shall develop will bear on this concern too, for I shall, in fact, be attempting a more radical shifting of the burden of theory than my imagined critics suppose. Though I shall, in a way, be suggesting what could be called "epistemological views," the outcome of the theoretical diagnosis I shall offer is not happily described as leaving one theoretical account of knowledge pitted against another, thereby allowing the sceptic to claim victory at second order. This is because, in tying scepticism to foundationalism, I shall not be tying it so much to a particular theory of knowledge as to the idea that knowledge is the sort of thing that might be the object of theory *at all*. I shall not be asking how our knowledge of the world should be understood but, in a sense, whether there is anything to understand; not whether there is a theoretical understanding of this knowledge that permits a positive assessment, to offset the sceptic's negative assessment, but why we think that there is anything to assess; not whether the battle can be fought to a stand-still, but why we suppose that is can even be joined.

I turn then to my main task: to show that sceptical doubts are un-natural doubts. Indeed, to show just *how* unnatural they are.

# 2

# The Priority of Experience

## 2.1 EPISTEMOLOGY AND RADICAL SCEPTICISM

Not even philosophers who see sceptical doubts as intuitive or natural think that the sceptical consequences of our ordinary ways of thinking about knowledge and justification are immediately evident. Somehow, involvement in ordinary pursuits conceals them. It takes philosophical reflection to bring them into clear focus, hence the clash between philosophy and common life.

For the would-be theoretical diagnostician, this is a significant concession. It indicates that scepticism does not fall automatically out of the truistic elements in the sceptic's case. Rather, his truisms, or seeming truisms, acquire sceptical significance only in the context of an extraordinary investigative project whose theoretical presuppositions will bear looking into. But the everyday ineffectiveness of sceptical doubts also suggests a quite specific line of attack for, as we shall see, it is not easy for the intuitive sceptic to explain the strikingly context-bound character of his doubts while preserving his sense that his conclusions clash with our everyday attitudes.

In the previous chapter, I accepted Stroud's identification of the four key elements in the traditional epistemological project. A philosophical examination of our knowledge of the world is an attempt to *assess* the *totality* of that knowledge, conceived as knowledge of an *objective* world, from a *detached*, external standpoint. Since I am advocating a theoretical diagnosis of scepticism, one question that comes immediately to mind is whether we have any understanding of the project of "assessing our knowledge of the world" that is independent of our familiarity with a certain kind of sceptical argument, which might then be examined for its theoretical commitments. If we take seriously the thought that scepticism represents a startling discovery, it is natural to suppose that we do: we begin naively with the idea of assessing our knowledge of the world and, to our surprise, find ourselves led to a negative verdict. But I am inclined to think that this gets things backwards. It is only because we are familiar with certain kinds of sceptical arguments that we can give content to the idea of such a project of assessment. To "assess" our knowledge of the world, at the proper level of generality, just is to decide whether certain arguments can be rebutted.

Let us consider the common characterization of the task of epistemology as that of showing that knowledge is possible. This can be misleading in several ways.

It is widely held today that justified true belief is not sufficient for knowledge. If knowledge is to be understood in terms of justification at all, there must be some fourth condition. This means that there are two ways of denying the possibility of knowledge. We could argue that we are never in a position to fulfil whatever condition needs to be added to justification and truth to make our beliefs add up up to knowledge strictly so called. Or, more radically, we could argue that we never even get so far as being justified.

*radical scepticism*

For the traditional epistemological project, the challenge of radical scepticism – the claim that our beliefs, or our beliefs belonging to some broad category, are never so much as justifiable – is by far the more significant. Certainly, philosophers who see scepticism as a disturbing discovery about the human condition must have radical scepticism in mind. They cannot take the sceptic to have shown only that, though we have all sorts of good reasons for the things we believe, our justifications are not quite as ironclad as we might have hoped. There is nothing disturbing in that.

Scepticism will present itself as a disturbing discovery about the human condition only if it clashes with essential features of our everyday epistemic attitudes. It must come into conflict with deeply entrenched commitments, with attitudes that we *need* to take up or claims that we need to make, not things we happen thoughtlessly to believe but can easily abandon. But justified belief is all we need for everyday purposes, so that the more that knowledge demands beyond truth and justification, the less we need knowledge. It follows that there will seem to be a deep clash between philosophy and common life only if the attempt to assess our knowledge of the world threatens to lead to radical scepticism. In common life, we can adapt to our justifications always being less than ironclad. Whether we can adapt to their being always utterly worthless is another matter entirely.

*non-radical*

To take an example of non-radical scepticism, it has been argued by Peter Unger that "know", like "flat" is an "absolute term." Strictly speaking, a surface is flat if and only if it has no bumps whatsoever, which means that no physical surface is ever really flat. Similarly, knowledge requires absolute certainty: I know something if and only if there is no possibility, however remote, that I am wrong. On this view, there is a kind of incoherence in combining a claim to know that P with an admission that one might nevertheless be in error. Of course, some error possibilities are so remote that, for ordinary practical purposes, we rightly disregard them.

This is the case with the sceptic's typical thought experiments, which involve our being victims of Descartes' Evil Deceiver or brains in vats. But something very similar can be said about bumps: for practical purposes, such as playing billiards, a surface's minute irregularities do not matter. Still, all this means is that the table is flat enough for playing billiards, not that it is really flat. So by the same token, our "knowledge" may be knowledge for all practical purposes; but unless we can rule out the sceptic's error possibilities it will not really be *knowledge*.[1]

I think it is clear that, if this were all there were to it, though the sceptic might well be able to argue that "scepticism" does not presuppose much in the way of contentious epistemological theory, scepticism would not be a very serious problem. This is because it would not point to any deep clash between philosophy and common life, or to any clash at all. Clearly, the discovery that nothing is absolutely flat is not disturbing. This is because, when we claim that a billiard table is flat, we mean that the surface has no irregularities that could disturb the path of a billiard ball; and if we claim that it is *really* flat, we mean flat enough to satisfy the standards of the most exacting player. But even if we mean more than this – even if, in our thoughtless way, we mean that it is free of even the most microscopic bump – showing us the error of our ways will not place us in conflict with anything we ordinarily *need* to claim, which means that we can accept correction without strain. Accordingly, if scepticism rested on no more than the analogy between "know" and "flat," scepticism would not point to a deep and unsettling truth about the human condition. To preserve the analogy, ordinary knowledge claims would have to stand to justification as ordinary flatness claims stand to flatness, demanding whatever measure is appropriate to the purpose in hand. Absolute certainty, like absolute flatness, would be an idealized condition that we do not expect to find realized in the actual world. So even if the sceptic succeeded in pointing out a conflict between features of our ordinary thinking about knowledge – say, our believing both that we have lots of knowledge and that knowledge demands absolute certainty – the crucial feature would not be one that, as Wright says, "goes deep."

Not that I mean to concede even this argument for scepticism. But the point I want to insist on here is that the *radical* sceptic's discovery that knowledge is impossible cannot be like the discovery that nothing in the physical world is ever absolutely flat. Ordinary, imperfect flatness is an approximation to real flatness. But if the radical sceptic is right, ordinary "knowledge" is not an approximation to real knowledge. What is ordinarily called knowledge does not involve *imperfect* justification, i.e. justification that approximates but falls short of some ideal. Rather, we have no justification *at all* for anything we ordinarily believe about the world. This suggests that we will miss the significance of sceptical alternatives to our ordinary views if we think of them as remote possibilities that, while they deprive us of absolute certainty, leave as with plenty of justification for what we ordinarily believe. Sceptical alternatives are *remote* possibilities only relative to our ordinary views about the world: if all those views are in question, the standards for calling a possibility "remote" are not so clear. This is one reason why I think that we will never get to the bottom of scepticism by tracing it to the quest for certainty. Abandoning the ideal of absolute certainty might free us from the threat of the sort of non-radical scepticism that depends on distinguishing sharply between knowledge and justified true belief. But for anything we have seen so far, it would leave the problem of radical scepticism untouched.

This brings us to the second way in which characterizing the traditional epistemological project as that of showing that knowledge is possible might be misleading. We might understand "possible" in a very weak sense as "logically possible." The task of epistemology would then be to come up with a definition of "knowledge" that covered enough of the intuitively right cases while remaining consistent. Alternatively, we might take possible to mean something slightly stronger: "humanly" possible perhaps. Then we would have to characterize knowledge in such a way that acquiring knowledge would not overstrain the capacities of creatures such as ourselves living in a world like ours. Our having knowledge would have to be consistent with the laws of nature as well as those of logic.

Again, I think it is clear that neither task answers to the traditional epistemological project. If this were all there were to showing that knowledge is possible, it would not be clear why the possibility of knowledge would be a *problem*. There is a problem about the possibility of knowledge because there are arguments purporting to show that knowledge is *im*possible. Putting the arguments of this section together, to show that knowledge is possible is to show how arguments for radical scepticism go wrong. It is to show how the considerations that the sceptic exploits do not, on reflection, amount to barriers to knowledge after all.[2]

This brings us back to the close connection between scepticism and traditional epistemology. As the epistemological quest was first described, it sounded as though we had an intuitively intelligible project of "assessing" our knowledge of the world that, disastrously, turned out to end in scepticism. We wanted to know whether our beliefs are all we take them to be and found out that they aren't. Now, however, it begins to look as if things are the other way round: because there are arguments for radical scepticism there is a project of showing that knowledge is possible. In other words, sceptical arguments are what breathe life into the idea of "assessing" our knowledge of the world as a whole. For what is it to "assess" this knowledge other than to determine whether or not such arguments are successful? This is just what the theoretical diagnostician suspects: thinking about knowledge in a certain way underwrites sceptical arguments, which in turn create space for the project of "assessing" our knowledge. There are no questions about knowledge that we understand naively, independently of contentious theoretical ideas, and which, when pressed, lead to the discovery that we never know any of the things we ordinarily take ourselves to know.

## 2.2  SCEPTICISM AND EPISTEMOLOGICAL PRIORITY

I am going to argue that sceptical doubts cannot be detached from a foundationalist conception of knowledge and justification. Its roots are not to be found in any metaphysical doctrine, such as realism, nor in the abandonment of the actor's standpoint for that of the spectator, nor even in the so-called "quest for certainty," but in a contentious epistemological theory, itself the product of mistaken analogies.

But does it really need to be *argued* that modern or "Cartesian" scepticism depends on foundationalism? Isn't it just obvious that it does? The traditional epistemologist, in the Cartesian mold, is concerned with assessing large classes of beliefs in an unusually general way. The assessment takes place in connection with the threat of radical scepticism, the possibility that these beliefs fail to amount to knowledge because they are completely without justification. But doesn't this project clearly stand or fall with a foundationalist conception of justification? If we are to "assess" all our knowledge of the world, all at once, it must be on the basis of knowledge that we take (or have argued) to be somehow more secure. What could this be, if not experiential knowledge?

This general suspicion appears to be readily confirmed by the way that arguments for scepticism typically proceed. Moreover, since the assessment of our knowledge of the world always centres on coming to terms with such arguments, we get further confirmation of my suggestion that the project of seeing where such arguments go wrong, if they do, exhausts our understanding of the idea of assessing the totality of our knowledge of the world.

Consider our knowledge of the external world. The sceptic argues that what we unquestionably know by means of the senses amounts to less than we want to know. What we know by means of the senses, "immediately" anyway, is how things appear to us. What we want to know is how they really are. Now *if* knowledge of how they are has to be derived from knowledge of how they appear, we have both the makings of a sceptical problem and room for a project of assessing out knowledge of the world as a whole. If it does not, it is not clear that we have either. Thus we find Stroud, who is as convinced as anyone of the intuitive character of sceptical problems, conceding that "The apparent obstacle to our knowledge comes from the doctrine of the epistemic priority of sensory experiences over independently existing objects."[3] This is as good as to say "The obstacle comes from our apparent need to provide knowledge of the world with sensory foundations."

Other sceptical problems about particular "kinds" of knowledge seem to depend on making analogous cuts between what we are allowed to know, at least for the sake of argument, and what we hope (or like to think) we know. The problem of other minds sets knowledge of the inner lives of other people against the "evidence" provided by their "external" behaviour; the problem of induction contrasts knowledge of general, future or otherwise unobservable facts with observational knowledge gained to date; the problem of historical knowledge challenges us to relate beliefs about the past to evidence available in the present; and so on. Sceptical arguments *begin* by partitioning propositions into privileged and problematic classes. Propositions in the (at least relatively) privileged class are taken to provide the (ultimate) evidence for those in the problematic class and sceptical arguments challenge us to explain how they manage to do this. This challenge is not easy to meet, which is why propositions in the problematic class are problematic.

We ought to wonder what justifies these initial divisions. But this much is clear: once the appropriate relations of epistemological priority are in place, scepticism is just around the corner. A clear perception of this is what lies behind Ayer's classic analysis of "the pattern of sceptical arguments."[4] As Ayer presents the case for scepticism, the sceptic reaches his conclusion in three stages. At the first stage, he insists that the knowledge claims he is examining do not simply recapitulate the data we have for them and so need some kind of inferential backing. Our knowledge of the external world, for example, rests in the end on sensory experience, but any proposition about the external world claims far more than is claimed by any proposition having to do only with the contents of experience. Familiar thought experiments show, or are supposed to show, that the entire course of my experience could be just what it has been even if the world were very different from the way I take it to be, or even if there were no external world at all. Perhaps I am the victim of Descartes's Evil Deceiver or, to recur to the modern variant, a brain kept alive in a vat, my entire stream of experience artificially stimulated by implanted microelectrodes and bearing no relation to events in my environment. Analogous possibilities arise in connection with knowledge of the thoughts and experiences of other people versus the data provided by their overt behaviour, predictions about the future course of events versus evidence provided by what has happened up to now, the course of history versus the traces it has left behind, and so on. Perhaps other people are like robots, with no conscious inner life: all they do is behave in their characteristically complex ways. Or perhaps the course of nature will suddenly change: what reason do I have to think it won't? And how do I know the world did not come into existence five minutes ago, complete with delusive memories on the part of its inhabitants and with all the outward marks of great antiquity?

Having shown the need for inferential backing, the sceptic argues at the second stage that the link between the disputed beliefs and the evidence we can adduce for them can never be deductive. We can never deduce anything about the external world from experiential data alone, or about another person's inner life from his overt behaviour. However, and this is the third stage, there is no acceptable form of inductive inference to bridge the gap either. So beliefs in the area under consideration never amount to knowledge.

This analysis has considerable explanatory power. Notably, it enables Ayer to classify competing strategies in the theory of knowledge according to which stage of the sceptical argument they object to.

Naive or direct realism objects to the first stage, denying that knowledge of the kind the sceptic aims to undermine is always inferential. But this position only amounts to a different view about what is prior to what: it involves no quarrel with the idea of epistemic priority as such. For Ayer's direct realist, the foundations of knowledge start higher up than is sometimes thought. However, it seems difficult to maintain such a view in the face of the sceptic's thought experiments. The case of the Evil Deceiver, or the brain in a vat, seems to show that I could have all the experiential knowledge I presently have even if I knew nothing whatever about the external world. If we fall in with the idea of general relations of epistemo logical priority, we will not be able to avoid conceding that experiential knowledge is prior to knowledge of the world.

Reductionist and related strategies – phenomenalism and logical behaviourism, for example – challenge the second stage, claiming that certain epistemologically problematic statements are in fact analyzable in terms of statements giving the proper evidence for them. Again, such strategies do not challenge the idea of general, deep-lying relations of epistemological priority: their aim is simply to narrow the gap between propositions in the problematic and those in the privileged class. Few philosophers today expect reductionist strategies to succeed. But though this would not be Ayer's view, even if they did succeed their succes would be a kind of failure. They are typical of responses to scepticism that involve us in the epistemologist's dilemma. Either a reductionist strategy fails, so that we end up giving in to the sceptic, or it succeeds, in which case the knowledge we save will seem to amount to less than we wanted. We wanted knowledge of an objective world but got a roundabout way of talking about experience: in other words, a roundabout way of agreeing with the sceptic.

Third comes the "scientific approach," which still has significant appeal. As we saw, Strawson thinks that if there is hope for a theoretical response to scepticism, this is where it lies. If we adopt this approach, we will see sceptical arguments failing at the third stage by taking too narrow a view of inductive inference: we can justifiably believe in the external world or other minds via an "inference to the best explanation," if our "hypothesis" best explains the kind of experience we have or the way we see others behave. Ayer himself seems sometimes to incline to this view, as for example when he suggests that in talking about external objects we are elaborating a theory with respect to our basic experiential data.

I do not myself expect much from this way of dealing with the sceptic. The crucial question is: what does the supposed inference to the best explanation explain? The answer, from Hume to the present day, is always the "coherence" of experience. Our experience is not chaotic but follows definite and repeated patterns, a fact best explained by our interacting with a world of stable, physical objects. Note, however, that this answer is given in the context of a response to scepticism that accepts the general epistemological priority of experiential knowledge over knowledge of the external world. It must therefore be possible to know that experience is coherent without leaning on knowledge of objective reality. That is to say, the coherence of experience must consist in its conforming to purely experiential regularities. It is beside the point to claim, as Hume does, that:

> Bodies often change their position and qualities, and after a little absence, may become hardly knowable. . . . But here 'tis observable, that even in these changes, they preserve a coherence, and have a regular dependence on each other; which is the foundation of a kind of reasoning from causation, and produces the opinion of their continu'd existence. When I return to my chamber after an hour's absence, I find not my fire in the same situation, in which I left it: But then I am accustom'd in other instances to see a like alteration produc'd in a like time, whether I am present or absent, near or remote.[5]

Though Hume is supposed to be telling us something about the course of our "impressions," he ends up telling us something about "bodies." All he points to is the existence of what we may call *dependent* experiential regularities: regularities in the appearance of external things under relevantly similar conditions of perception. What the argument needs, however, is *independent*, hence *purely*, experiential regularities. However, as I have argued elsewhere, the problem is that we can find no stable regularities in experience unless we are already in a position to allow for the objective conditions of perception. Hume's error is forced: he comes up with inappropriate examples of the coherence of experience because there are no appropriate examples. So far as I can see, experience is coherent *only* within certain objectively fixed limits, having to do with the environment and the perceiver: purely experiential regularities collapse with every blink of the eye and turn of the head. So if all physical object talk is proscribed pending validation, not merely is there no way to identify the regularities in which the coherence of experience is supposed to consist, there is no reason to think that experience even *is* coherent in the required sense.[6] Even in pointing to the regularities that constitute the coherence of experience, we subtly beg the question against the sceptic, helping ourselves to the very knowledge he has called in question.

This brings us to the fourth approach, the "method of descriptive analysis." This does not try to refute the sceptic, at least not directly, but settles instead for an account of the inferential practices that we actually follow. We might expect such a method to lead Ayer to question the idea of fixed, underlying relations of epistemic priority for, as we noticed, when Wittgenstein looks at ordinary practices of giving evidence, he does not find that they follow the lines laid down by foundationalists. However, Ayer does no such thing. In his hands, this approach turns into a variant of the second: descriptive analysis reveals that though, say, statements about external objects cannot be *analyzed* into experiential statements, state ments of these two kinds are linked by evidential relations that are some how *a priori* or analytic. This too is a suggestion for how to cope with the epistemological constraints that underlie sceptical arguments, not a challenge to them.

Once again, then, though Ayer himself would dissent, we have a strategy that seems to play into the sceptic's hands. Obviously, the doctrine of analytic evidential connections is no stronger than that of analytic truth generally. But even waiving this, propositions connecting how things apear with how they are do not appear to be analytic. The sceptic's thought-experiments seem to show that the way the world objectively is has no logical connection with the way it appears to be. If I were a brain in a vat, my experiences would be a completely unreliable guide to my surroundings. So how can it be *analytic* that experience of a certain kind constitutes good evidence for the external world's being one way rather than another? And if it were, wouldn't we be back in the epistemologist's dilemma? That is to say, wouldn't we have retreated from our claim to have knowledge of an objective world, the facts of which are what they are irrespective of how we experience them as being or what we happen to think about them?

It seems fair to conclude that Ayer's account of sceptical arguments explains a lot about how the main anti-sceptical strategies arise. But more than this, supplemented along the lines I have indicated, it provides the outlines of a powerful case for what Stroud calls "the conditional correct-ness of scepticism." If we really are constrained to understand the epistemological status of the knowledge-claims the sceptic examines in the way he suggests, it is hard to see how scepticism is to be avoided. If our knowledge of the external world really does need to be derived, in some general way, from prior experiential data, we ought to be able to explain how. But it is difficult to see how we could give an account of a warrant-conferring form of inference connecting how things appear with claims about how they are in the external world which would be adequate to meeting the sceptic's challenge while doing justice to our sense of the objectivity of the world. The doctrine of the epistemological priority of experiential knowledge over knowledge of the world seems to disconnect our beliefs about the external world from the only evidence available to support them. The problem – seemingly insoluble – is to reconnect them without compromising their objectivity.

The account of sceptical arguments we are considering explains how scepticism can so easily come to seem inevitable. The fact is that, once the initial concession has been made, it *is* inevitable. The *conditional* correctness of scepticism cannot in the end be denied. But the account even does some justice to the apparent intuitiveness of the sceptic's argument. For what is striking is that the same considerations underlie each stage. The basic thought is that, if the world is an objective world, statements about how things appear must be logically unconnected with statements about how they are: this lack of connection is what familiar sceptical thought experiments dramatically illustrate. At the first stage of the sceptic's argument, this thought underwrites the claim that our beliefs about the external world commit us to much more than we are guaranteed by experience alone, and so needs some kind of inferential backing. But the very same thought that opens up the gap between experiential knowledge and knowledge of the world also prevents our ever closing it in a way that satisfies us. Either we fail to close it at all, or we close it in a way that changes the character of the knowledge we are trying to save.

We can even make room for the sceptic's sense of discovery. He *has* discovered something: namely that because there is no hope of placing our knowledge of the world on an experiential foundation, we will never be able to explain to ourselves how it is that we have *any* knowledge of the external world. Granting ourselves some such knowledge, we will be able to explain how we acquire more. But we will never understand the posibility of knowledge of the external world *as such*.

Putting these points together, there is no denying that an account of sceptical arguments that traces scepticism to a foundational conception of knowledge and justification explains a lot. So have I made the case for scepticism's depending on foundationalism? Unfortunately not: the argument has barely begun.

## 2.3 PRESUPPOSITION OR BY-PRODUCT?

Anyone familiar with sceptical arguments will recognize the pattern Ayer describes. But does this analysis really do justice to the case for scepticism? Does it go to the heart of the matter? No philosopher who thinks of scepticism as a powerfully intuitive problem can suppose so.

As I argued in chapter 1, it is essential to scepticism that sceptical doubts be natural or intuitive. If scepticism comes to be seen as simply the artifact of certain contentious theoretical ideas about knowledge or justification, its character as a philosophical problem is changed beyond recognition. This means that any account of his arguments that presents the sceptic as simply taking for granted a foundationalist view of knowledge plays into the critic's hands by making scepticism appear to rest on a gratuitous theoretical assumption. A foundationalist to the bone, Ayer has no qualms about simply handing the sceptic the idea that beliefs of one broad kind are "epistemologically prior" to those of another. So, though Ayer would not himself have seen it this way, his analysis offers the critic of scepticism exactly what he needs: a handle for a theoretical diagnosis of sceptical arguments.

However, although no one who thinks of scepticism as an intuitive problem can be happy with Ayer's account of sceptical arguments, it can hardly be denied that there are familiar sceptical arguments that *do* follow Ayer's pattern. Accordingly, the defender of the naturalness of sceptical doubts must hold that the considerations Ayer brings into prominence are not fundamental. This is a possibility that the theoretical diagnostician cannot ignore. No one denies that, given foundationalist views of knowledge and justification, sceptical arguments are readily constructed, so no one denies that there are familiar sceptical arguments that presuppose foundationalism. But what we need to know is whether there are any that do not.

This question is made pressing by the availability of an alternative account of the relation between scepticism and foundationalism. On this account, the sceptic deploys his strongest and most intuitive arguments to make us realize that our beliefs about the external world are intrinsically more vulnerable than our experiential data. Thus he does not, as Ayer's account suggests, simply help himself to the appropriate relations of epistemological priority: he argues for them. More precisely, the suggestion on the part of the sceptic (or traditional epistemologist) is that, in the course of a distinctive kind of examination of our knowledge of the world (the precise character of which will occupy us in subsequent chapters), seemingly harmless considerations, truisms even, force this realization upon us. The epistemological hierarchy characteristic of foundational theories of knowledge and justification, which makes experiential knowledge in some quite general way epistemologically prior to knowledge of the world, emerges as a by-product of the fundamental motives for scepticism. I take this to be what Stroud has in mind when he remarks that the "familiar criticism" of the sceptical problem concerning our knowledge of the external world – that it rests on the mistaken assumption that there must be sensory foundations for knowledge – "does not penetrate very deeply into the sources of scepticism": indeed, that it gets things "almost entirely upside down."[7] The lure of scepticism explains the temptation to be a foundationalist, the very opposite of what I want to argue.

So the key question becomes: is epistemological foundationalism a presupposition of sceptical argument or just a by-product? There is no avoiding the issue. As I just agreed, it is certainly fair for a philosopher impressed by the apparent naturalness of sceptical doubts to object that simply pointing out that a powerful case for scepticism can be mounted *given* a foundationalist view of knowledge and justification is not at all the same as showing that scepticism *depends* on foundationalism. Adopting foundationalism may be *sufficient* for ending up a sceptic, but what needs to be argued is that it is *necessary*. Obviously, it won't be necessary if there are other, less theoretically loaded ways of subjecting our knowledge of the world to sceptical doubt. More than this, it may even turn out that scepticism and foundationalism spring from the same roots. Indeed, I think they will have to, if there are to be any arguments for foundationalism at all: for how else are we to establish the natural epistemic priority of experiential knowledge over knowledge of the world except by showing that beliefs about the world are intrinsically more dubitable, that is, more vulnerable to sceptical assault, than beliefs about external reality? Stroud's suggestion, that foundationalism is a by-product rather than a presupposition of sceptical argument, is exactly the right view both for philosophers intent on upholding the intuitiveness of the case for scepticism and for those attracted to foundationalism.

If this position can be satisfactorily defended, we will have to see foundationalism as a strategy, perhaps in the end the *only* strategy, for answering the sceptic and not, as I want to claim, as a precondition for making sense of his problems. Notice too that the view of foundationalism as a by-product of an initial encounter with scepticism has no difficulty explaining why so many familiar sceptical arguments follow the pattern Ayer describes. If foundationalism offers the main, and still more if it offers the only, strategy for responding to scepticism, it is obvious why the sceptic needs arguments starting from foundationalist premises, hence why he so often seems to take foundationalism for granted: to complete his case, he needs to show that the antisceptical options foundationalism offers all fail.

The view that foundationalism is a by-product rather than a presupposition of sceptical argument thus invites us to see the sceptic as following a two-stage strategy, first forcing a retreat and then preventing any subsequent advance. Thus at the first stage he deploys his most intuitive arguments in order to force us to recognize that we can answer him only by grounding knowledge of the world on experiential knowledge, in effect by carrying through some foundationalist project. But then, at the second, he argues that all such projects inevitably come to grief. If this is right, we shall conclude that philosophers who think that the case for scepticism rests on foundationalist preconceptions go wrong by concentrating exclusively on arguments belonging to the second stage. They mistake the presupposition of a project the sceptic forces on his opponents for the presuppositions of scepticism itself. Or so the argument will go.

If this defence of the naturalness of scepical doubts can be made out, there will be no avoiding scepticism. The very same considerations that force us to recognize the priority of experiential knowledge over knowledge of the world will also leave us facing the epistemologist's dilemma. Any residual hope for defusing scepticism will have to lie in attempts to find fault with the sceptic's originating questions, where finding fault will not mean questioning their theoretical presuppositions but something more like finding them less than fully intelligible, as it does for Stroud and the other new Humeans. We will be left, as I argued in chapter 1, with the hopeless task of meeting the sceptic with a definitive refutation. The task is hopeless because, although it commits us to finding the sceptic's questions less than fully intelligible, they do not seem defective in point of intelligibility. Indeed, the very step that *commits* us to arguing against the intelligibility of scepticism – the concession that scepticism is, in the sense I explained at the beginning, an intuitive rather than a theoretical problem – is what *prevents* us from making the argument convincing. For how can we agree that the sceptic's deepest questions or arguments invoke only familiar platitudes, the sort of thing we understand if we understand anything, and at the same time hold that they are less than fully intelligible? Wouldn't they have to inherit their lack of intelligibility from the platitudes they depend on?

On the other side, however, the suggestion that foundationalism is a by-product rather than a presupposition of scepticism will be tenable only if the considerations that force the initial retrenchment to experiential knowledge, or which set up the context in which intuitive considerations force such a retrenchment, do not themselves simply take foundationalist ideas for granted. Since, as I hope to show, they do take such ideas for granted, proving quite ineffective otherwise, the claim that foundationalism is a by-product of an initial encounter with an intuitive case for scepticism is not tenable. True enough, foundationalism emerges out of a sceptical assessment of our knowledge of the world, but only in the way the rabbit emerges out of the conjuror's hat.

## 2.4   AGRIPPA'S TRILEMMA

One of the most ancient and most intuitive sceptical arguments is what we may call "Agrippa's trilemma," after the ancient sceptic who appears first to have given it formal expression.[8] The idea behind it is devastatingly simple. When any proposition, advanced as a claim to knowledge, is challenged, there are only three ways of responding:

1   Refuse to respond, i.e. make an undefended assumption.
2   Repeat a claim made earlier in the argument, i.e. reason in a circle.
3   Keep trying to think of something new to say, i.e. embark on an infinite regress.

Since there is no fourth option, any attempt to justify a given belief will fail, either by being interminable or by terminating in an evidently unsatisfactory way. It is hard to imagine a sceptical argument starting with more minimal presuppositions than this. All that appears to be taken for granted is that any claim can be challenged: a request for justification always *can* be entered, even though normally it might not be.

We may note, in passing, that in its ancient presentation, the trilemma appears as three of five "modes" leading to suspension of judgment. The other two are "discrepancy" and relativity." I think that these can be seen as devices for maneuvering us into a position where we are confronted by the fatal trilemma. Agrippa's thought, it seems to me, is that any claim can be met with a counter claim plausible enough to sow seeds of doubt (the mode of discrepancy). Alternatively, anyone who advances a claim about how things objectively are can always be offered an unfriendly qualification: "According to you that is how things are" or "That is how they seem to be in such and such circumstances" (the mode of relativity). In both instances, we have a way of making a request to say more seem in place. Once we agree that it is in place, we come face to face with the trilemma.

Although about as simple and intuitive as an argument for scepticism can get, even the argument from the trilemma may be less simple than it looks. For example, is it really true that all rejections of demands for further evidence amount to making *assumptions*? Or, going right back to the beginning, is it really the case that any claim can *reasonably* be challenged? In connection with the mode of "discrepancy," it is worth recalling Wittgenstein's dry comment that "If Moore were to pronounce the opposite of those propositions which he declares certain, we should not just not share his opinion, we should regard him as demented."[9] We should not respond by offering him evidence.

However, since my anti-sceptical strategy centres on shifting the burden of theory, the problem for me is that, in the case of questions like those just raised, it is not immediately clear where the burden of theory finally lies. The sceptic might ask "Isn't an undefended proposition *at bottom* an assumption, even though we may ordinarily be reluctant to admit it?" At least, he may argue, the claim that it is is plausible enough to face us with a problem. If there is a defensible distinction between mere assumptions and propositions reasonably advanced without evidential backing, it is up to the critic to explain what it is. If no such explanation is forthcoming, a sceptical conclusion surely stands.

We may also wonder whether the sceptic needs any *general* way of sowing seeds of doubt, or needs to suppose that such seeds can always reasonably be sown. After all, when we lay claim to knowledge, we surely do more than announce what we believe: we imply that what we say can be relied on. So, the sceptic may argue, he doesn't (unreasonably) *impose* the question "How do you know?." Rather, we *invite* it by the mere fact of laying claim to knowledge, even if neither we nor anyone else has doubts, reasonable or otherwise, about *what* we claim to know. At least, if we don't invite it, it is up to us, not the sceptic, to explain why not.

In any case, however these issues are finally decided, the argument from the trilemma seems a lot *more* general and *more* formal than arguments conforming to Ayer's pattern. Such "foundational" arguments start by imposing unexplained restrictions on what can be advanced in defence of what, thereby inviting theoretical diagnosis, whereas the problem posed by the trilemma threatens to arise *whatever* we are allowed to say.

So far, I have been treating the trilemma as a particular sceptical argument. But it is really a general strategy, susceptible of wide application. This is how the ancient sceptics see it, for they follow the Agrippan strategy in connection with at least two distinct problems.

The first is the familiar "regress of justification." Trying to justify a given proposition by citing a further proposition as evidence gets us nowhere. Since that proposition will itself need to be justified, as will anything we cite as evidence for it, and so on, we run straight into the trilemma. So chains of justification either fail to terminate or terminate in one of two unsatisfactory ways.

The second is what was known as "the problem of the criterion." Suppose that, instead of offering some particular piece of evidence, I back up a given belief by citing its supposedly authoritative source ("the senses," "reason," etc.) or by claiming it meets some condition that distinguishes justified beliefs from unjustified (e.g. increasing the overall coherence of one's belief-system): surely I can be challenged to explain why beliefs issuing from that source, or meeting that condition, are likely to be true. Again, we face three options: we can refuse to explain; we can justify our reliance on a given source or standard by appeal to the same source or standard ("I know by observation that observation is reliable," "A coherence theory of justification maximizes coherence"): or we can try to cite a different source ("I can show *a priori* that observation is reliable/that coherence is truth-conductive"). I suppose, however, that given our limited epistemological ingenuity, there is not much chance of our embarking on an infinite regress: circularity and mere assumption are the chief dangers here.

We should add a third application: the problem of evidential connection. When evidence E is entered in support of a proposition P, we can ask why it is that E, even if true, supports P? What is the connection between E and the truth of P? Various regresses threaten. But one kind seems especially significant: can I defend the evidential connection between E and P without either taking some evidential connections as primitive or relying, eventually, on the very kind of evidential connection that is in dispute? Here again, the prospects for a regress seem remote, but those for brute assumption or circularity very real.

All three problems represent important applications of the trilemma. But the first is the most fundamental. The second and third problems only take on specific forms, and possibly only present themselves as problems at all, once the first has been dealt with. For example, it makes all the difference to the problem of evidential connection whether we do, or do not, accept foundationalist restrictions on evidence.

A clear illustration of this point is provided by Crispin Wright's account of how a sceptic can argue that a proposition like "There are material objects" is utterly beyond evidence. Wright invites us to consider the following inference:

*from*:   Jones has kicked the ball between the two white posts,
*to*:   Jones has scored a goal,
*to*:   A game of football is taking place.

In this inference, the first line provides evidential support for the second only if we already know, or justifiably believe, that what is claimed at the third line is true. If we have no reason at all to think that a game of football is taking place, Jones's action may mean anything or nothing. But now consider Moore's attempt to prove the existence of external things by holding up his hand in good light. According to Wright, the sceptic will claim that it involves an inference from:

some proposition describing his experiences,
*to*:   Here is one hand and here is another,
*to*:   Material objects exist.

And the objection is that this is just like the football example: the first line only offers *any* evidential support for the second given that the third is true. If, as in Descartes's example, the "material world" is an elaborate hallucination, Moore's experiences have no evidential value whatsoever. There is, however, one crucial difference. Whereas in the football example it is easy to imagine how independent support for what is claimed at the third line could be gathered, this is not so in Moore's case. We have no evidence for the existence of material objects that is not evidence for the existence of particular material objects. If, therefore, we could establish the existence of such things, it would only be as a consequence of particular material-object propositions which, as we have seen, cannot be supported by evidence unless the existence of the material things is already taken for granted. It follows that, if it isn't taken for granted, it cannot be supported by evidence, which is as good as to say it cannot be supported by evidence at all. Any attempt to argue for the existence of the material world is doomed to circularity.[10]

A distinguished ancestor of this strategy is to be found in Hume's way of setting up the problem of induction. Having made an initial cut between the data provided by our knowledge of past and current fact and our beliefs about the future or general beliefs, Hume argues that the supposition on which inferences from the one to the other depend cannot be supported. Knowing about the future, on the basis of data about the past, depends on the belief that the future will resemble the past, which can be argued for only on the supposition that the future will resemble the past. Here the sceptical difficulty is that the course of Nature may change.

Given their presuppositions, these are impressive arguments. They suggest that, when it comes to knowledge of the external world, or knowledge of the future, the problem of evidential connection is insoluble: the evidence we must ultimately rely on for knowledge of the world has no evidential value unless knowledge of the world is already available to us. Once more, however, for present purposes these arguments are beside the point. They show the sorts of sceptical difficulties that *result from* foundationalism's way of partitioning our beliefs into privileged and problematic classes. But from the standpoint of showing that scepticism is an intuitive problem, this way of arguing for scepticism is no improvement on – in fact only highlights certain aspects of – Ayer's.

So, to pick up the main theme, I have suggested two points: that the trilemma, though perhaps most familiar through the problem of the regress of justification, represents a general strategy rather than a single problem, and that future possibilities for applying the Agrippan strategy may be decisively affected by theoretical reactions to previous applications. For a theoretical diagnostician such as myself, these points are absolutely crucial. In particular, it may be that, when it comes to the sceptical problems central to modern philosophy, the problem of our knowledge of the external world *et al.*, the Agrippan strategy works *in conjunction with* foundationalist conceptions of knowledge and justification. But this will not mean that those problems can be generated out of Agrippan considerations alone, though, if it sometimes seems that they can, this will explain why they can appear so intuitive, natural, lacking in theoretical commitments.

Of course, things would be different if these foundationalist conceptions were themselves forced on us by Agrippan considerations: in effect, if the only escape from the regress of justification were via the postulation of intrinsically credible, basic beliefs. Now it may be that the regress does show that, if justification is to be possible at all, some things must "stand fast": there must be some "fixed points." (As we shall see, it is difficult even for coherence theorists to expunge from their views all traces of epistemological privilege.[11]) But I take it to be a familiar and elementary observation that this point falls far short of justifying the various partitions of our beliefs into privileged and problematic classes that underlie the modern canon of sceptical problems. All chains of justification stop some-where: let us even agree that they stop at propositions or beliefs which, in some sense, cannot reasonably be doubted. It still does not follow that these terminating propositions fall into any simple, theoretically coherent kind such as "propositions about the contents of immediate experience." As we saw, the problem of evidential connection is going to be decisively affected by our openness or resistance to foundationalist ideas about evidence. We can say exactly the same for the problem of the criterion. If we agree that empirical knowledge has to be traceable to a single source – e.g. "experience" – that problem may well arise in an acute, even insoluble, form. But so far we have not seen any reason to suppose that the class of propositions that "stand fast," thereby making empirical justification possible, shows any kind of theoretical integrity. Nor have we yet seen why it should matter whether it does or not.

Though elementary, this point is easy to miss; and if it is missed, Cartesian scepticism will appear to arise out of less in the way of epistemo-logical theory than in fact it requires. There is a good example of how this can happen in the recent account of scepticism offered by Marie McGinn. McGinn begins with the Humean point that the sceptic's first step is to take up a critical, reflective attitude towards our ordinary way of accepting knowledge claims. Having taken up this attitude, she notes that, ordinarily, knowledge claims are accepted (or rejected) within a framework of judg-ments that are themselves accepted without special testing so that, if these cannot be grounded, nothing can. But, she argues, when it comes to judgments like "Here is one hand," we must look for evidence that commits us to no claims about the nature of objective reality, if we are to avoid begging the question at issue. This, McGinn claims, is the point at which "the idea of evidence that is epistemologically prior to any knowledge of the external world emerges." Thus:

> The sceptic is not to be seen as *starting* from a sense that objective reality may be forever beyond his reach, but rather the idea of confinement within experience is something that develops in the course of his reflections. . . . [T]he first stage in this process involves the sceptic's being led to cast his ordinary framework judgments in the form of knowledge claims. This leads, in turn, to the development of a purely subjective conception of experience. Given this conception of experience, our ability to make any judgments concerning the objective world can quickly be made to appear problematic. Thus, we are to see the idea that the sceptic is confined within the perspective of his own subjective experience as something that emerges as a *consequence* of the sceptic's initial assessment of judgments of the frame as knowledge claims which stand in need of a justification.[12]

This is exactly the sort of argument we are looking for, an argument in which foundationalism emerges out of an initial encounter with scepticism in a form that does not take foundationalist ideas for granted.

The suggestion here is that we are forced to concede the fatal "subjective conception of experience" as soon as we give in to the sceptic's Agrippan strategy of pressing for justifications where they are not normally given but where, he suggests, they ought to be available. However, the argument does not work, for it trades on a wholly undefended equation of "framework judgments," in the sense of "judgments affirmed without special testing," with "commonsensical claims about physical objects." If we concede this equation, it will indeed seem that the sceptic has shown that there is something specially problematic about our commonsense knowledge of the world. And once we have got this far, there will be no resisting his insistence that we look to some other kind of judgment altogether for the required evidence: a form of judgment that has (so far) not been called in question. However, if the Agrippan strategy is followed in its pure form, unconstrained by prior foundationalist commitments, there is no reason to suppose that there is any form of judgment that has not been called in question. Going back to the idea of "framework judgments", it is clear that the judgments we ordinarily affirm without special testing *include* those pertaining to "subjective" experience. So far as the regress argument itself goes, it is perfectly in order to ask questions like "How do you know that what you seem to see looks *red*?" Of course, we may try to argue that these judgments are in fact privileged. But my point is, the regress argument alone does not require us to suppose that our "framework" or "terminating" judgments fall into any simple, epistemological kind. That argument, because it is fully general, does not underwrite a particular sceptical problem about our knowledge of the external world or "objective reality." That problem arises only if we are determined to halt the regress in a special way, the way characteristic of foundationalism. This means that McGinn's argument can either remain true to its simple basis in the regress argument, and so fail to generate the required problem, or generate the required problem, but only by surreptitiously importing foundationalist ideas about evidence that the argument does not enforce.

In case this seems unfair, let me try to put the point a slightly different way. The key equation in the argument is effected by the introduction of "Here is one hand" as a paradigm of a framework judgment. We are meant to think that the sceptic has given us reason to think that all our claims to knowledge of the world are hollow because this judgment *and all judgments like it* are inevitably groundless. The question is, however, "Like in what way?" This Moorean example involves the kind of judgment that we ordinarily advance and accept without evidence. But it is also a judgment about an "external object," what Austin used to call an ordinary middle-size specimen of dry goods. This duality is what makes the example so useful and so misleading.

To return to the question, "Like in what way?," the abstract notion of a framework judgment, which is all the argument supposedly has to go on, requires that the answer be "Like in point of being affirmed without special testing." This gets us nowhere, since the judgments we affirm this way are so various that there is no obvious kind of judgment to retreat to in our attempt to provide our framework judgments with evidential backing. This means that the argument does nothing to establish the *contrast* between "framework judgments" and "subjective experiential judgments" that it subsequently takes for granted. For anything that has been shown, these classes may overlap, so that the possibility of retreat from one to the other in the face of sceptical questioning has already been blocked. This brings us back to the central point that the ancient problem of the regress has no particular connection with the modern problem of our knowledge of the external world. In the argument we are considering, the transition to that problem requires that we focus on a certain narrower class of framework judgment typified by "Here is one hand," for which the relevant likeness to the paradigm is a matter of affirming some obvious truth about the exernal world. But it does nothing to justify this.

The equation of framework judgments with judgments about the external world is helped along by treating judgments as if they were (abstract) propositions, rather than statements formulated and advanced in particular circumstances. Treating them this way is an important first step in the direction of the foundationalist idea that propositions can be partitioned, *a priori*, into privileged and problematic classes, without regard to context. Wittgenstein has some useful reminders here. He writes:

One may be wrong even about "there being a hand there." Only in particular circumstances is it impossible. "Even in a calculation one can be wrong – only in certain circumstances one can't."

But can it be seen from a rule that circumstances logically exclude a mistake in the employment of rules of calculation? . . .

If . . . one wanted to give something like a rule here, then it would contain the expression "in normal circumstances." And we recognise normal circumstances but cannot precisely describe them. At most, we can describe a range of abnormal ones.[13]

The account of terminating judgments hinted at in these remarks contrasts sharply with traditional foundationalism. For foundationalism, a judgment derives its epistemological status from some highly abstract feature of the content of the proposition it contains. Any judgment about experiential data is intrinsically more secure than, hence epistemologically prior to, a judgment about the external world. Given foundationalism, we might as well talk about basic propositions as about basic judgments (expressed by propositions advanced in particular circumstances). But if Wittgenstein is right, the distinction is crucial: a terminating judgment derives its status from its context, and not just from its content. Moreover, not merely is there no simple rule for identifying the relevant contextual determinants, there is no rule for determining what propositions can enter into terminating judgments, even supposing the context fixed. As Wittgenstein puts it: "[The] situation is . . . not the same for a proposition like 'At this distance from the sun there is a planet' and 'Here is a hand' (namely my own hand). The second can't be called a hypothesis. But there isn't a sharp boundary between them."[14] "Here is a hand" may be a paradigm candidate for entering into a terminating judgment, but it yields no clear-out criterion for establishing an epistemologically basic kind of proposition, hence no pressure to construct "the subjective conception of experience" as our only remaining evidential source. Whatever the merits of this response to the regress, it is nothing like traditional foundationalism.

The contrast we have just noted provides the first hint of what I shall claim to be foundationalism's decisive feature, its commitment to a strongly realistic conception of epistemological relations. For the foundationalist, there are relations of epistemological priority that hold between propositions independently of the circumstances in which those propositions are advanced, the interests that govern their assessment, or any other such "contextual" factors. The priority of experiential knowledge over knowledge of the world is, as it were, *just a fact.* The foundationalist, I suggest, is an *epistemological realist,* an extreme realist with respect to the objects of epistemological inquiry. But we needn't go into this just now. For the present, the conclusion is that, to find support for the view that foundationalism is a by-product rather than a presupposition of scepticism with respect to our knowledge of the world, we shall have to look beyond the ancient trilemma.


## 2.5   KNOWLEDGE AND THE SENSES


If foundationalism is to be a by-product rather than a presuppostion of sceptical argument, it must be possible to mount a sceptical challenge to our knowledge of the world without simply taking foundationalist ideas for granted. However, it is not easy to see how this is to be done, particularly once we realize that the obstacle to knowledge of the external world it generally thought to consist in the fact that experience could be just what it is, even if the world were very different. Certainly, this will be an obstacle to knowledge of the world if experiential knowledge is, in some general and objective way, epistemologically prior to knowledge of the world. But if we are sceptical of this doctrine of epistemological priority, matters are much less clear.

I think that as we look at the details of sceptical arguments, we shall find a tendency, on the part of those who think of sceptical doubts as natural or intuitive, to underestimate the theoretical resources needed to generate sceptical conclusions. A clear and important example of a deceptive quasi-truism is the claim that sets Descartes on the road to scepticism about knowledge of the external world: "all that up to the present time I have accepted as most true and certain I have learned either from or through the senses."[15]

Setting aside methematical knowledge, which many philosophers think has nothing to do with sensory evidence, isn't Descartes's claim undeniable? But if we concede it, can't we apply the Agrippan strategy to generate the problem of our knowledge of the external world by way of the problem of the criterion? For how do we know that the senses deserve this authoritative status? By means of the senses? Or some other way? (And why rely on that?) But if we can't justify reliance on the senses, how can we lay claim to knowledge of the external world. We can't, and no contentious foundationalist ideas are needed to show this. We simply combine a truism with the least theoretically loaded sceptical strategy available.

This won't do. Whatever sceptical problem is formulated here, it is not the problem of our knowledge of the external world. This argument, like the one rejected in the previous section, applies as much to immediate experiential knowledge as to knowledge of external things, to "inner" as well as "outer" sense. I can just as well ask "How do I know I can even trust my awareness of the experiential data: by experience?" The point is: the sense of "the senses" has to be narrowed if there is to be some special problem about knowledge of external reality. And this leads to the question: can we narrow it without forfeiting the seemingly truistic character of the claim that knowledge depends on "the senses"?

To illustrate the problem, here is Stroud on "the Cartesian problem of our knowledge of the external world." The dependence of such knowledge on "the senses" gives rise to a sceptical challenge to our knowledge of the world, he claims, because: "What we gain through the senses is on Descartes's view only information that is compatible with our dreaming things about the world and not knowing anything about that world. How then can we know anything about the world by means of the senses?"[16]

This takes a lot for granted. In fact, it equates "knowing by means of the senses" with "inferring from information about how things appear." But this equation, dubious enough in itself, provides the basis for a challenge to our knowledge of the world only if the one kind of knowledge is in some quite general and objective way epistemologically prior to the other. Here, then, the assumption that we know about the world "by means of the senses" is simply shorthand for a foundational view of knowledge and justification. This is an example of what I suggested is a recurrent pattern in supposedly intuitive arguments for scepticism: a seeming truism (all empirical knowledge is *in some sense* dependent on the senses) serves to introduce a contentious epistemological doctrine (all knowledge of the world must be derived from more basic, experiential knowledge). Notice that nothing in our earlier presentation of the problem of the criterion demanded that "the senses" be understood like *that*.

This much is perhaps a truism: that without functioning sense organs, I would never form any beliefs about the external world and so would never come to know anything about it either. But all this shows is that possessing functioning sense-organs is a causal precondition for possessing knowledge of the world: it establishes nothing whatsoever about the general *evidential* basis of such knowledge, not even that it has one. Consequently, it offers no inkling as to how any such supposed basis might be inadequate.

The reply will be that Descartes is not just thinking of sense organs but of sensory experience. Moreover, he is right to think of it. Someone who was permanently anesthetized would never come to know anything about the world outside. As H. H. Price once put it, at the very opening of his study of perception: "Every man entertains a great number of beliefs concerning material things. . . . It is plain that all these beliefs are based on sight and touch . . . in the sense that if we had not had certain experiences, it would be neither possible nor reasonable to entertain these beliefs."[17] This shows that knowledge depends on experience.

Suppose for the sake of argument that what Price claims is true, e.g. that no one who is blind can (reasonably) form beliefs about material things, even with extensive help from others. It is still not obvious that any epistemological issue has even been broached. If it is never *reasonable* to form such beliefs in the absence of certain experiences, for all that has been shown, this may be because it is not even *possible*. True, we are now talking about sensory experience, awareness of how things appear, and not just about physiological systems, but, even so, nothing has emerged to suggest that we have done more than identify a causal precondition for our coming to know things about the world. Casting experience for this role will not entitle us to think that our beliefs about how things are do not count as knowledge unless they can be inferred from "experiential data." There is no move from experience as causal precondition to experience as ground.

Recall once more Wittgenstein's remark that "My having two hands is, in normal circumstances, as certain as anything I could produce in evidence for it."[18] It might well be that, if I had spent my entire life in a coma, I would never have come to think of myself as having two hands. But, at least in normal circumstances, this does not put me in a position to treat its looking to me as if I have two hands as evidence for my having two hands. The experiential "evidence," the (apparent) sight of my hands, is not normally any more certain than the belief about how things objectively are, which is why it is not a ground for that belief, even if it is a causal precondition.

Of course, we might argue that Wittgenstein is just wrong: that my having two hands is *never* as certain as a report on my current experience. However, it is hard to see what such a claim could be based on, if not on the thought that my experience could be just what it is even if all my beliefs about how things objectively are were false. And this will not be an argument for my beliefs about the world being always less certain than my experiential beliefs unless we have already agreed to the general evidential dependence of the former on the latter. What we see here is that the contextual conception of relations of epistemic priority towards which Wittgenstein is pushing clashes with the strongly realistic conception characteristic of foundationalism. But this does not show that the one conception is to be preferred to the other, though it does reinforce the suggestion that sceptical arguments are always more theoretically loaded than they sometimes appear.

Although crucially important, the distinction between experience as cause and experience as ground is easily overlooked, with the result that sceptical conclusions can seem to emerge from truistic considerations. Here once more is Stroud, now defending the *prima facie* reasonableness of Descartes's "principle" and also echoing the line of thought that was so convincing to Price:

A person blind and deaf from birth who also lacked taste buds and a sense of smell would know very little about anything, no matter how long he lived. To imagine him also anaesthetised or without a sense of touch is perhaps to stretch altogether too far one's conception of a human organism, or at least a human organism from whom we can hope to learn anything about human knowledge. The importance of the senses as a source or channel of knowledge seems undeniable.[19]

But, to repeat, this does nothing *at all* to justify thinking of the senses as a source or channel of *knowledge*, rather than as merely playing a crucial causal role in the genesis of beliefs. The point of the phrase "source or channel of knowledge" is to insinuate the thought that all beliefs about the world have some kind of uniform evidential basis, in fact a basis in experience. But this epistemological doctrine is not established merely by the fact that someone with severe sensory disabilities would find it difficult to learn anything at all. The way in which the importance of the senses is undeniable does nothing to underwrite the conceptions of "what the senses tell us," that figures in Descartes's sceptical argument.

So is this what needs to be shown: that entertaining beliefs about material things, in the absence of certain experiences, would never be reasonable, even if it were possible? And isn't this just plainly so, as Price suggests? But if it is, the indispensability of experience is not merely causal: experience always plays a crucial evidential role in empirical knowledge.

I am inclined to doubt "experience" is always so indispensable. But even if it were, we would not yet be under pressure to concede the fully general priority of experiential knowledge over knowledge of the world. Experiential evidence can be indispensable without being, in the way the sceptic imagines, ultimate. This will be so if experiential knowledge plays its indispensable evidential role only in the context of collateral, *non*-experiential knowledge. This will mean that, in the Cartesian sense of "the senses," we never learn anything about our surroundings via the senses alone. But it is not "plain" that we ever do.

How can this be? Again, it is important not to conflate genetic and epistemic considerations. But, lightly sketched, the picture of empirical knowledge that emerges from philosophers like Wittgenstein and Sellars is this: in being trained to accept a certain system of judgments (or perhaps several more or less loosely related systems), we are also trained in techniques for making and assessing judgments. This is a causal matter and any role played by experience is a causal role. When and only when we have mastered the system are we in a position to treat experience as evidence for judgments about how things objectively are and to explain how and why certain experiences are evidentially significant. In other words, we are initiated into a system of judgments in which beliefs about the world and experiential evidence are interdependent. But this is not a matter of being indoctrinated with mere assumptions since, once the system has been mastered, its components can be corrected in the light of further experience.

This picture of empirical knowledge tends to suggest, and is certainly meant by some of its advocates to suggest, that while any element in our putative knowledge of the world can be subjected to critical scrutiny, there is no question of our ever assessing it as a whole. We shall discuss in due course whether this is really so, when I take up the question of whether rejecting foundationalism commits me to a coherence theory of justification. For now, let me just note that, if there are views of empirical knowledge that are not friendly to the sort of general assessment of knowledge characteristic of traditional epistemology, the attempt to conduct such an assessment cannot be treated as theoretically naive: it must involve some other conception of knowledge more congenial to the traditional project. We come back, not to an intuitive argument for scepticism, but to a clash of theoretical perspectives.

We do not need to press these issues at this point since it is clear that, if scepticism is to threaten, the "undeniable importance" of the senses as a "source" of knowledge cannot consist simply in experience's always playing *some* evidential role in our acquiring knowledge of the world. As Stroud concedes, scepticism threatens when: "we try to understand how the things we believe . . . are connected with and warranted by the bases or grounds on which we come to believe them. All possible evidence is ultimately sensory; our knowledge of the world is empirical."[20]

The crucial move is the equation of the thought that knowledge of the world is empirical, which may be some kind of truism, with the thought that all evidence is *ultimately* sensory. The role played by experience has to be not just indispensable but ultimate. But this is just what the argument we have been considering fails to show. At the very most, it suggests, though it hardly proves, that experience plays *some* crucial evidential role in our knowledge of the external world. It does not show that experience is the foundation of empirical knowledge. The question thus remains, why suppose that *any* abstractly categorized body of "evidence," sensory or otherwise, is ever "ultimate"? To call sensory evidence "ultimate" is to claim, but not yet to justify, the general and objective epistemic priority of experiential knowledge over knowledge of the world. This reinforces the thought that both scepticism and the project of assessing our knowledge of the world as a whole are inextricably bound up with a foundational conception of knowledge and justification.

In a nutshell, the point is this: that, *a priori*, there is no reason to think that there is any single answer to the question "What information do we get from the senses?" The answer might just be: it depends on the circumstances – for example on the state of the environment and the state of the perceiver (including his background knowledge). The uncontroversial fact that, without functioning sense organs, it would be difficult or impossible to learn anything about one's surroundings does not imply that there is some proprietary brand of "information" that it is the special office of "the senses" to transmit, still less that nothing else counts as empirical knowledge unless it can be inferred from such restricted data. To suppose that it does is to graft a contentious epistemological doctrine on to a causal truism.

## 2.6  THE NEUTRALITY OF EXPERIENCE

Perhaps the most striking illustration of the tendency to underestimate the theoretical commitments of sceptical arguments is what seems to be an almost irresistible temptation to think that, to raise the specter of scepticism, it is sufficient to point to the "logical gap" between statements about appearances and statements about reality. But this cannot be right. It is not the logical gap alone that threatens us with scepticism but the thought that, pending heroic efforts, we are stuck on one side of it.

What needs to be shown, in defence of the naturalness of sceptical doubts, is that the logical gap between appearance and reality provides the basis for an argument for the general and objective epistemic priority of experiential knowledge over knowledge of the world. But how could it? No purely logical claim, not even one having to do with statements about appearance and statements about reality, has any intrinsic epistemological significance. The epistemological significance of the logical gap between experiential knowledge and knoweldge of the world derives entirely from the thought that there must be some natural dependence of the latter kind of knowledge on the former. The difficulty of deriving statements about how things really are from information about sensory appearances would not matter if we were not already inclined to think that knowing how things really are depends on effecting some such derivation. This means that we cannot argue from the existence of a logical gap between experiential beliefs and beliefs about how things objectively are to the general evidential dependence of objective on experiential knowledge. The existence of the logical gap is perhaps non-controversial. But what is at issue is its epistemological significance: its mere existence decides nothing.

With this in mind, consider Stroud's claim that the sceptical philosopher's "reason for declaring the truth of scepticism" is that "all possible experience is equally compatible with the existence and with the non-existence of the world."[21] This is a perfectly representative account of the main obstacle to knowledge of the world: as we saw, its seeming insurmountability is Strawson's reason for settling for a defeatist version of naturalism. And, if not quite a truism, it seems very hard to deny. At least, if typical sceptical counter-possibilities – I am dreaming right now (or have always been dreaming), I am a brain in a vat, etc. – are even coherent, they seem to establish it conclusively. To realize our vulnerability to scepticism, we need only recognize the simple logical point that our experience could be just what it is and *all our beliefs about the world could be false*. When it comes  to knowledge of the world, the sceptic argues, experience is *evidentially neutral* (neutral, for short).

One way to react to this would be to deny the sceptic's logical point. This would involve trying to argue, as Davidson has done, that all our beliefs about the world could *not* be false: belief is *essentially* veridical.[22] I shall defer detailed discussion of this anti-sceptical strategy to a later chapter.[23] The point I want to make here is that there is no immediate and compelling reason to take up the challenge in quite this way. For the fact is, the reason given for declaring the truth of scepticism cannot be anyone's *sole* reason, since the sceptical philosopher's logical point does not, in itself, suggest *any* epistemological morals. Its sceptical potential derives entirely from its being conjoined with the further assumption that knowing anything whatsoever about the world depends on the availability of some completely general method for inferring statements about the world from information about "experience," for only if some such general method for giving our beliefs about the world an experiential grounding is required will its absence be a threat to knowledge. Since the absence of clear logical or conceptual connections between experiential statements and statements about the world has no *intrinsic* epistemological significance, without such a require-ment, no sceptical conclusion can be made to follow. But, equally, to insist on one is obviously just another way of enforcing a foundationalist concep-tion of knowledge and justification. So whether or not we *should* concede that all our beliefs about the world could be false, we can *afford* to concede it if we are careful not to swallow the epistemological thesis that gives the conceptual point its sceptical bite.

The lack of intrinsic epistemological significance in the sceptic's logical-conceptual point is sometimes obscured by proceeding as if the mere possibility of the world's being very different from the way we take it to be, the course of experience remaining the same, itself sufficed to show that statements about the world are "proleptic" or "go beyond experiential data." This was always Ayer's practice,[24] which explains why he felt free to present sceptical arguments in the way that he did. We have seen that Ayer's analysis of the pattern of sceptical arguments makes such arguments appear to rest on gratuitous theoretical assumptions, which is why it is unsatisfactory to a philosopher who thinks of scepticism as a natural or intuitive problem. But I doubt that Ayer ever saw it that way. I think he tended to see his first stage of a sceptical argument, the stage that points up the logical gap between statements in the privileged and those in the problematic class, to be itself an argument for the general evidential dependence of the latter on the former. The first stage establishes that the statements belonging to one class are more ambitious than those belonging to another. It thereby shows that they are (at least relatively speaking) problematic.

In fact, it shows no such thing. There is no automatic inference from one sort of statement's being more ambitious than another to some general relation of evidential dependence. If, in normal circumstances, my having two hands is as certain as anything I could produce in evidence for it, I am under no obligation, because I am in no position, to produce *anything* by way of evidential support, no matter how unambitious. Again, the reply will be that my having two hands is *never* as certain as my experiential data, but the reason had better not be that "experience could be just what is is even if . . . etc." or we will be starting to run in a *very* small circle.

The danger in writing as Ayer does is that it hides the fact that *two* claims are being advanced when statements about the world are said to "go beyond" experiential data: one conceptual and (relatively) uncontroversial, the other epistemological and highly contentious. Moreover, the contentious point is in no way supported by the uncontroversial. The transition from one to the other is effected by the phrase "go beyond" which superimposes an epistemological asymmetry on what is initially only a conceptual *gap*. Statements about the world "go beyond" experiential statements in that the world could be very different, and perhaps not exist at all, even if my experience were just what it has been: the facts of experience do not require the world to be any particular way. But if this is all there is to "going beyond," experiential statements go beyond statements about the world, for the world's being one particular way does not *logically* determine how, or even whether, it will be experienced. (Think, for example, of the inverted spectrum problem). "Going beyond" has to mean "transcending the appropriate evidence." But this alleged epistemological ambitiousness cannot be made to follow from a purely conceptual point: highlighting a conceptual gap does not establish a standing obligation to traverse it in a particular direction.

None of this is meant to imply that those who hold to the intuitiveness of scepticism never acknowledge the central importance of the idea of epistemic priority. As we noted, Stroud makes it quite clear that "The apparent obstacle to our knowledge comes from the doctrine of the epistemic priority of sensory experiences over independently existing objects." He is well aware that the compatibility of all possible experience with various views about the objective world, which he regards as "an apparently harmless truism,"[25] needs to be conjoined with this doctrine to generate a sceptical problem. However, given my argument to this point, what should puzzle us is that this recognition of doctrinal dependence seems not to affect his sense of the naturalness of sceptical doubts. Perhaps this is the result of an inclination to identify the doctrine with the deceptively truistic equation of "our knowledge of the world is empirical" with "all possible evidence is ultimately sensory," an equation which, as we saw, holds only for those already committed to foundationalism. But whether or not this is so, the real problem at this stage of the argument is to see how the admission that scepticism with respect to our knowledge of the world depends on the doctrine of the epistemic priority of ideas over independently existing objects is to be combined with the view, to which all who think of sceptical doubts as natural doubts are committed, that foundationalism is a by-product of scepticism rather than a presupposition. The response envisaged to my preliminary case for thinking that sceptical arguments take founda-tionalist ideas for granted was that these ideas arise out of, or are forced on us by, an initial encounter with the sceptic's deepest and most intuitive reasons for thinking that knowledge of the world is beyond us. The ad-mission that the apparent obstacle to knowledge of the world "comes from" the doctrine of the epistemic priority of ideas over external objects thus reverses what the intuitive sceptic must take to be the true direction of explanation. His view simply *must* be that, in the last analysis, the doctrine comes from our recognition of an obstacle to knowledge of the world, not the other way round.

Stroud demonstrates a firm grasp of what needs to be shown when he claims that "Those considerations that are thought to lead to scepticism are precisely those that lead to the doctrine of the epistemic priority of 'ideas' over objects."[26] But what are these considerations? According to Stroud:

> Descartes arrives at his sceptical conclusion from the recognition that all our experience could be just the way it is now whether there were any external things or not. What we can know on the basis of the senses therefore is something that could be known to be true without our knowing anything at all about objects existing independently of us in space. This general gap between appearance and reality is an expression of what can be called the "epistemic priority" of sensory experiences . . . over those independent objects that exist in space.[27]

To serve their purpose, these considerations must force an initial retrench-ment from experiential knowledge to knowledge of the world without relying on foundationalist assumptions. What we find is that they lead us straight back into the same small circle of ideas.

One way to understand this argument is to see it as trying to go from the neutrality of experiential knowledge to its priority. But, as I have already argued, this move is invalid. Let us concede both that there is a "general gap" between appearance and reality and that "the senses," as the source of "experience," only tell us about appearance: still, for anything that has been shown so far we might just as well conclude that, since we do know all sorts of things about objects existing in space, that knowledge is not derived from the senses, in the Cartesian sense of "senses." That is to say, we might take the neutrality of experience to count *against* its general epistemic priority. The mere fact, if it is a fact, that we could retain all our experiential knowledge while knowing nothing of objects existing in space simply does not decide the matter. Of course, a big step towards deciding it will be taken if the appeal to the fact that we do know all sorts of things about external objects can be blocked. But, in the argument under consideration, the only given reason for thinking that it is blocked is that "experience could be just the way it is whether there were external things or not," a point which, I have insisted, has *no* epistemological significance unless the epistemic priority of experiential knowledge over knowledge of the world is already established.

I have been claiming that there is no move from a logical gap to an epistemological asymmetry. For one thing, propositions about experience and propositions about the external world seem to be on a par: if the course of experience does not determine the way the world is, neither does the way the world is dictate the course of experience. But perhaps my argument fails to do justice to the sceptic's discovery. What he calls our attention to, someone might say, is the more-than purely-logical point that I could *know* all about how things appear without knowing anything about how they are, whereas I could not know anything about how they are without knowing about how they appear. This is not to say that how they are determines how they appear, hence what precise experiential knowledge I must have. The point is that I could not know *anything* about how the world is without knowing *something* about how it appears; whereas I could know all about how it appears and yet know nothing about how it is. So there is a fundamental asymmetry here after all.

Suppose that we agree that there is this much of an asymmetry: what follows? So far as I can see, nothing to the point. At most, the argument will establish what we might call the *autonomy* of experiential knowledge: that it is possible to have experiential knowledge without having any objective knowledge, but not the other way around. This is not equivalent to showing that experiential knowledge is the ultimate basis for objective knowledge. The fact that objective knowledge always brings some experiential knowledge in its train does not show that it is, or ought to be, derived from it.

By way of illustration, consider Sellars's thought that "looks" talk is a guarded form of "is" talk.[28] On this view, whenever we are in a position to make an "is" statement, we are automatically in a position to make a more guarded "looks" statement. Equally clearly, the reverse does not hold. But this epistemological asymmetry does not go straight over into general evidential dependence. For it might be that, in many cases, when I am in a position to make a less guarded assertion, I am in no *better* position to make its more guarded cousin, in which case there will be no question of the more guarded backing up the less. This is exactly what we found Wittgenstein suggesting in connection with my belief, in normal circumstances, that I have two hands: the more guarded claim that it looks to me as if I have two hands would be peculiar precisely because it would be more guarded without being more certain. So the conclusion seems to be not only that there is no direct move from the neutrality of experience to its epistemic priority but also that there is no indirect move, via its autonomy, either.

Stroud couches the argument in terms of "knowledge." Older forms of it tend to aim at revealing the different degrees of certainty attaching to experiential beliefs and beliefs about external objects. Presumably, Stroud avoids this formulation because he does not want to encourage the charge that a misguided quest for certainty lies behind the entire sceptical problem, a charge he is inclined to equate with the claim he is most concerned to rebut, that scepticism presupposes foundationalism. However, I do not regard this difference of formulation as particularly significant. Everything I have just said applies to attempts on the part of older theorists, such as Price, to demonstrate the "indubitability" of a certain kind of experiential belief by means of a quasi-introspective investigation. When Price looked at the tomato in front of him, he found that:

> there is much that I can doubt. I can doubt whether it is a tomato I am seeing and not a cleverly painted piece of wax. I can doubt whether there is any material thing there at all. Perhaps what I took for a tomato was really a reflection; perhaps I am even the victim of some hallucination. One thing however I cannot doubt: that there exists a red patch . . .[29]

But of course, it is not really a matter of what Price finds that *he* (psychologically speaking) can bring himself to feel uncertain about. If there is a clear point here at all, it is the neutrality of experience: because Price's experience could be just what it is even if there were no tomato there at all, experience does not determine how things are in the world. If there is more, it is at most an argument for the autonomy of experiential knowledge. To convert either point into an argument for the general epistemological priority of experiential knowledge over knowledge of the world, we have to step right back into the circle. The epistemic priority of experiential knowledge over knowledge of objects is supposed to derive from the latter's but not the former's being subject to radical doubt. But why suppose that beliefs about objects are always, in themselves, more dubitable than experiential beliefs? Because our experiences could be just what they are even if there were no external objects. However, as Stroud seems on occasion to concede, this logical claim points to no immediate epistemological morals. To get it to point in the right direction, we need to assume the general epistemological priority of experiential knowledge over knowledge of objects, which is what we were supposedly trying to derive. It is no surprise to find that a doctrine of epistemological priority can be extracted from sceptical doubts that take it for granted. But so far the case for seeing the doctrine as a by-product rather than a presupposition of scepticism has advanced not at all.

## 2.7   SCEPTICAL HYPOTHESES

Presentations of arguments for scepticism often make use of vivid thought-experiments in which the world is imagined to be very different from the way we generally take it to be but which, it is claimed, cannot really be ruled out by evidence. The original example, of course, is due to Descartes, who imagines that what he naturally takes to be experience of the material world is an elaborate hallucination, induced in him by an Evil Deceiver. The familiar modern variant is to suppose one's brain removed from one's head and kept alive in a vat of nutrients, with the appropriate afferent nerves connected to an array of microelectrodes that exactly mimic the pattern of stimulation that would be produced by one's current interactions with the environment. In both cases, the question is: how do you know that the situation envisaged isn't your actual situation? Is this the intuitive argument we are looking for?

We must go carefully here. The question to ask is: why are these alternatives to our usual way of looking at things *sceptical* hypotheses? Here it is crucial to remember that we are looking for an intuitive argument for *radical* scepticism. As I argued at the outset, if we were only interested in showing that, in a sense, nothing we believe about the world is ever *absolutely* certain, perhaps it would be enough to point out that it is always logically possible for the world to be very different from the way we take it to be. Thus the familiar thought experiments could be seen as barriers to knowledge, hence as sceptical hypotheses, to the extent that knowledge requires absolute certainty. But the issue now is radical scepticism, and it is not easy to see why bare logical possibilities should be taken to exclude even the slightest measure of justification.

The standard thought experiments are designed to accommodate any experiential data that we might cite in support of our ordinary outlook. Arguably, then, they show that such data do not really count in favour of our ordinary views. But this isn't to the point. This argument will accord the hypotheses in question the right sceptical significance only if it has already been established that, in the end, all our beliefs about the world depend for their justification on experiential data. The most natural – indeed, so far as I can see, the only – account of why sceptical hypotheses are *sceptical* forces us to treat foundationalism as a presupposition of sceptical argument. But we were looking for a reason to think of it as a by-product.

Linking up with the previous section, we can say that sceptical hypotheses must amount to more than vivid illustrations of a purely conceptual point: the neutrality or autonomy of experiential knowledge. It follows from my argument there that, if this is all they are, they are not, in and of themselves, arguments for scepticism. In fact, the lesson of that section was that, only on condition that justifying any belief about the world depends, in the last analysis, on deriving it from "experiential data," do such examples threaten to compromise the possibility of objective knowledge. To get from the mere logical possibility of my being a brain in a vat to the impossibility of my ever knowing that I am not, even when I am not, it is essential that this knowledge be stipulated to depend on whatever knowledge *would* be left to me *even if I were*. I have to establish that I am not a brain in a vat on the basis of whatever knowledge I and such a brain can be presumed to share. Perhaps there are ways of enforcing this requirement that do not depend on taking foundationalism for granted. But for all we have seen so far, the requirement is just another way of insisting on the general epistemic priority of experiential knowledge. To follow Nagel in simply describing sceptical puzzle cases as "possibilities . . . according to which the world is completely different from how it appears to us, and there is no way to detect this"[30] is to beg the question in favour of this doctrine by equating "detection" with justification according to foundationalist standards.

Given the difficulties we have encountered, it is not surprising to find philosophers who lay stress on sceptical alternatives tending to take a view of the sceptic's fundamental strategy that is very different from Ayer's. Letting $P_E$ be any proposition about the external world and $H_S$ be some suitable sceptical hypothesis, such as that I am dreaming right now or that I am a brain in a vat, they see the sceptic as arguing:

> I know that $P_E$ entails not-$H_S$;
> I do not (cannot) know that not-$H_S$;
> therefore I do not know that $P_E$.

The general significance of this argument lies in the fact that I could substitute anything for $P_E$. I do not need to start with any general thesis about knowledge of the external world. In particular, I do not need to start from an *a priori* partitioning of beliefs into privileged and problematic classes.

This way of putting things tends to bring into prominence a question that has excited considerable controversy: namely, is knowledge "closed under known logical entailment"? The sceptic seems to take it for granted that if I know that P and know that P entails Q then I know that Q. Some philosophers have suggested that this apparently plausible principle is in fact false, indeed that it fails precisely in connection with sceptical hypotheses. The sceptic is right to claim that I can't know that I am not a brain in a vat – sceptical hypotheses are designed to exclude knowing that they do not obtain – but wrong to conclude that I do not know that this is my hand (when like Moore I hold it up in good light, etc.). Seeing why the principle of closure fails, they suggest, gives us a satisfying diagnosis of scepticism. For one thing it explains why the sceptic's arguments can so easily come to seem irrefutable: for not merely do they trade on a *prima facie* plausible principle, their central contention – that we cannot know that sceptical alternatives do not obtain – is actually correct. But it also explains the puzzling character of Moore's proof of an external world, which everyone feels is misguided even while finding it difficult to say exactly why. The suggestion is that Moore and the sceptic rely on the very same plausible but false closure principle, the only difference being that, where the sceptic wants to contrapose, Moore suggests we detach.

Before we contemplate denying closure, however, we need to ask why it is that we cannot know that sceptical alternatives do not obtain. If the reason turns out to be that the course of experience could be just what it is even if some sceptical alternative did obtain, recasting the sceptic's argument into the form just given will get us nowhere. We shall be back to trying to argue from the neutrality of experience to the impossibility of knowledge of the world, which will succeed given a foundationalist view of knowledge and justification but not otherwise. Non-closure, so to say, will be a by-product of a concession to scepticism that itself presupposes the foundationalist doctrine of the priority of experience. For now, however, we can set the issue aside. In due course, I shall discuss the question of closure at length. We have still found no compelling reason to think that foundationalism is a mere by-product of scepticism, rather than an essential presupposition.

This is a good point at which to recall another argument of Moore's, briefly scouted in chapter 1. Moore agrees that the epistemological principles espoused by Hume and Russell, which amount to a version of the doctrine of the priority of experiential knowledge over knowledge of the world, apparently entail that no one ever knows anything about external objects. But he replies that the fact that he does know that there is a pencil in his hand shows that those principles are false. Or at the very least, even if the principles are not definitely false, it is so much more certain that he knows that his pencil exists than that any general epistemological principle is true, that it could never be rational to deny his knowledge on the basis of such a principle. I suggested that this argument does not work if, as the intuitive sceptic believes, the "principles" that lead to scepticism are implicit in our most ordinary ways of thinking about knowledge. If this is so, Moore has not, as he thinks he has, produced a *reductio ad absurdum* of Hume's or Russell's principles but simply another illustration of the clash between our ordinary attitude and the conclusions that we naturally come to when we reflect on our pretensions to knowledge of the world.

I agreed that Moore's argument, as offered by Moore, is a failure. But I proposed taking it as a suggestive first step on the road to a theoretical diagnosis of scepticism. Then Moore is right: it is more certain that I know that my pencil exists than that the sort of principles Hume and Russell accept are true; and even if this does not definitively refute those principles, it does begin the process of shifting the burden of theory. Although we cannot simply assert the commonsense outlook against the results of philosophical reflection, the fact that our ordinary epistemic attitudes are at variance with the sceptic's conclusions is *prima facie* evidence that the sceptic's principles do not reflect our ordinary way of thinking about knowledge. In getting the sceptic to admit that there is something to be explained here, Moore strikes a significant blow for the cause of theoretical diagnosis.

Stroud, however, objects more radically. He thinks that Moore has not even given an instance of the "eminently rational" procedure of rejecting the less certain on the basis of the more certain. Imagine a murder committed in a country house, and compare two cases of this procedure. In the first case, the detective's eager assistant argues that the duke must have been murdered by one of the guests, who dashed in and out of the room while the butler was answering the telephone, but is refuted by the detective who points to what they know about the physical layout of the room to show that no one would have had time. In this case, a hypothesis is quite properly ruled out by an appeal to something antecedently known. But now consider a second case, in which the assistant goes back over the list of guests and concludes that the butler *must* be the murderer since only he had an opportunity. Here the detective points out that, since they have no reason to think that the list of people in the house is complete, they still do not know the murderer's identity. The assistant cannot reply that the list must be complete, or he would not know what he does know, namely that the butler did it. Stroud suggests that although Moore means his argument to be like the first case, it is really like the second.

Why are the cases so different? The crucial factor is that, in the second case, the detective, in pointing out an overlooked possibility, exposes a deficiency in the way the assistant reached his conclusion. The assistant cannot rebut the detective's suggestion simply by reiterating his conclusion, once the detective has entered an objection to his inference. Similarly with Moore and the sceptic. Since the sceptic's counter-possibilities strike at Moore's capacity for knowledge of the world, Moore cannot cite examples of such knowledge to rule them out. However, this means that it will be proper to assimilate Moore's reply to the sceptic to the assistant's absurd reply to the detective only if Moore's certainty that his pencil exists also depends on some kind of inference, which is the very point at issue. Moore's argument is analogous to the assistant's inept response only if Moore's knowledge that his pencil exists is governed by principles of the kind that Hume and Russell advance.

The detective raises a possibility that is "compatible with all the apprentice's evidence for his claim" and which "if realised, would mean that he does not know that the butler did it." Moreover, he does not have to know whether the possibility is in fact realized since we recognize that the apprentice does not know what he claims to know "unless he has established that the list is complete."[31] Once the deficiency in the asistant's inference is exposed, the burden of proof lies with him.

Presumably, we are meant to think that the sceptic follows a similar course. He raises possibilities – that Moore is dreaming or a brain in a vat – that are compatible with all the evidence that Moore has for his claim to know that his pencil exists; and he does not have to know whether or not they are realized to show up the deficiency in Moore's inference. What he must take for granted, however, is the priority of experiential knowledge over knowledge of the world. Bracket this doctrine and there is no reason to regard Moore's certainty as inferential, at least in any way that makes it vulnerable to the sceptic's bare logical possibilities. And if there is no reason to so regard it, there is no reason to assimilate it to the assistant's foolish reply.

This much is true: Moore cannot both concede that his knowledge of the existence of external objects is always inferential in the way that Hume and Russell suggest and suppose that he can refute the sceptic by appealing to the greater certainty of his knowing that his pencil exists. Once the detective raises the possibility that the list is incomplete, the assistant's certainty that the butler did it is no longer warranted: indeed, it ought to dissipate. It is not an example of denying the less certain on the basis of the more. Equally, however, if Moore's argument really is an example of this, it must be analogous to the first case rather than the second. All Stroud's argument brings out, then, is that Moore's claim to certainty clashes with the consequences of the sceptic's principles. If Moore's point does not reduce the sceptic's argument to absurdity, neither does Stroud's reply refute Moore's claim that his commonsense convictions are more certain than the principles that lead to scepticism. Still less does it amount to a defence of those principles. That defense is what we are still looking for.

## 2.8   DREAMING AND KNOWING

I am sure that the feeling will persist that I have not done justice to the sceptical potential of sceptical hypotheses. Of course, there is a way of exploiting sceptical alternatives that takes foundationalism for granted. We can take, say, the Cartesian dreaming argument as starting from the assumption that knowledge of the world rests ultimately on experience and moving to the claim that any amount of experience is compatible with the hypothesis that we are always dreaming and therefore never know anything about external reality. But there is a way of using the dream possibility so that the resulting argument's dependence on foundationalism is, to say the least, much less evident.

Anyone who levels this objection will have in mind something like the following: I can come to know something about the world, through perception, only if I can know that I am not dreaming; but I can never know that I am not dreaming; therefore I can never come to know anything about the world through perception. Unless I have access to empirical facts by way of something other than perception, which presumably no one does, this means that I have no knowledge of the world.

Notice that the sceptic can put forward knowing that one is not dreaming as an independent and intuitively plausible condition on acquiring perceptual knowledge of the world, so that his argument need not invoke any general principle of closure. The sceptic need not claim that knowing P implies knowing the falsity of everything incompatible with P (or with our knowing that P). He claims simply that coming to know a proposition P through perception requires knowing that one is not merely dreaming that P. Since his argument does not invoke any general principle of closure, it cannot be met by denying such a principle. This seems to mean that, if the argument is to be met at this point, it must be by rejecting the proposed condition on perceptual knowledge. But it is doubtful whether this could be done convincingly, since the condition seems likely to prove as plausible as any theoretical account of knowledge conjured up to rebut it.

So what about the second premise? We might defend it by invoking Descartes's discovery that there are no "marks and traces" by which dreams can be decisively distinguished from waking experiences. But if all this means is that it is logically possible that any stretch of experience, no matter how long and coherent, is a dream, we have reverted to the type of argument we are trying to get away from. We are back to using the dream possibility to argue for the neutrality, and perhaps also the autonomy, of experiential knowledge; and there is no getting from either thesis to a sceptical conclusion except by way of foundationalism.

However, the sceptic has another defence of his second premise, which seems at first glance intuitive and compelling. He can argue that, if we are ever to know that we are not dreaming, there must be a test that, at least in some circumstances, we can apply to determine whether we are dreaming or not. But now suppose that there were such a test – any test, not just one conforming to foundationalist preconceptions – pinching oneself perhaps. This test will be of use only if we can determine that we have really applied it, indeed applied it properly, and have not just dreamed that we have done so. That is, it will be of use only if we already have some way of determining that we are not dreaming, which leads us into a regress, no foundationalist assumptions required.[32]

This line of thought assimilates the argument from dreaming to the Agrippan problem of the criterion. So I could invoke my earlier conclusion that Agrippan considerations alone will not lead us to see a *special* problem concerning knowledge of the external world. However, I prefer to press on and to take another look at the first premise: that (perceptual) knowledge that P requires knowing that one is not dreaming that P. It seems to me that it can be read two ways. On one reading, it is a truism, or at least something I shall not dispute, but useless to the sceptic. On the other, it gives the sceptic the argumentative leverage he needs, but at the cost of ceasing to be truistic.

On the first reading, premise one makes the purely logical point that my acquiring, at a given time, perceptual knowledge that P is incompatible with my then not knowing whether I am merely dreaming that P. Like all logical points, this is epistemologically neutral. It says nothing about what we have to know in order to know what else. On the contrary, it is entirely compatible with our holding that, since we often do come to know things about the world, we often know that we are not merely dreaming them: that is, we know that we are not dreaming in virtue of what we know about the world. Notice that if this possibility is admitted, the absence of "marks and traces" also ceases to be a worry. If we generally know that we are not dreaming by way of various things we know about the world, we do not have to be worried by the lack of a decisive experiential marker by which to distinguish dreaming from waking. There will, in a sense, be "tests" for whether or not we are dreaming (=ways of knowing that we aren't), though not necessarily any single procedure or criterion that applies in all situations.

Obviously, the sceptic intends premise one to make more than the innocuous logical point just canvassed. He takes it to require that, if we are to be capable of acquiring knowledge of the world, we must *first* be capable of knowing that we are not dreaming: that is, of ruling out the dream possibility in some way that is independent of all knowledge of the world. On this reading, premise one certainly promises to be useful to the sceptic, but only because it introduces a general dependence of knowledge of the world on whatever knowledge we can have whether or not we know we are dreaming. So premise one is either truistic and useless or useful but just another way of insinuating a foundationalist constraint on knowledge of the world. Once more, the sceptic's argument turns out to start from the very thing it is supposed to generate: the epistemological priority of "ideas" over knowledge of the world. It is only by oscillating between the two readings of its first premise that the sceptic's argument produces the illusion of scepticism's emerging from a truism.

It is absolutely crucial here to remember that we are looking for an argument from which the priority of experiential knowledge over knowledge of the world emerges as a by-product. So, in approaching the present argument, we must not suppose ourselves antecedently persuaded by this traditional doctrine. We may, in fact, approach it disposed to agree with Wittgenstein that:

> My having two hands is, in normal circumstances, as certain as anything I could produce in evidence for it.
> That is why I am not in a position to take the sight of my hand as evidence for it.

And that:

> One might grant that Moore was right if he is interpreted like this: a proposition saying that here is a physical object may have the same logical status as one saying that here is a red patch.[33]

But it is clear that, if we approach the dreaming argument disposed to agree with remarks like this, the second reading of the sceptic's premise will strike us as imposing a completely unreasonable condition on worldly knowledge. If there are judgments about external objects that, in the right circumstances, stand at the outer limits of certainty, there is no reason why they themselves should not be what excludes the possibility that we are dreaming. Indeed, not merely would it be unreasonable to insist that the dream possibility be excluded independently of the sort of knowledge expressed by such judgments, if Wittgenstein is right it would be pointless even to attempt so to exlude it. If, in the right circumstances, some worldly knowledge is as certain as any experiential knowledge, we would add nothing to its certainty even if the attempt succeeded. Of course, the disputed condition on knowledge of the world would be entirely reasonable if we had already decided that experiential knowledge enjoys some kind of universal and absolute priority. But this is just what we are supposed not to have done.

The reply will be that neither scepticism nor the priority of experiential knowledge over knowledge of the world is meant to follow from premise one alone. Rather, both arise from premise one in conjunction with the claim that there could not be a test, foundationalist or otherwise, for determining whether or not we are dreaming. This reply would be ineffective if the second premise itself depended for its plausibility on the disputed doctrine of epistemic priority. But the sceptic will claim it doesn't: its defence turns on two much less contentious points: (1) that no test or procedure is worth anything unless we can ensure that we have really carried it out, and have not merely dreamed that we have; and (2) that anything we can do we can dream that we have done. However, I think we are now in a position to see that the two premises in the sceptic's argument are not really independent. Unless we accept the strong form of premise one, the form that presupposes foundationalism, the argument for premise two will fail: for, as we saw, if we generally know that we are not dreaming in virtue of what we know about the world, there is no reason to admit that there can be no test for determining whether or not we are dreaming. The regress apparently forced on us by premise two depends on the thought that, whatever we claim to know about the world, and whatever the circumstances in which the claim is made, our knowledge claim must fail unless, independently of that knowledge – or indeed anything like it – we can exclude the possibility that we are dreaming. If this requirement is not imposed, the regress is blocked by our capacity, in appropriate circumstances, for non-inferential knowledge of the world.

In effect, what the argument for premise two really shows is that there is no way of knowing that we are not dreaming that is independent of all knowledge of the world: there is no purely experiential test by which to exclude the dream possibility. But this conclusion poses no threat to knowledge of the world unless we have already been given reason to think that such knowledge, by its very nature, always requires grounding in some more primitive stratum of knowledge. The argument for there being no test for determining whether or not we are dreaming turns out to be another way of making the point that knowledge of the world cannot be given a grounding in experiential knowledge, which is not a step on the road to scepticism unless it has been established that knowledge of the world stands or falls with the possibility of giving it such a grounding. Once again, we have an argument that shows that foundationalist ambitions are likely to be disappointed, but gives no particular reason for entertaining them in the first place.

However, although I think that my remarks to this point are correct as far as they go, I am aware that they will strike many people as unconvincing, or even beside the point. For what they ignore is the special context of inquiry in which the sceptic enters the arguments we have been considering. The threat of scepticism arises in the course of the attempt to reach a reflective, philosophical understanding of our knowledge of the world. Moreover, what is at stake is the totality of our knowledge of the world, the philosophical task being to assess all of it, all at once. As philosophers, we are not just interested in how, ordinarily, we determine that we know this or that particular worldly fact: rather we want to know how it is that we are ever in a position to know anything whatsoever about external reality. This shows why the sceptic is entitled to understand the premises of his argument in the way he does, for example as requiring that the dream possibility be excluded independently of knowledge of the world. For if our aim is to understand how we are ever in a position to know anything at all about the world, we cannot remove apparent obstacles to such knowledge by appealing to the very knowledge in question. Our next task, then, is to examine the questions that animate the traditional epistemological project – the quest for an understanding of human knowledge in general – questions which, once asked, seem to lead ineluctably to a sceptical conclusion. We shall need to know two things: how we have to think of "human knowledge" if we are to suppose that such questions can be asked at all; and what results obtained in the context of reflective, epistemological inquiry imply about the status of the knowledge claims made in the course of our other (ordinary and even not so ordinary) pursuits. We shall approach these questions by way of a closer look at the totality condition that the tradional epistemological project imposes on a philosophical understanding of knowledge of the world. Does it really give the sceptic what he needs, or something less?

# 3

---

# Epistemological Realism

## 3.1 GENERALITY AND EPISTEMIC PRIORITY

Although a defender of the naturalness of sceptical doubts must hold that foundationalism is a by-product of scepticism, not a presupposition, so far we have seen nothing to suggest that the case for scepticism can be understood apart from the doctrine of the priority of experiential knowledge over knowledge of the world. This result would not be decisive if this essential doctrine could itself be derived from the truistic elements in the sceptic's arguments. But we have seen nothing to suggest this either. On the contrary, everything points the other way.

This leaves one option: to see how the truistic elements in the sceptic's arguments take on sceptical significance, we must look to the distinctive character of the traditional epistemological project. The sceptic (or traditional epistemologist) must argue that, in the context of a distinctively philosophical investigation of our knowledge of the world, the crucial ideas about epistemic priority are *forced* on us by our ordinary understanding of knowledge or justification. If he can do so, he will have rebutted the charge that he simply takes them for granted.

In trying to explain how what might otherwise seem to be truisms take on a surprising significance, it is natural to look first to the traditional epistemologist's aim of assessing the *totality* of our knowledge of the world. Because he wants to explain how we are able to know anything at all about the external world, his plan is to assess all such knowledge, all at once. But surely, the argument now goes, if we are to understand how it is possible for us to know *anything at all* about external reality, we must trace that knowledge to knowledge we should still have even if we knew nothing about the world. No explanation of how we come to have knowledge of the world that depended on our already having some would show the required generality: it would not be an explanation of how we have *any* such knowledge. But this is as good as to say that, once we accept the legitimacy of the epistemologist's question – and we have seen no reason to suppose that it is unintelligible – we must also accept the priority of experiential knowledge, since experiential knowledge is what remains when knowledge of the world is set aside.

This is Stroud's view, which explains why he thinks that the diagnosis of scepticism that traces it to foundationalism gets things upside down. According to Stroud:

> What we seek in the philosophical theory of knowledge is an account that is completely general in several respects. We want to understand how any knowledge at all is possible – how anything we currently accept amounts to knowledge. Or less ambitiously, we want to understand with complete generality how we come to know anything in a certain specified domain.[1]

It is the distinctively philosophical goal of understanding certain kinds of knowledge with "complete generality" that leads to attempts to ground knowledge of a given kind on some "epistemologically prior" kind of knowledge, and the reason is that no other strategy will yield the right kind of generality. Unfortunately, the lesson of scepticism seems to be that such attempts are bound to fail, so that there is no hope of understanding human knowledge in general.

In chapter 1, I characterized the unusual generality of the traditional epistemological undertaking by saying that the traditional epistemologist imposes a *totality condition* on a properly philosophical understanding of our knowledge of the world. Acceptance of this condition, I believe, is what lies behind the feeling that my arguments in the previous chapter are unfair to the sceptic. There I claimed that purely conceptual points – the neutrality of experience or the "non-dreaming" implication of ordinary perceptual knowledge – have no intrinsic epistemological significance. Moreover, since such sceptical significance as they possess depends entirely on a tacit commitment to the priority of experiential knowledge over knowledge of the world, they themselves give no grounds for accepting any such general relation of epistemological priority. But perhaps they do not have to. Perhaps the very nature of epistemological investigation forces us to recognize that relation; and once it is recognized, the sceptic's truistic conceptual points are all he needs to reach his conclusion.

For example, I argued that the (truistic) claim that my knowing (perceptually) that P implies my knowing that I am not dreaming that P is not equivalent to the claim the sceptic must assimilate it to: that my knowing that P requires my being able to rule out the possibility that I am dreaming that P independently of my knowledge that P (or indeed anything like it). But the suggestion now is that the totality condition, rather than the non-dreaming condition alone, is what imposes the crucial restriction.

So, in the context of the traditional attempt to understand our knowledge of the world, an otherwise innocuous claim gives the sceptic what he needs.

Acceptance of the totality condition on a properly philosophical understanding of our knowledge of the world is also the deep source of the epistemologist's dilemma, for the dilemma springs from a fatal interaction of the totality condition with the objectivity requirement. This is the requirement that the knowledge we want to explain is knowledge of an objective world, a world that is the way it is independently of how it appears to us to be or what we are inclined to believe about it. Now, as we have seen, the totality condition requires us to try to trace our knowledge of the world to something more fundamental, which can only be experiential data. But, as a sceptical argument along Ayer's lines reveals, it is impossible to explain how such data could ever function as evidence. They cannot be linked empirically with any facts about the world for, in accepting such linkage, we would be crediting ourselves with knowledge of the world, in violation of the totality condition. On the other hand, conceptual connections between experiential data and worldly fact seem to be ruled out by the familiar thought-experiments that the sceptic appeals to to establish the neutrality and autonomy of experience. And if, in a desperate attempt to avoid scepticism, we insist on such connections, we make the way the world is depend on how it appears to us, in violation of the objectivity requirement. Accordingly, in the context of the attempt to assess the totality of our knowledge of the world, it seems impossible either to respect or violate the objectivity requirement: whatever we do looks like succumbing to the sceptic.

Nevertheless, although the epistemologist's dilemma arises from the interaction of the totality condition and the objectivity requirement, I take the totality condition to be fundamental. Many philosophers would disagree, for they see the objectivity requirement, with its commitment to a "realistic" view of truth, as the deep source of sceptical problems. But it is not clear, to me at least, that the objectivity requirement, any more than its relative the neutrality of experience, has any particular sceptical potential outside the context of an assessment of worldly knowledge governed by the totality condition. I shall say more about this in due course.[2]

I say that the totality condition is fundamental. More strictly, however, what is fundamental is the attempt to conduct an *assessment* of our knowledge of the world in the light of that condition. If the priority of experiential knowledge over knowledge of the world is implicit in the traditional epistemological project, this is not solely on account of that project's unusual generality. Also crucial is the kind of understanding it suggests we seek. As Quine has argued, if all we want is some kind of causal or developmental account of the emergence of our knowledge of the objective world, there is nothing viciously circular in our appealing to what

we now know about the world in an explanation of how we came to be in
our current position.[3] And where there is no threat of circularity, there is no
pressure to accede to a general doctrine of epistemic priority.

As Quine is of course well aware, traditional epistemology is under
pressure to accept such a doctrine because it seeks a different kind of
understanding. Its aim is to explain how it is that our beliefs about the
world amount to knowledge. Thus when Stroud says that what we want
from a theory of knowledge is an account of how our knowledge of the
world emerges out of something that is not our knowledge of the world,[4] he
does not mean that we want an explanation of how our current way of
looking at things developed out of some some previous way: i.e. out of
knowledge (or what out ancestors thought of as knowledge) that is not *ours*.
This is a task for historians and anthropologists. Nor is he thinking of an
account of how our knowledge emerges out of something that is not our
*knowledge*. Quine's idea of a naturalized epistemology is a gesture in this
direction, for it is supposed to issue in a causal explanation of how our
interactions with the environment lead us to form certain beliefs; and if
there is a worthwhile project here, it is presumably one for psychologists
and neurophysiologists. What is missing from both these projects is the idea
of an assessment. Each could as well, in fact more properly, be offered as an
account of the emergence of our *beliefs*. But only a legitimating account of
the basis or emergence of our beliefs will give an account of our *knowledge*.
 The sort of theory Stroud has in mind is therefore one that traces our
knowledge of the world to something that is *ours*, and that is *knowledge*, but
not knowledge *of the world*. What could this be except experiential knowledge? As we shall see, even Quine is forced to something like this position
when he tries to connect his "naturalized" epistemology with traditional
sceptical problems.[5]

It seems, then, that something very like foundationalism falls out of
a methodological constraint on a properly philosophical examination of
knowledge of the world. So we have, apparently, found what we were
looking for: a defence of the claim that foundationalism is a by-product of
scepticism, not a presupposition. When this possibility was first mooted,
I suggested that it would have to turn out that scepticism and foundationalism have a common root. We have now located that common root in the
 attempt to gain a certain kind of understanding of our knowledge of the
world. In effect, we have glossed Hume's thought that we set foot on the
road to scepticism as soon as we ask distinctively philosophical questions
about knowledge. True, this will not yield a defence of the naturalness of
sceptical doubts unless, as Hume thought, that form of questioning is itself
fully natural. However, even on this point, the sceptic has strengthened his
position. It is hard to see how there could be anything *unintelligible* in what
seems only to be an attempt to understand knowledge in an unusually

general way, so the prospects for a convincing therapeutic diagnosis of scepticism seem bleak. But it is not obvious offhand that the prospects for a satisfactory theoretical diagnosis are any brighter, for how can mere generality entail extensive theoretical commitments?

This is not all. Suppose that we agree that the traditional epistemological project leads inevitably to the conclusion either that we have no knowledge or that, if we do, we will never understand how we do; and suppose we insist that, since this is its outcome, it *must* involve some distortion of our epistemological position: can we say that identifying this distortion will let us see how knowledge is possible after all? Stroud suggests not. We should not think that:

> if we did come to see how and why the epistemological enterprise is not fully valid, or perhaps not even fully coherent, we would then possess a satisfactory explanation of how human knowledge in general is possible. We would have seen, at best, that we cannot have any such thing. And that too, I believe, would leave us dissatisfied.[6]

This is a powerful objection to any theoretical diagnosis of scepticism. Attempts to answer the sceptic directly run into the epistemologist's dilemma. But, if Stroud is right, attempts at diagnostic responses meet a similar fate. Suppose we find that we cannot hope to ground our knowledge of the world in the way that traditional epistemology has invited us to, because of some defect in the ideas about justification involved in the notion of even trying: we would still not have explained to ourselves how it is that we ever come to know anything about the world. Unless we show that the sceptic's question is actually unintelligible, it will remain dissatisfyingly unanswered. So this is our new dilemma: if the traditional epistemological project is coherent, it is doomed to fail; and if it isn't, we are still left in a position hard to distinguish from scepticism. It may be scepticism at second order, but it is scepticism for all that. We may *have* knowledge of the world, but we will never be able to explain to ourselves how we do. We may know things about the world, but we will never know that we know them.

## 3.2  EXTERNALISM AND TRADITIONAL EPISTEMOLOGY

Much recent work in the theory of knowledge has been inspired less by the problem of scepticism than by the apparent demonstration, due originally to Edmund Gettier, that the traditional "justified true belief" analysis fails to state a sufficient condition for knowledge.[7] To take a simple (and much discussed) "Gettier example," imagine that I have very good evidence that my colleague Jones owns a particular make of car, and that I infer from this that at least one of my colleagues owns such a vehicle: this conclusion seems to be something I am justified in believing. But suppose that, all my evidence notwithstanding, Jones does not own such a car though, entirely unknown to me, another of my colleagues does. Then my conclusion will be true as well as justifiably believed. But my belief will not amount to knowledge: my reasons for what I believe do not mesh appropriately with what makes it true.

A conservative reaction is to take Gettier cases to show that only certain kinds of justifying inference yield knowledge and so to look for some additional constraint on the justification requirement. Thus Gilbert Harman proposes that a justifying inference cannot yield knowledge if it depends essentially on any false lemmas.[8] In the example just given, I reach the conclusion that one of my colleagues owns a particular kind of car by way of the false intermediate conclusion that Jones does, so my inference does not yield knowledge.

Such an approach works only where knowledge depends on inference. However, there are Gettier examples where inference is not obviously present. For example, suppose that an arrangement of mirrors makes it look to me as if there is a candle in front of me; and suppose further that everything looks the way it would if things were entirely normal, so that I have no reason to suspect that the appearance is produced by mirrors: filling in the details appropriately, it will seem that I am justified in believing that there is a candle in front of me. But now suppose that someone has left a candle behind one of the mirrors, so that my belief is true. Do I know that there is a candle in front of me? It seems not. But do I go through any reasoning, defects in which might be blamed for my failure to know? Not consciously. My belief that there is a candle in front of me seems more like an immediate reaction to how things look than the result of inference.

Harman handles cases like this by attributing unconscious inference. Perhaps I reason that things appear as they do because there *is* a candle where there seems to be one, and this is false: there *is* a candle there, but this is *not* why things appear as they do.[9] However, to some philosophers, this all seems artificial and unnecessary. The point of the no false lemmas requirement is to prevent beliefs counting as knowledge when they are only accidentally true. But there is no need to *supplement* the justification condition with a "non–accidental truth" requirement, since this is itself sufficient. Thus the justification condition can be dropped entirely: knowledge is simply non-accidentally true belief. There are competing suggestions as to how to fill in the details, but an appealing and recurrent idea is that knowledge is belief that results from some kind of truth–reliable method or process. For convenience, I shall refer to all theories of knowledge that propose eliminating justification in favour of some "non–accidental truth" condition as "pure reliabilist" theories.

On a pure reliabilist theory, in order to have knowledge a believer need only as a matter of fact stand in some appropriate relation to the facts. He need not know, or on some versions of the view even believe, that he does. A typical example is Goldman's causal theory of knowledge. According to Goldman, my belief that the rug in my room is green amounts to knowledge if any only if it is caused in an appropriate way by the rug's being green. In a case like this, appropriate causation will involve (at least) the normal operation of my senses in more or less ordinary circumstances. Whether a belief amounts to knowledge therefore depends essentially on the believer's situation and external relations, rather than on his internal state alone. Thus theories of this type are generally thought of as "externalist."[10]

Now although responding to scepticism has not always been the prime motive for developing externalist theories of knowledge, it is worth asking what happens to scepticism once externalism is recognized as an option. I identified "Showing that knowledge is possible" with responding to radical scepticism and explained radical scepticism in terms of justification. But if certain externalists are to be believed, justification has nothing to do with knowledge. As one contemporary externalist puts it, the concept of knowledge is "more primitive" than that of justified belief.[11] So can the project of showing that knowledge is possible be detached from that of responding to the radical sceptic? Do externalist theories of knowledge make it possible to hold that, in so far as the sceptic's barriers to knowledge are barriers to justification, they do not need to be overcome for us to be able to understand how knowledge is possible?

A first reaction is that detaching the concept of knowledge from that of justification leaves radical scepticism untouched. If the concept of justification remains important to us, radical scepticism remains to be confronted. We might even think that the effect of externalism is to drain the concept of knowledge of most of its traditional epistemological importance. However, we might also think that some of the urgency goes out of the problem of scepticism if we can show that, however things turn out with justified belief, knowledge remains secure. But will an externalist account of knowledge really allow us to think of even knowledge as secure, in the face of arguments for radical scepticism?

One reason for answering "No" might be that, even if there exists a primitive kind of knowledge – the kind possessed by animals and young children – fully-fledged human knowledge is bound up with justification, and thus vulnerable to sceptical challenge. This view has been defended by Colin McGinn, who argues that the move from "subrational" to "rational" cognitive states makes it harder to know things.[12] But other externalists think that, even at the level of fully fledged human knowledge, there can be knowledge without justifying reasons. Do theories like this offer a satisfying response to scepticism?

Before tackling this question head on, we need to get clearer – or perhaps I should say make a decision – about what to count as an externalist theory of knowledge. I think that, although externalism entered current epistemological debate by way of pure reliabilist, hence radically non-justificational, accounts of knowledge, it would be a mistake to equate "externalist" with "radically non-justificational." As I see things, the crucial feature of an externalist account of knowledge is that it denies, with respect to some essential conditions on knowing, that knowing that P requires knowing or justifiably believing that those conditions are fulfilled. For externalists, the relevant conditions must *be* fulfilled, but the believer need not (though in some circumstances he may) *know* (or justifiably believe) that they are. Externalism thus drives a wedge between knowing something or other and knowing that one knows it. So, for example, my acquiring perceptual knowledge that the rug is green, may depend on the conditions of perception being more or less normal. But according to an externalist, it will not depend on my knowing that they are normal. Knowing that they are normal is relevant to my knowing that I know that the rug is green, but not to my simply knowing that the rug is green.

This crucial feature of externalism is not the exclusive possesion of radically non-justificational accounts of knowledge. Consider, for example, Austin's view that, while knowledge involves justification, justification depends only on ruling out certain specially relevant alternatives to what one has claimed, not anything and everything that would be incompatible with it.[13] All that is ordinarily required for me to back up my claim that the bird on the fence is a goldfinch is reason to believe that it is not woodpecker or any other kind of bird that, in the circumstances, it might be. I do not have to be able to show that it is not a stuffed goldfinch, a possibility that, in normal circumstances, it too far fetched for me to have to take it into account. Still less do I have to show that it is not a hallucinatory goldfinch. Though obviously not radically non-justificational, this view of knowledge has definite affinities with reliabilist accounts. Provided circumstances are normal, ruling out certain alternatives is a reliable way of forming true beliefs; and Austin requires only that circumstances be normal, not that we know them to be so. Of course, if they are in some way abnormal, then what would otherwise have been an acceptable justification may be defective, and whatever claim or belief it was used to justify will have to be revised or withdrawn, should the problem be detected. Otherwise, however, my justification is not defective and my belief amounts to knowledge, but not in such a way as to guarantee that I know that it does.

Wittgenstein too often seems to betray externalist leanings. He rejects the idea that experiential knowledge is always and everywhere intrinsically epistemologically prior to any knowledge of the world, on the grounds that in normal circumstances my having two hands is as certain as anything I could produce in evidence for it. But, notably, he does not require that circumstances be known to be normal. This suggests that he saw knowing that circumstances are normal as primarily relevant to knowing that one knows rather than to simply knowing. Similarly with propositions that stand fast in ordinary practices of inquiry and justification. Though such propositions are said by Wittgenstein to form a kind of framework for ordinary practices, he is conspicuously reluctant to think of them as either known or not known. Perhaps, then, for ordinary practices of inquiry and justification to yield knowledge, propositions that stand fast only have to *be* true, not *known* to be true. Perhaps this is why "It is always by favour of Nature that one knows something."[14]

In light of this, McGinn's suggestion that we may become more vulnerable to scepticism simply in virtue of connecting knowledge with justifying reasons is too hasty. According to McGinn:

> if we suppose a child to move from the subrational to the rational while possessing knowledge during both phases, we have to say that justification gets a purchase only in the rational phase; and so we have the prospect that what was knowledge ceases to be, because it comes to rest upon an inadequate foundation.[15]

However, this particular prospect opens up only if we construe "foundation" in the most traditional sense. If we allow an externalist element in our account of justifying reasons, as Austin and Witgenstein seem willing to do, there is no immediate move from connecting knowledge with justification to an increased vulnerability to scepticism.

But does any of this mean that the way to deal with radical scepticism is to develop an externalist conception of knowledge, and perhaps even of justification? Does an externalist outlook provide the key to an understanding of how knowledge of the world is possible? The answer depends on what we expect from an argument for the possibility of knowledge. If an externalist account of knowledge is consistent with the principles of logic and the laws of nature then, in a sense, it makes for the possibility of knowledge: such an account, supposing it to be otherwise adequate, will show that knowledge is humanly possible. But this does not mean that, by itself, it shows a way around sceptical obstacles to the possibility of knowledge.

Part of the problem is that "showing" is essentially connected with justification. To show that knowledge is possible is to give ourselves reasons to think that we are in a position to know things; and if we are taken by an externalist account of knowledge, this means giving ourselves reasons to think that we are in a position to meet the relevant external conditions. The radical sceptic therefore shifts his point of attack from the question of whether we can know things to the question of whether we can have any justification for thinking that we do. The sceptical obstacles to knowledge simply reassert themselves at second order. If they are genuine, but cannot be overcome, it will not be a satisfactory response to scepticism to point out that though we may well know all sorts of things, we do not have the slightest reason to suppose that we really do know any of them. On the other hand, if they do not need to be overcome, this needs to be shown *before* we can settle for an externalist understanding of knowledge.

However, the problem is not so much with the concept of showing as with what the sceptic challenges us to show. We are challenged to explain how it is possible for us to know anything at all about the external world and we cannot meet this challenge by way of a theory of knowledge that makes some actual relation to the external world constitutive of knowledge. For can we know that such a relation ever obtains? If we do not suppose that we can, we will not have explained how we have knowledge of the world. We shall indeed have described conditions such that *if* they obtain, we will know various things; but we will not have given ourselves any reason to suppose that they do obtain, and so our explanation will remain fatally incomplete. On the other hand, if we just help ourselves to the assumption that we can know that such conditions obtain, we will not have explained how we come to know anything at all about the external world. We will simply have appealed to some (putative) knowledge of the world in order to account for the rest, and so our explanation will again be incomplete. These considerations lead Stroud to the conclusion that "enlightened," externalist theories of knowledge leave scepticism untouched.[16]

Matters here are not completely straightforward. Since they allow us to know things, or in some cases have justified beliefs, even when we do not know that the appropriate reliability conditions are met, externalist theories of knowledge drive a wedge between knowing and knowing that one knows. But they do not *preclude* knowing that one knows: they insist only that knowing that one knows that p is neither guaranteed nor required by one's knowing that p. Provided that our belief that they do obtain satisfies *its* appropriate reliability conditions, we will know that the conditions for knowing obtain, and so know that we know, in addition to simply knowing. My belief that my beliefs about the world have been formed in a reliable way may itself have been formed in a reliable way.

This problem is clearly recognized by Stroud. Although he feels convinced that externalist theories of knowledge do not offer a satisfactory response to scepticism, and so do not speak to the demand for understanding that lies at the heart of traditional epistemology, he concedes that it is "difficult to say precisely what is inadequate about this kind of response, especially in terms that would be acceptable to an externalist."[17]

Equally, however, it is difficult not to sympathize with Stroud's perception. It is all very well for an externalist to note that we may know that we have knowledge of the world, provided that our belief that we do is reliably formed: the fact remains that, if we have felt the force of radical scepticism, the sceptical challenge will simply re-emerge at this new remove. We will want to know what reason we have for thinking that we know anything about the relations between our beliefs and the world. This challenge too can be met with an externalist response – we do not need a reason, just an appropriate connection between our belief and the facts – which will be met with a renewed challenge, and so on. But at no point will we reach the fully general understanding of our knowledge of the world that the traditional epistemological project invites us to seek. We will never reach the position of seeing how it is that we know anything whatsoever about the world. Rather, we will have embarked on a familiar regress. Hence Stroud's verdict on the new "enlightened" theorist's position, a verdict that acknowledges the complexity of the issue without withdrawing the charge of inadequacy: "Perhaps it is best to say that the theorist has to see himself as having good reason to believe his theory in some sense of 'having good reason' that cannot be fully captured by an 'externalist' account."[18]

On this point, it is surely important that the traditional assessment of knowledge takes place from an uncompromisingly first-person standpoint. This retreat into subjectivity is an immediate consequence of accepting the totality condition on a properly philosophical understanding of knowledge of the world. If all knowledge of the world is up for assessment, I cannot take for granted anything having to do with my or anyone else's worldly situation. By contrast, externalist theories of knowledge are developed from a third-person perspective. To the traditional epistemologist, then, an externalist will seem to be describing how I might assess someone else's capacity for knowledge, taking my own capacity for granted. Knowing how things are in the world, what that other person believes, and how he comes to believe it, I can appreciate that his beliefs are formed in a way that makes them non-accidentally true. From my standpoint, he is a reliable informant, and so in that sense worthy of being treated as someone who knows what he is talking about. What seems impossible, however, is that I should assess my own capacity for knowledge of the world this way, for I could do so only by begging the question in my own favor. It seems that once we accept the totality condition on a philosophical understanding of knowledge of the world, no externalist theory of knowledge can provide the sort of understanding we seek.

However, while I think that Stroud is in a sense quite right, it is important to be clear about the way in which externalist responses to scepticism are inadequate. They are inadequate if offered as direct answers to scepticism, or as attempts to respond on its own terms to the traditional demand for an understanding of how knowledge is possible. But this does not mean that they cannot make an important contribution to a theoretical diagnosis both of the traditional project and of the scepticism that seems to be its inevitable outcome. A theoretical diagnosis of scepticism must reveal how the case for scepticism depends essentially on theoretical ideas which are not forced on us by acknowledged facts regarding everyday epistemic practices. It is therefore an essential part of theoretical diagnosis to suggest new ways of looking at or interpreting those facts. The way to make the theoretical commitments underlying a given approach to a problem stand out is to develop an alternative theoretical perspective. Externalism, as an alternative approach to understanding epistemic concepts, promises to be important at just this point.

This result was implicit in the connection we noted in Wittgenstein – and which can also be traced in Austin – between a willingness to accept a measure of externalism in one's account of knowledge and suspicion of the doctrine of the priority of experiential knowledge over knowledge of the world. As we saw in the previous section, any attempt to understand in a properly general way how knowledge of the world is possible seems to force that doctrine on us. Thus to respond directly, on its own terms, to the traditional demand for an understanding of our knowledge of the world is necessarily to accede to that doctrine, hence to forgo being satisfied with an approach to knowledge that is hostile to it. Agreement on how to draw the distinction between externalist and internalist theories of knowledge is far from complete. But in the context of the challenge to explain how it is possible to have any knowledge whatsoever of the external world, the issue between externalism and internalism reduces to the question of whether knowledge of the world can and must be traced to some more primitive kind of knowledge: in other words, to the question of whether experiential knowledge is always and everywhere epistemologically prior to knowledge of how things objectively are. Thus externalist accounts of knowledge can bear on scepticism, but as part of an attempt to undermine the doctrine of the priority of experiential knowledge. They may thus contribute to, but cannot substitute for, a theoretical diagnosis.

Perhaps it will clarify matters to recall the use the sceptic makes of sceptical hypotheses. The sceptic constructs cases where enormous external differences have no distinctive internal consequences. Such thought-experiments pose a difficult problem for anyone who thinks that knowledge must be traced to cues available from the "inside." If we think of knowledge this way, my epistemic situation seems identical with that of a brain in a vat: we both have only our experience to go on, and, if the sceptic is right, experience does not settle how things are objectively. However, externalist theories of knowledge permit a sharp distinction between the epistemic situation of a normal human being and that of brain in a vat. Since a normal human being may stand in a truth-reliable relation to the facts of his world, in a way that a brain in a vat will not, he will know all sorts of things that the brain in a vat doesn't. For an externalist, the fact that their respective situations are indistinguishable "from the inside" need not be decisive. But even if I accept all this, I still have no *reason to conclude* I know things about the external world, even though perhaps I do know them, unless I have some reason for thinking that I am not a brain in a vat. This takes us right back to the challenge of radical scepticism.

Once more, then, we see that an externalist theory of knowledge is not a direct answer to that challenge, which must be met or turned aside before we can be content with any version of externalism. But the prospects for doing either will be bleak indeed if the doctrine that makes the challenge seemingly unmeetable, that of the priority of experiential knowledge over knowledge of the world, is forced on us by any attempt to understand our knowledge of the world in a properly general way.

However, we must go slowly here. The argument that traces what seem to be the sceptic's foundationalist presuppositions to the essential character of the traditional epistemological project is a version of the Humean thought that we are doomed to scepticism as soon as we ask distinctively philosophical questions. But this argument will favor the view that scepticism is a natural or intuitive problem only if those questions themselves are naively intelligible, which I doubt.

The line of thought we have been exploring apparently makes the absolute priority of experiential knowledge impossible to deny, if we want a properly general understanding of our knowledge of the world. But it rests on two assumptions. The first is that there *is* something, our knowledge of the world, to examine, so that although we cannot account for knowledge of the world given the priority of experiential knowledge, rejecting that doctrine will also leave us dissatisfied, because just as much unable to answer what seems to be a perfectly intelligible question. The second is that examining our knowledge of the world, by way of charting its relation to "experience," is tantamount to assessing it, so that a failure to ground knowledge of the world, at this level of abstraction, will reflect badly on all particular, detailed knowledge-claims. Both will stand looking into. We shall find that they are closely related.

## 3.3 KNOWLEDGE AS AN OBJECT OF THEORY

In asking whether there is such a thing as knowledge of the world, I am not asking the very same question the sceptic asks but one that I think cuts deeper. I am asking how we have to think about "knowledge of the world" for that phrase to pick out a proper object of theory. So if it sounds too strange even to hint that there might not be anything for the theory of knowledge to be a theory of, my question can be rephrased. What matters is whether "our knowledge of the world" picks out the kind of thing that might be expected to be susceptible of uniform theoretical analysis, so that failure to yield to such analysis would reveal a serious gap in our understanding.

To raise these questions is to begin to examine a move that gets made before epistemological arguments, and particularly sceptical arguments, even get started. This is the introduction of the objects of epistemological inquiry. We shall be trying to isolate views that, for the most part, even the most determined anti-sceptics share with their adversaries. Philosophers who respond to scepticism do not doubt that there is something to defend against the sceptic's attacks. If they are dubious about our prospects for giving a direct refutation of scepticism, they call for a diagnosis of the sceptic's questions which will reveal them, first impressions to the contrary, as less than fully coherent. Even Stroud, who thinks our most pressing need as epistemologists is to understand how traditional epistemological inquiry misrepresents our epistemic position, if it does, seems not to doubt the existence of its objects. For the idea that there is something called "our epistemic position" is just another aspect of the idea that there is such a thing as "human knowledge" or "our view of reality." But is there? Or are there fewer things in heaven and earth than are dreamt of in our epistemology?

Now, it is tempting to use "human knowledge" and "our knowledge of the external world" as though it were obvious that such phrases pick out reasonably definite objects of study. But it isn't obvious, or shouldn't be. We can talk of "our knowledge of the world," but do we have any reason to suppose that there is a genuine totality here and not just a loose aggregate of more or less unrelated cases? My sense is that the totality condition is far more problematic than it first seems.

Consider, for example, Nagel's characterization of the aim of epistemology as "to form a conception of reality which includes ourselves and our view of reality among its objects."[19] This offhand allusion to "our view of reality" takes a lot for granted. To suppose that there is such a thing as "our view of reality," which might then be the "object" of a single theoretical enterprise, is to assume that human knowledge constitutes some kind of surveyable whole, an idea that is not, on the surface, very promising. There are no clear criteria for individuating beliefs and, even if there were, it is far from clear that there would be any systematic way of enumerating all the things we believe. Phrases like "our system of beliefs" and "our view of reality" are so vague that we cannot be confident they refer to anything.

Nothing changes if we pull back to narrower categories such as knowledge of the external world. When it comes to such "specified domains," whether there is anything to understand will depend on how the domains are specified. To try to understand all knowledge in the standard epistemic domains is to suppose that the beliefs in those domains hang together in some important way. But how? "Knowledge of the external world" covers not only all the natural sciences and all of history, it covers all everyday, unsystematic factual claims belonging to no particular investigative discipline. Since, even within a single subject, theories, problems and methods tend to proliferate with the progress of inquiry, so that even the most systematic disciplines tend to become less rather than more unified, it is doubtful whether we can take a synoptic view of physics, never mind everything we believe about the external world. It is not obvious that it makes sense even to try.

Recall Stroud's claim that in the philosophical study of human knowledge we want "to understand how any knowledge at all is possible – how anything we currently accept amounts to knowledge." He finds that engaging in this project "feels like the pursuit of a perfectly comprehensible intellectual goal.[20] Perhaps it does once we have grown familiar with theoretical ideas that we shall be examining shortly. But we must try to recover some naivete here. Then I think we see that, when we first encounter the challenge to show how any knowledge of the world is possible, we cannot tell whether we have been given a perfectly comprehensible goal or not. In fact, the obvious difficulty in commanding a synoptic view of our worldly beliefs suggests that we haven't. We cannot, therefore, just *see* whether the epistemological challenge makes sense. What we can do, however, is to ask how we might make sense of it.

I think that we can find a somewhat oblique recognition of this problem even in Descartes. Descartes admits that getting to a general doubt by questioning his beliefs one at a time would not be easy: perhaps the examination would never be completed. Hume too dismisses a piecemeal approach as a 'tedious lingering method."[21] But these grudging concessions are misleading: for they imply that the main obstacles to going over our beliefs *seriatim* are time and energy, whereas the question is certainly not one of convenience. If we are to make sense of the project of explaining how anything we believe about the world amounts to knowledge, we need a way of reducing our beliefs to order. We have to bring them under principles or show them as resting on commitments that we *can* survey. We must reveal some kind of *theoretical integrity* in the class of beliefs we want to assess.[22] If we can do this, human knowledge is a possible object of theoretical investigation. But not otherwise.

The very nature of the traditional project demands that the principles in question be all-pervasive. For example, if we are to assess the totality of our beliefs about the world, there must be principles that inform all putative knowledge of the world *as such*. But what could they be? I take it to be obvious that, in one way, our beliefs do not show any kind of theoretical integrity. They do not, that is, add up to an ideally unified theory of everything. There is no way now, and none in prospect, of integrating all the sciences, much less all of anyone's everyday factual beliefs, into a single coherent system: for example, a finitely axiomatized theory with specified rules of inference. In this way, Nagel's phrase "our view of reality" borders on the absurd. We have not got a "view of reality" but indefinitely many. The idea, taken for granted by coherence theorists of justification, that we have a "system" of beliefs ought to be suspect.

"Our beliefs," then, do not amount to a single, integrated "view of reality." They are not *topically integrated*. But this need not be fatal to the project of understanding human knowledge in general. For even if our beliefs are not topically integrated, they might be *epistemologically* integrated. This to say: they might be subject, in so far as they are meant to be justified or to amount to knowledge, to the same fundamental, epistemological constraints. This is what is usually suggested, or rather assumed. Thus Descartes ties his pre-critical beliefs together, thereby constituting their totality as an object of theoretical inquiry, by tracing them all to "the senses." No matter how topically heterogeneous, and no matter how unsystematic, his beliefs have this much in common: all owe their place to the authority of the senses. If this authority can be called in question, each loses its title to the rank of knowledge.

We have seen that this talk of "the senses" is poised between a causal truism and a contentious epistemological doctrine. Now we see more clearly why the epistemological doctrine is and must be what is intended. Only by tracing our beliefs about the world to a common "source," which is to say a common evidential ground, can we make "beliefs about the world" the name of a coherent kind. In the absence of topical integration, we must look to epistemological considerations for the theoretical integrity we require.

Hume may have seen, though perhaps dimly, that an epistemologically based form of theoretical integrity is a precondition for a properly general, hence "philosophical," understanding of human knowledge. He compares assessing particular beliefs and particular sciences one at a time to a strategy of "taking now and then a castle or village on the frontier"; and he contrasts this "tedious" method with marching up to "the capital or center of these sciences, to human nature itself." In explaining the principles of human nature, he tells us, "we in effect propose a compleat system of the sciences." But the completeness envisaged does not involve topical integration. It derives rather from the fact that all sciences, whatever their subject matter, "lie under the cognizance of men, and are judged of by their powers and faculties." Their subjection to the same underlying epistemological constraints, rooted in our "powers and faculties" is thus what makes possible a sweeping evaluation of "all the sciences."[23]

Hume sees the fact that all sciences lie "under the cognizance of men" as showing that all are "in some measure dependent on the science of MAN." But it seems clear that the science of man is not, or ought not to be, dependent on the other sciences. (Hume is apologetic about his occasional excursions into natural philosophy.) This asymmetry belongs to the logic of Hume's project, indeed to the logic of the traditional epistemological enterprise. Since he is attempting, with a view to its reform, a wholesale assessment of our knowledge of both the physical and the moral world, he cannot take any of that knowledge for granted. This means that it must be possible to investigate our "powers and faculties," the epistemological aspect of the human condition, without relying on any worldly knowledge. Our epistemological self-knowledge must be both autonomous and fundamental. Thus the project of assessing the totality of our knowledge of the world does more than presuppose that experiential knowledge is in some very deep way prior to knowledge of the world. It also assigns a definite privilege to knowledge of such epistemological facts. These features of the traditional project point to very extensive theoretical commitments.

The fact that the traditional epistemological enterprise is committed to the autonomy of epistemology sheds further light on the significance of externalism in the theory of knowledge. By suggesting that our capacity for knowledge depends on our situation in the world, and not just on our own "internal" capacities, externalism challenges the idea of our "epistemic position" as an autonomous object of theory. If our epistemic position is not something that can be investigated without knowing something about how we are placed in the world, there can be no question of our assessing the totality of our knowledge of the world on the basis of insights into our epistemic position. Perhaps we do not even have a fixed epistemic position. And if we find that we do not, it is doubtful whether we will be able to retain a clear conception of "our knowledge of the world" as an appropriate object of theory.

Unlike Hume, Descartes aspires to topical as well as epistemological integration: hence his metaphor of the tree of knowledge whose roots are metaphysics, trunk physics, and branches medicine, mechanics, and morals, a figure that contrasts interestingly with Hume's citadel of reason. But even for Descartes, topical integration is something to be achieved rather than assumed. His initial survey of his beliefs takes for granted only their epistemological integrity. As is familiar, he makes the point in terms of the metaphor of foundations: undermine the foundations and the whole edifice crumbles. The metaphor is a very natural one for, as we have seen, there is a clear sense in which epistemology, understood as the attempt to comprehend how any knowledge is possible, is intrinsically foundational. To see human knowledge as an object of theory, we *must* attribute to it some kind of systematic basis. This may involve inference from some class of fundamental evidence-conferring beliefs, as traditional foundationalists maintain; or it may involve governance by certain "global" criteria of explanatory integration, as coherence theorists think. But *something* must regulate our knowledge of the world: something that we can identify and examine independently of any such knowledge. We should therefore not be too eager to *oppose* the account of scepticism that traces it to the generality of the epistemological enterprise to that which traces it to foundationalism. (Nor, for that matter, should we be too eager to oppose foundationalism to the coherence theory.) If we give up the idea of pervasive, underlying epistemological constraints; if we start to see the plurality of constraints that inform the various special disciplines, never mind ordinary, unsystematic factual discourse, as genuinely irreducible; if we become suspicious of the idea that "our powers and faculties" can be evaluated independently of everything having to do with the world and our place in it: then we lose our grip on the idea of "human knowledge" as an object of theory. The clear contrast between castles on the frontier and the fortress at the centre dissolves. Perhaps there is no capital, each province, as Wittgentein said of mathematics, having to take care of itself. The quest for an understanding of human knowledge as such, no longer feels like "the pursuit of a perfectly comprehensible intellectual goal."

The same is true of more modest aims, such as understanding how our beliefs about the external world amount to knowledge. As a way of classifying beliefs, "beliefs about the external world" is only quasi-topical, bringing together beliefs belonging to any and every subject, or no well-defined subject at all. They are united only by their supposed common epistemological status. The essential contrast to "beliefs about the external world" is "experiential beliefs" and the basis for the contrast is the general epistemic priority of beliefs falling under the latter heading over those falling under the former. "External" means "without the mind"; and it is taken for granted that we have a firmer grasp of what is "in" the mind than of what is outside it.

There is no doubt that this epistemological distinction is readily mastered: readily enough for arguments based on it to strike us as "immediately gripping." But a teachable distinction does not guarantee theoretical integrity in the kinds of things distinguished. There are various ways of failing. I discuss two examples in this section and one in the next.

My first example illustrates a relatively mild form of failure. In his natural history of heat, Bacon gives a long list of examples of heating. It includes examples of heating by radiation, friction, exothermic reactions and by "hot" spices that "burn" the tongue.[24] Everything he mentions is ordinarily said to involve "heat," so we cannot deny that his list reflects ordinary usage. But what we have here is is a clear case in which a nominal kind, comprising all the things commonly called "hot," has no automatic right to be considered a natural kind. It is no objection to the kinetic theory that it doesn't cover the tremendous "heat" produced in my mouth by a chicken vindaloo, never mind the heat often generated by philosophical arguments. We don't complain that, since the theory doesn't apply to hot curries or heated arguments, it fails to explain heat in a satisfactorily general way.

Given that we want to know whether there is any such thing as, say, "our knowledge of the world," this kind of failure may seem too weak to be of interest. Failure to take in hot curries and heated arguments does not tempt us to say that there is no such thing as heat. But we could say that there is no such thing as *nominal* heat, the nominal kind being *merely* nominal. We can tie together some of the examples of heat and, having done so, treat them as the only genuine examples, discarding the others as resembling the genuine examples only superficially, hence as not really, but only metaphorically, hot. This is, indeed, what Bacon himself goes on to do when he argues that heat is a form of motion. Anyway, it is clear that there need be no theory of all the things commonly called "hot": a hot curry is hot even when it has gone cold. Nor need the lack of such a theory be cause for intellectual dissatisfaction. It is just another example of an ordinary principle of classification failing to cut nature at the joints. By the same token there does not *have* to be a theory of all the things normally called "examples of knowledge." And if there isn't, it has to be shown that this reveals a lack. It may be that there is no such thing as knowledge (or knowledge of the external world, etc.) in just the way that there is no such thing as Bacon's nominal heat.

All this notwithstanding, I agree that the example of heat doesn't get me very far. All that happens in this case is that a nominal kind fails to coincide exactly with a theoretically coherent kind. So I move to my second example: the supposed division of sentences into analytic, or true by virtue of meaning, and synthetic, or true by virtue of fact. Quine is famously sceptical about this distinction because he is dubious about the atomistic conception of meaning that he takes to lie behind it.[25] Quine's view of meaning is holistic – the meaning of a given sentence depends on its role in a wider theory – and this holistic conception of meaning suggests that there is no privileged way of distinguishing a theory's "meaning postulates" from its empirical assumptions, any more than there is a way of determining which out of alternative complete axiom sets is the right one.

Against Quine, Grice and Strawson argue that the analytic/synthetic distinction must be genuine and significant because it is teachable in such a way as to enable the student to apply it to new cases.[26] The reply, well known by now, is that all kinds of dubious distinctions have proved to be teachable in this way, for even terms belonging to a false theory can admit of consensual application on the part of those who accept it. If the fact that,

*[margin annotation: analytic/ synthetic dist.]*

at one time, everyone could agree on who was the village witch does not mean that there really were witches, the fact that appropriately trained students can pick out examples of analytic sentences does nothing to show that any sentences are genuinely analytic. But the point I want to make does not require agreement on this particular example. Whether or not we agree with Quine on the question of analyticity, the fact remains that distinctions can be teachable and projectible while failing to correspond to any theoretically coherent division of objects. When a classification rests on an implied background theory, there is no immediate inference from the existence of an easily mastered kind-term to the theoretical integrity of its associated kind.

The application to our current problem is obvious. In accordance with my project of theoretical diagnosis, I have been arguing that the kinds of knowledge investigated by the traditional epistemologist are theoretical kinds. So, just as the ability of believers in the analytic/synthetic distinction to agree on what to count as paradigm instances of analytic sentences does not mean that there are analytic sentences, the fact that we can agree on what to count as examples of knowledge of the external world does not mean that there is knowledge of the external world. The underlying principle of classification, whatever it is, might be bogus. As a result, we cannot simply help ourselves to classifications of this kind on the grounds that nothing else promises the right kind of generality. That such principles of classification pick out coherent objects of theoretical investigation needs to be shown.

In the case of heat, to sort out the genuine from the spurious examples we rely on a physical theory which identifies some underlying property, or structure of more elementary components, common to hot things. Explaining theoretically significant kinds this way is typical of scientific realism. For the scientific realist, deep structural features of the elementary components of things determine the boundaries of natural, as opposed to merely nominal or conventional, kinds. This suggests an analogy. Since, if human knowledge is to constitute a genuine kind of thing – and the same goes for knowledge of the external world, knowledge of other minds, and so on – there must be underlying epistemological structures or principles, the traditional epistemologist is committed to *epistemological realism*. This is not realism as a position within epistemology – the thesis that we have knowledge of an objective, mind-independent reality – but something quite different: realism about the objects of epistemological inquiry.

The epistemological realist thinks of knowledge in very much the way the scientific realist thinks of heat: beneath the surface diversity there is structural unity. Not everything we call knowledge need be knowledge properly so called. But there is a way of bringing together the genuine cases into a coherent theoretical kind. By so doing – and only by so doing – we make such things as "knowledge of the external world" the objects of a distinctive form of theoretical investigation. We make it possible to investigate knowledge, or knowledge of the world, *as such*.

I expect that at first it seemed bizarre to question the existence of the objects of epistemological inquiry. Who can deny that we evaluate claims and beliefs epistemologically, sometimes deciding that they express or amount to knowledge, sometimes not? And who can deny that these claims or beliefs concern such things as objects in our surroundings, other peoples' thoughts and experiences, events in the past, and so on? No one. So it is easy to assume that, if our claims ever warrant positive assessment, there must be knowledge of the external world, knowledge of other minds, knowledge of the past, and so on. Even more obviously, there must be knowledge. But I hope the examples just considered make plausible the thought that there doesn't *have* to be. All we know for sure is that we have various practices of assessment, perhaps sharing certain formal features. It doesn't follow from this that the various items given a positive rating add up to anything like a natural kind. So it does not follow that they add up to a surveyable whole, to a genuine totality rather than a more or less loose aggregate. Accordingly, it does not follow that a failure to understand knowledge of the world with proper generality points automatically to an intellectual lack. To sum up, though I readily admit that we have teachable distinctions here, all this ensures is that there will be things that we can agree on as *examples* of, say, knowledge of the external world. It does not guarantee any theoretical integrity of the kind to which the examples are assigned. This is the sense in which there need be no such thing as knowledge of the world.

At this point, someone is likely to object that there is no immediate inference from the lack of a certain type of theoretical integrity in a given kind to its spuriousness. Still less is there an inference to the non-existence of things of that kind. Take the sort of loose, functional classification of things that is common in everyday life, such as the division of dining room furniture into table and chairs. We do not expect to be able to formulate a physical theory of what makes an object a chair. But we are not tempted to conclude that chairs do not exist.[27]

This objection assumes that "knowledge of the external world" is like "chair" rather than like "witch" (or "analytic"). But is it? The distinctive feature of terms like "witch" is that they are *essentially theoretical*. Essentially theoretical distinctions are distinctions that we see no point in continuing to make, or even no way of drawing, once the theory behind them has been rejected. If Quine is right, "analytic/synthetic" is like this, for he holds that giving up a certain conception of meaning involves losing all sense of how to make a fixed, objective division between a theory's meaning postulates and its empirical assumptions. Essentially theoretical classifications must therefore be distinguished from classifications that have been theoretically rationalized but which retain independent utility. Distinctions like this are apt to survive the rejection of theories with which they have become associated. Our first example, heat, is a case in point. Rejecting the caloric theory of heat, or the phlogiston theory of combustion, did not tempt us to conclude that there are no hot things or that nothing burns. Some philosophers would take this view of "analytic," for they think that there is a robust and useful pre-theoretical notion of synonymy that survives Quinean scepticism about meanings. If they are right, the analytic/synthetic distinction is not essentially theoretical. But where a classification is essentially theoretical, we are happy to say that there are no things of that kind, if we once become convinced that the background theory is false. Thus there are no witches (or, if Quine is right, analytic sentences).

Though I do not claim that the concept of an essentially theoretical classification is knife-edged, I do want to say that "knowledge of the external world" is quite clearly essentially theoretical. There is no common-sense, pre-theoretical practice that this way of classifying beliefs rationalizes: its sole function is to make possible a certain form of theoretical inquiry, the assessment of knowledge of the world as such. As we have seen, this classification cuts across all familiar subject-matter divisions and, in addition, presupposes the autonomy of epistemology. Even the sense of "external" is unfamiliar from a commonsense standpoint. "External" does not mean "in one's surroundings," for even one's own body, with its "internal organs," is an "external" object. It was a radical innovation on Descartes's part to externalize his own body.[28] As I have already remarked, "external" in "external world" means "without the mind." And since being within the mind depends on being given to consciousness, the essential contrast to "knowledge of the external world" is "experiential knowledge": the classification is epistemological through and through.

But what if the proper analogy for "knowledge of the external world" were not "witch" but "heat?" I do not believe that it is because I do not see that there is any pre-theoretical utility to the concept, or any theory-independent way of drawing even approximately the right boundaries round it. But this is not all. In bringing to center-stage the issue of epistemological realism, I am not questioning particular theories of the structure of empirical knowledge, as we might question particular theories of heat, but the very idea that knowledge has any fixed, context-independent structure. The analogy is therefore not with cases where one structural theory replaces another but with those where we abandon any idea of coming up with a theory of that kind. If there are no witches, we may debate witch-crazes and witchcraft beliefs, but not whether sympathetic magic is superior to contagious.

Suppose, however, that I am wrong about all this. Suppose, that is, that "knowledge of the external world" is like "chair": then what? So far as I can see, nothing to the purpose. In connection with such loose, functional classifications, we do not expect theoretical understanding, which is why such classifications survive the recognition that no such understanding will be forthcoming. We do not feel that there is an irremediable intellectual lack because there will never be a science of chairs. But that is exactly what we are supposed to feel in the absence of a suitably anti-sceptical theory of knowledge of the external world. This shows that, even by the traditional epistemologist's own standards, "knowledge of the external world" cannot be like "chair." It must pick out something in which theoretical integrity is to be expected, and this means that the existence of the objects of traditional epistemological inquiry is far less assured than that of furniture.

## 3.4  EXPLANATION OR DEFLATION?

Let me suggest one further case for comparison. It has to do with deflationary views of truth. Philosophers who take a deflationary approach want no more from a theory of truth than a description of the logical behavior of "true" and some account of why it is useful to have such a device in our language. Quine is a good example of such a philosopher. According to Quine, if we consider a sentence like " 'Snow is white' is true if and only if snow is white" we see that: "To ascribe truth to the sentence is to ascribe whiteness to snow. . . . Ascription of truth just cancels the quotation marks. Truth is disquotation."[29]

Applied to a given sentence, the truth-predicate is dispensable. It comes into its own, however, with respect to sentences that are not given, as when we say that all the consequences of a given theory are true. But even here, to say that certain sentences are true is just to say that the world is as they say it is. As Quine remarks, "one who puzzles over the adjective 'true' should puzzle rather over the sentences to which he ascribes it. 'True' is transparent."[30]

Though I am very sympathetic to this view, my interest here is less in its correctness than its character. This view of truth is striking on account of what it does *not* say. Compared with traditional theories of truth, it says nothing about what makes all true sentences true. On the contrary, a deflationist will hold that his remarks on the behaviour and utility of the truth-predicate say just about everything there is to say about truth. To approach truth in a deflationary spirit is emphatically not to think of "true" as denoting a theoretically significant property, explicating which will illuminate what is involved in any sentence's being true. What is involved in a given sentence's being true is exhaustively captured by the sentence itself. On a deflationary view, then, true sentences constitute a merely nominal kind. We could even say that, for a deflationist, though there are endlessly many truths, there is no such thing as truth.

The traditional theorist sees things quite differently. In his eyes, "truth" *is* the name of an important property shared by all true sentences, a property that can be expected to repay theoretical analysis. This property may be correspondence to fact, incorporability in some ideally coherent system of judgments, or goodness in the way of belief, depending on whether he favors a correspondence, coherence or pragmatic theory. But whatever his theoretical preference, he will hold that, since true sentences constitute not just a nominal but a theoretical kind, no theory of truth is satisfactory which does not explain what makes true sentences true. We set our sights too low if we aim only to capture the use of a word or explain the point of a concept: there is more to understanding truth than appreciating the utility of the truth-predicate.[31]

We see, then, that traditional and deflationary theories are not theories of exactly the same kind. As Stephen Leeds puts it, the traditional theories are genuinely theories of truth whereas deflationary theories are theories of the concept of truth (or, we could say, accounts of the use of "true").[32] Leeds's illuminating distinction is readily applied to epistemological theories. We can distinguish theories of knowledge from theories of the concept of knowledge. I think that the debate sparked by Gettier's demonstration that the standard "justified true belief" analysis fails to state a sufficient condition for knowledge is best seen as concerning the concept of knowledge. The kind of extra constraint on justification that seems to be required – for example that an inference cannot yield knowledge if it involves a false lemma essentially – is rather formal, nothing being said about what beliefs can serve as justifying evidence for what. This is why it is possible to discuss issues raised by the Gettier problem without ever getting entangled in sceptical problems. Theories that say nothing about whether examples of justified beliefs about objective states of affairs reveal any essential similarities, beyond highly formal ones of the "no false lemmas" variety, are neutral with respect to whether we should think of our knowledge of the world as an appropriate object of theory. By contrast, traditional foundational and coherence theories, which are much more closely involved with scepticism, put forward general, substantive constraints on justification and so make room for a project of assessing our knowledge of the world as a whole. They are theories of knowledge and not just theories of the concept of knowledge.[33]

Of course, there is no obstacle in principle to supplementing one's views about the concept of knowledge with views about knowledge itself.[34] But one could also advance such views in a deflationary spirit. One philosopher who has done so, I believe, is Austin. Wittgenstein may be another.

The availability of deflationary accounts of a notion like truth changes the whole problem-situation. Naively, we might be inclined to suppose that just as in physics we study the nature of heat, so in philosophy we study the nature of truth. But once plausible deflationary views are on the table, the analogy between truth and things like heat can no longer be treated as unproblematic, for the question raised by such views is precisely whether there is any need to think of truth as having a "nature." We can conclude, *mutatis mutandis*, that if we have a plausible account of the concept of knowledge, it is a further step to insist on an account of knowledge as well. A deflationary account of "know" may show how the word is embedded in a teachable and useful linguistic practice, without supposing that "being known to be true" denotes a property that groups propositions into a theoretically significant kind. We can have an account of the use and utility of "know" without supposing that there is such a thing as human knowledge.

What makes this suggestion particularly pointed is that appearances certainly do not favour the view that a phrase like "knowledge of the world" picks out a theoretically coherent kind. For one thing, justification, like explanation, seems interest-relative, hence context sensitive. This is in part what Austin is driving at in insisting that demands for justification are raised and responded to against a background of specifically relevant error possibilities. What is relevant will depend on both the content of the claim in question and the context in which the claim is entered. If all evidence is relevant evidence, then, abstracting from such contextual details, there will be no fact of the matter as to what sort of evidence could or should be brought to bear on a given proposition.

If context-sensitivity goes all the way down, there is no reason to think that the mere fact that a proposition is "about the external world" establishes that it needs, or is even susceptible of, any particular kind of evidential support. No proposition, considered in abstraction, will have an epistemic status it can call its own. To suppose that it must is precisely to fall in with what I call "epistemological realism." To treat "our knowledge of the world" as designating a genuine totality, thus as a possible object of wholesale assessment, is to suppose that there are invariant epistemological constraints underlying the shifting standards of everyday justification, which it is the function of philosophical reflection to bring to light. Exposing this epistemological deep structure will be what allows us to determine, in some general way, whether we are entitled to claim knowledge of the world. But if this is so, foundationalist presuppositions are buried very deeply in the Cartesian project. They do not just fall out of the totality condition's exclusion of any appeal to knowledge of the world in the course of our attempt to gain a reflective understanding of that knowledge. They turn out to be involved in the very idea of there being something to assess.

These are my suspicions in outline. Now we must look at some details.

## 3.5  FOUNDATIONALISM

My main concern is the relation between scepticism and foundationalism. So having distinguished between theories of knowledge and theories of the concept of knowledge, I must say what kind of a theory I take foundationalism to be.

One way to understand foundationalism is to see it as a doctrine about the formal character of justifying inferences. Formal foundationalism, as we may call it, is the view that justification depends on the availability of terminating beliefs or judgments, beliefs or judgments which amount to knowledge, or which are at least in some way reasonably held to, without needing support from further empirical beliefs. Formal foundationalism is sometimes thought to contrast with "coherentist" theories of knowledge or justification. According to theories of this type, a given belief becomes justified through incorporation in some suitably "coherent" system of beliefs or "total view." Empirical inference is thus a matter of moving from one total view to another. The terminating judgments, which the foundationalist sees as fixed points constraining the possibilities of inferential justification, are unnecessary. Some philosophers see the commitment to beliefs that function as fixed points as *the* essential feature of foundationalism, hence the complaint, prominent in a recent systematic defence of the coherence theory, that the key error in foundationalism is its "linear" conception of inference.[35]

I have my doubts about the contrast between foundationalism and the coherence theory, but they can wait. The point I want to make here is that anyone who traces scepticism about our knowledge of the external world to the foundationalist doctrine of epistemic priority must have more than formal foundationalism in mind. We can call this stronger doctrine "substantive" foundationalism. The distinction between formal and substantive foundationalism turns on the account given of terminating beliefs or judgments. Substantive foundationalism involves more than the formal doctrine that inference depends on letting certain beliefs function as fixed points: it adds a distinctive account of the kind of beliefs capable of performing that function. Since I think that a genuinely foundationalist view of knowledge and justification must be substantive, whenever I refer to foundationalism *simpliciter* I shall have substantive foundationalism in mind.[36]

Substantive foundationalism is a theory of knowledge, whereas formal foundationalism is only (a contribution to) a theory of the concept of knowledge. One way to see this is to recall that Wittgenstein's view of knowledge, which concedes that all justification takes place against a background of judgments affirmed without special testing, can be seen as *formally* foundationalist. But as I argued in the previous chapter, this point about our ordinary practices of justification, while it might offer a way into the fully general problem of the regress of justification, gives no basis for supposing that there is a particular sceptical problem about our knowledge of objective reality. The transition to that problem depends on the tacit assumption that the fixed points recognized by commonsense justifications fall into some fairly obvious kind, so that once they have been questioned there must be some other, more primitive kind of judgment that we are forced to look to for their support. The thought that the functional role recognized by formal foundationalism corresponds to some kind of broad topical division of our beliefs is what I take to be the essential characteristic of substantive, as opposed to merely formal, foundationalism.

This is the way, then, in which there is more to what I am calling (and what has generally been called) "foundationalism" than the purely structural doctrine of formal foundationalism. What is missing from formal foundationalism is any hint as to the kinds of beliefs that function as fixed points or as to what qualifies a belief to play that role. But we have not yet got quite to the heart of why formal foundationalism is too weak a doctrine to capture all that is essential to a foundationalist conception of knowledge and justification. They key point is this: that not only does formal foundationalism give no account of what sorts of beliefs are epistemologically prior to what, and why, it does not even imply that any such account needs to be given. If foundationalism is a *purely* formal or structural doctrine, we have no reason to think that a given belief has *any* particular or permanent epistemological status. Perhaps the same belief can be a fixed point at one time, or in one particular context of inquiry or justification, but a candidate for justification at another time or in another context. Nothing in formal foundationalism excludes this.

By contrast, substantive foundationalism presupposes epistemological realism. I first introduced the idea of epistemological realism by way of analogy with scientific realism. We can now get a clearer sense of the appropriateness of the analogy. A micro-structural theory of a physical phenomenon is not purely structural. It will identify both certain structures and the types of entities fitted to occupy appropriate places in them. (Think of models of the atom.) Similarly with the foundationalist: he both attributes to justifying inferences a certain structural character *and* identifies the types of beliefs fitted to play the various structurally defined roles: basic, inferential, etc. Thus for the (substantive) foundationalist beliefs have an *intrinsic epistemological status* that accounts for their ability to play one or other of the formal roles the theory allows. Beliefs of one kind can be treated as epistemologically prior to beliefs of some other kind because they *are* epistemologically prior; some beliefs play the role of basic beliefs because they *are* basic; others receive inferential justification because they *require* it; and all because of the kinds of beliefs they are. According to foundationalists, our beliefs arrange themselves into broad, theoretically coherent classes according to certain *natural* relations of epistemological priority. Beliefs to which no beliefs are epistemologically prior are epistemologically basic. Their credibility is naturally intrinsic, as that of all other beliefs is naturally inferential. This is a much more peculiar doctrine than is generally recognized.[37]

On the foundationalist view, a belief's intrinsic epistemological status derives from the content of the proposition believed. The foundationalist's maxim is "Content determines status." Not, however, the details of content: what matter are certain rather abstract features, for example that a belief is about "external objects" or "experience." Thus it comes naturally to foundationalists to talk of basic propositions or basic statements, as well as of basic beliefs. Propositions recording the data of experience are held to be, by their very nature, epistemologically prior to propositions about external objects, which is why they are apt for the expression of basic beliefs. In light of this, we can characterize foundationalism as the view that our beliefs, simply in virtue of certain elements in their contents, stand in *natural epistemological relations* and thus fall into *natural epistemological kinds*. The broad, fundamental epistemological classes into which all propositions, hence derivatively all beliefs, naturally fall constitute an epistemic hierarchy which determines what, in the last analysis, can be called on to justify what. This means that, for a foundationalist, every belief has an inalienable epistemic character which it carries with it wherever it goes and which determines where its justification must finally be sought. The obvious illustration is the thought that any belief whatever about "external objects" must in the end derive its credibility from the evidence of "the senses," knowledge of how things appear.

I call the foundationalist's supposed relations of epistemological priority "natural" to emphasize the fact that they are supposed to exist in virtue of the nature of certain kinds of beliefs and not to depend on the changing and contingent contexts in which beliefs become embedded. For the foundationalist, in virtue of his epistemological realism, there is a level of analysis at which epistemic status is not, as Quine once said of one important epistemic feature, conventionality, "a passing trait." Beliefs are more like the members of a highly class-conscious society in which a person, no matter what he does, always carries the stigma or cachet of his origins. The quest for epistemic respectability is thus never entirely *une carrière ouverte aux talents*. A given belief, though useful in all sorts of ways, generally and quite properly (in appropriate contexts) taken for granted, and beyond any specific reproach, can never be allowed quite to forget that it *presupposes the existence of the external world* and is therefore, by that fact alone, subject to some kind of residual doubt, unless it can trace its lineage to more respectable data.

The foundationalist conception of fundamental epistemological relations, cutting across ordinary subject divisions and operating independently of all contextual constraints, receives an early articulation in Descartes's notion of "the order of reasons." Descartes writes, "I do not follow the order of topics but the order of arguments. . . . [In] orderly reasoning from easier matters to more difficult matters I make what deductions I can, first on one topic, then on another."[38] However, it is far from obvious that there is such an order of reasons, operating independently of the division of topics. It is not at all clear that some matters are intrinsically – that is to say independently of all circumstances and all collateral knowledge – "easier" than others. The way that justification and inquiry proceed in common life, or for that matter theoretical science, is far from evidently favorable to the foundationalist conception of epistemological relations. In both science and ordinary life, constraints on justification are many and various. Not merely that, they shift with context in ways that are probably impossible to reduce to rule. In part, they will have to do with the specific content of whatever claim is at issue. But they will also be decisively influenced by the subject of inquiry to which the claim in question belongs (history, physics, ornithology, etc.). We can call these *topical* or, where some definite subject or distinctive form of inquiry is involved, *disciplinary* constraints. Not entertaining radical doubts about the age of the Earth or the reliability of documentary evidence is a precondition of doing history *at all*. There are many things that, as historians, we might be dubious about, but not these.

Disciplinary constraints fix ranges of admissible questions. But what is and is not appropriate in the way of justification may also be strongly influenced by what specific objection has been entered to a given claim or belief. So to disciplinary we must add *dialectical* constraints: constraints reflecting the current state of a particular argument or problem-situation. In this respect justification is closely akin to explanation, which is also context-sensitive because question-relative.

I shall have more to say about disciplinary constraints and about the relation between justification and explanation. But for now let me note that, in ordinary examples of requiring and producing justifications, the epistemological status of a given claim can also depend on the particular situation in which the claim is entered, so that justification is also subject to a variety of *situational* constraints. Here I have in mind the worldly and not just the dialectical situation. Consider yet again Wittgenstein's remark that "My having two hands is, in normal circumstances, as certain as anything I could produce in evidence for it."[39] Entered in the right setting, a claim to have two hands might function like a foundationalist's basic statement, providing a stopping place for requests for evidence or justification: hence the element of formal foundationalism in Wittgenstein's view. But in other circumstances *the very same claim* might be contestable and so might stand in need of evidential support. The content of what is claimed does not guarantee a claim some particular epistemic standing. Not merely is status often dependent on the details of content, it is *never* determined by content alone. As Wittgenstein notes:

> If a blind man were to ask me "Have you got two hands?" I should not make sure by looking. If I were to have any doubt of it, then I don't know why I should trust my eyes. For why shouldn't I test my *eyes* by looking to find out whether I see my two hands? *What* is to be tested by *what*? (Who decides *what* stands fast?)[40]

The point is that, in the absence of a detailed specification of a particular context of inquiry, the sort of specification that would fix the relevant contextual constraints on justification, the question "What is to be tested by what" has no answer. Questions about justification are essentially context-bound. This is something a foundationalist will deny. He must of course make allowances for the way that what tests what can shift with context. But – and this is the crucial point, he cannot allow that such contextual determination goes all the way down. At the fundamental level, what is to be tested by what is objectively fixed, which is why there is no question of anybody's *deciding* the matter. The answer is determined by the epistemological facts themselves: by fundamental, objective relations of epistemological priority. This is not exactly an "intuitive" view.

Continuing with the example of my knowing (in normal circumstances) that I have two hands, recall also that there is no obvious way to generalize from an example like this. In normal circumstances, the proposition that I have two hands is as certain as anything we could cite as evidence for it. But there is no obvious, non-trivial way of saying what other propositions are, in normal circumstances, as certain as anything we could cite as evidence for them. Normally, I am as certain as I could be of anything that my name is Michael Williams: but beyond this, what does the proposition that my name is Michael Williams have in common with the proposition that I have two hands? What feature of their content explains their belonging to the same epistemic kind? As far as I can see, there isn't one. So even if someone said that the claim to have two hands did have a kind of intrinsic status – that of being certain in normal circumstances – we would still not be able to treat the example as *paradigmatic* of propositions belonging to a definite epistemic kind, for which we could articulate some alternative, non-trivial criterion of membership.[41] Again, the foundationalist sees things quite differently. For him, highly abstract divisions of propositions according to content (propositions about external objects versus experiential propositions, propositions about the past versus propositions about the present, etc.) have to coincide with fixed differences in epistemological status. But what we should learn from the example under discussion is that no such coincidence can be simply assumed. To cite again another of Wittgenstein's reminders, "a proposition saying that here is a physical object may have the same logical status as one saying that here is a red patch."[42] Without natural epistemological kinds, the foundationalist's permanent underlying structure of epistemological relations goes by the board.

We see from this that the antidote to foundationalism, indeed to epistemological realism generally, is a *contextualist* view of justification.[43] To adopt contextualism, however, is not just to hold that the epistemic status of a given proposition is liable to shift with situational, disciplinary and other contextually variable factors: it is to hold that, independently of all such influences, a proposition has no epistemic status whatsoever. There is *no fact of the matter* as to what kind of justification it either admits of or requires. Thus stated, contextualism implies a kind of externalism, for though appropriate contextual constraints will have to be met, if a given claim is to express knowledge, they will not always have to be known, or even believed, to be met.[44] But when we realize that the point of contextualism is to oppose the sceptic's or traditional epistemologist's epistemological realism, the externalist element in contextualism ought to be more palatable. The problem with externalism was that it seemed to deprive us of the possibility of answering a perfectly intelligible question: how do we come to know anything whatsoever about the external world? What we now see is that this question is not at all intuitive but reflects theoretical presuppositions that are not easy to defend. Contextualism, with its implied externalism, is not offered as a question-begging direct answer to an undeniably compelling request for understanding, but as a challenge to justify the presumption that there is something to understand.

What adds strength to the contextualist position is that, putting recent points together with the results of chapter 2, it looks as though there could not possibly be non-question-begging reasons for acceding to the key presupposition of the traditional project of assessing our knowledge of the world as a whole: namely, that propositions about physical objects belong intrinsically or naturally to a different epistemological category from those about appearances or "sense-data." As we saw, the familiar arguments for this distinction go from the neutrality or autonomy of experience to the intrinsic dubitability, which is to say intrinsic inferential status, of all beliefs having to do with external objects. Thus they implicitly assume what they supposedly prove. But now we see that the appeal to the totality condition, as a way of establishing the necessary epistemological asymmetry, is equally question-begging. The traditional epistemologist's charge that the contextualist begs the question can be met with the reply that the boot is on the other foot.

Though the idea of intrinsic epistemological status – alternatively, the idea of natural epistemological kinds and natural epistemological relations – is the absolutely crucial feature of the foundationalist conception of knowledge and justification, this is not how matters have always been seen. Many traditional defences of foundationalism have revolved around arguments for the existence of basic beliefs that are incorrigible, absolutely certain. The thought has been that, if nothing is certain, nothing else can be so much as probable. For inferential justification to be possible at all, there must be data that are absolutely beyond question. If there are not, the regress of justification has not really been halted.

If commitment to incorrigible basic beliefs is the hallmark of foundationalism, the diagnosis of scepticism that I favour – that scepticism arises from a foundational view of knowledge and justification – collapses into that which traces scepticism to the so-called "quest for certainty." This account of the basis of scepticism is not what I intend. The crucial question for me is whether sceptical arguments essentially involve a foundationalist, hence epistemological-realist, understanding of epistemological priority. Incorrigibility is a secondary issue, best left to foundationalists to sort out for themselves.

That this is so is evident from the fact that its contemporary defenders of foundationalism themselves often advocate detaching what they see as its real insights from the traditional "quest for certainty." These philosophers readily concede that no beliefs are absolutely incorrigible: even basic beliefs can be overridden by "higher level" beliefs, once we have got a working system of beliefs off the ground. The initial, non-inferential credibility of basic beliefs need only be *prima facie*, making them defeasible. Nevertheless, even according to this "modest" foundationalism, a measure of initial credibility belongs intrinsically to some beliefs and not to others. This is therefore genuine foundationalism, however modest in other ways.[45]

If foundationalism is tied to incorrigibility, tracing scepticism to foundationalism will be neither convincing as a diagnosis nor effective as an entering wedge for criticism. It will be unconvincing as a diagnosis because it is enough for the sceptic's purposes if experiential knowledge is, in the last analysis, prior to knowledge of the world, whether or not experience is a source of absolute certainty. So if commitment to incorrigible basic beliefs is made definitive of the foundationalist outlook, the sceptic can argue with some plausibility that he is not wedded to foundationalism. And no criticism will be effective if it is directed at a view which, while no doubt associated with some particular formulations of the sceptic's case, is not essential to it.

So, to sum up, foundationalism presupposes the more general outlook that I have called "epistemological realism." To repeat, this is not realism as a position within epistemology (the view that we have knowledge of a "real" or objective world) but rather a form of extreme realism with respect to the typical objects of epistemological reflection: knowledge, justification, and so on. The foundationalist is an epistemological realist because his view involves more than openness to the idea of an epistemological hierarchy, cutting across ordinary subject-matter divisions and operating independently of all contextual factors: it involves a definite conception of the *status* of this hierarchy. The hierarchy of epistemological kinds is supposed to capture the fundamental, underlying structure of all empirical justification and so is conceived by the foundationalist as *fully objective*. He does not see the partitioning of our beliefs into, say, beliefs about the external world and experiential beliefs as something that he imposes for the purpose of carrying out a particular kind of investigation but rather as corresponding to an objective structure of epistemic relations: mirroring the epistemological facts, so to speak. For a foundationalist, to suggest that his constraints on justification are imposed for a particular purpose, and have no compelling force in abstraction from it, would be to detract from their objectivity. Constraints that are fully objective cannot be interest-relative. So when I said that, according to foundationalism, our beliefs *arrange themselves* into a certain hierarchy of classes, I meant to be taken literally. This realist conception of the objectivity of justificational structure is what I mean to capture through the notions of natural epistemological kinds and natural epistemological relations. It is this conception that makes possible the move from formal foundationalism as a theory of the structure of inference to genuine substantive foundationalism as a theory of the structure of knowledge. It may well be that knowledge- or justification-yielding inferences, entered in a wide variety of contexts, show common structural features. But the claim that human knowledge, or knowledge of the world, considered as some kind of integrated totality, has a permanent structure, or indeed any definite structure at all, is a far different and far more theoretically ambitious claim.

## 3.6  METHODOLOGICAL NECESSITY

We have already seen that, to flesh out the idea of "human knowledge" as a possible object of theoretical investigation, we have to suppose that there are pervasive epistemological constraints or relations. That is to say, at least some constraints on what propositions demand evidential support and on what propositions can provide it must be *context-invariant*. If we do not always insist on respecting these constraints in a fully rigorous way, this need not mean that they do not apply. To admit that certain constraints are often waived is different from, indeed incompatible with, claiming that they are inapplicable.

This is a very substantial commitment and it is not clear why we should accept it. An examination of ordinary practices of justification strongly suggests that constraints, governing what sorts of evidence can properly be brought to bear on a disputed claim, what needs to be defended and what can safely be taken for granted, though subject to other kinds of contextual determination as well, are at least *topic-relative*, which is to say determined in part by the subject under discussion.

In chapter 1, I criticized, in passing, Hume's offhand suggestion that only carelessness and inattention save us from a permanent, debilitating awareness of the truth of scepticism, hence from lapsing into a state of chronic, paralyzing doubt. My point was that, in particular contexts, disciplines etc., exempting certain propositions from doubt is what determines the *direction* of inquiry. As Wittgenstein remarks: "It may be... that all enquiry on our part is set so as to exempt certain propositions from doubt, if they are ever formulated. They lie apart from the route travelled by enquiry."[46]

If some of these propositions cease to lie apart from the route travelled by inquiry, then inquiry travels by a different route. Or perhaps no clear route remains for it to travel by. This is obviously the case with investigations in particular scientific or scholarly disciplines. Disciplinary constraints have a great deal to do with the kinds of questions that can and cannot legitimately be raised without radically affecting the direction of inquiry. Thus, introducing sceptical doubts about whether the Earth really existed a hundred years (or five minutes) ago does not lead to a more careful way of doing history: it changes the subject, from history to epistemology. So when Wittgenstein asks: "am I to say that the experiment which perhaps I make to test the truth of a proposition presupposes the truth of the proposition that the apparatus I believe I see is really there?"[47] he is clearly inviting the answer "No." And the reason for answering "No" is that the possibility mentioned, while relevant to certain general, epistemological problems, is completely beside the point in the context of a specific experiment in chemistry or physics. To bring it up is not to introduce greater rigor into the investigation in hand but to shift attention to another kind of investigation entirely.

"[T]hat something stands fast for me," Wittgenstein remarks, "is not grounded in my stupidity or credulity."[48] We now see that this is so, at least in part, because it is grounded in my *interests*. It is not that I think that no proposition that stands fast could ever be questioned, though in certain cases I should be likely to feel, as Wittgenstein says, "intellectually very distant" from someone inclined to raise questions. It is just that some doubts are logically excluded by forms of investigation that I find significant, important, or perhaps just interesting. This has nothing to do with dogmatism, credulity or carelessness. Wittgenstein sums up the key points in the following well-known passages:

The questions that we raise and our <u>doubts depend on the fact that</u> <u>some propositions are exempt from doubt</u>, are as it were like hinges on which those turn.

That is to say, it belongs to the logic of our scientific investigations that certain things are in deed not doubted.

But it isn't that the situation is like this: We just can't investigate everything, and for that reason we are forced to rest content with assumption. If I want the door to turn, the hinges must stay put.[49]

Of course, I if I do not want the door to turn I can nail it shut; or I might want it to open the other way, in which case I will move the hinges. But if I want the door to turn this way, it is not just more *convenient*, if a little slapdash, to place the hinges where they are: there is nowhere else to put them.

<u>By fixing a range of admissible questions, we determine a form of</u> <u>inquiry</u>. But this means that a form of inquiry is determined by more than purely formal constraints. As Wittgenstein puts it: 'The question doesn't arise at all.' Its answer would characterise a *method*. But there is no sharp boundary between methodological propositions and propositions within a method."[50] For a subject like history, there is more to method than abstract procedural rules. This is because the exclusion of certain questions (about the existence of the Earth, the complete and total unreliability of documentary evidence, etc.) amounts to the acceptance of substantial factual commitments. (These commitments, which must be accepted, if what we understand by historical inquiry is to be conducted at all, have the status, relative to that form of inquiry, of *methodological necessities*.)

I have introduced the idea of a proposition's being exempted from doubt as a matter of methodological necessity in connection with the disciplinary constraints that determine the general directions of highly organized forms of inquiry. (But it is evident that something similar goes on in more informal, everyday settings.) <u>Asking some questions logically precludes asking others</u>: all sorts of everyday certainties have to stand fast if we are to get on with life. Again, however, I want to emphasize that our situation is misread both by the Humean naturalist and by the sceptic. (The naturalist sees our everyday inability to entertain radical doubts as showing that nature has simply determined us to believe certain things, however groundless they seem to us in our more reflective moments.) <u>By contrast, I want to</u> <u>claim that exemption from doubt – epistemic privilege – is a matter of</u> <u>methodology, not psychology</u>. In a specific context, certain exemptions will be *logically* required by the direction of inquiry. We are therefore determined by Nature to hold certain things fast only in so far as we are naturally inclined to interest ourselves in matters requiring us to exempt them from doubt.

This is far from the only point that we must emphasize. It is also crucial to note that, if epistemic status is determined by the direction of inquiry, the reason why, in a given inquiry, certain propositions have to stand fast has to be separated from the reason why that inquiry results in knowledge, if it does. Here we recur, from a slightly different angle, to the externalist element in contextualism. In particular contexts of inquiry, certain propositions stand fast as a matter of methodological necessity. But inquiries informed by them will yield knowledge only if those propositions are true, which they need not always be.

The general moral here is that questions about a proposition's epistemic status must always be separated from questions about its truth. If epistemic status is fixed by the direction of inquiry, epistemic status is context-sensitive. Truth however is not. A proposition is either true or not. But, according to the contextualist view I favor, we cannot say, in a similarly unqualified way, that a proposition is either open to doubt or not. Sometimes it will be and sometimes it won't. Generally speaking, a proposition is neither true because it stands fast nor stands fast because it is true.

We can also see why it was so important at the outset to distinguish between formal and substantive foundationalism. If foundationalism is equated with a certain view of the formal structure of justification – i.e. with the view that inferential justification always requires beliefs that function as "fixed points – a contextualist view of justification can be seen as (formally) foundationalist. But it certainly need not be substantively foundationalist. There are no limits as to what might or might not, in an appropriate context, be fixed.

If a proposition's epistemic status is determined by the direction of inquiry, its status is interest-relative. This is the sense in which epistemic status is not fully objective. This has nothing to do with its being subjective. If I want the door to open, the hinges must stay put: there is nothing subjective about this. However, needing to stay put is not an intrinsic property of these pieces of metal: they must stay put only in so far as I want them to function as hinges. In abstraction from my purposes, there is simply no fact of the matter as to what these pieces must or must not do. But when the sceptic singles out experiential beliefs as epistemologically prior to beliefs about the external world, the kind of epistemic privilege he assigns them has nothing to do with how I want them to function. Experiential knowledge is prior to knowledge of the world whatever my other interests and whether I like it or not. There is a fundamental level at which epistemic priority, hence epistemic status, is determined by the epistemological facts and not by anyone's interests.

When I say determined by the *epistemological* facts, I mean determined by certain *purely* epistemological facts. We encountered this idea in Hume's insistance on the autonomy of the science of man. If there is to be room for a project of assessing our knowledge of the world as a whole, there must be facts about our epistemic situation which hold, and can be seen to hold, independently of our knowing anything about the external world. So to the context-invariance and full objectivity of fundamental epistemological relations we must add their autonomy. As we have seen, ordinary constraints on justification seem to operate rather differently. Because they reflect substantive factual commitments (e.g. the existence of the earth time out of mind), they are not autonomous. On the contrary, they are deeply implicated with views about the world. This means that, for the traditional epistemologist, they cannot be fundamental. In chapter 5, we shall look more closely at his explanation of how this might be. Right now, we must return to the argument with which this chapter began.

## 3.7  PRIORITY RECONSIDERED

The contextualist account of epistemic status just sketched may seem at first to play right into the sceptic's hands. It claims that exemption from doubt is often a function of the direction of inquiry. But it concedes, indeed insists, that this kind of epistemic privilege does not guarantee truth. Propositions that stand fast as a matter of methodological necessity do not have to be true, which means that inquiries guided by them do not have to result in knowledge. Doesn't this amount to conceding that, in the end, what we are pleased to call knowledge rests on assumptions, just as the sceptic says? I do not think so: letting a proposition stand fast as a matter of methodological necessity is quite different from *merely* making an assumption.

The sceptic, or traditional epistemologist, can agree with this, at least to an extent. He can agree that methodological necessities are not assumptions in the sense of arbitrary or gratuitous assumptions. But he will argue that the distinction is not all that important *from a purely epistemological standpoint.* His point is that though there may well be a way in which we have to take certain things for granted, this has nothing to do with their being justified.

I think that this reply derives much of its force from a standing ambiguity in the phrase "justified belief." What is supposed to be justified: the proposition believed or our believing it? We may well be justified in believing propositions that cannot themselves be justified, in the sense of derived from evidence more certain than they. Wittgenstein remarks that to use a word without justification is not necessarily to use it without right.[51] A similar point can be made about believing: to be justified in accepting a proposition is not always a matter of being able to marshal evidence for the proposition accepted. I think that this is what philosophers have in mind when they speak of our special "non-epistemic" relation to certain "framework judgments" or "presuppositions."

The sceptic ignores this ambiguity in the notion of justified belief, not out of carelessness but out of his commitment to epistemological realism. As we saw, an epistemological realist is apt to think that content determines status. This is why it comes as naturally to foundationalists to speak of basic propositions as it docs to speak of basic beliefs. For a foundationalist, certain broad features of the content of what is believed determine whether what is believed can be epistemically justified. And, in light of the autonomy of epistemology, *epistemically* justified believing must be derivative from the justifiability, in the sense of proper derivability, of the propositions believed. There may, of course, be ways in which my letting a given proposition stand is entirely justified: for example, exempting it from doubt may be essential to the pursuit of important goals. But this kind of justified believing, we shall be told, is not a pure case of epistemic justification. For a foundationalist, the distinction between believing propositions justifiably and believing justifiable propositions operates significantly only at the level of everyday, practical concerns, where more than the purely epistemic aspects of justification are involved.

My reply to this will not be complete until chapter 5, where I examine the suggestion that what is ordinarily called "knowledge" is really only knowledge-for-all-practical-purposes. A central concern of that chapter will be whether there is a "purely epistemological standpoint" from which the distance between methodological necessities and arbitrary assumptions shrinks to the vanishing point. However, even at this juncture we can see that the sceptic's way with the suggestion that methodological necessities are in no sense unjustifid assumptions is no more compelling than his epistemological realism, which in fact it takes for granted. But this is not all. The considerations just explored show that the sceptic himself is committed to recognizing the distinction between methodological necessity and truth. And this distinction, far from advancing his cause, is lethal to it. To see why, we must rehearse the argument to date.

In chapter 2, I tried to show that arguments for radical scepticism presuppose the priority of experiential knowledge over knowledge of the world. This enabled me to conclude that attempts to establish the intrinsic epistemological priority of experiential knowledge on the basis of the greater intrinsic dubitability of objective knowledge are question-begging. The only reason for thinking that such knowledge is intrinsically more dubitable is provided by the existence of sceptical arguments which, when unpacked, turn out to take the doctrine of the priority of experiential knowledge for granted.

This result did not allow us to conclude straight away that scepticism rests on a gratuitous epistemological assumption. What it did suggest, however, is that the source of the doctrine of the priority of experiential knowledge is not evidence from our ordinary justificational practices

but rather the distinctively philosophical project of trying to understand
how it is possible for us to know anything whatsoever about the external
world. The totality condition that the sceptic (or the traditional philosopher) imposes on a philosophical understanding of our knowledge of
the world is what forces us to see that knowledge as somehow derivative
from experience. No other way of seeing it permits an assessment, hence a
legitimating explanation, at the proper level of generality.

We are now in a position to see why this argument does not prove
what it needs to prove. All it shows is that the doctrine of the priority of
experiential knowledge over knowledge of the world is *a methodological necessity
of the traditional epistemological project*. But since the sceptic himself is irre-
vocably committed to distinguishing between methodological necessity and
truth, it does not show, nor by his own standards can the sceptic take it to
show, that that doctrine is true.

The result is that the inference from the essential generality of the
traditional epistemological project fails to establish the kind of relations of
epistemological priority needed to threaten us with scepticism. To yield
sceptical results, these relations must reflect more than *mere* methodological
necessities: they must correspond to fully objective epistemological asymmetries. It is not enough to point out that if we are to attempt an assessment of our knowledge of the world as a whole we must *take* experiential
knowledge to be epistemologically prior to the knowledge we want to assess.
Success or failure in the enterprise will have the significance the sceptic and
the traditional epistemologist mean it to have only if experiential knowledge
really is, as a matter of objective epistemological fact, more basic than
knowledge of the world. If it isn't, or more generally if no epistemological
relations are in the sense I have indicated fully objective, no attempt to
ground knowledge of some allegedly problematic kind on some appropriately
prior kind of knowledge will amount to an attempt at assessment. So, as we
saw in chapter 2, should the attempt fail, or even inevitably fail, the sceptic
will be left with a harmless logico-conceptual point but with no way of
advancing to his pessimistic epistemological conclusion.

I remarked that the argument from the totality condition to the absolute
prority of experiential knowledge over knowledge of the world rests on two
assumptions: that there is something to assess, and that charting its relation
to experience amounts to assessing it. I have concentrated on the first, but
by so doing have shown what to say about the second. As a pure methodological proposal, there is nothing wrong with setting propositions about the
world against experiential propositions, for the purposes of exploring possible relations between them. Like Goodman, we could think of phenomenalism as an interesting constructive project. We could ask, "To what extent
can a phenomenalist reconstruction of the world be carried through?"
without thinking that we were even addressing any questions of epistemic

legitimacy.[52] Think of the way we can model arithmetic in set theory: though this is an interesting piece of mathematics, we need ancillary epistemological assumptions to think of it as relevant to an "assessment" of arithmetic. But this is not the spirit in which the sceptic thinks of the relation between experiential knowledge and knowledge of the world. He needs a fully objective epistemological asymmetry, and this is what no argument from methodological necesity will ever yield.

We saw in chapter 1 that some philosophers treat scepticism as a paradox exploiting deep tensions in our ordinary way of thinking. Given our results so far, it would be better to locate the tensions in the sceptic's own theoretical presuppositions. One of those key presuppositions is realism, and according to realism when it comes to true and false, thinking does not make it so. To say that we must believe something is one thing; to say that it is true is something else again. But when combined with his view of epistemological relations, which involves commitment to a realm of autonomous epistemological fact, his own realism works against any attempt to trace the epistemological constraints he exploits to the character of the traditional epistemological project. No argument of that kind can show more than that we have to accept certain views in order to undertake a project of the kind in question. It does not and cannot show that they are true.

Think back to Moore's attempt to confront the sceptic's assumptions with commonsense certainties. Stroud thinks that Moore does not refute these assumptions, any more than the eager assistant refutes the detective, "if those 'assumptions' are nothing more than truths unavoidably involved in any general assessment of our knowledge of the world."[53] Exactly. But this kind of unavoidable involvement does not guarantee truth. I agree with Stroud that these assumptions are unavoidably involved in a general assessment of our knowledge of the world, but I deny that this is any argument for them. My argument here thus reinforces my previous verdict on Moore's strategy. This strategy fails if the appeal to commonsense convictions is meant as a direct rebuttal of the sceptic's conclusions. But it succeeds if it is intended to bring out the need for a theoretical diagnosis of his questions. Those questions, we have now seen, depend essentially on foundationalist preconceptions. But foundationalism is more than a particular response to a traditional epistemological problem: foundationalist ideas are built into the traditional epistemologist's very conception of his enterprise. So if we ever concede that the traditional conception of a philosophical assessment of our knowledge of the world is naively intelligible, we implicitly accede to the sceptic's foundationalist presuppositions. This will mean both that his questions are perfectly in order and that there is no hope of answering them as Moore tries to do. In accepting the questions at face value, thus accepting the constraints on justification they implicitly impose, we undermine the commonsense certainties that Moore tries to hold fast to. In the context of the traditional assessment of our knowledge of the world, Moore's certainties cease to be available. Again, however, this does not show that Moore is wrong to be so certain. It shows only that, in challenging the sceptic, he fails to clearly locate what Wittgenstein calls "the right point of attack." Though Moore's certainties cannot be directly opposed to the sceptic's conclusions, they can form the basis of a theoretical diagnosis of the way he reaches them. Or to probe even deeper, they offer a way into a diagnosis of the very conception of epistemological understanding that animates the sceptic's apparently most intuitive questions.

## 3.8  SCEPTICISM IN CONTEXT

Suppose I am right and that the argument from methodological necessity does not establish the existence of a fully objective relation of epistemological priority between experiential knowledge and knowledge of the world: someone might still press the question of why, exactly, the sceptic needs that relation to be fully objective. And I agree that the question should be pressed. To appreciate fully the sceptic's commitment to epistemological realism we need to backtrack, this time all the way to the Humean biperspectivalism that we encountered at the very beginning of our discussion.

According to Hume and his many contemporary followers, we have two outlooks, both natural in their way. On the one hand, there is the commonsense, everyday attitude, which is free of radical doubts about the existence of the external world; and on the other, there is the profoundly sceptical attitude which seems to be the natural outcome of attempts to philosophize. Sceptical doubt and commonsense certainty seem to be equally context-bound, which is why scepticism cannot be refuted simply by appealing to common sense against the results of philosophical reflection. A correct diagnosis of scepticism, I suggested, should give a satisfying explanation of its context-sensitivity and that of common sense too.

We now have the explanation in hand: characteristic possibilities of certainty and doubt will not detach from a given form of inquiry because they are fixed by that form of inquiry's characteristic direction. Or as I have put it, what can and cannot be called in question is a matter of methodological necessity. Whether we are engaged in the topical inquiries of everyday life (and the special sciences) or whether we are attempting to philosophize in the manner of the traditional epistemologist, the direction of our investigation imposes limits on what can be questioned and what can be brought in evidence. Acceptance of the priority of experiential knowledge over knowledge of the world is a methodological necessity of traditional epistemological inquiry in exactly the same way that acceptance of the existence of the world time out of mind is a methodological necesity of doing history. But if this is so, the sceptic's inference to the general impossibility of knowledge of the world from his demonstration that such knowledge can never be experientially grounded is blocked. The sceptic takes himself to have discovered, under the conditions of philosophical reflection, that knowledge of the world is impossible. But in fact, the most he has discovered is that knowledge of the world is *impossible under the conditions of philosophical reflection*. It is not human psychology that prevents scepticism's escaping from the study into the street but the shift in epistemological constraints that accompanies a shift in the direction of inquiry. The discovery that knowledge of the world is impossible under one set of conditions does not license the conclusion that it is never possible, even when conditions are entirely different.[54]

When I first introduced the suggestion that we have a special "non-epistemic" relation to framework judgments I said that the sceptic is likely to think that the critic has shown at most that our relation to them is not *ordinarily* epistemic. Indeed, he is likely to think that all that has been shown is that our relation to them is not ordinarily *treated* as epistemic. However, we are now in a position to see that this reply may be less potent than it first seems. If different forms of inquiry impose different constraints on justification, but if no constraints are more fundamental than others, sceptical results obtained in the course of philosophical reflection will not necessarily point to defects in results obtained in other circumstances.

There is only one way to meet this argument. The sceptic must hold that the constraints on knowledge of the world that emerge in the course of his philosophical reflections have a completely uniquely privileged status. He must hold that philosophical reflection brings to light constraints which, though they may for various reasons be ignored or overridden, apply to knowledge of the world as such. These constraints must be context-invariant, rather than context-sensitive; they must derive from the essential nature of knowledge of the world; and since they cannot be in any way interest-relative, they must be fully objective. In other words, the sceptic must be an epistemological realist. Only epistemological realism can validate his inference from results obtained in his very special context of philosophical reflection to the general impossibility of worldly knowledge.

Many philosophers have been tempted by the thought that there may not really be a clash between the sceptic's discoveries and commonsense claims to knowledge of the world. But they have tended to think that, to avoid a clash, they must point to a systematic difference in meaning between that we say in everday life and what we say in the course of philosophical reflection. Perhaps Kant originated this strategy when he distinguished between the "empirical" claims made by the special sciences and the "transcendental" theses that are the business of philosophy.

Some philosophers, Carnap for example, hold that the sceptic fails to undermine ordinary knowledge of the world because his statements, as he intends them to be taken, mean nothing at all. As a statement "internal" to our everyday linguistic framework, "There are material objects" is a trivial consequence of any statement about the world. But as an "external" statement about that framework, an attempted statement, though made in the very same words, will lack "cognitive significance." However, the sceptic might be equally unsuccessful if his statements, as they must be understood in the unusual context of philosophical reflection, mean something different from what they ordinarily mean. Thus Thompson Clarke suggests that the very general commonsense propositions with which Moore confronts the sceptic can be taken two ways, the "plain" way and the "philosophical" way. For example:

> Suppose a physiologist lecturing on mental abnormalities observes: *Each of us who is normal knows that he is now awake, not dreaming or hallucinating, that there is a real public world outside his mind which he is now perceiving, that in this world there are three-dimensionsal animate and inanimate bodies of many shapes and sizes.* . . . In contrast, individuals suffering from certain mental abnormalities each believes that what we know to be the real public world is his imaginative creation.[55]

The italicized, plain propositions are "verbal twins" of propositions typically attacked and defended in discussions of philosophical scepticism. But in plain contexts, nobody doubts that they are true, even though plain common sense recognizes the very phenomena – dreaming, hallucinating, and so on – that the sceptic appeals to in his attempt to show that we can never know that we are in touch with "a real public world." Whether there is a clash between philosophy and common sense will depend, therefore, on the relation between philosophical and plain knowing.

*clash*

Here Clarke is more subtle than Carnap, for he recognizes that the sceptic has an account of the relation between philosophy and common sense which both preserves the relevance of philosophical discoveries to ordinary plain knowing and makes it hard to think that sceptical claims are less than fully meaningful.[56] Ordinary, plain knowing is hemmed by practical considerations. By contrast, to philosophize is "to step outside the nonsemantical practice" and, meaning simply what one's words mean, ask whether we really know what we (plainly) take ourselves to know. Compared with our philosophizing, ordinary thinking is "restricted." All the sceptic has to do is to get us to look beyond the restrictions. This is easy enough since there is a standing invitation to look "beyond the plain" in our conception of knowledge as knowledge of an objective world. We want to know what there is: not just relative to this and that particular restriction, imposed by this or that practical purpose or limitation, but *absolutely*.

Still, the final distance between Clarke and Carnap is not as great as their initial divergence might suggest. Clarke too holds that, in the end, both "philosophical common sense" *and* its sceptical denial "are a spurious fiction if our conceptual-human constitution is not standard." Amongst other things, a conceptual-human constitution of the standard type requires that "Each concept or the conceptual scheme must be divorceable intact from our practices, from whatever constitues the essential character of the plain" and that we, as concept users, are "purely ascertaining observers who, usually by means of our senses, ascertain, when possible, whether items fulfill the conditions legislated by concepts."[57] But the sceptic himself shows that our conceptual-human constitution cannot be of the standard type. Our plain knowledge that we are not dreaming right now – the sort of knowledge expressed by the physiologist – cannot be undermined by the plain possibility that we might, in fact, be asleep. But it would be if our conceptual-human constitution were of the standard type. For on this point the sceptic is right: there are no marks or features that conclusively distinguish waking experience from dreaming. So the fact of plain knowing, combined with the sceptic's point about dreaming or hallucinating, shows that our conceptual-human constitution is not of the standard type. This insight is part of the legacy of scepticism.

In representing the sceptic as helping bring about his own undoing, Clarke prefigures the strategy followed by Wright. Wright, we may recall, argues that the sceptic does indeed show that his target-propositions – for example, that there is a real, public world – are beyond justification. They are beyond justification because the sole evidence we can bring to bear on them only functions as evidence if they are already known to be true. Thus sensory experience only counts in favour of any proposition about the public world on assumptions that already commit us to that world's existence. But the lesson to learn from this is that the propositions the sceptic represents as groundless, factual assumptions, are not really factual at all. If a proposition's factuality requires some account of the cognitive powers that would be required for knowing that proposition to be true, and if the sceptic shows that, in the case of some propositions, no such account can be given, scepticism is self-undermining. This argument shares with Clarke's more than just structural similarities.

None of these arguments appeals to me. I do not want to distinguish between internal and external questions or between plain and philosophical meanings of statements. Nor do I wish to claim that, for deep philosophical reasons, apparently factual statements are really not factual at all. The reason is that I think that all these reactions to scepticism reveal the deep and pervasive influence of epistemological realism. I suggested earlier that one of the epistemological realist's central commitments is to the doctrine that content determines status. Now I claim that the attempt to insulate common sense from sceptical undermining by finding a different meaning, or no factual meaning at all, in the apparently commonsensical propositions the sceptic examines is driven by that same doctrine. If a statement is certain in one context but not in another, the argument assumes, this can only be because a change in context induces a change in meaning. So if, plainly speaking, we do know that we are awake at the moment, whereas, philosophically speaking, we don't, our plain and philosophical propositions can only be "verbal twins." But if, as I have argued, epistemological status is never determined by content alone, there is no such easy inference from a difference in status to a difference in content. We can explain the context-boundedness of sceptical doubts without getting entangled in this baroque apparatus of plain and philosophical meanings. As we shall see in a moment, this is all to the good.

Once again, I must emphasize that my argument on these matters will not be complete until I have examined the sceptic's own favored account of the nature of philosophical reflection. Even so, however, I think it is fair to conclude that we are well on the way to accomplishing the primary goal of theoretical diagnosis, which is to get the sceptic to share the burden of theory. But there is a nagging question that is likely to surface again at this point. If we are left with one theory of knowledge confronting another, and we will never be able to determine conclusively which is correct, doesn't the sceptic win ties and so triumph at second order?

When I first raised this question, towards the end of chapter 1, I hinted that it would not be quite right to describe the outcome of the theoretical diagnosis I would defend as "one theory of knowledge confronting another." I hope that I have now clarified what I had in mind. If we abandon epistemological realism, there is a clear sense in which we no longer see such things as "knowledge of the world" as appropriate objects of theory. At most, we will have a theory of the concept of knowledge. We will not have a theory of knowledge as well. *A fortiori*, we will not be left confronting the sceptic's theory with a theory of our own.

Perhaps this will look like a purely verbal maneuver, for we shall certainly be left with epistemological views, whether or not we want to think of them as a theory of knowledge. But the point isn't just verbal. For what we have seen is that the sceptic's theoretical commitments are in fact far more extensive than those of his contextualist opponent. Contextualism simply takes seriously and at face-value what seem to be evident facts of ordinary epistemic practices: that relevant evidence varies with context, that content alone never determines epistemological status, and so on. The theoretical resources required to explain these appearances away belong entirely to the sceptic. So it might be reasonable to object that the sceptic wins ties, if the outcome of my theoretical diagnosis were a tie. And if I had followed philosophers like Carnap, Clarke, or Wright and rested my diagnosis on difficult and controversial views about meaning, perhaps it would have been. But as things stand it isn't.

This is not all. It seems to me entirely reasonable to hold that extra theoretical commitments demand extra arguments. But where will the sceptic find them? Not in evidence from everyday practice, which fits in as well or better with contextualism. Presumably, then, in some kind of general, theoretical considerations. Here, however, we run into the fallaciousness of the argument from methodological necessity: by the sceptic's own standards, there is no inference from the fact that we must *take* experiential knowledge to be generally prior to knowledge of the world, if we are to make room for a project of assessing our knowledge of the world as a whole, to its really being so. But if the argument from methodological necessity does not show that the sceptic's principles are true, what would? It is hard to say: for although the argument from methodological necessity is fallacious, it is not as if there are other ways of arguing for the priority of experiential knowledge. On the contrary, as we have seen repeatedly, attempts to argue for it directly beg the question. So the doctrine has to be true but unarguable.

I think that the sceptic's difficulties are compounded when we turn from this relatively particular doctrine to epistemological realism in general. It is not easy to imagine what a convincing argument for epistemological realism would even look like, or what evidence it could appeal to. This is where the clash between scepticism and our ordinary attitudes really does work to the sceptic's disadvantage. It does so because our ordinary practices of justification not only tolerate but invite a contextualist construction: and contextualism is the antidote to epistemological realism.

True, a contextual view of knowledge and justification will seem unsatisfactory to a philosopher who continues to feel the lack of an understanding of human knowledge in general. But if my argument to this point is correct, he will feel this lack only if he is already predisposed to epistemological realism. Once more, we are starting to run round a very small circle of ideas. The sceptic's foundationalism, together with the epistemological realism it embodies, is a brute metaphysical commitment. The theoretical diagnostician could hardly ask for more.

# 4

# Examples and Paradigms

## 4.1 THE BEST-CASE ARGUMENT

I have connected the traditional project of assessing our knowledge of the world as a whole with a definite theoretical outlook: foundationalism interpreted in the light of epistemological realism. But there is a way of presenting the case for scepticism that tends to conceal the extent of the sceptic's theoretical commitments, thus permitting him to argue that his conclusions derive from a respect for our most ordinary ideas about what it is to know something. The strategy I have in mind is this: focussing on a single carefully chosen case of knowledge, with a view to arguing that if knowledge fails here, it evidently fails everywhere.

Arguably, this is how Descartes reaches his general doubt. Having determined that his putative knowledge of the world is entirely dependent on the reliability of his senses, Descartes looks for a way to call their reliability in question. His first thought is that an uncritical reliance on appearances sometimes leads us to form false beliefs. Seen from a distance, a round tower may look square. How the tower looks can therefore mislead me into thinking that it is square. If it does, my "senses" will have "deceived" me.

Descartes sometimes writes as though susceptibility to such errors were a sufficient ground for a general distrust of the senses. For example, he reports in the *Discourse on Method* that: "because our senses sometimes deceive us, I wished to suppose that nothing is just as they cause us to imagine it to be."[1] But if this were his argument, it would be an obvious fallacy. From the fact that our senses have sometimes deceived us, it does not follow that they might do so always. They might mislead us in some circumstances while remaining completely reliable in others. Perhaps, however, the conclusion is not meant to follow from the fact of perceptual error alone, for Descartes turns to examples of error only after he has laid down an important guiding principle. Thus:

inasmuch as reason already persuades me that I ought no less carefully to withhold assent from matters which are not entirely certain
and indubitable than from those which appear to me manifestly to be
false, if I am able to find in each one some reason to doubt, this will
suffice to justify my rejecting the whole.[2]

Given this principle, no belief based on the senses can be regarded as
absolutely "certain and indubitable," if even the barest possibility of
perceptual error is allowed, Even at the best of times there will be a chance,
however slight, that things are not as they seem. By Descartes's standards,
this will be enough to justify witholding assent.

Whatever it is worth, this argument has nothing to do with *radical*
scepticism. Perhaps none of our beliefs about the world are, in the sense
indicated, absolutely certain. But this does not preclude their being justified,
even to the point of *virtual* certainty. Indeed, not only is there nothing
particularly threatening, or even interesting, in this kind of scepticism, to
offer it as revealing the chief obstacle to knowledge would be to damage
rather than advance the sceptic's cause. For this argument invites just the
sort of criticism he needs to head off: that since absolute certainty is not
ordinarily required for knowing, scepticism results from distorting ordinary
epistemic standards, and so reveals nothing about knowledge as we ordinarily understand it.

Let me concede straight away that, once the force of the sceptic's
distinctive questions is taken into account, it is not immediately obvious
that an insistence on a much higher than usual degree of certainty *would*
involve a distortion of ordinary standards. This is an issue I shall return to
in the next chapter. For now, however, I want to set it aside because, even
if Descartes is tempted to argue in the ways just mentioned, it is clear that
neither argument fully represents his reasons for thinking that the senses
are, in some quite general way, not to be trusted. He recognizes full well
that it would not be reasonable to base a general distrust of the senses
on the fact of their "deceiving" us in certain special circumstances: for
example, when the objects we are interested in are small or far away or
observed under poor conditions. Even in the passage quoted above, where
Descartes indicates his willingness to withold assent from all propositions
that are less than certain, he insists on finding a ground for doubt that
applies to each. Accordingly, errors that are evidently tied to particular
circumstances will not give him what he wants.

The crucial step in Descartes's argument is taken when he turns from
ancient and familiar examples of perceptual error to a situation in which he
seems ideally well placed for knowing what is going on in his surroundings.
This is the situation he currently finds himself in, sitting by his fireside. He
finds himself assured of many things: e.g. that he is sitting by the fire, in his

dressing gown with a book on his lap. Here his assurance presupposes no special expertise, which he might lack. Furthermore, there is no question of his going wrong because his knowledge concerns objects that are small or far away, or because the conditions of perception are unfavorable. Everything is familiar, near to hand and in full view, and the conditions of perception are as good as they get. Nevertheless, Descartes is astonished to discover that he does not know what he thought he knew. He finds that, even in apparently ideal conditions, he cannot rule out the possibility that he is dreaming; and dreaming that something is so is incompatible with knowing it.

It is interesting to note, in passing, what a new twist this gives to the ancient sceptical argument from dreams. Dreaming, so crucial for Descartes, is mentioned only incidentally by Sextus Empiricus as one of the "conditions or dispositions" influencing judgment. Sleeping and waking, Sextus tells us:

> give rise to different impressions, since we do not imagine when awake what we imagine in sleep, nor in sleep what we imagine when awake; so that the existence of our impressions is not absolute but relative, being in relation to our sleeping or waking condition. Probably, then, in dreams we see things which to our waking state are unreal, although not wholly unreal: for they exist in dreams, just as waking realities exist, although nonexistent in dreams.[3]

This is one of a series of arguments against the claim that the senses are the source or "criterion" of objective knowledge. The claim is that since sleeping and waking reveal different worlds, there is no reason to take the objects of the waking world as uniquely real, hence no reason to make the senses the criterion of knowledge. True, the objects of the dream world do not exist in the waking world. Equally, however, the objects we encounter in waking life do not exist in dreams, for in dreams even familiar objects are capable of fantastic transformations. So all we can conclude is that the two worlds are different, not that one is unreal. There is no non-question-begging way of establishing that waking perception, as opposed to dreaming, is what puts us in touch with reality.

The striking feature of this argument, when compared with that of Descartes, is its emphasis on the *difference in content* between dreams and waking experience. Because of this emphasis, the argument contains no suggestion that it might be difficult, or even impossible, to distinguish the two. By contrast, Descartes is taken with the apparent difficulty of ruling out the possibility that one is dreaming even when one is in fact awake. He therefore does something that never occurs to Sextus: he stresses the possibility of a dream's replicating any experience we might have while awake. For Descartes, the crucial feature of dreams is their potential for simulating waking experience.

It is the significance of this alleged possibility of simulation that I have been concerned to challenge. The neutrality of experience, I have argued, does not establish its epistemological priority, and without the doctrine of epistemological priority, there is no route from a bare logical possibility to a sceptical conclusion. In my view, Descartes's transformation of the ancient argument from dreams is mediated by, and so is indicative of, his commitment to foundationalism, hence to epistemological realism.

However, since we are exploring what may prove to be another route to the sceptic's conclusion, let me waive this argument for the time being and concede that, if Descartes really does fail to know the things that, at the outset, he takes himself to know, knowledge of the world is never possible. Taking that argument at face value, his conclusion depends neither on a hasty generalization from a single case nor on a fallacious inference from the fact of occasional error to a ubiquitous epistemological disability. Descartes has chosen a case which, as Stroud puts it, is "meant to be the best kind of case there could be of sensory knowledge about the world around us."[4] If the senses fail to give us knowledge in these circumstances, they will not yield knowledge when conditions are even less favorable.

We may still wonder why Descartes cannot exclude the possibility that he is dreaming, supposing that he really is in the best possible position for knowing things about his surroundings. Won't being ideally placed involve having discovered that dreams have a characteristic feel, a dreamlike quality which waking experience can only approximate, and even then only in highly unusual circumstances? For example, if Descartes's perceptions were affected by some powerful drug, he might be unsure whether he is dreaming. Let us even concede that, if he were *dreaming* he might on occasion be unsure whether he was dreaming or not. But why does this prevent his knowing that he is not dreaming when he is wide awake and not drugged? Surely, to be under the influence of a powerful drug, or to be asleep and dreaming, is not to be in the best possible position for knowing things about one's surroundings. Conversely, if Descartes is in the best possible position, he will be able to exclude the dream possibility.

This reply will not work, the sceptic will say, if we agree that Descartes really has described a case that is representative of the best possible position for knowing something about the world. The discovery that dreams have a special feel implies a capacity for knowledge of the world. Descartes cannot discover that there is typically a different feel to his experience when he is awake unless he can identify at least some instances of wakefulness. So all we have shown is that, once Descartes has some knowledge of the world, he can acquire more. But how did he come by his initial knowledge? In similar "ideal" situations, where learning things about the world also requires background knowledge? To suppose so would be to embark on a vicious regress. To avoid the regress, we will have to say that the situation in which Descartes imagines himself placed is not really representative of the best possible situation for knowing things. This is in effect Descartes's own solution: we are best placed when we withdraw from the senses and concentrate on the deliverances of reason. Then we can divine certain highly general facts about the world which allow us to assess experiential evidence, thus to come to know further particular facts. But if we are not attracted by the idea of "reason" as an independent source of knowledge of the world, it will not be possible to say this. We shall have to admit that the case Descartes examines really is a best case. This means that there could not have been a more favorable situation in which he could have acquired the knowledge he needs to exclude the dream possibility.

It seems, then, that the sceptic does not have to embark on his assessment of our knowledge of the world with any general epistemological ideas. In particular, he does not need to suppose, as I have charged, that our beliefs about the world constitute a class with some definite kind of theoretical integrity. All he needs to reach his general conclusion is a properly chosen particular case. The "best-case" argument does not mention the priority of experiential knowledge over knowledge of the world. That foundationalist doctrine emerges as a by-product of an encounter with scepticism. Have we at last found the intuitive argument we have been looking for?

## 4.2  KNOWLEDGE BY EXAMPLE

In responding to the best-case argument, an obvious first move is to cast a critical eye on the sceptic's examples of things that he knows. Are they really acceptable cases of knowing, or is there something defective, misleading or unrealistic about them? Do they subtly violate some essential features of the ordinary use of words like "know". The "ordinary language" critic of traditional epistemology is likely to think that they do.

The classic attempt to rebut scepticism by way of close attention to our ordinary use of epistemic concepts is to be found in the work of J. L. Austin. It is particularly appropriate to discuss Austin in connection with the best-case argument because of the close parallel between this route to scepticism and Austin's way of defending his resolutely anti-sceptical outlook. Like the sceptic, Austin conducts his argument by way of examining a typical or paradigm instance of a claim to knowledge, investigating the conditions in which such a claim may reasonably be advanced, how it can reasonably be objected to, and when it ought to be withdrawn. But whereas Descartes uses his case to illustrate a general defect in our putative knowledge of the world, Austin uses *his* to argue that there is no reason to suppose that there is any such thing.

Austin thinks that he can show that the sceptic's attempt to get us to withdraw a claim to knowledge violates our ordinary standards of reasonableness. As Stanley Cavell points out in a perceptive discussion of the best-case strategy, the requirement of reasonableness is one that the sceptic willingly accepts.[5] This acknowledgment of the need for reasonableness is closely connected with what I have put forward as the requirement of naturalness. Scepticism loses its paradoxical character if it depends essentially either on arbitrary stipulations about what it is to "really" know facts about the world or on contentious epistemological or metaphysical theories. The sceptic must reach his conclusion by steps that we can all recognize as acceptable on the basis of our everyday conception of what is required for knowledge of the world. If that is justification beyond a reasonable doubt, the sceptic's doubts must be reasonable.

Cavell argues that the very fact that the sceptic accepts this requirement makes it unlikely that he will be vulnerable to any simple charge of "misusing language." From the word go, sceptical arguments are formulated with an eye to the demands of our ordinary understanding of "knowledge," demands which by their very nature any competent speaker, even a sceptic, can be expected to recognize. Far from resulting from a distortion of our ordinary epistemic concepts, scepticism is what, in the face of the considerations the sceptic deploys, our mastery of those concepts demands. This is what a sceptic will think, and we should expect him to be able to defend himself.

Cavell stresses the fact that the steps by which the sceptic reaches his conclusion are modeled on a completely familiar procedure. The procedure is one that we follow when the question "How do you know" is asked, as Austin says, "pointedly": that is to say, not out of curiosity or a desire to learn but out of a suspicion that you might not *know* at all. Faced with such a challenge, someone who implies that he knows something needs to explain *how* he knows it; and if his explanation proves inadequate, we will feel that his claim ought to be withdrawn. Thus in the sceptic's example we find:

> *Claim*:   Here I am, seated by the fire, etc.
> *Request for basis*:   How do you know?
> *Basis*:   I can see that I am. Or, by means of the senses.
> *Ground for doubt*:   That's not enough; you could be having just the same experiences even if you were dreaming or hallucinating.

But Austin's example of an assessment of a claim to knowledge seems, as Cavell says, "in essentials" and "at first glance" to proceed no differently. In Austin's case we have:

*Claim*:   There is a goldfinch in the garden.
*Request for basis*:   How do you know?
*Basis*:   From the red head.
*Ground for doubt*:   But that's not enough; woodpeckers also have red heads.[6]

In both cases, "an example of a claim is given; its basis articulated; a ground for doubt is raised which, unanswered, repudiates the claim." So, since in Austin's instance we all recognize that unless the deficiency in the basis can be remedied the knowledge claim must be withdrawn, why don't we have to recognize it in the sceptic's instance too? Formally at least, the sceptic's exchange fully accords with our ordinary conception of how knowledge claims are advanced and withdrawn. There is no hint of a misuse of language or a distortion of ordinary procedures. The impression of naturalness is reinforced, rather than undermined, by the way Austin tries to reach his quite different conclusion.

Austin takes the sceptic to be challenging our knowledge of the world on the grounds that the evidence we ordinarily adduce to support it is "not enough." This evidence, the sceptic points out, fails to exclude possibilities which, if realized, would falsify what we claim to know; and he takes this observation to neutralize the force of what we ordinarily regard as adequate evidence. In response, Austin isolates certain conditions that govern our ordinary notion of adequate evidence, two of which seem especially important. One is the *definite lack* condition: it is not reasonable to complain that someone's evidence is not enough unless one is prepared to specify, in some fairly definite way, *how* it is deficient. Thus:

> If you say "That's not enough," then you must have in mind some more or less definite lack. "To be a goldfinch it must have the characteristic eye markings"; or "how do you know it isn't a woodpecker? Woodpeckers have red heads too." If there is no definite lack which you are at least prepared to specify on being pressed, then it's silly (outrageous) just to go on saying "That's not enough."

But we are not ordinarily thought to be obliged to consider even every *definite* error possibility. Some possibilities can be, in the circumstances, too far fetched to deserve consideration. So, according to our ordinary notion, evidence is adequate if it satisfies a condition of *reasonable sufficiency*. That is:

> Enough is enough: it doesn't mean everything. Enough means enough to show that (within reason, and for present intents and purposes) it "can't" be anything else, there is no room for an alternative, competing description. It does *not* mean, for example, enough to show that it isn't a *stuffed* goldfinch.[7]

Reasonable sufficiency is not logical conclusiveness.

I think that both observations are correct. The problem is to see what the sceptic has to fear from them. The first point seems evidently harmless. The sceptic does not just mindlessly ask for more, no matter how much evidence is offered him. Rather, he challenges us to rule out certain specific counter-possibilities: "You might be dreaming," "You could experience all that even if you were a brain in a vat," and so on. These possibilities are admittedly unusual, but it would not be easy to show they are not "definite."

This throws the weight on the second point, where I think it belongs anyway. The real issue is not the definiteness of the sceptic's worries but their contextual appropriateness. According to Austin, whether the evidence offered on a given occasion is "enough" depends on "present intents and purposes." However, this means that, unless pressed much farther, Austin's observations do the sceptic no damage at all. For the sceptic can perfectly well reply that his counter-possibilities are entirely appropriate to *his* "intents and purposes." Doubts that would be out of place in ornithology may be very much in place in epistemology. The point that grounds for doubt must be contextually appropriate gets us nowhere unless combined with an investigation of the context of inquiry apparently created by the sceptic's attempt at a general assessement of our knowledge of the world and an examination of how results obtained in that context might prove to have significance for knowledge claims entered in other, more ordinary contexts. Such an investigation will take us beyond Austin's "ordinary language" objections and, once more, into the realm of theoretical diagnosis. However, the interesting fact here is not *that* Austin's objections fail but *why*. At least at first sight, they are self-defeating. What prevents their amounting automatically to a damaging criticism of scepticism is an aspect of the concept of knowledge they themselves bring to the fore.

When I introduced the notion of epistemological realism, I distinguished between theories of knowledge and theories of the concept of knowledge. My point was that we can have an account of the behavior and significance of the concept of knowledge without supposing that the class of known propositions has any kind of theoretical integrity. We should not just assume that we can get, or even need, a substantive theory of what all known propositions have in common – e.g. that all known proposition are warranted by members of a special class of basic propositions. In particular, phrases like "our knowledge of the world" cannot simply be *assumed* to designate appropriate objects of theory. So even though we know all sorts of things about the world, there still may be no such thing as our knowledge of the world. As I said, the examples can be genuine while the kind is bogus.

My suggestion that the epistemic status of a belief or proposition is a functional (hence contextually varying) matter, which need not be explained by the belief's or proposition's intrinsic character, offers a further account of how this might be so. The concept of knowledge imposes certain formal or procedural constraints on the advancing and withdrawing of claims: for example that advancing a knowledge claim (often) commits one to backing it up with appropriate evidence. But what counts as appropriate evidence depends on what one has claimed to know and the situation in which one claims to know it and is thus not determined by the concept of knowledge (or even the concept of knowledge of the external world) alone. The same point is implicit in Austin's conditions: whether a lack is sufficiently definite and whether evidence has to be enough to exclude it depends (at least) on "present intents and purposes" and not simply on the concept of knowledge.

If this is right, we should not be surprised at the procedural similarities shown by Cartesian and Austinian examples. Indeed, we should be sympathetic to the claim on the part of Descartes – our personification of the traditional epistemologist – to be respecting the demands of our ordinary concept of knowledge. Anyway, if the constraints imposed by the concept of knowledge are largely functional and procedual, attempts to convict the sceptic of misusing them are quite unlikely to succeed. Advancing a claim to knowledge may commit us, if challenged, to providing appropriate grounds for the claim. But if what is, in a given context, an appropriate ground, or an appropriate challenge, is determined neither by our mastery of the concept of knowledge nor by some highly abstract feature of the content of what we claim to know; if, rather, further constraints on justification are to be sought in the character of the particular form of inquiry in which a given claim is embedded, the precise content of the claim itself, and any relevant features of the situation in which the question of justification arises: then the traditional philosopher can say that, when it comes to his examples, the main determinant of appropriateness is his project of assessing the totality of our knowledge of the world. This means that, to see our way beyond scepticism, we must find reasons for objecting to this project. We will get nowhere by trying to impugn the sceptic's grasp of epistemic concepts.

In light of this, it is only to be expected that Descartes and Austin should draw such different morals from their respective examinations of claims to knowledge. We can explain the difference in terms of Austin's disregard for the demands of Descartes's distinctively philosophical project. This disregard allows Austin to select an example of putative knowing in which there are many, highly specific ways of going wrong. But an example like this is useless to the traditional epistemologist, who is constrained by his philosophical task to focus on a case that represents the best possible situation anyone could be in for knowing something about the world. In effect, Austin first changes the subject and then presents the results of this investigation as evidence of the traditional epistemologist's insensitivity to

the nuances of the concept of knowledge. /But the nuances Austin himself isolates prevent our taking demands on knowledge discovered in one
imagined context to show that a philosopher has misused or distorted our
ordinary concept simply because he has discovered different demands in
another. /

The result is that Austin and the traditional philosopher are talking past
each other. What Austin says about his case is entirely correct: failure to
respond to what is a reasonable ground for doubt in his example will reveal
only a deficiency on the part of a particular claimant or a problem in that
claimant's particular circumstances: for example that he doesn't know
enough about goldfinches, or could only get a fleeting glimpse of the bird in
question. Naturally, when a claim to knowledge fails for a reason like this,
there will be no suggestion of a general obstacle to knowledge of the world.
To sustain such a suggestion, another kind of example entirely is required:
the kind of example offered by Descartes, which prescinds from idiosyncratic
sources of error.

Since he starts from an example that will not sustain a general conclusion, it is inevitable Austin should charge the would-be sceptic with the
sort of fallacies we noted earlier. Saddled with an example lacking inbuilt
general significance, the sceptic will only be able to get to a general
conclusion either fallaciously or by way of some gratuitous and doubtless
implausible principle. Accordingly, Austin sees epistemologists as "prone to
argue that because I *sometimes* don't know or can't discover I *never* can."
Admittedly, there is some justification for this, in that Descartes does make
the reasonableness of his general doubt depend in part on the principle
that:

> All that up to the present time I have accepted as most true and
> certain I have learned either from the senses or through the senses;
> but it is sometimes proved to me that these senses are deceptive, and
> it is wiser not to trust entirely to any thing by which we have once
> been deceived.[8]

This argument offers an easy target for Austin, who replies that of course
"the senses" can let us down: the bird might fly away before I get a close
enough to look at it, so that what I see is not enough to establish that it is a
goldfinch and not a woodpecker. But when I do know enough about birds,
and can inspect the supposed goldfinch thoroughly, then I can be wholly
certain that is a goldfinch. We cannot argue from the possibility of error to
the impossibility of knowledge.

We have agreed to this already. We must, however, also agree with
Cavell that the traditional epistemologist is not "arguing" anything of the
sort. Indeed, we shall think that there is something left for him *to* argue
only if we ignore the special character of the knowledge claim he examines.

The sceptic's example is chosen so that questions of special expertise, unfavorable viewing conditions and so on do not arise: this is what makes it a *best* case. So precisely because it lacks scope for the highly specific ways of failing to know that Austin calls attention to, the example has general significance built in. If we accept it for what it purports to be, there is no further step to be taken. If knowledge fails here, it fails everywhere.

Putting matters this way, it seems that the ordinary language philosopher, more than the sceptic, is the one who puts his arguments in a deceptive light. The ordinary language philosopher is not blind to the special character of traditional examples, but he is inclined to represent what is in fact a strategic requirement as evidence of ignorance or simple-mindedness. Thus Austin presents his examination of a claim to know as more thorough than that of the typical epistemologist. Austin pays close attention to the details of the situation, to the multifarious ways in which knowledge claims may prove to be defective, making Descartes seem by comparison hasty and superficial. Austin's examples are rich, detailed, "realistic": those of Descartes and other epistemologists schematic, abstract and under-described.[9]

Neither the sceptic nor traditional epistemologist will be impressed by this. He will reply that, while well aware of the details that Austin reminds him of, he ignores them because they are irrelevant to his purposes. We will never see whether there is some general obstacle to knowledge of the world if we immerse ourselves in the details of knowledge claims involving gold-finches, for of course there is no general lesson to be drawn from highly specific examples. To see if any general points can be made, we must concentrate on things that everyone knows, if anyone does. This has nothing to do with ignorance. If such examples are defective, the source of the defect must somehow lie in their very generality. But this will take some showing, since generality is not in and of itself an objection.

Austin's criticisms are blunted, therefore, by the sceptic's ability to concede that Austin's examples are bound to be more familiar, more "ordinary" than his own. Because a sceptic's example must be representative of the best situation anyone could be in for knowing facts about the world, it will necessarily involve requesting a basis, and entering a ground for doubt, where ordinarily we never do. By the same token, the grounds for doubt the sceptic brings up will be out of the way by comparison with those Austin mentions. Austin concentrates on the sort of knowledge that commonly does *not* go without saying. But this does not show that the sceptic's grounds for doubt are inappropriate to his purposes. They may be entirely appropriate, *even by the most ordinary standards*, once the less than ordinary intent behind them is allowed for. Someone who asks questions that are not normally asked may be led to say things that are not ordinarily said. This is not evidence of ignorance or conceptual ineptitude.

## 4.3  GENERIC AND SPECIFIC

Since, on a purely formal or procedural level, Austin and Descartes do not disagree about how knowledge claims come to be withdrawn, it is natural to conclude that their examples have such different significance because of the contents of the claims involved. However, though there is some truth in this, we must not stress the distinctive content of the sceptic's claims to the point of ignoring the special context of inquiry in which those claims are entered. This is Cavell's mistake.

According to Cavell, the crucial difference is that whereas Austinian examples of knowledge-claims typically involve the *identification* of *specific* objects ("The bird on the fence is a goldfinch"), Descartes sets the pattern for the traditional investigation of knowledge by concentrating on a claim to know that a *generic* object *exists*. Generic objects are things like hands and tables, items for which there are no special identifying features and which anyone can be expected to recognize. Cartesian examples derive their general significance from their concentration on generic objects. Austinian examples, because they concern specific objects, point to no general morals.

This account of the difference between the two sorts of examples ties in well with Wittgenstein's observation that the things that Moore insists he knows are not propositions Moore has arrived at "by pursuing some line of thought which, while it is open to me, I have not in fact pursued."[10] "Here is one hand" asserts the existence of a generic object, in full view; and there cannot *be* any particular line of inquiry into the truth of such a claim. Lacking special identifying features, the object offers nothing that could be the subject of such an investigation.

Though both are often classed as "ordinary language" philosophers, on this point there seems to be a significant difference between Wittgenstein and Austin. Wittgenstein seems more sensitive to the peculiarities of the examples that figure in epistemological discussions, hence less willing to trace sceptical utterances to straightforward fallacies. This is reflected in his puzzlement at Moore's claiming to know his propositions of common sense: that the earth has existed for many years past, that he has never been far from it, and so on. Wittgenstein is struck by the fact that these propositions are not arrived at by special investigations that not everyone will have carried out, and he connects this with their apparently exemplary character. Thus: "The truths that Moore says he knows, are such as, roughly speaking, all of us know, if he knows them."[11] Indeed, *On Certainty* begins with the concession that: "If you do know that *here is one hand*, we'll grant you all the rest. . . ." The message seems to be that, to deal with scepticism, we must investigate examples like this. It will not do to concentrate exclusively on examples of knowledge that result from special investigations.

We can see also that it would be wrong to associate Austin's appeal to ordinary language too closely with Moore's appeal to common sense. Austin's cases are the opposite of Moore's. Austin's examples of knowledge claims do imply special expertise, do result from pursuing lines of thought which not everyone has pursued. This is why they illustrate only some particular person's knowing or failing to know this and that. So whereas Moore at least meets the sceptic on the right terrain, Austin argues from cases that seem not to be relevant to philosophical questions about the possibility of knowledge.

Austin is of course aware that the sceptic is concerned with establishing the reality of objects rather than with identifying them. But here too he is suspicious of the attempt to establish a general conclusion. Just as when we suggest that someone's evidence is "not enough" we must have in mind a definite lack, so when we suggest that something may not be real, we must have in mind some definite contrast, a specific way of not being real. The contrast will vary from case to case – "Those 'diamonds' are *paste*," "That's a *decoy* duck," "It's a *reproduction* Chippendale" – as will the way of determining whether the object in question is "real." However:

> The wile of the metaphysican consists in asking "Is it a real table?" (a kind of object which has no obvious way of being phoney) and not specifying or limiting what may be wrong with it, so that I feel at a loss "how to prove" it *is* a real one.[12]

That is, the metaphysican uses generic objects to issue a challenge that is baffling, not because it is so general, but because it is vacuous. An examination of ordinary usage reveals that a question about whether something is "real" always presupposes a particular way of being "abnormal" or "phoney," a way that depends "essentially upon the nature of the matter which I have announced myself to know." The sceptic's general conclusion thus depends on the illusion that "real" has "a single meaning . . . , and that a highly profound and puzzling one."[13]

Once more, I think that what Austin says is correct but acceptable to the sceptic. One way to see this is to note how his remarks bring out similarities between "real" and "know." In both cases, he shows that the use of the term is governed by certain procedural constraints: "real" implies a contrast with some appropriate way of being phoney; "know" (often, if not always) implies the possession of appropriate evidence. But what counts as an appropriate contrast or appropriate evidence depends on both the claim's content and the context in which it is entered, not just on the concept of reality or knowledge. Austin's anti-sceptical argument will seem to work, therefore, only if we ignore the special context apparently created by the traditional project out of which scepticism seems to develop. Once we take account of that project, it is far from clear that the sceptic is

incapable of meeting the procedural constraints Austin brings out. Substantively, his contrasts and error possibilities may be quite out of the
ordinary. But this does not make them inappropriate to their own context,
since when unusual questions are on the table, unusual possibilities may
have to be considered. Austin's argument stops where serious criticism
must start: with the traditional epistemological project, its theoretical presuppositions, and its claim to produce insights that apply to other contexts
of justification.

If this is right, we again reach the conclusion that Austin fails to pursue
the implications of his contextualist views to the point where they might
threaten the sceptic's procedure. As Cavell points out, asked how you know
that there is an envelope (or tomato or table) here, in full view, you will not
offer an Austinian feature ("from the shape," "by the texture," "because of
the legs") as the basis of your claim: "Generic objects have no Austinian
features in terms of which they are identified."[14] Since there is no question
of misidentification, the knowledge that is at stake, when such objects are
introduced, is knowledge that one of them really exists and *has not been
dreamt, imagined, hallucinated or anything like that.* In other words, the sceptic
can claim with some plausibility, that his use of existence claims involving
generic objects does limit the "particular ways" in which the objects in
question can fail to be real. Austin may be right to insist that "If the
context doesn't make it clear, then I am entitled to ask 'How do you
mean?'... '*What are you suggesting?.*'" But what he has not shown is that
"the metaphysician" has no answer. If we ask whether a goldfinch is real,
we may well be wondering whether it is stuffed. But this is evidently not
what Descartes intends when he questions the reality of the hands that he
seems to see. The use of the generic object establishes a context in which it
is clear that the ground for doubt is appropriate to the knowledge in
question.

Cavell concludes that, once the philosopher's "How do you know?" is
accepted as reasonable, you will *have* to give "Because I see it" or "By
means of the senses" as the basis of the claim. And "have to" means "in
order to remain reasonable," i.e. "in order to honour as fully as possible the
most natural demands of ordinary language." The traditional philosopher
thinks that: "Given his context and object and his question reasonably
asked, *the basis is as determined by ordinary language* as the kind of basis we can
offer about an Austinian object is."[15] This is exactly what the defender of
the view that scepticism is an intuitive problem needs to be able to say. The
traditional epistemologist cannot be accused of constructing a problem by
imposing artificial demands on knowledge of the world, if he can plausibly
represent himself as honoring the demands of ordinary language, though
admittedly in the context of an extraordinary undertaking. As Cavell says,
his procedure, while not "fully natural," is not "fully unnatural" either. It

looks more and more as if we have finally found what the intuitive sceptic is looking for.


## 4.4  KNOWING AND CLAIMING

If we agree that the sceptic's grounds for doubt are appropriate to his examples and that his examples are appropriate to his purposes, how can we then avoid his negative verdict on our putative knowledge of the world? Only, it seems, by locating some defect in the examples. It will not do to offer different examples, manifestly inappropriate to the sceptic's purposes, in order to argue that *they* do not suggest any general obstacle to knowledge of the world.

If Cavell's account of the difference between Austinian and Cartesian examples is correct, a diagnosis of scepticism will have to show that propositions asserting the existence of generic objects cannot be used as the sceptic tries to use them. Perhaps it will even have to show that they are inappropriate objects for knowledge claims. This is just what Cavell tries to do. He wants to argue that something about the sceptic's own enterprise prevents his "meaning what he wishes to mean", indeed "what he *must* mean if his conclusion is to mean what he says."[16] Clearly, Cavell is aiming at a therapeutic rather than a theoretical diagnosis of scepticism, hence at a form of definitive refutation. This is a severe task to set oneself. As I argued in chapter 1, agreeing on this point with those who find scepticism a deeply intuitive problem, we will never find it easy to convince ourselves that we do not understand the sceptic. In fact, our sense that we do understand him is so powerful that it tends to undermine the credibility of theories of language that imply we do not. One of the advantages of theoretical as against therapeutic diagnosis is that it frees us from the need to pretend not to understand what, in some way and to some extent, we evidently do understand.

That there is a genuine difficulty here is suggested by the air of paradox that surrounds Cavell's own conclusions. It is not easy to grasp how one can wish or be required to mean something that one cannot mean at all. But one of the strengths of Cavell's diagnosis is that it gives him something to say about this, for it offers an explanation of how the sceptic's procedure generates an illusion of meaning.

Attempts to convict the sceptic of advancing meaningless claims are usually made in the context of a broadly verificationist conception of meaning. Verificationists challenge what has been called "the classical pre-understanding of meaning."[17] As its name implies, this presupposition of much traditional philosophy is not an articulated theory. Indeed, philosophers who have taken it for granted – Descartes or Hume for example –

*meaning*

have often shown scant interest in the theory of meaning. Nevertheless, the argument goes, the classical pre-understanding of meaning is what makes conceptual space for scepticism. The classical pre-understanding treats the contents of our thoughts, hence of the sentences used to express them, as fixed independently of any procedures for determining whether they are true. Thus we can believe what we believe, even if we have no reason for supposing that anything we believe is actually correct, indeed even if everything we believe is false. This is the position Descartes finds himself in at the end of the *First Meditation*.

According to verificationists, the classical pre-understanding of meaning needs to give way to the "epistemic" conception. There are competing versions of the epistemic conception of meaning, but running through all of them is the thought that the meaning of what we say is a function of what we recognize as appropriate conditions for saying it. The sceptic's implied divorce between meaning and the possibility of verification cannot be arranged.

From time to time, we have touched on a classic articulation of this view: Carnap's distinction between "internal" questions raised within a given "linguistic framework" and "external" questions about the framework as a whole. Only the former, according to Carnap, are "cognitively" significant, for only within a given framework are there rules for verifying statements, thus answering questions. So are there external things? The answer is that, as a statement internal to our commonsense framework of external things, the statement that there are is a trivial deductive consequence of any correctly asserted statement, which means that when the sceptic denies that we know that there are, we can refute him in the way of Moore. If the sceptic cannot be refuted this way, it is because his intention is to question the legitimacy of our entire commonsense framework. But then he does not need to be refuted. As an external statement, the claim that there are external things is not a theoretical or factual statement at all. There is thus no failure of knowledge either to demonstrate or rebut. At most, there remains the pragmatic question of the utility of speaking as we do, an issue which is to be settled in the end by a decision, not a discovery.[18]

As we saw in chapter 1, this approach to scepticism not only invites the response that our sense that we do understand the sceptic is far stronger than our sense that any such recondite theory of meaning is true, it also walks into the epistemologist's dilemma: for because it removes our belief in the reality of the external world from the realm of the factual, it looks like a roundabout way of agreeing with the sceptic. But at this stage in the argument, we can say a little more about what this removal involves. The external question of the "utility" of the framework of external things is not raised, and so cannot be answered, within that framework. This means that the utility of the framework as a whole can only consist in the way it helps us anticipate the course of experience. Thus to substitute for the illusory factual question of whether the framework of external things really answers to reality some pragmatic question that must be answered without invoking talk of external things is to reduce the framework of external things to a device for coping with experience. What begins as an attack on the sceptic's implied pre-understanding of meaning modulates into a rejection of his – and it seems our – pre-understanding of objectivity. We may begin by thinking that talking about the world is quite different from talking about our experience of the world; but in order to avoid scepticism we end up admitting that talking about exernal things is just a roundabout way of talking about experience. This looks like scepticism under new colours. Significantly, however, it does so because it implies a version of the doctrine of the priority of experiential knowledge over knowledge of the world.

Cavell tries to avoid all such problems. Though he finds an ultimate failure of meaning in the sceptic's assertions, he does not, at least on the surface, invoke anything like Carnap's verificationism. On the contrary, from Cavell's standpoint, the epistemic conception of meaning, as embodied in such verificationist theories, shares a fatal error with the classical pre-understanding it is meant to supplant, namely, a tendency to forget the very thing that ordinary language philosophy so forcefully reminds us of: the ordinary human subject, the utterer of sentences and maker of claims. So whereas verificationists focus on the sceptic's words, asking what they might mean, Cavell thinks we should turn our attention to the sceptic himself, asking what *he* might mean *by them*. On this approach, the meaning of sentences is not primary but rather derived from what sentences are used to mean on particular occasions. The meaning of words, as a function of their role in sentences, is therefore an abstraction from an abstraction. The critical potential in this thought lies in its opening up the possibility that uttering a meaningful sentence – i.e. a grammatically correct sentence composed of meaningful words – does not guarantee fully meaningful speech. So in Cavell's eyes, though the sceptic uses meaningful sentences, and even uses them in ways that are recognizably analogous to familiar uses, an essential feature of his enterprise forces him to enter his claims in a way that violates the conditions for fully meaningful speech. Though his words mean what they always mean, there is nothing that he means by them. In this way, the sceptic's procedure generates an illusion of meaning.

This illusion of meaning is the source of a further illusion: an illusion of depth. Philosophical perplexity arises, as Wittgenstein says, when language goes on holiday. But it is difficult to accept that we mean nothing by what are apparently unexceptionable sentences. Thus we can come to feel that we must mean something, even though we cannot easily say what it is. We must mean something strange and profound, something obscured by the concerns of ordinary life. I may see that *normally* I would mean nothing by asserting, say, that I know that the object in front of me is a tree, when it is perfectly apparent that it is. As for my saying that I did not know that it is a tree, that would be even stranger: evidence perhaps of mental disturbance. But maybe when such things are said in the course of doing philosophy, we do mean something by them. Thus it is precisely by saying things that he could not normally mean anything by that the sceptic seems give voice to insights that are, are Cavell says, deeper than our everyday, average ideas. This is reminiscent of Austin's comment on the metaphysician's use of "real": what is in fact under-specified to the point of vacuity so easily takes on the air of being profound and puzzling. But both the illusion of meaning and the illusion of depth to which it gives rise are shattered by the reminder that meaningful speech requires more than meaningful words.

Cavell's key notion is that of a "concrete" claim. A concrete claim is one that has a definite point: it is a claim that is made to inform, to warn, to amuse, or whatever. It is, for Cavell, a matter of "grammar" that an utterance must enter a concrete claim if it is to count as an intelligible act of assertion. This means that truth alone does not guarantee intelligible assertibility, for a statement can be true without its assertion having any point at all. If truth were sufficient for intelligible assertion, one could go around all the time uttering Moore-like propositions – "That's a tree," "I know I have never been very far from the Earth," "Here is one hand" – without giving anyone cause to wonder. But since one cannot do any such thing, truth is evidently not sufficient.

In Cavell's reconstruction, to reach his general conclusion the sceptic enters a claim that asserts the existence of a generic object. This means that the very generality of his enterprise requires him to assert propositions that, when he asserts them, do not enter concrete claims. Thus he faces a dilemma. His investigation:

> must be the investigation of a concrete claim if its procedure is to be coherent; it cannot be the investigation of a concrete claim if its conclusion is to be general. Without that coherence it would not have the obviousness it has seemed to have; without that generality its conclusion would not be sceptical.[19]

Again, being "coherent" demands more than involving only meaningful sentences: it requires whoever asserts them to mean something by them; and the sceptic cannot mean anything by the sentences he asserts. So Cartesian examples purchase their essential generality at the cost of ceasing to be imaginable cases of claiming to know anything. Although the sceptic, or traditional epistemologist, uses ordinary words with their ordinary meanings, so that there is no doubt as to what they mean, it is impossible to see what he means by them. The sceptical conclusion to the traditional investigation involves a kind of hallucination of meaning.

If an "ordinary language" criticism of scepticism is one that accuses the sceptic of some specific misunderstanding or distortion of our everyday epistemic terms, this is not an ordinary language criticism. As much as Carnap's verificationism, it is based on a general theoretical view of the conditions for meaningful assertion. This is why, as Cavell recognizes, what he offers is at best a sketch for a refutation of scepticism. The main difficulty is to be certain that his strictures on claiming apply to every way of asserting or thinking something. As Stroud points out, there is a gap between the general point that claiming, asserting, remarking and so on all have special conditions, limiting when such speech acts can intelligibly be performed, and the conclusion that the sceptic's performance is incoherent. To close it, we would have to show that, in the kind of example he must make use of, a philosopher cannot meet the conditions for any way of saying or thinking something: not just claiming, but believing, assuming, remarking, and so on. This would not be easy.[20]

Not only would it not be easy to convert Cavell's sketch into a full dress refutation, the outcome of an attempt to do so would certainly be very complicated; and the more complicated our theoretical views become, the less certain we shall be that they are correct. Thus Cavell's response to the sceptic faces the obstacle that confronts all attempts at definitive refutation: our feeling that we do understand the sceptic's particular claims, hence that they involve more than an illusion of sense, is apt to carry more conviction than any theoretical argument for their incoherence. However, I think that Cavell's response faces more than this general difficulty, for his argument illustrates and confirms the incompatibility of theoretical and therapeutic diagnosis that I argued for in chapter 1. The more we do to embed the sceptic's claims in a definite intellectual project, informed by its own distinctive theoretical presuppositions, the more we make sense of them. But the more we do to make sense of them, the less room we leave for arguing that they are not really meaningful. Because of this, Cavell's own criticisms of Austin, which show a lively awareness of why the sceptic proceeds as he does, return to haunt him.

Let us look more closely at the suggestion that the sceptic's knowledge claims violate the conditions for intelligible claiming. Something very like this seems to be behind Wittgenstein's suspicion of Moore's claims to know his various commonsense propositions. He writes:

I know that a sick man is lying here? Nonsense! I am sitting at his bedside, I am looking attentively into his face. – So I don't know, then, that there is a sick man lying here? Neither the question nor the assertion makes sense. Any more than the assertion "I am here," which I might yet use at any moment, if suitable occasion presented itself.[21]

If I have an appointment to meet you at your house, I might call out "I am here" to let you know I have arrived. This would be a "suitable occasion" for making this "assertion." But after we have been together for an hour, most likely the occasion would not be suitable, though in special circumstances it could be. Perhaps someone arrives whom you would rather not see and I say in a reassuring tone "I am here," implying he will not stay or that nothing much will happen with someone else around. However, if there are no such special circumstances, it will be impossible to see me as meaning anything by such an announcement. This will be so even though the sentence I come out with means what it always means and is true.

How far is Descartes's claiming to "know" that he is sitting by his fire, etc. etc., or alternatively his entering the claim that he is sitting by the fire as an instance of something he knows, like my announcing "I am here," out of the blue? Certainly there can be "suitable occasions" for asserting that one is sitting in front of the fire, in one's dressing gown, etc. Perhaps someone calls from another part of the house "Where are you?" and I reply "By the fire." "Are you busy?" "No, just sitting in my dressing gown, with a book." Clearly, the situation Descartes imagines is not like this. But can we conclude that his example cannot be made the object of a concrete claim? And if we could, would this prevent the sceptic reaching his conclusion?

I envisage the traditional epistemologist making two points. The first is that to charge Descartes with failing to enter a concrete claim is to subtly change the subject. Descartes aims to present a representative case of *knowing*, not *claiming* to know. Perhaps (and only perhaps) if Descartes is alone in front of the fire, we cannot imagine him making a concrete claim to that effect. But even so, the reply will continue, since Descartes *could* make a concrete claim along the lines imagined, should a suitable occasion present itself, he must *at this moment* know what he says or implies that he knows, even if he couldn't properly *claim* to know it. He could never inform anyone of his whereabouts if he did not know where he is.

Cavell anticipates something like this objection. Of course, in the sort of situation the sceptic imagines, no one would have *said*, "This is a hand." But this is just because it is:

> so flamingly obvious that he knows, and if you're going to try to convince us that just because it is odd in that sense, that therefore we cannot or ought not to say it, then you're trying to convince us that we cannot or ought not say something which is true, true in spades. And that is just outrageous.[22]

What Cavell goes on to say in reply is quite correct: we cannot always intelligibly utter truths. But it doesn't meet the point at issue, which is that the sceptic intends to put forward an exemplary case of knowing – of something that is known if anything is – not an exemplary case, or indeed any case, of claiming to know. Inevitably, he will choose the sort of "flamingly obvious" fact that everyone will concede and which, consequently, no one could normally be informed of, warned about or whatever. Normally, therefore, there will be no question of a sceptic's exemplary proposition featuring in a concrete claim and no possibility of its being imagined as so doing.

The key word here, "normally," brings us to the second point. When a sceptic offers an exemplary case of knowing, it will not involve a proposition that anyone could, in normal circumstances, be imagined as intelligibly claiming to know. But this does not mean that no claim is entered when such an example is introduced into a philosophical inquiry as a best case of knowing. The claim is made *now*, in the context of philosophical reflection, that when I am of sound mind, apparently alert, have no reason to expect any unusual circumstances. etc., and it seems to me that I am sitting by my fire, then I know that I am. I do not have to imagine that, if I were in that situation and were *not* engaged in philosophical reflection on my knowledge of the world, I would be able intelligibly to enter a claim to know where I was and what I was doing. Cavell conflates the question of whether I can use such an example *now* to enter a claim to know with that of whether the example itself must be imagined as involving such a claim. Like Austin, Cavell ties meaning to context. But also like Austin, he does less than justice to the possibility that the extraordinary context of epistemological investigation confers meaning on the sceptic's extraordinary claims.

## 4.5 THE SCOPE OF KNOWLEDGE

I think it is fair to conclude that, if the sceptic fails to mean anything by his words, it cannot be because "no suitable occasion" has presented itself for their use. By Cavell's own showing, a proposition to the effect that a generic object exists, entered in the context of philosophical reflection as a best case of knowing, is precisely tailored to the epistemologist's aim of assessing our knowledge of the world as a whole. If the sceptic's utterances fail to be fully meaningful, it cannot be because his words are situationally inappropriate: his claims must harbour some hidden but intrinsic defect.

What Cavell or any other ordinary language critic needs to show, then, is that we simply cannot think of ourselves either as knowing or not knowing that a generic object exists, no matter what we are up to, philo-sophizing included. He must show that the sceptic's exemplary propositions fall outside the scope of the concept of knowledge.

This will be difficult. It is easy to show that they would not ordinarily be

regarded as appropriate vehicles for knowledge claims, but this will fall far
short of showing that they are not exactly what is required, by our ordinary
understanding of "know" even, in the context of the sceptic's distinctively
philosophical project. For example, we must not slip into the very strategy
Cavell dismisses, plausibly enough when Austin tries to follow it, of charging
the "metaphysician" with failing to offer a definite contrast to our supposed
conviction that the objects we think we see are "real." Indeed, Cavell's
challenge to the epistemologist to say what he means by the claims he enters
is very much of a piece with Austin's challenge to the metaphysician to say
what contrast he has in mind, and there is no more reason to suppose that it
cannot be met. When the metaphysician suggests that an apparent object of
perception might not be real, he is suggesting that it might be dreamed or
hallucinated, rather than actually seen. When the traditional epistemologist
raises the possibility that his exemplary truths might not be known, he is
suggesting that perhaps they are only taken for granted, found undeniable,
assumed for practical purposes, or something of the sort. In their appropriate
context, his generic knowledge claims look to be, by Cavell's own standards,
sufficiently "concrete." If so, they should be both perfectly intelligible and
charged with general implications.

One possible argument, perhaps derivable from Austin, is that, as a
matter of the ordinary meaning of "know," a claim to know implies that
one has some special expertise or is somehow especially well-placed to
assert the proposition in question. Accordingly, any use of "know" in
connection with the existence of a generic object will be incoherent because
involving a claim to particular credentials where none are possible. But
why accept this? The phrase "common knowledge" is not an obvious
oxymoron. True, in the kind of example favored by Austin, the point of
claiming to know will often be to imply some sort of special qualification.
But again, the sceptic can claim plausibly that this has more to do with the
highly specific character of the knowledge claimed than with the meaning of
"know." The evidence linking "know" with claims to special credentials
reveals only that one cannot ordinarily *claim* to know something that anyone
can be expected to realize, not that such things can never intelligibly be
said to be known. In the context of the traditional epistemologist's general
assessment of our knowledge of the world, we may claim knowledge that
(we hope) we always have, even if we cannot always intelligibly lay claim to
it.

Apparently more promising is the thought that certain propositions
lie outside the scope of the concept of knowledge because there is no way
*at all* of explaining how we know them. It is not just that there are no
special ways: there are no common ways either. This idea certainly tempts
Wittgenstein who writes:

"I know" often means: I have the proper grounds for my statement. So if the other person is acquainted with the language-game, he would admit that I know. The other, if he is acquainted with the language-game, must be able to imagine how one may know something of the kind.[23]

However, Moore "chooses precisely a case in which we all seem to know the same as he, and without being able to say how."[24] But rather than concluding with the sceptic that, being unable to cite appropriate grounds, we do *not* know them, Wittgenstein suggests that the concept of knowledge does not apply in connection with such propositions. To suppose that it does is to mistake their logical role. Thus:

Moore does not know what he asserts he knows, but it stands fast for him, as for me; regarding it as absolutely solid is part of our method of inquiry. When Moore says he *knows* such and such, he is really enumerating a lot of empirical propositions which we affirm without special logical testing; propositions, that is, which have a peculiar logical role in the system of our empirical propositions.[25]

This peculiar role is to establish the framework within which all genuinely empirical questions are raised and answered, which is why no one can say how he knows propositions that play this role to be true. Anything that we recognize as inquiry or justification takes them for granted. Accepting them is built into our very practice of judgment, belongs to the nature of (what we call) judgment. They are the hinges on which all empirical investigation turns. But the difficulty is to see why this is a refutation of radical scepticism rather than another expression of it. Suppose we give Wittgenstein the concept of knowledge: still, aren't we explaining the restriction on its scope in terms of the impossibility of justifying certain propositions? If this is not to amount to conceding the sceptic's point, it must be shown that this absence of justification is not a lack.

As we have seen, philosophers like Strawson and McGinn think that the way to do this is to argue that our relation to "framework judgments" is "non-epistemic." Once we see that such judgments are not properly thought of as known or not known, justified or unjustified, we also see that the sceptic induces a sense of lack only by wrongly presenting them as if they were. But the only evidence for this view is that we do not ordinarily treat such judgments as open to question, and this falls short of showing that they are unquestionable, hence completely outside the scope of the concept of knowledge. As I remarked when we first encountered it, this "naturalist" response to the sceptic invites the reply that, though in

ordinary circumstances our relation to such judgments may well be all that
Wittgenstein says it is, this does not show that the sceptic is wrong to treat it
differently in the unusual circumstances of philosophical reflection.

So far as I can see, this is a reply that the sceptic can make to any attempt to base a definitive refutation of scepticism on observations about
our ordinary use of "know." Such remarks only point unquestionably to
something that the sceptic does not deny: that our ordinary use of "know"
reflects our everyday insensitivity to sceptical problems, which is itself
rooted in our thoughtless conviction that we know all sorts of things about
the world. They do not show that because, when he invites us to project
our mastery of the concept of knowledge into the context of certain less-
than-usual questions, the sceptic reaches results that conflict with our
usual attitude, he distorts the meaning of "know."

Given all these difficulties, I think we should abandon efforts to convict
the sceptic of conceptual incompetence. As I see it, the significance of the
contextualist approach to knowledge and justification implicit in much
ordinary-language philosophizing lies in its challenge to the sceptic's epistemological realism. The evidence garnered by Austin and Wittgenstein
is important because it calls attention to how context determines the substance of epistemic constraints. But this means that to appeal to this evidence to argue that certain propositions are, as it were, intrinsically outside
the scope of the concepts of knowledge and justification is to move in
exactly the wrong direction. To reject epistemological realism is to hold
that a proposition's epistemic status is a functional matter, not an intrinsic
characteristic. Certain propositions may well enjoy a privileged status in
all ordinary inquiries – may play, as Wittgenstein says, a peculiar logical
role – but this does not mean that they cannot shed that role when wrenched
from ordinary contexts.

It will not do to object that Wittgenstein shows more than that we do
not treat certain hinge propositions as open to question but that, since
their standing fast for us constitutes what we understand by judgment,
we cannot so treat them. At least, it will not do unless we have a way of
meeting the reply that "cannot" only means "cannot if we are to get on
with ordinary pursuits." As historians, we cannot entertain radical doubts
about the reality of the past. But this does not mean we cannot entertain
them as epistemologists.

What Wittgenstein's remarks *can* make us wonder, however, is what
results obtained in the extraordinary context of philosophical reflection
imply about knowledge claims entered elsewhere. My suggestion is that
unless we concede epistemological realism, they imply nothing. If this
doctrine is not conceded, the contextualist defence of the sceptic against
his ordinary language critic forces the sceptic to buy the intelligibility of
his project at the cost of its general significance. This is because, although

he needs the propositions that must stand fast if his project is to proceed to state fundamental epistemological truths, he has no way of showing that they are more than methodological necessities of that project. So I think that Cavell is right: the intelligibility of the sceptic's procedure is in tension with the general significance of his results. We disagree over the explanation.

The strain in Wittgenstein emphasized by Strawson and McGinn does not go unnoticed by Cavell. As we saw in chapter 1, it is his candidate for what he calls "the truth of scepticism," a truth the sceptic is groping for but which he presents in a distorted form. The deep truth behind the sceptic's reflections is that "our relation to the world as a whole is not one of knowing, where knowing construes itself as being certain." So let me recall another point, also touched on in chapter 1, that the "naturalist" position Strawson and McGinn try to occupy, perhaps now along with Cavell, is not easily maintained. Forgetting for the moment how it could be shown, let us suppose we decide that there are propositions that we cannot ever intelligibly claim to know, even in the context of philosophical reflection. The question to ask is whether these propositions, to which our relation is ineluctably non-epistemic, are nevertheless genuinely factual? Wittgenstein seems to vacillate on this point. On the one hand, he refers to the peculiar logical role of certain "empirical" propositions and suggests that "The truth of certain empirical propositions belongs to our frame of reference"; but he also gives voice to the suspicion that "not everything with the form of an empirical proposition is one."[26]

This uncertainty is one more manifestation of the epistemologist's dilemma. If we say that the propositions in question are factual, how have we really rebutted the sceptic, who claims that what we think of as knowledge rests on factual presuppositions that cannot be justified? We will never suppress the feeling that this solution to the problem of scepticism amounts only to a verbal maneuver. It is hard to think that scepticism can be refuted by insisting that there are fundamental factual commitments that lie outside the scope of the concepts of knowledge and justification: such "conceptual" points seem, in the end, to amount either to a dogmatic assertion of the claims of common sense against the results of philosophical reflection – Moore's intransigence in the idiom of linguistic philosophy – or else to a roundabout expression of agreement with the sceptic. Awareness of this is what creates the pressure on those who take this approach to acknowledge a certain "truth in scepticism."

Because of this, the thought that the sceptic's exemplary propositions lie outside the scope of knowledge inevitably induces doubts about whether such propositions are genuinely factual. Thus we find Wittgenstein suggesting that: "Really 'The proposition is either true of false' means only that it must be possible to decide for or against it." Thus: "If the true is what is grounded, then the ground is not true, nor yet false."[27]

This is the Wittgensteinian thought, that, according to Crispin Wright, shows the sceptic's arguments to be self-defeating. The sceptic is right when he notices that the propositions that, as Wittgenstein says, function as the "hinges" on which all inquiry turns cannot themselves be either verified or falsified. But that there should be some naturalistically acceptable way of saying how a proposition could come to be known is a reasonable criterion of that proposition's being genuinely factual. Thus, the argument continues, the sceptic cuts the ground from under his own feet. He tries to argue that empirical knowledge is impossible because it rests on factual presuppositions that are incapable of verification, but succeeds only in showing that the hinge propositions on which empirical inquiry turns are not really factual.[28]

To stress this aspect of Wittgenstein's thought is to narrow, if not entirely to close, the gap between him and Carnap. When it comes to our relation to the world as a whole, or as Carnap would say favoring the formal mode of speech, our acceptance of the framework of external things, there is no theoretical issue to be decided, the reality of the world not being a factual matter. To philosophers who find scepticism a deeply intuitive problem, this will look like a radical departure from commonsense realism, and so just another way of giving in to scepticism. As we saw in chapter 1, Wright himself is in two minds as to whether he is explicating or revising our commonsense conception of factuality.

The ordinary language approach to the dissolution of scepticism seems attractive because it promises to invoke only facts that anyone must acknowledge. Since the ordinary language philosopher offers to meet the sceptic on his own ground, with an intuitive dissolution of what is presented as an intuitive paradox, he promises to avoid the problem that seems to bedevil more theoretical replies to the sceptic, such as verificationism, which is that our sense of the intelligibility of the sceptic's claims will in the end always outweigh any theoretical case for their incoherence. What we have seen, however, is that, if they retain pretensions to amount to a definitive refutation of scepticism, ordinary language criticisms tend to collapse into the verficationism we might have hoped they would enable us to avoid.

I think that this tendency is visibly close to the surface of Austin's work as well as Wittgenstein's. Recall his remarks on the "wile of the metaphysician" who challenges us to prove that something is "real," without offering a definite contrast. According to Austin:

> If you ask me, "How do you know it's a real stick?" How do you know it's really bent?" ("Are you sure he's really angry?"), then you are querying my credentials or my facts . . . in a certain special

way. . . . These doubts are all to be allayed by means of recognised procedures . . . , appropriate to the particular type of case.[29]

The crucial thought here is that doubts are legitimate only where there are recognized procedures for allaying them. It follows that if the metaphysician's doubts cannot be allayed, they must be induced by a wile. They could not be both coherent and unassuageable.

But we have seen enough to conclude that it is better not to look to ordinary language for a therapeutic diagnosis of scepticism. The prospects for a theoretical diagnosis are much more hopeful. This said, let us return to the best-case argument.

## 4.6 EXAMPLES AND PARADIGMS

We have seen that, if we pay attention to the special context created by the traditional attempt at a general assessment of our knowledge of the world, we are unlikely to be convinced by the charge that the sceptic means nothing by his words. But this defense of the sceptic points to what is *really* problematic about his procedure. The appropriateness of his examples and the relevance of his distinctive error possibilities, to which he appealed in defense of the intelligibility of his procedure, seem tightly bound to the special context of philosophical reflection. But since he wants to establish a general point about human knowledge, the significance of his results must not be. As we have seen, the sceptic must claim to have discovered, under the conditions of philosophical reflection, that knowledge of the world is impossible: it is not enough for him to have discovered that knowledge of the world is *impossible under the conditions of philosophical reflection*. This puts him in a difficult position. On the one hand, in order to defend himself against the ordinary language philosopher's charge that he is speaking a subtle and sophisticated (or perhaps, if Austin is to be believed, a not so subtle and not so sophisticated) form of nonsense, he seems bound to invoke the contextual appropriateness of his claims and error possibilities. But, on the other hand, he cannot let the contextual variability of relevant error possibilities insulate more ordinary knowledge claims from the results of his reflections. Put it this way: the sceptic's investigation of his carefully chosen example is supposed to show that we never know anything about external objects. Thus, the differences between them notwithstanding, a failure to know in a Cartesian case must imply failure in all Austinian cases too.

Given Cavell's account of the difference, this implication may seem unproblematic. Surely, we will never be in a position to identify specific objects if we are incapable even of assuring ourselves of the existence of generic objects. Identification of specific objects presupposes knowledge of the existence of generic objects. In claiming to know that the bird on the fence is a goldfinch, we take it for granted that (we know that) there is a bird on the fence. So, if whenever we make an Austinian claim, we implicitly advance a less ambitious Cartesian claim, Cartesian examples show that knowledge fails even in Austinian instances, though for generic, Cartesian rather than specific, Austinian reasons.

This tells us something important about the Cartesian conception of a best case of knowing. A Cartesian example is not just representative of the best situation one could be in for knowing something about the world: it is also, in some important way, representative of all situations in which we might pretend to such knowledge. Thus we are invited to think of a specific Austinian claim as simply adding detail to an implicit, generic Cartesian claim. If an Austinian situation is less than optimal, this is because it involves advancing a claim that introduces more ways of going wrong, ways that supplement but do not replace those already introduced by the embedded generic claim. However, if we do not go wrong in any of those additional ways, an Austinian claim will be just as good, though of course no better, than its Cartesian core. Cartesian examples of knowing are intended to be representative of certain ubiquitous and fundamental features of empirical knowing generally, not just of knowing at its easiest or best. They are, so to speak, not just *examples* but *paradigms* or *prototypes*. They are intended to capture everything essential to knowledge of the world and nothing else. This is why they provide the basis for a general (sceptical) conclusion.

Since the examples the sceptic examines are meant to be paradigmatic of empirical knowing, it is obvious that another anti-sceptical maneuver, much associated with ordinary language philosophy, is bound to be inconclusive. I am thinking of the argument from the paradigm case. It is no good meeting the sceptic with the claim that, if this isn't a case of knowledge, nothing is. This conditional is not just acceptable to the sceptic, it is integral to his argument. The question, then, is whether a given paradigm of what we ordinarily *call* knowledge is a genuine case of knowledge, and once the argument has got to this point, the critic seems to have only two options. One is to insist that it is, in the manner of Moore. The other is to argue that a paradigm of what we *call* knowledge must be the genuine article. That is, the choice is between a non-explanatory insistence on the correctness of our ordinary outlook and a problematic verificationism. (The argument that a paradigm of what is *properly* called knowledge must be the real thing is just another version of dogmatism, for the sceptic claims that we can see, on reflection that by our most ordinary standards we should not call such things knowledge.)

Still, it is not insignificant that the sceptic himself is in the paradigm case business. For once we notice the paradigmatic character of Cartesian examples, a new question comes to mind: under what conditions can we reach a general conclusion about something by considering a single representative case of it? Better yet, what kinds of things lend themselves to this kind of representation? Even defenders of the naturalness of sceptical doubts must admit the importance of such questions. Indeed, according to Stroud, understanding the sense in which Descartes's example can be treated as representative is "the key to understanding the problem of our knowledge of the external world."[30]

Clearly, there are plenty of concepts that do not lend themselves to paradigm case arguments: for example concepts whose instances are united by "family resemblance," thus by criss-crossing networks of similarities rather than any single essential feature or set of features. Wittgenstein's familiar example of "game" makes the point. There are games for various numbers of players and games one plays alone; competitive and non-competitive games; games that demand physical and games that demand mental abilities; light-hearted games and deadly serious games; games requiring elaborate equipment and games requiring none; and on and on. There is no question of selecting a "best" or "representative" example of a game for the purpose of arguing that, since there are obstacles to our playing this game, there is no game that we could possibly play.

Functional concepts also require careful handing. We cannot generalize, at least not without great care, about the material characteristics of paradigm instances of functional concepts, if we should even think of such concepts as admitting paradigm instances. The thing I am sitting on is a paradigm of a chair (if anything is). But I cannot infer that, because this chair is made of wood, all chairs must be wooden, so that the metal object against the wall isn't a chair.

This example suggests that danger lurks in any defence of the sceptic's procedure that appeals to the exigencies of the traditional epistemological project. Implicit in that defence seems to be the view that constraints on knowing imposed by our ordinary concept of knowledge are functional and procedural, rather than substantive. Knowing (often, though perhaps not invariably) requires being able to provide appropriate backup when one's knowledge is challenged. But what is appropriate varies with context (and along more than one dimension). Thus failure to meet the substantive constraints appropriate to one context, hence a failure of knowledge under those conditions, tells us nothing about the prospects for knowledge in other contexts. To suppose it did would be like examining the chair in my study and concluding that all chairs must be made of wood.

Seeing what concepts won't serve a paradigm-case argument reveals what will. To argue from a representative case, we need a concept whose instances, however diverse on the surface, are united by some underlying,

natural
kinds

essential similarity. Moreover, the property that fixes this similarity must be categorical rather than functional. We need a concept that picks out (what we take to be) a natural kind.

Here is a typical contemporary account of natural kind terms:

> A natural kind term . . . is a term that plays a special kind of role. If I describe something as a lemon, or as an acid, I indicate that it is likely to have certain characteristics (yellow peel, or sour taste in dilute water solution, as the case may be); but I also indicate that the presence of those characteristics, if they are present, is likely to be accounted for by some "essential nature" which the thing shares with other members of the natural kind. What the essential nature is is not a matter of language analysis but of scientific theory construction; today we would say it was chromosome structure, in the case of lemons, and being a proton donor, in the case of acids. Thus it is tempting to say that a natural kind term is simply a term that plays a certain kind of role in a scientific or pre-scientific theory: the role, roughly, of pointing to common "essential features" or "mechanisms" beyond and below the obvious "distinguishing characteristics."[31]

Whatever the merits of the notion of a natural kind, this seems to me to capture its central features. In any case, the merits of the notion are not my concern. The point is that this way of conceiving natural kind terms such as "lemon" or "acid" corresponds exactly to the way the traditional epistemologist does and must think of "knowledge of the world" if he is to be able to treat a failure of knowledge in a prototype instance as implying a failure of knowledge generally.

When we have a natural kind, we can learn general things about the kind by investigating the properties of appropriate samples. The procedure is legitimate because of the supposed underlying hidden structure. Where there is such a structure, what goes for one sample will go for all; where there isn't, no general lessons can be drawn. If the objects, or samples, falling under a given kind term are united only by certain "superficial characteristics" and do not share a common underlying essence – that is to say, if we have a kind term that does not pick out a genuine natural kind – we cannot treat a particular example of the kind in question as paradigmatic of the kind as a whole. Since this is just how Cartesian examples of "knowledge of the world" are meant to be treated, the traditional epistemologist must think of terms of epistemic appraisal as strongly analogous to natural kind terms.

Of course, samples can be misleading. Sulphuric acid has properties that are not shared by all acids, so that we cannot, without special precautions, treat a sample of sulphuric acid as a prototype of an acid generally. And even when treating it as a prototype of sulphuric acid, we have to be careful that it does not contain impurities apt to effect the experiment in hand. This need for caution gives the traditional epistemologist a handle on the contrast between Austinian and Cartesian examples. In focussing on failures to know that result from special features of the particular proposition under dispute, Austin is like a chemist studying an impure sample of an acid. Clearly, in neither case can general conclusions validly be drawn. But Cartesian examples, so it is assumed, focus on failures that result from common, underlying epistemological constraints, constraints operative in all cases of empirical knowing. They manage this, supposedly, by their concern with the existence of generic objects, rather than the identification of specific objects. This shift of focus functions as a kind of experimental control, like those that ensure we are studying acidity and not the properties of some specific acid. It operates as a kind of filter for removing contextual impurities, leaving the ultimate basis of empirical knowledge exposed to view.

We see, then, that the strategy of arguing from a representative case, far from sidestepping the traditional epistemologist's realist presuppositions with respect to epistemic kinds and relations, brings us right back to them. His procedure is legitimate only if it is reasonable to treat terms like "empirical knowledge" as natural kind terms. There must be something in the epistemic realm analogous to the hidden structure or essential characteristics of naturally occurring substances, such as gold. There has to be a microstructure, a hidden essence, of empirical knowledge. We have already seen what this is: context invariant, fully objective and autonomous epistemological constraints: in particular, natural relations of epistemological priority. These relations are what make it possible to suppose that there could be a prototypical case of "empirical knowledge." Subjection to underlying and universal epistemological constraints is what binds examples of such knowledge into a genuine kind, so that an appropriately chosen case can represent all. Given this epistemological realism, the sceptic can explain why he takes himself to have discovered, under the conditions of philosophical reflection, that knowledge of the world is impossible, and not just that knowledge of the world is impossible under the conditions of philosophical reflection. When we reflect philosophically, we prescind from all demands on knowing that are merely interest-relative, and so presuppose knowledge of the world, concentrating exclusively on the fundamental demands that remain. These are demands on knowledge of the world as such. The function of Cartesian examples, as paradigm cases, is to bring them to centre stage.

However, given that our aim is theoretical diagnosis, this maneuver leaves the sceptic with only a Pyrrhic victory. He can turn aside the charge of having distorted our ordinary concept of knowledge, by arguing that an ordinary concept can impose extraordinary demands when projected into an unusual context. But in so doing, he exposes himself to danger from another quarter, for the charge now becomes that a failure of knowledge in one context need not imply failure in another, still less in all. To defend the general significance of his procedure – indeed, to defend the very possibility of following it – the sceptic is compelled to invoke epistemological realism. He must do exactly what the theoretical diagnostician wants him to do, which is to share the burden of theory. Accordingly, he has to sacrifice all the advantages that accrue from the apparent intuitiveness of the case for scepticism. Scepticism no longer appears as a paradox embedded in our most deeply entrenched ways of thinking but as an artifact of theoretical ideas we might do well to abandon.

## 4.7 ORDINARY LANGUAGE AND PHILOSOPHICAL DIAGNOSIS

Austin and Cavell fail to refute the sceptic because they attempt too much. They want to appeal to the facts of ordinary usage, or to general constraints on ordinary communicative discourse, to show that what the sceptic says, or tries to say, is incoherent. They want a definitive refutation, by way of a therapeutic diagnosis. The problem is that the very facts that ordinary language philosophers bring to light suggest a contextualist alternative to the sceptic's epistemological realism; and contextualism itself works against any claim that the sceptic's considerations are so out of the way as to be unintelligible. The conclusion to draw is that attention to ordinary language is important as an adjunct to theoretical diagnosis, not as the key to definitive refutation. Definitive refutation may have been the goal of most ordinary language philosophy, but this was a mistake.

*contextualism*

The real lesson to learn from Austin, then, is that our everyday, or for that matter not so everyday, practices of epistemological assessment, do not especially favour the view that there are underlying, topic-invariant, autonomous epistemological constraints, binding on all forms of factual knowledge. Both Austin and Wittgenstein are at pains to indicate how the error possibilities relevant to the assessment of a given claim to knowledge are influenced by the specific content of the proposition in question, by the direction of inquiry, and by the actual circumstances in which the claim is entered. Indeed, though they do not couch their discussions in these terms, they effectively take issue with the three aspects of epistemological realism I identified in the previous chapter. They invite us to see demands on justification, hence on reasonable doubt, as interest-relative rather than fully objective, situational rather than context-invariant, and world-dependent rather that autonomous. Taken seriously, their reminders reveal the possibility of conceiving of knowledge and justification in a way quite different from that which informs the traditional epistemological project. To put it no more strongly, Austin and Wittgenstein show that our ordinary use of epistemic terms at least tolerates this alternative conception, which is all that theoretical diagnosis requires of them.

If this is right, Cavell's objections to Austin, though seemingly powerful at first sight, do less than justice to Austin's insights. According to Cavell, Austin fails to engage the concerns of the traditional epistemologist because he confines his attention to highly specific examples of claims to know, where failures imply no general conclusion. Accordingly, he has nothing to tell us about what, if anything, is wrong with the examples that feature in the traditional assessment of knowledge, examples whose paradigmatic character gives them inbuilt general significance. However, this reply misses the most serious implications of Austin's challenge to the  sceptic's procedure. Austin's view of the concept of knowledge ties the appropriateness of various grounds for doubt to present intents and purposes, the suggestion being that no grounds are universally appropriate. True, Austin does not press this insight as hard as he should. But once we appreciate the possibility he points to, we cannot blunt the force of his criticism by a simple insistence on the sceptic's need to consider a representative case, for what has now become problematic is the very possibility of representativeness. Again, and perhaps contrary to Austin's own intentions, these remarks should not be seen as the key to a definitive refutation. But they do point us in the direction of a correct theoretical diagnosis.

I have suggested that only given an analogy between natural kind terms and terms of epistemic appraisal – that is, only given epistemological realism – does the traditional procedure make sense. If we reject the analogy, Cartesian examples no longer generalize. Knowledge may well fail under Cartesian conditions, but we will no longer be in a position to take those conditions as representative, still less as "best." Rejecting epistemological realism leaves us with examples of knowledge but no paradigms. Accordingly, I think that in his defence of the traditional epistemologist against his ordinary language critic, Cavell concedes too much. The question to press is not "Can a claim be both generic and concrete?" but "Why suppose that a knowledge claim becomes representative simply by being generic (i.e. by involving only the existence of a generic object)?" The answer must be that there is *room* for the sceptic's doubts even in Austinian cases, even though (because of pressure from other interests) they are not normally pressed. The error possibilities the sceptic exploits are always, strictly speaking, relevant, even though they are ordinarily and in a way justifiably, ignored. But as I have said, what I think Austin means to claim is that there are no universally relevant error possibilities. In ordinary circumstances, the sceptic's doubts are not suppressed, ignored or overridden: they are strictly irrelevant. The most the sceptic can show is that knowledge of the exernal world cannot be based on exclusively experiential data. If the conditions of philosophical reflection require that we restrict ourselves to this impoverished basis, it will follow that we cannot know anything about the world under the conditions of philosophical reflection. But this does not mean that we *never* really know anything, since no basing on experience is generally required.

When he traces the difference between Descartes's and Austin's conception of a representative case to the differing claims that figure in their examples, Cavell concedes a lot to the sceptic. If I am right about Austin's contextualism, the difference does not lie simply in the kinds of claim that they examine but in their conceptions of the factors that affect our epistemic position. Cavell's concentration on the claims, to the exclusion of the conditions of claiming, obscures this. Not only that, his own doubts about Descartes's conception of "the senses" notwithstanding, it lets in the foundationalist conception of evidence on which scepticism about our knowledge of the world depends.[32]

On a thoroughgoing contextualist understanding, our capacity for knowledge can vary with our situation. For example, it may be crucial whether conditions really are normal or only appear to be so. Whether Descartes is in a position to know what he claims to know may depend on his actually being awake, sitting in front of the fire, etc.; for it may be that, when I am not dreaming, I know that I am not, even though, when I am dreaming, I am in no position to know anything. The actual situation in which a claim is entered may be important independently of the content of the claim.

Descartes does not argue against this possibility for he never considers it. From the word go, he takes his actual, worldly situation to be irrelevant to his "epistemic position." This, far more than his introduction of the generic object, is what sets his investigation on the road to its sceptical conclusion. It is a large assumption that, independently of our place in the world, we have *any* epistemic position at all. But if we do, there is only one thing for it to be: confronting experiential data while, as yet, knowing nothing about the world. Accordingly, for Descartes, an example of the best position anyone could ever be in for knowing something about the world is not given by his *being* awake and sitting in front of the fire. Rather, if it *seems* to him that he is awake and sitting in front of his fire, he is already in a position that cannot be improved on. The best position we can ever be in for knowing about the external world is to be presented with various experiential data from which we might hope, vainly as it turns out, to draw inferences about the world. Our epistemic situation is the same whether we are normal human beings or brains in vats. That is why Descartes can present his case as not just a best case but as representative of any possible case of empirical knowing.

In fact, if we fall in with Descartes's conception of our epistemic position, it is misleading to speak of the "best" position anyone could ever be in for knowing something about the world. To speak this way is to imply that our position is subject to change whereas, for the sceptic, in its fundamentals it is always the same. As Descartes sees things, the essential feature of our epistemic position is our dependence on "the senses" for knowledge of how things are in the world. Our task is therefore always one of inferring how things are from information about how they appear to be. If that task is sometimes harder, it can only be because some claims introduce more ways of going wrong than others. Thus, given that our epistemic position with respect to knowledge of the world never changes, the only way to pick out the knowledge claims that have the best chance of succeeding is in terms of their lack of ambition. This is how Cavell understands the difference between Austinin and Cartesian examples. He goes along with Descartes at just the point where Austin invites us to ask questions.

I think, however, that Descartes does a lot to muddy the waters. The seemingly progressive character of his argument is deeply deceptive. He begins by considering examples of error under less than optimal epistemic conditions, errors made when objects are small or far away, or otherwise not clearly visible. Since such errors imply no general epistemic disability, he apparently moves to a case from which such errors are excluded. This suggests a commonsensical conception of "our epistemic position" which allows that position to vary with our worldly situation. Perhaps we easily make mistakes when dealing with objects that are far away but do much better with objects that are close to hand. But when Descartes considers familiar objects, in good light, close to hand, he introduces a radically different conception of our epistemic position. He does not ask, as we may have been led to expect, what he can know when he is sitting in front of the fire, etc. but, as we have seen, what he can know given that he *seems* to be sitting in front of the fire, *seems* to be awake, and so on. Our epistemic position is taken to be one of confronting the hopeless task of recovering knowledge of the world starting from a purely experiential basis. This "position" does not improve with a change of location.

The reply will be, of course, that we cannot take worldly circumstances to be relevant to our possessing knowledge of the world if we are to assess the totality of that knowledge. But this shows where Descartes's conception of a best case, or of our epistemic position, comes from: not from our ordinary understanding of the concept of knowledge but from the methodological exigencies of his distinctively philosophical project. Once more, we find ourselves going round in a small circle. It is only by ruling out the fundamental or essential relevance to empirical knowledge of circumstantial factors, problem-situation, disciplinary constraints and collateral knowledge, that we give colour to the idea that there is such a thing as "our epistemic position" and thus, since our beliefs about the world are not topically integrated, to the idea that they constitute a genuine totality, susceptible of wholesale assessment. Having once persuaded ourselves that "knowledge of the world" in an autonomous object of theory – in other words, having once opted for epistemological realism – we can close the circle by ruling that a properly representative case of empirical knowing must prescind from all particular contextual influences, influences which we will now see as impurities in our sample.

We can conclude that the best-case strategy offers no real alternative to sceptical arguments that simply take foundationalism for granted. The Cartesian notion of a case that represents our optimal epistemic position is just one more vehicle for a foundationalist conception of knowledge and justification. But this brings us to another way in which Cavell's defense of the traditional epistemologist concedes too much. He argues, we may recall, that once the sceptic's prototypical knowledge claim is accepted as reasonably entered, the basis offered and objections advanced are as much "determined by ordinary language" as their counterparts in an Austinian case. Asked "How do you know," having claimed existence for a generic object, we can only reply "Because I see it" or "By means of the senses." But these phrases are not equivalent. "By means of the senses" is the sceptic's code for his foundational view of knowledge, whereas "Because I see it," which if nothing else is taken into account is the most that is "determined by the demands of ordinary language," is not. The commonsensical reply, "Because I see it," does not commit one to setting all background knowledge aside and tracing the disputed claim to experiential data alone. But only if this commitment is accepted do the sceptic's error possibilities ("You might be dreaming") become automatically relevant, and indeed insurmountable.

Put it this way: why isn't "Because I see it" the *rejection* of the demand for a basis (in the sense of evidence), whereas "By means of the senses" is the attempted provision of a basis that is highly restricted and so, as it turns out, inadequate? Cavell makes the fatal concession – which it is the rhetorical function* of the generic object to extract – that just as specific claims have a specific evidential basis, so generic claims have a generic evidential basis (in our permanent epistemic position). But ordinary language does not enforce any such idea. It is consistent with the evidence of ordinary usage to hold that generic claims, though subject to various situational constraints – e.g. that conditions be normal – have no evidential basis at all. When, in an attempt to philosophize, we are required to prescind from all situational factors, we are, in effect, asked to specify a basis for asserting a proposition given nothing beyond the semantic content of the proposition itself. The correct response is that given by the contextualist, in his role as critic of epistemological realism: that this information is insufficient to determine a basis. To suppose that it is sufficient is to fall in with foundationalism and with epistemological realism.

The conclusion, once more, is that the demands that determine the crucial commitment to a fatally inadequate evidential basis for the sceptic's supposedly representative knowledge claim do not come straight from ordinary language but from the traditional epistemological project of assessing the totality of our knowledge of the world. At most, the concept of knowledge demands appropriate backup for knowledge claims, backup which need not always take the form of evidence. But the concept of knowledge does not determine what counts as appropriate, not even in conjunction with the semantic content of what we claim to know. In determining this, other factors always come into play, in the sceptic's case the requirements of the philosophical project he is engaged in. However, as I have argued, the essential restriction on our evidence for beliefs about the world emerges from that project only as a methodological necessity, and this is far less than the sceptic needs.

A philosopher who continues to feel an intuitive force in the demand for a total assessment or our knowledge of the world will be dissatisfied with this outcome. However, my argument still has some way to go. I have examined the idea of assessing the totality of our knowledge of the world, but I have not yet looked into the thought that an examination of knowledge derives its character, including perhaps its unusual generality, from the distinctively detached or external standpoint from which it must be conducted. My next task, then, is to explore the sceptic's understanding of the context of philosophical reflection and, in particular, the way he conceives the relation between the discoveries made there and the knowing that is characteristic of ordinary life.

# 5

# Scepticism and Reflection

## 5.1 PHILOSOPHY AS REFLECTIVE UNDERSTANDING

Close to the heart of Humean epistemological pessimism lies the thought that we set foot on the road to scepticism as soon as we begin to philosophize. Having once started down this path, there is no turning back: scepticism is the *terminus ad quem* of all our philosophizing. This is why, according to Hume, the only antidote to scepticism is distraction, involvement in other pursuits, which is a palliative not a cure. But although this thought does a lot to sustain the conviction that scepticism is a natural or intuitive problem, it does so by virtue of incorporating a particular conception of philosophy and its relation to common life. In brief, whereas the business of common life is practical activity, that of philosophy is reflective understanding.

Pursuing everyday practical goals, the argument goes, involves taking many things for granted or accepting them on less than adequate evidence. Because time and resources are limited and because even pausing to deliberate can exact heavy costs in lost opportunities, we are bound to act as if we knew all sorts of things that we may not really know at all. In philosophy, however, none of this applies, for the philosophical stance goes with the meditation, not action. As Hume tells us, scepticism results when reason acts "alone," when pressures to act and the natural inclination to believe what one sees are in abeyance. Once our aim is reflective understanding, we can step back from our everyday projects and practices and ask whether the beliefs that inform them really amount to knowledge. Evidently, then, the standpoint we assume for the purpose of philosophizing must be quite alien to any we occupy in the course of common life. Whereas ordinary projects imply an "engaged," "internal," "subjective" outlook, the standpoint from which the philosophical examination of knowledge is carried on is "detached," "external," or "objective." This difference in standpoints explains, in turn, the strikingly context-bound character of sceptical doubts. Since involvement in practical activity is incompatible with radical uncertainty, we can keep hold of the sceptic's insights only for as long as we can maintain our detachment: that is, for as long as we can ignore the pressures to act. To seek philosophical understanding, we must withdraw from the concerns of common life; and to get on with common life, we must ignore our philosophical insights. But although philosophy and common life become, in some measure, insulated from each other, this is not because the sceptic is wrong about ordinary knowing.

Hearing this, philosophers with a pragmatic turn of mind may think that the sceptic stands condemned out of his own mouth. Indeed, for them, philosophy of any kind, in so far as it is intrinsically reflective or contemplative, is a suspect undertaking. Significant thought, we are told, helps us cope with life's concrete problems, and now it seems, by the philosopher's own admission, that scepticism inevitably leaves the concerns of common life untouched. Whoever tells it, the sceptic's tale signifies nothing, for all its sound and fury.

As I have said, I doubt that a serious encounter with scepticism leaves us completely untouched. But in any case, a dismissive attitude contributes little to our understanding of scepticism, let alone philosophy. It can only be satisying to someone who has never experienced the force of sceptical arguments and who therefore has no intellectual need to be satisified. More than that, however, it seems to rest on a misconception of the Humean view of philosophy's relation to "life." True, philosophy is at home only in the study. But this means only that the standpoint and the concerns of philosophy are alien to *common* life, not life as such. For the reflective individual, the sifting humor that impels him down the road to scepticism is as much a part of life as ordinary dogmatic certainty. The urge to step back from everyday problems and projects, so as to get some broader or deeper understanding of them, is not something we choose to have. It is there, to be coped with.

An abrupt dismissal of scepticism does not substitute for a proper diagnosis. But does a pragmatic approach to philosophy perhaps suggest a promising diagnostic strategy? I think not. It is not much help to be told, say, that scepticism results from abandoning the standpoint of the actor for that of the spectator, since this is something the sceptic willingly acknowledges. More traditionally minded philosophers agree that detachment is a defining characteristic of philosophy as they understand it, but they do not see why this is automatically an objection. To break out of the impasse, we would have to explain what is wrong with trying to take up a reflective stance with respect to everyday practices. For example, if we suspect that this stance cannot really be assumed, we should say why. However, I am happy to leave such questions to others. My quarrel is not with the sceptic's urge to reflect but with the object of his reflections.

I do, however, have one further reservation about hasty dismissals of

scepticism. This is that they are apt to concede what I see as a very significant Cartesian–Humean point: the assimilation of the ordinary to the
practical. This point cannot simply be let go, for it suggests an account of
the nature of philosophical reflection that, at first sight, offers powerful
support for the sense that scepticism is a deeply intuitive problem, latent
in our most ordinary ways of thinking about knowledge and justification.
If philosophy leads to scepticism, and if the essential feature of philosophical reflection is withdrawal from all *practical* considerations, scepticism
*must* be an intuitive problem. For the sort of thinking that makes scepticism seem a real possibility, if not completely unavoidable, will be *methodologically distinctive* but not, as I claim, *theoretically loaded*. Thus we are
told, for example, that Descartes confronts scepticism in the course of an
inquiry that is distinctively "pure," an inquiry that is subject to no practical constraints or limitations whatsoever. If pursuing this project is what
leads to scepticism, scepticism will result not from assenting to some particular theory or doctrine, but simply from taking up a distinctive stance
or attitude towards everyday convictions and practices.

We saw in the previous chapter that, although the sceptic's grounds for
doubt are highly unusual, this need not mean that he distorts the ordinary
meaning of epistemic terms. His considerations may be entirely appropriate, even by the most ordinary standards, once the context provided
by his extraordinary intellectual project is taken into account. Now we
must face the possibility that the step into this context can be taken without assuming any particular burden of theory, all that is required being
a detached attitude towards everyday practices. If it is possible to take
on this attitude, it is possible and reasonable – perhaps even inevitable
– to ask the sort of questions the sceptic asks. So the argument goes.

If this is conceded, the sceptic's position is strengthened immeasurably.
Consider Cavell's argument that, since an intention to speak the truth is
not sufficient for pointed assertion, the sceptic cannot defend the intelligibility of his entering an apparently pointless knowledge-claim on the
grounds that the claim is meant to be true. Is it so obvious that an intention to speak the truth is not sufficient for pointed assertion, once reflective
understanding and not goal-directed action is the order of the day? If all
we mean to ask is whether we really know certain things, why does our
sample knowledge claim need any purpose beyond that of being true? Or
take the thesis that we have a distinctive non-epistemic relation to certain
"framework judgments," propositions which inform all our everyday judgmental practices and so lie apart from the route travelled by inquiry: why
doesn't their occupying this privileged position simply show that ordinarily
we have more on our minds than truth and justification? If to get on with
practical activities we must take some things for granted, we cannot in
everyday contexts treat those things as requiring evidential support. But

suppose we raise questions of justification in a context where truth is the only consideration: then what?

This, then, is the possibility I must address: that the traditional philosopher's methodological purity, rather than any contentious ideas about knowledge and justification, is what forces him to face the possibility that no one ever knows anything about the world.

## 5.2 DIAGNOSIS AND DISAPPOINTMENT

Given what we have just seen, there are clear dangers attached to conceding the sceptic's preferred account of philosophical reflection. If his initial reflective turn is so natural, it is not going to be easy to block his arguments at a later stage. Nevertheless, the thought that it is natural seems to attract philosophers who are otherwise highly critical of the sceptic's procedure. Thus Stanley Cavell tells us that:

> the philosopher's originating question – e.g. "(How) do (can) we know anything about the world..." – ...is a response to, or expression of, a real experience.... It is not "natural" in the sense [of being] a response to ordinary practical contexts, framed in language which any master of a language will recognise as ordinary. But it is ...a response which expresses a natural experience of a creature complicated or burdened enough to possess language at all.[1]

There are two important concessions here. The first is that the experience of detachment or estrangement from our everyday knowledge of the world, an experience that takes hold of us in, or perhaps even constitutes, the context of reflective philosophical inquiry, is not only "real" but natural. Because this experience is in an important way pre-philosophical, it can explain and motivate systematic inquiry into the possibility of knowledge in a way which it could not if it were an artifact of contentious theoretical ideas. But that it is not an artifact of such ideas is implied by Cavell's tracing its roots to our possession of language. If to possess language belongs essentially to the human condition, sensitivity to the philosopher's "originating" question belongs to it too, just as the intuitive sceptic claims.

I take it that Cavell intends a response to a natural experience to be quite different from a response to a theoretically loaded question. This brings us to the second concession. If "ordinary" contexts are "practical" contexts, the context of philosophical inquiry is distinguished by its pure theoreticity: that is, by its methodological character rather than any theoretical presuppositions. As we have seen, this equation of the ordinary with the practical lies at the heart of the sceptic's preferred account of his philosophical project.

These are larger concessions to the naturalness of sceptical doubts than Cavell can afford to make. Cavell, we know, hopes to defeat the sceptic farther down the road by arguing that, though the sceptic's words mean what they always mean, there is nothing that he means by them. The things he claims to know are too "flamingly obvious" for claiming to know them to have any intelligible point. But as McGinn points out, this criticism depends on treating the epistemologist's entering of a knowledge claim regarding the existence of a generic object as *initiating* his investigation. Given what we have just seen, this is wrong even by Cavell's own standards. Cavell himself insists that the traditional investigation of knowledge begins with a sense that something may be dreadfully amiss with our knowledge of the world as a whole, systematic investigation of the possibility of knowledge coming later. In the context of responding to a natural experience of distrust in our capacity for knowledge of the world, we cannot charge the sceptic with entering claims that are so "flamingly obvious" that they cannot be understood as knowledge-claims at all. To the extent that we can become detached from everyday practices, banal assertions can become detached from their everyday obviousness.

In view of her willingness to advance this criticism of Cavell, it is perhaps surprising to find McGinn at one with him on the natural origins of the philosophical quest. "It is extremely important," she writes, "that we regard the sceptic as beginning, not with any specific demands concerning the standards of knowledge or reasonable belief, but by taking a reflective attitude towards our practice of making and accepting knowledge claims."[2] But why is it so important? The answer has to do with what McGinn is willing to count as a satisfying response to scepticism. The problem with Cavell's argument, as McGinn sees it, is that it collapses into an attempt to rebut the sceptic simply by *insisting* on the certainty of everyday certainties, a strategy that is bound to fail once the sceptic has persuaded us to look at everyday certainties in a new way. In reminding us of what would ordinarily be the "flamingly obvious" character of the judgments the sceptic calls in question, Cavell is not so much showing how the sceptic goes wrong as underlining the violence of the clash between common life and the results of philosophical reflection. The same applies to Moore and Austin: they too, in the end, meet the sceptic simply by insisting on commonsense certainties and so offer no real insight into how he goes astray. By contrast, Wittgenstein's dissolution of scepticism is at least on the right level. Wittgenstein offers a "naturalistic" conception of our knowledge of the world that can serve as a counterweight to the conception that informs the sceptic's argument. It is in the interests of this philosophical naturalism, then, that she refrains from criticizing the sceptic's first step: his attempt to take up a reflective stance with respect to our knowledge of the world. It is important to the Wittgensteinian response to scepticism, as she understands it, that the sceptic's false step come at a later stage, when he treats "framework judgments," the unquestioned propositions which provide the background for all ordinary inquiries and justifications, as if they were straightforward empirical propositions requiring evidential backing. A naturalistic examination of our ordinary use of concepts reveals that this is not how such judgments are ordinarily treated. We lose this insight if we cut off the sceptic's questioning too soon.

As I have insisted throughout, this does not avoid the problem that defeats Cavell. Though the thesis that our relation to framework judgments is "non-epistemic" must amount to more than that our relation to them is *ordinarily* non-epistemic, what prevents the traditional sceptic replying that our relation to such judgments *becomes* epistemic, once his initiating question is accepted as reasonable? But although this question always presented a serious problem, the problem becomes acute once the naturalness of the sceptic's initial detaching move is conceded. If the sceptic's initial (and apparently legitimate) step back from ordinary problems and projects is sufficient to detach everyday certainties from their everyday obviousness, it is sufficient to transform our everyday relation to them.

This is not the only difficulty. If reflection demands detachment, why isn't a "naturalistic", third-person account of our ordinary practices of justification, undertaken within the "framework" that we are supposed to be reflecting on and assessing, simply question-begging? The answer, according to McGinn, is that Wittgenstein's naturalistic response to scepticism:

> does not come in after the sceptic's argument has been constructed, to show that our unshakeable conviction in the judgments of the frame makes the argument idle. Rather, the naturalism forms a background to an account of the nature of our conviction and of the role of the judgments of the frame, that allows us to see why the absence of justification for these judgments is not a failure or lack.[3]

But how far does this get us? From what position are we able to see that the absence of justification is not a lack? Certainly not from the standpoint of common life. Not only does the question of justifying "framework judgments" never normally arise, the presuppositions of ordinary practices are normally invisible. Wittgenstein himself remarks that:

> I do not explicitly learn the propositions that stand fast for me. I can discover them subsequently like the axis around which a body

rotates. This axis is not fixed in the sense that anything holds it fast, but the movement around it determines its immobility.[4]

Only in the context of philosophical reflection do we even become aware of our deepest presuppositions. It must therefore be from the detached or reflective position of the philosopher that we see that the absence of evidence for them is not a lack. However, this means that we must be able to combine a naturalistic outlook with philosophical detachment, and how are we to do this? Taking up a detached position freezes the everyday movement around our axial propositions, which presumably now float free. This implies that we cannot assume a philosophical stance while retaining the confident grip on framework certainties that the naturalistic attitude requires. In the context of reflection, a naturalistic attitude is not even *available*.

Significantly, McGinn finds another strain in Wittgenstein's outlook, though she does not distinguish it from the straightforward espousal of naturalism just questioned. She is responding to this strain when she claims that:

> In so far as Wittgenstein provides an alternative assessment of the fact that we do not possess or require justifications for the judgments that form the frame of our practice, he prevents scepticism from arising, and we never find ourselves deprived of either the natural attitude or unqualified common sense.[5]

This is quite different from the suggestion that naturalism provides a response to scepticism "on the same level," the level of a reflective understanding of our knowledge of the world as a whole. If this kind of reflection is to be possible, we must be able, somehow or other, to distance ourselves from the natural attitude. If the significance of naturalism is that it shows that this is not possible, then the aim of the naturalist is not to show that, once his reflective examination of our knowledge of the world has got under way, the sceptic crucially misrepresents our epistemic position. It must rather be to show that something goes wrong at the very first step, at which we try to take up a reflective attitude towards ordinary certainties. If we cannot deprive ourselves of the natural attitude, the reflective stance cannot really be assumed.

There is a strange tension here, an inclination to concede the naturalness of the sceptic's initial reflective turn coexisting with a temptation to argue that his supposed detachment from everyday certainties is illusory and impossible. We can find the same tension in Wittgenstein's own writings. Wittgenstein tells us that "If Moore were to pronounce the opposite of those propositions which he declares certain, we should not just not share his opinion: we should regard him as demented". But consider the following situation: "I am sitting with a philosopher in the garden; he says again and again, 'I know that's a tree,' pointing to a tree that is near us. Someone else arrives and hears this, and I tell him: 'This fellow isn't insane. We are only doing philosophy.' "[6]

Scepticism is not a clinical condition and the things said while discussing it are not evidence of dementia. In the context of having withdrawn from practical concerns, for the purpose of seeking reflective understanding, they are far from pointless. However, having handed the sceptic his starting point, thus apparently the intelligibility and even the reasonableness of his questions, it is hard to see how to avoid his conclusions. Perhaps, then, the mistake was to hand him his starting point. Thus we find Wittgenstein suggesting that:

> The statement "I know that here is a hand" may ... be continued "for its *my* hand" that I'm looking at. Then a reasonable man will not doubt that I know. – Nor will the idealist; rather he will say that he was not dealing with the practical doubt which is being dismissed, but there is a further doubt *behind* that one. – That this is an *illusion* has to be shown in a different way.[7]

Here the claim is that there is no doubt behind the ordinary doubt: the thought that there is is simply an illusion. But this can be so only if there is something defective about the context in which that doubt seems to arise and in which it seems to be perfectly intelligible. More precisely, if that context is created simply by taking a step back from everyday judgmental practices, there must be something deeply wrong with the very idea of such a detaching move.

But what? Here we must be careful not to read too much into talk of "depriving ourselves of the natural attitude." On first hearing, it sounds as if, in order to philosophize, we must strip ourselves of our most deeply entrenched beliefs, which is surely impossible. But just as philosophical scepticism is not a clinical condition, neither is philosophical detachment a spectacular psychological achievement. To become detached from our everyday beliefs is simply to be willing, for a time and in very special circumstances, to be open to the possibility that they are largely or even wholly false, however deeply entrenched. It is to be willing to ask whether we have or even could have any evidence for them. It is to ask questions *about* what we normally and perhaps in some sense inevitably just rely on.

If detachment is not a feat of mental gymnastics, the impossibility of detachment must be conceptual rather than psychological. But where is the conceptual defect in what is apparently a simple methodological proposal? Moreover, how could an incoherent proposal be a potential source of valuable philosophical insights? Nevertheless, giving the sceptic his first step seems to make it very unlikely that we will be able to impede his progress later. We seem to be caught in a dilemma, hence the tension.

One possibility is this: that in attempting to take a detached view of the propositions that express framework judgments we change the propositions themselves. The thought here is that, when it comes to propositions that stand fast, standing fast contributes essentially to making them the propositions they are. This seems to be Clarke's idea, when he argues that Moore's propositions belong to "philosophical" common sense, and so are only "verbal twins" of their "plain" counterparts. Perhaps there are hints of it in Wittgenstein too. But this approach does not really resolve the tension in the Wittgensteinian approach. If wrenching the presuppositions of common sense from their ordinary setting inevitably changes or distorts them, it seems that we cannot comment on their character *at all*. If the sceptic's claim that they are mere assumptions is incoherent – because in the context of philosophical reflection we cannot comment on them, but only on their verbal twins – then so is the anti-sceptical claim that our relation to them is in fact non-epistemic. Again, we find the urge to deny the sceptic his detached, reflective standpoint colliding with the need to assume it for the purpose of rebutting him.[8]

Earlier, I found a clue to the source of the temptation to concede the sceptic's initial methodological innocence in McGinn's suggestion that, because it engages the sceptic "on the same level," the level of philosophical understanding, Wittgenstein's naturalism is a satisfying response to scepticism in a way that the responses of Moore, Austin and Cavell are not. Why, however, is it so important to find a response on the same level? The answer, I think, is that the urge to find such a response points beyond dissatisfaction with particular philosophers to a feeling that no purely diagnostic response to scepticism will ever be satisfying. It is not just that, since the sceptic's questions do not seem to be unintelligible, it is difficult to resist conceding the naturalness of his starting point. Rather, as Stroud argues, to be told that the traditional epistemological project is misconceived, that from the very outset it distorts or misrepresents our epistemic position, is not to be given the kind of reflective understanding of human knowledge that it appears to us natural to seek.[9] Diagnosis seems to leave us with nothing where we still feel that something is required. It would be more satisfying to allow the sceptic his initial reflective turn and to meet him later on with an account of human knowledge on the same level.

I see no hope of this. If the sceptic is allowed his account of his enterprise, there will be no resisting his conclusions. This is why the temptation to concede that account only produces tension. In Wittgenstein's and McGinn's case, the tension takes the form of sometimes seeming to allow the sceptic his intial move and sometimes seeming to argue that no such move is possible. In Cavell, it takes the form of arguing that, though the sceptic's utterances are unintelligible, there is nevertheless a truth in scepticism. In my view, however, such tensions reflect a false dilemma: that the sceptic either succumbs to a therapeutic diagnosis or triumphs. What we need, then, is to extend our theoretical diagnosis to the sceptic's understanding of philosophy. In this way, we may be able to see that we can take a purely diagnostic approach to scepticism without reconciling ourselves to there being an important kind of understanding that we want but can never have.

## 5.3   REFLECTION AND DETACHMENT

Let us take a closer look at the thought that what is distinctive about the "detached," philosophical attitude is its intention to examine our beliefs about the world in abstraction from all practical consideration: that like no other form of inquiry, philosophy is a *purely* theoretical undertaking. This account of philosophy in terms of its methodological purity is a powerful weapon in the sceptic's arsenal.

In common life, the argument begins, limitations on time and resources, not to say our need to cope with pressing problems, compel us to accept or reject propositions on the basis of evidence that is often recognizably less than adequate. Thus, in everyday practical situations, we may often quite reasonably claim to be justified in accepting things without having looked into everything that, strictly speaking, would be relevant to their truth or credibility. We will be justified in the sense of having done all that could reasonably be expected *in the circumstances.* But from a strictly theoretical standpoint, our justification may be quite weak. Indeed, in extreme cases we may have nothing at all that could reasonably be described as *epistemic* justification. The sceptic(or traditional epistemologist) thus sees everyday justification as influenced by considerations of two quite different types: epistemic considerations, having to do with everything that is relevant to the truth of our beliefs, and practical considerations, having to do with the costs and benefits attached to decision-making.

Given this understanding of justification and its relation to practicality, it is clear that philosophy begins only when practical considerations are set aside. When our aim is to command a reflective understanding of our knowledge of the world, we are interested only in the epistemological status of our beliefs in that area. The question is not whether such beliefs are pragmatically necessary, not whether they are psychologically irrepressible, not whether *we* are justified in holding them, but whether *they* are really justified. And this means: do they really meet the criteria that we can see to be appropriate when no practical considerations cloud the issue? However, we cannot answer this question unless we can isolate the exclusively epistemic constraints on knowledge and justification. Detachment, by eliminating all practical considerations, does just this.

As well as being purely theoretical, the reflective understanding we seek in philosophy is unusually general. But what makes its unusual generality reasonable and possible, it will now be said, is its purely theoretical character. Propositions that have to stand fast if we are to get on with the practical affairs of common life appear in a new light when we step back to reflect. They appear as commitments that need evidential backing if they are to amount to more than ungrounded assumptions.

By explaining how ordinary justification is subject to practical constraints, the sceptic neutralizes anti-sceptical argumens drawn directly from the ordinary use of epistemic terms. True, I do not ordinarily suppose that a justified claim about an object in the external world demands exclusion of the possibility that I am dreaming right now. But this possibility remains truth-relevant, even if practical concerns ordinarily compel me to ignore it. We cannot, therefore, claim that the sceptic imposes artificially strict conditions on knowing and so fails to state a truth about knowledge as we ordinarily understand it. Recall Austin's charge that the sceptic violates the "definite lack" and "reasonable sufficiency" conditions on ordinary justification.[10] Even according to Austin himself, what counts as a definite lack or a reasonable sufficiency in one's evidence is determined by "present intents and purposes." So, when "present intents and purposes" have nothing to do with practical decision making, a stricter than usual standard may be appropriate, even according to our ordinary concept of knowledge.

With this argument in place, the evidence Austin culls from examples of everyday epistemic assessment itself becomes hard to assess. The trouble is that in Austin's examples practical constraints operate at full force. When bird-watching, I need to give my full attention to whatever identifying marks my fleeting glimpses of birds afford me. As a result, I cannot worry about whether the birds are clever radio-controlled models, still less about whether I might be hallucinating every one of them. But if my purposes have nothing to do with the practicalities of bird identification – if my choice of an example involving bird identification is purely illustrative – then perhaps I can and should consider such possibilities. The sceptic's stricter-than-usual standards are not extraordinary standards: they are just ordinary standards freed from ordinary limitations.

The significance of Austin's and Wittgenstein's reminders about ordinary usage begins to look deeply equivocal. What they present as constraints on knowledge and (epistemic) justification may point to something quite different: namely, constraints on when it is (ordinarily) reasonable *to lay claim to* knowledge or justified belief. As Barry Stroud argues, Austin's data always concern what it would be reasonable or appropriate to *say*, rather than the epistemic status of what is said. Of course in an ordinary practical context it would be absurd to *say* that someone didn't know that the bird on the fence was a goldfinch on the grounds that, for all he knows, he might himself be a brain in a vat. But this does not show that the sceptical alternatives are irrelevant to the question of whether he really does know it. In fact, the sceptic will argue,when we appreciate the special conditions under which philosophical inquiry takes place, we can recognize that they are highly relevant to whether our knowledge of the world is all we take it to be, just as clearly as we can recognize the ordinary inappropriateness of bringing them up.

According to Stroud, one important reason why it would not normally be completely misplaced. He would not, by ordinary standards, have been hasty or careless and it would be wrong to imply that he had. However, would normally imply (in Grice's sense of conversational implicature) some criticism of him: that he had been hasty, or careless or whatever. But if, in ordinary contexts, hastiness and carelessness are themselves relative to various practical concerns and limitations, such criticism would be competely misplced. He would not, by ordinary standards, have been hasty or careless and it would be wrong to imply that he had. However, from the fact that it would not normally be appropriate to say to someone that he does not know something, because this would imply a misplaced criticism of *him*, it does not follow that he *does* know it. Appropriateness of utterance does not entail truth and inappropriateness does not entail falsity. What the sceptic says might well be true, even though it would be absurd or offensive to be constantly reminding people of it. It might be true even if its assertion would normally carry false implicatures.[11]

Thompson Clarke invents an ingenious example, which Stroud also appeals to, to illustrate how the sceptic sees the relation between the context of philosophical reflection and more ordinary contexts. We are to imagine that certain "humanoids" are taught to identify enemy aircraft according to checklists of distinguishing features. (Clarke calls them "humanoids" because he does not himself think that our human situation is really analogous to theirs.) Unbeknownst to them, the checklists do not suffice to distinguish the types of aircraft they are taught to recognize from certain very rare, obsolete types that are, in any case, not so dangerous. If they were modified to cope with the obsolete types, the recognition procedures would be so cumbersome that identification of various truly dangerous types of aircraft would be seriously delayed. So a spotter, using his checklist,will identify an aircraft as type A, which it may well be; but the features on which he bases his judgment do not in fact distinguish it from an obsolete type X. Thus, though his claim to have spotted a type A will be accepted and acted on, and though he has acted in a competely

unexceptionable way, we will all agree that strictly speaking, and abstracting from practical concerns and limitations, he does not know that
the aircraft he has seen is a type A, even though he thinks he does. But
according to the sceptic, Clarke says, all our "knowledge" is like this. Our
"plain" knowing is the sceptic's "restricted" knowing. If we cannot rule
out the possibility that we are dreaming, or victims of evil deceivers, then
strictly speaking we never know any of the things we think we know. Of
couse, we are perfectly entitled, in ordinary situations, to take it that we
know such things, claim that we do, and so on, for to cope with the world
we have to take all sorts of things for granted. Still, all claims to knowledge are false. What we have is knowledge-for-all-practical-purposes, not
the genuine article.[12]

The example of the spotters does more than show how the standards for
assessing claims to knowledge can change, perhaps becoming more severe
depending on various practical contingencies: it also reveals the source of
such shifts in standards. If justification has more than just an epistemic
dimension, how much evidence we take as adequate may depend in part,
for example, on the costs of collecting it. But when we raise philosophical
questions about knowledge, we are interested in the epistemic dimension
alone. So when we prescind from all practical considerations, the question
about whether a given spotter knows what he claims to know naturally
turns into the question of whether the identification procedure guarantees
true belief. The analogy of the spotters is a dramatic illustration of the
sceptic's two-factor conception of justification.

The sceptic's account of the character of philosophical inquiry supports
Stroud's sense that the charge that scepticism results from a quest for
certainty, which Stroud associates closely with the charge that the sceptic is
an antecedent foundationalist, gets things upside down. The basis for the
charge is that the sceptic insists on considering error-possibilities that
would ordinarily be regarded as too far fetched to take seriously. But
neither the sceptic nor the traditional epistemologist comes to his investigation already committed to this strategy. Rather, having taken up a
detached, reflective attitude, he *discovers* the relevance of sceptical hypotheses
to the fundamental questions about human knowledge that it is the business
of philosophy to ask.

All this reinforces the sceptic's sense that he in no way distorts the
demands of our ordinary epistemic concepts by imposing unreasonably
strict standards on knowledge and justification. Rather, he invites us to
consider what those demands come to when our ordinary concepts are
projected into an unusual context. However, the context is not so unusual
that results obtained there bear no obvious relation to our more ordinary
views. On the contrary, since the effect of philosophical detachment is
simply to abstract the properly epistemic dimension of knowledge and

justification from extraneous practical considerations, what we learn through philosophical reflection concerns knowledge as we always understand it, not knowledge according to some invented criterion. Nor does the sceptic's conception of philosophical method conceal tendentious theoretical assumptions. The detachment from practical considerations that is the precondition of philosophical reflection is just an extension or radicalization of a perfectly familiar procedure. Scepticism is a natural, intuitive problem through and through.

The sceptic can also back up his suspicions about the naturalist response to scepticism, which claims that we have a distinctive, non-epistemic relation to the everyday platitudes the sceptic tries to question. The sceptic can admit that there is some truth in this, but without in any way retreating from his position. The truth is that, in ordinary circumstances, our relation to such judgments is not *purely* epistemic. Practical considerations require us to take all sorts of things for granted and, in a practical sense, justify our so doing. But this does not mean that the sceptic makes an error when, for philosophical purposes, he looks beyond ordinary practical concerns and finds that we do not really know the things we so effortlessly accept.

Finally, that sceptical alternatives are at home only in a highly rarefied, theoretical context, explains the fact that so impressed Hume: that the conviction attaching to sceptical conclusions cannot be sustained outside the study. We can see that this conviction will survive only while we maintain a detached, philosophical attitude. The moment we relax our detachment, practical pressures and interests will intervene to direct our attention away from the considerations that sustain a sceptical assessment of our knowledge of the world. Everyday practical affairs do not allow us to dwell on sceptical hypotheses. But this does nothing to show that the sceptic's conclusion is not the final truth about human knowledge. The conclusion to draw seems to be Hume's: that "carelessness and inattention," not theoretical insight, are all that stand between us and a consistent acknowledgment of the truth of scepticism.

## 5.4 RELEVANT ALTERNATIVES AND EPISTEMIC CLOSURE

Hinted at in the remarks quoted from Austin is a version of what has come to be known as the "relevant alternatives" account of knowledge. On this view, it is wrong to think that justification, even when taken purely epistemically, depends on ruling out any and every alternative to what one believes to be the case. What matters is the exclusion of certain *relevant* alternatives. Obviously, I have a good deal of sympathy with this view, though I would hesitate to say that knowledge always depends on the ability to rule out alternatives. But whether this account of knowledge has any force against scepticism depends entirely on what makes an alternative relevant or irrelevant.

The "relevant alternatives" view of knowledge suggested by Austin has been developed with considerable sophistication by Fred Dretske, who regards it as intimately connected with the failure of knowledge to be closed under known logical entailment.[13] I shall discuss the issue of closure at length in chapter 8. I mention it here to show how the sceptic's account of philosophical inquiry helps him respond to this diagnosis too.

For those who deny closure, we can allow that the sceptic is right to insist that no one ever knows that he is not a brain in a vat, or not always dreaming. But this does not mean that he never knows, say, that he is sitting at his desk. For although he knows that if he is sitting at his desk then he is not a brain in a vat, once closure is denied there is no way to get from his inability to know that this sceptical alternative does not obtain to an inability to know a commonplace particular fact.[14]

What makes an alternative relevant? According to Dretske, relevance has to do with what I intend to be the *dominant* contrast to whatever claim I have advanced. This will vary with context. The claim that I am sitting at my desk may imply that I am sitting at *my* desk (not yours), that I am *sitting* at my desk (not standing), that I am sitting *at* my desk (not on it), or that I am sitting at my *desk* (not in the armchair). Knowing what I mean by the claim that I am sitting at my desk is a matter of knowing, which contrasting possibilities I have in mind. Relevance depends on speaker's meaning.[15]

This way of excluding certain alternatives as irrelevant, so it is claimed, has nothing to do with their being *known* not to obtain. That they do not obtain is something that is presupposed, taken for granted. Given present intents and purposes, they are simply not in play, so that the question of whether or not they obtain does not arise. Affinities with Wittgenstein, as well as with Austin, are evident here. When we do history, we set aside radical doubts about the age of the earth, the reliability of documentary evidence, and so on. We do this to focus attention on particular historical claims. This focussing of attention requires that certain ways in which these claims could fail to be true be kept in the background.

Further reflection on the presuppositions of particular claims, questions and inquiries reveals a general reason for thinking that knowledge cannot be closed under known entailment. At least some of the presuppositions of a particular knowledge claim will concern the *reliability conditions* for the evidence on which the claim is based. Wittgenstein's examples are often like this. The presuppositions of doing history have to be true for the evidence we regard as relevant to have the force we attribute to it. If, as in Russell's fantasy, the earth came into existence five minutes ago, complete with misleading indications of great antiquity, everything we regard as historical evidence would be worthless. But surely, one might say, this does not mean that, since we know all sorts of historical facts, we also (thereby) know that the earth has existed for many years past. Where the presuppositions of a particular knowledge claim determine the reliability conditions for the evidence on which the claim is based, knowledge that a given proposition is true cannot yield knowledge that these conditions are fulfilled, even when that proposition entails that they are. That Napoleon was victorious at Austerlitz in 1805 entails that the earth has existed for more than one hundred and fifty years. But because inquiries into the career of Napoleon presuppose the past existence of the earth, their results confer no justification on our belief in it. This is, *prima facie*, a very plausible view.

According to Wittgenstein, such presuppositions, because they lie apart from the route travelled by inquiry, are neither known nor not known, even though they may be known to be entailed by things we do know. Wittgenstein seems to be committed to denying closure, even though he does not underline the issue in the way that Dretske does. The same seems to be true of Strawson and Marie McGinn. To say that our relation to framework judgments is non-epistemic is to say that they neither amount nor fail to amount to knowledge. But surely they can be entailed by judgments to which we do have an epistemic relation, in which case knowledge fails to close under known entailment.

Not surprisingly perhaps, given their common roots, Dretske's response to the sceptic also has a lot in common with Cavell's. Cavell, as we saw, thinks that the sceptic tries to operate in a "non-claim context." He wants simply to mean what his words mean, without meaning anything particular by them, which would involve having no particular contrast in mind. Cavell, however, does not get involved with the issue of closure. But of course he doesn't have to. If what the sceptic says is less than fully intelligible, he has failed to make his case however the question of closure is decided. Still, the impossibility of knowing whether or not sceptical alternatives do or do not obtain finds an echo in Cavell's thought that, though we know all kinds of things about the world, our relation to the world as a whole is not one of knowing. Cavell and those who make closure a central issue are at one in finding a large measure of truth in scepticism.

This suggests, however, that closure isn't the main issue even for Dretske. The view that knowledge depends only on the exclusion of relevant alternatives is what really blocks the sceptic's attempt to undermine our knowledge of ordinary empirical facts. On this account, whether or not we *can* rule out sceptical counter-possibilities, we don't *have* to in order to secure everyday factual knowledge. Whether or not we deny closure, depends on what we go on to say about sceptical counter-possibilities. If we agree that they cannot be excluded, failure of the principle of closure will be a (surprising) consequence of our response to the sceptic, but more a by-product of our response to scepticism than its basis.

So how effective an anti-sceptical weapon is the relevant alternatives account of knowledge? It will be effective at all only if the sceptic's alternatives are generally irrelevant to ordinary knowledge claims, which is not easy to show once the sceptic's conception of philosophical inquiry is taken into account.

For a start, the sceptic can concede that his alternatives are not usually *salient*, and so not usually considered. But he can insist, with some plausibility, that not being salient is not the same as being completely irrelevant. He can admit, therefore, that what we *mean by* a given claim is a function of what we intend to pick out as the dominant contrast: what I meant by what I just said was that I was *sitting* at the desk, not standing. But the full range of relevant alternatives to what I have claimed is determined by what the sentence I use to state my claim means, by everything it excludes and not just those things I choose to emphasize. If I were sitting, but at the table not the desk, my claim would have to be withdrawn or at least rephrased, whatever I happened to have in mind when I made it.

Of course, it is not accidental that the sceptical alternatives are not usually salient: for they are not *specifically* relevant to any particular claim about how things stand in the world, and so unlikely when some specific claim is on the table to belong to the range of dominant contrasts. However, the sceptic will think that this lack of specific relevance is what gives the arguments he bases on them their essential generality. He will not concede that lack of specific relevance is *irrelevance*. In the sceptic's eyes it is universal hence usually non-salient relevance.

This leads to the main point: alternatives are never just relevant or irrelevant, they are relevant or irrelevant to something or another. Relevant alternatives are determined by dominant contrasts, and the dominant contrasts to a given claim reflect what questions we think an audience might have in mind, what specific doubts we think might need to be resolved, and so on. But now the sceptic can easily explain, indeed concede, how his alternatives might be "irrelevant" (in ordinary contexts) without retracting to the smallest degree his claim that they undermine all our knowledge of the world (even the knowledge we take ourselves to have in contexts where sceptical counter-possibilities are admittedly irrelevant). Ordinary contexts are shot through with practical concerns and limitations. This means, first, that in ordinary contexts we are likely to be more interested in particular claims about the world than in whether any such claim ever amounts to knowledge, properly so-called. Accordingly, the dominant contrasts, hence the relevant alternatives, will be fixed by quite restricted aspects of what is claimed. But even when we are interested in epistemic assessment, the form our interest takes will itself be restricted by the range of error-possibilities that our practical concerns make especially salient, which is simply to say that even epistemic assessment is ordinarily practically constrained. However, all this shows is that we are not ordinarily interested in general epistemological questions: that ordinarily when a claim is made we are interested in whether it is correct in respect of some quite definite aspect of its content, or whether the claimant has credentials or evidence specifically relevant to that aspect. When we do take an interest in more general epistemological questions, the relevance of sceptical counter-possibilities becomes apparent. In fact, they emerge as *the* relevant alternatives. And if we cannot rule these out when epistemological questions are on the table, we fall short of knowledge even when they are not.

All this is illustrated by the example of the aircraft spotters. For spotters with limited training, the differences between type A and type X aircraft are not at all salient, if they are recognizable at all. But they don't have to be, since they are not even relevant to the pressing practical task of rapid identification of potentially hostile planes. They are, however, relevant to whether a spotter with limited training really knows what kind of aircraft he sees, no matter how practically effective he may be.[16]

We must conclude that, if there is a context in which the sceptic's alternatives are the relevant ones, and if that context is what the sceptic says it is – namely, one created solely by detachment from ordinary practical concerns and limitations – then neither the "relevant alternatives" nor any other broadly contextual conception of knowledge and justification will make headway against scepticism unless it is backed up by an alternative account of the relation between the context of reflection and more ordinary contexts. But that there is such a context seems hard to deny. When Moore claims "Here is one hand," he doesn't mean as opposed to *two* hands or one *foot*. He means that here is one real-external-thing hand, as opposed to a dream hand, hallucinatory hand or anything else of that sort. So if the sceptic is right to claim that in this context, when the question is whether we really know that here is an honest to goodness hand, that the relevant alternatives cannot be excluded, we need to know what prevents his concluding that we never really know anything about the external world. The sceptic has traced the everyday irrelevance of his counter-possibilities to the fact that our interests are not confined to epistemological questions, leaving us with no reason to think that the epistemological questions to which his possibilities are relevant can be answered other than sceptically.

The sceptic's context, then, is one in which we raise the question of whether we ever really know the sort of thing Moore would like simply to treat as an example of empirical knowledge. What we need to know is what results obtained in this context imply for our putative knowledge elsewhere or on other occasions. What do results obtained when sceptical counter-possibilities are relevant imply about our pretensions to knowledge when they aren't? A philosopher who associates the "relevant alternatives" analysis with a failure of closure might reply that he does not need to answer this question, since no such sceptical results can be obtained once the sceptic is denied the closure principle. But a moment's reflection should stifle this temptation. Denying closure does not remove the need to investigate the relation between everyday life and philosophical reflection.

As Dretske notes, some sentential operators are not transmitted across entailments at all. An example might be "It is surprising that ..." It may be surprising that P; P may entail and be known to entail Q; but this is no indication that it is surprising that Q. Others, such as "It is necessary that ..." are invariably transmitted. Dretske calls these two types of operators "non-penetrating" and "penetrating" respectively. He claims that "S knows that ..." must be different again. Knowledge is not invariably or undiscriminatingly transmitted across known entailments, but not completely non-transmissible either. Knowledge that P must to some extent be transmitted across known entailments, and in a systematic way, or knowledge that P will not even exclude relevant alternatives to P. This is why Dretske characterizes "S knows that ..." as "semi-penetrating": it "penetrates" to the relevant alternatives to P, excluding them but not others.[17]

If knowledge "penetrates" even to this extent, we cannot claim that, in the sceptic's favored context, we still know that here is one hand even if we do not and cannot know that we are not dreaming or not brains in vats. Since, in this context, the sceptic's counter-possibilities constitute the relevant alternatives, any knowledge of the world will penetrate to them. We seem forced to admit, therefore, that, when the question on the table is whether we ever really know anything about the world, the sceptic is right to conclude that, if his characteristic counter-possibilities cannot be excluded, the answer to the question must be "No."

Does the answer remain "No" even in contexts where sceptical alternatives are irrelevant, because general epistemological questions are not on the table? I think it does, if the sceptic is allowed his account of philosophical reflection, hence of what makes for relevance and irrelevance. In fact, if the sceptic is allowed this account, the apparent failure of closure is an illusion. Those who deny closure claim that, in an ordinary context, I can know that there is a *hand* in front of me even if I do not know that I am not merely dreaming that there is. But the sceptic will reply that this is not really a case in which I know that P, know that P entails not-Q and yet fail to know that not-Q. Rather, it is a case in which I know-for-all-practical-purposes that P, and so would ordinarily quite properly be *said* to know that P, even though, strictly speaking, I fail to know that P precisely because I fail to know that not-Q. The absence of knowledge is compatible with the presence of knowledge-for-all-practical-purposes. To the extent that the sceptic's account of philosophical reflection takes the anti-sceptical edge off contextual accounts of knowledge, it also undermines the arguments against closure they may seem to support.

## 5.5  THE TWO-FACTOR THEORY

Once we appreciate how the sceptic puts it to work, we can see straight away that his proposal to set aside all practical considerations is less innocent than it first sounds. Behind it lies a definite epistemological thesis. For the sceptic, everyday justification can be resolved into two components: an epistemic component, which has to do solely with factors relevant to the truth of our beliefs, and a second component which affects, in light of practical exigencies, how high a standard of evidence it is (practically) reasonable to insist on. Here "practical" considerations include everything that is, in the broadest sense, "economic"; i.e. all costs and benefits attaching to decisions and to the decision-making process itself. Thus the sceptic sees the severity of ordinary demands on justification as a kind of resultant, the sum of an epistemic and an economic vector. It is central to his understanding of his inquiry that this resultant be resolvable, indeed uniquely resolvable, into these two entirely distinct components. Even more important, however, is his account of their character.

We must not confuse the sceptic's account of the two components in justification with other distinctions. In particular, the epistemological/practical distinction, as drawn by the sceptic, does not line up with the distinction between justified belief and justified believing. No doubt he would treat justified believing as a species of practical justification. But, as we have seen above, he also intends the epistemological/practical distinction to account for variations in constraints on evidence. That is, he means to apply the distinction *within* the area of the justification by evidence of propositions believed. He does not intend his distinction to mark a contrast between that kind of justification and some other kind.

We have seen that the sceptic is apt to treat ordinary language examples of reasonable and unreasonable objections to knowledge claims as indicative only of restrictions on *saying* that someone does or not know. The distinction between justification as it applies to acceptance and as it applies to the propositions accepted is relevant here. We may be entitled to *say* that we know something because *we* are (practically) justified in *accepting* it, even though our evidence for the proposition accepted is less than complete. But again, though the sceptic can appeal to the practical/epistemological distinction to explain the contrast between justified believing of propositions and believing justified propositions, the two distinctions are not co-extensive. In fact, the main use the sceptic finds for the practical/ epistemological distinction has to do with the justification by evidence of propositions believed. The examples presented by Austin are not all accounted for by the claim that they have to do with the reasonableness of saying, or even believing. The fact is that ordinarily, even when interested in providing evidential backing for what we believe, we do not suppose that we need to exclude the outlandish error-possibilities that are the sceptic's stock in trade. Austin's definite lack and reasonable sufficiency conditions are constraints on justification by evidence, not just on reasonable saying or believing, possibly in the absence of evidence. This is where the two-factor view of justification finds its most important application, for it offers a way of defending the introduction into discussions of human knowledge error-possibilities that would ordinarily be considered too far fetched to be taken seriously. At the same time, it explains why the traditional assessment of our knowledge of the world so easily becomes entangled with questions about certainty. When we are under pressure to come to a decision, it would be irrational to investigate every way we might go wrong, no matter how far-fetched. But it is not so obviously irrational when practical constraints have been temporarily set aside. From this point on, then, the practical/epistemological distinction as it applies to justification by evidence will be our central concern.

A second distinction not to be confused with the sceptic's distinction between practical and strictly epistemological considerations is that between formal and substantive aspects of justification. Austin's 'reasonable sufficiency" and "definite lack" conditions illustrate the kind of formal constraints that we might take to be imposed simply by the concept of knowledge. But what counts as a reasonable sufficiency or a definite lack will have to do with our interests, situation and background knowledge in some particular context of justification, and so will be determined neither by the concept of knowledge alone, nor simply by that concept in conjunction with the content of the belief to be justified. But though this is a kind of two factor view, it is not the sceptic's. The sceptic holds that, *within the area of substantive constraints*, we can factor out the influence of epistemological or truth-relevant factors from that of economic or cost-relevant factors. His vector-addition model explains fluctuations in substantive constraints and is not intended merely to distinguish them from formal constraints.

If the source of one vector lies in economic considerations, where should we locate the source of the other? The answer can only be: in our concepts, epistemic and otherwise. Presumably, setting aside all practical considerations leaves only theoretical considerations behind. But this step alone will not guarantee the traditional epistemologist an object for his reflections. We saw in chapter 3 that stepping back from the methodological necessities of, say, historical inquiry does not yield a more cautious way of doing history but a different form of inquiry altogether. However, a more cautious form of disciplinary inquiry is the most we can get out of imagining away practical limitations, where the practical is identified with the economic. This shows that, in his attempt to reflect on our knowledge of the world generally, on what Thompson Clarke sees as the whole field of "the plain," the sceptic also means to step outside all disciplinary constraints, which imply substantive factual commitments. But why suppose, when this step is taken, that there remains anything to reflect on?

This question brings to light a crucial ambiguity in the idea of detachment. Those who see detachment as a precondition of reflective philosophical understanding have at least two things in mind, which they are not always careful to distinguish and are perhaps even inclined to identify. The first is what we have been concerned with thus far: the setting aside of all economic constraints. By itself, however, the setting aside of practical concerns and limitations explains very little of what goes on in philosophical reflection on our knowledge of the world. How could it? Detachment from practical projects and limitations may yield purely theoretical inquiry. But purely theoretical inquiry is not, in and of itself, epistemological inquiry. The problematic transition in the sceptic's account of philosophical reflection is from the purely theoretical to the purely epistemological.

Accordingly, it is the second, less emphasized aspect of detachment that really does the work. This aspect of detachment is nothing less than the totality condition all over again. If we are to assess our knowledge of the world in its entirety, we must set aside not only all our practical interests but all our ordinary beliefs about the world and our relation to it. We must "detach" ourselves from the commitments implicit in our everyday outlook or our assessment will not be properly general. By sliding from detachment as the taking up of a purely theoretical attitude to detachment as a step outside all knowledge of the world, the sceptic creates the impression that "detachment" exposes to view epistemic constraints inherent in our concepts alone. He creates the impression that a withdrawl from practical concerns is enough to make knowledge an object of theory.

The two aspects of detachment are of course related, though not as closely as perhaps some philosophers think. Without question, the pursuit of practical interests requires taking lots of things for granted. Accordingly, detachment from practical considerations is a necessary condition for detachment from all everyday beliefs about the world. But it is certainly not a sufficient condition. It may well be that we cannot perform the radical detachment from our natural outlook that is required by philosophical reflection on our knowledge of the world unless we first set practical considerations aside. But it may be that we still cannot manage it even after we have done so. Or it may be that, though we can manage it, detachment from the natural attitude leaves us either with nothing to examine or something other than what we wanted. So for our concerns here, the most important connection between epistemological realism and the idea of a "reflective understanding" of human knowledge is the one forged by the sceptic's need to guarantee an object for his reflections. If knowledge and justification depend on the the ways that specific beliefs and judgments are embedded in particular contexts, and if contextual factors include our interests, collateral knowledge and worldly situation (known or not), there will be no possibility of reflecting on "knowledge" in abstraction from everything we know, including things we know about the world. There will be no possibility of reflective understanding if, in taking the crucial step back, we deprive ourselves of anything to reflect on. This is why epistemological realism is indispensable. There must be, as I have said, a realm of autonomous epistemological fact — for example, as constituted by context-invariant relations of epistemological priority — if the radical detachment from worldly knowledge envisaged by the traditional epistemologist is to leave him with anything to assess. This is why I said earlier that my objection to the traditional epistemologist, as to his *alter ego* the sceptic, is not aimed at his attempt to reflect but rather at the object of his reflections.

I have argued at length that the project of assessing our knowledge of the world as a whole, and all at once, is not to be dissociated from epistemological realism in its specifically foundationalist form. So if philosophical reflection on our knowledge of the world necessarily involves detachment, and if insisting on detachment is just another way of enforcing the totality condition, the appeal to the demands of reflective understanding is just another way of introducing, though not of arguing for, epistemological realism. This is why it is crucial to distinguish detachment as the totality condition under another name from the bland suggestion that the quest for philosophical understanding should not be overly burdened with immediate practicalities. The possibility of purely theoretical inquiry does not guarantee the possibility of purely epistemological inquiry. Only epistemological realism does that.

If detachment is understood as detachment from our beliefs about the world, the connection with foundationalism, hence with epistemological realism, is easy to discern. After all, detachment cannot be a step into the void. A detached examination of our knowledge of the world inevitably proceeds on the basis of whatever knowledge remains to us after detachment, and there is nothing for this to be except knowledge of our own thoughts and experiences. But, as I have argued, neither recovering nor failing to recover knowledge of the world from such limited resources will be relevant to an assessment of our knowledge of the world unless knowledge of our own thoughts and experience is generally and objectively prior to knowledge of the world. It is not enough that we have to *treat it as such* if we are to make room for the kind of project of assessment that the traditional epistemologist envisages.

As a way of exploring this point further, let us return to the thought-experiment of the aircraft spotters, which Clarke uses to illustrate the sceptic's conception of the relation of philosophy to everyday life. Clarke means this example to capture "the significant part of a small, independent universe of humanoids." He adopts this odd description because he wants to explain what it is to have "a conceptual-human constitution of the standard type." We do not have such a constitution, which is why the spotters are humanoids, not humans. Roughly – we shall get to details shortly – a conceptual constitution is standard when knowledge results from the correct identification, according to some checklist of features, of members of some independent domain of "items." This is how we imagine the spotters: their task is to identify enemy aircraft by checking planes against a list of distinctive features, and we can suppose that they check off features without error. The human epistemic situation is more complicated. Whereas the spotters' domain includes only such things as aircraft, ours includes items like dreams. To say the least, the identification of such "items" is problematic, a fact the sceptic exploits to the full.

Clarke thinks that the possibility that I might be dreaming right now can be cited two ways, depending on whether its target is a "plain" or a "philosophical" claim to knowledge. Citing the dream possibility in an everyday or "plain" way, I presuppose that I can determine, if not now then later, whether this possibility is realized. Thus the plain possibility that I am dreaming represents an "epistemic" possibility, which Clarke writes "$P_e$." This possibility, which we certainly understand, gives the sceptic his starting point. However, he wants to use this plain possibility to undermine philosophical common sense, $CS_{ph}$. $CS_{ph}$ is given by the sorts of things Moore claimed to be quite certain of and which he advanced, without any ulterior motive, as examples of things we know: that there is an external world, inhabited by beings with thoughts and feelings very like my own, and so on. Clearly, plain $P_e$, precisely because it is an epistemic possibility, will not do the job. The sceptic therefore moves to $P_{ne}$, again the possibility that I might be dreaming, but now with no implication that I can ever find out whether I am or not. However, according to Clarke, even $P_{ne}$ remains too plain for the sceptic's purposes. When I try to imagine that I might never find out whether or not I am dreaming, I still take it for granted that my environs "could be observed, known to be real, by outsiders, if any, in appropriate positions." Even the arch outsider, Descartes's Evil Demon, "is so natural-seeming because he fills the shoes built into our conception: he knows in fact what must, as . . . we conceive of $P_{ne}$, be know*able*." So could there be a yet more extreme possibility,

$P_x$, lacking even this epistemic condition? According to Clarke, "We have no satisfactory techniques for handling a question like this objectively: we are forced winetasters of the conceivable." Nevertheless, Clarke feels confident that $P_x$ is not really conceivable.[18]

With this result in hand, Clarke asks how the philosophical question $(Q_1)$ "Can we ever know we're awake, not dreaming?" is to be answered. If the answer is "Yes," the epistemic requirements for philosophical $P_e$ and $P_{ne}$ are met. However, since the sceptic is able to show that we have no way of ruling out his possibilities, and so are incapable of knowledge of the world, the answer to $Q_1$ must be "No." But if the answer is "No," $P_e$ and $P_{ne}$ are not genuine, since their epistemic requirements cannot be met, so the answer to $Q_1$ is "Yes" after all. Clarke concludes that $Q_1$ can be answered neither affirmatively nor negatively, hence that the "proposition" of $CS_{ph}$, that we can know we're not dreaming, can be neither affirmed nor denied.[19]

Eliminating philosophical $P_e$ and $P_{ne}$, and with them $CS_{ph}$, leaves us with only plain sceptical possibilities and plain claims to knowledge. Plainly, I might be dreaming and, in an extreme situation, might never find out. But what state I am in must be knowable, if not to me then to someone else: and how can this be if Descartes is right and "there are no features of his experiencing, no marks incompatible with his being asleep, dreaming"? Clarke does not say he is wrong: on the contrary, plain $P_e$ and $P_{ne}$, hence our ordinary concept of Dream, support Descartes. But he concludes that this concept is "not designed along the lines of 'marks and features' concepts" and hence that our conceptual-human constitution is not standard. Our relation to veridical experience is not like that of the spotters to hostile aircraft.

On one level, Clarke offers a straight verificationist response to the sceptic. Like a misfiring straight answer to a Carnapian "external" question, Clarke's $CS_{ph}$, philosophical common sense, amounts to an attempt to affirm the reality of our knowledge of the world from a standpoint outside all such knowledge. That such talk is meaningless is shown by the inconceivablity of what would be the proper counter-possibilities to $CS_{ph}$, if the propositions of $CS_{ph}$ really made sense. This seems to me redolent of paradox in just the same way as Cavell's claim that the sceptic cannot mean what he wants to mean: we seem able to say exactly what it is we cannot conceive. So it is not surprising to find Stroud claiming against Clarke that he *can* make sense of the dreaming possibility as the sceptic characterizes it. Stroud asks:

> Could it be that I am now dreaming? Not only does the right answer
> seem to me to be "Yes" but, more importantly, it seems to me that the
> possibility continues to make sense even if I go on to imagine that no

one on the face of the earth or anywhere else could ever know that I am dreaming because they too could never know whether they were awake or dreaming. Adding the further thought that the truth about my state is unknown or even unknowable to everyone does not seem to me to affect the possibility I originally tried to imagine at all. Of course, I might be wrong about this, but how is one to tell?[20]

Stroud tastes the conceptual wine and finds a different flavor. That is all there is to say about it: not a very satisfactory result.

More promising is Clarke's attempt to trace the sceptic's sense of the problem to his assumption that our conceptual-human constitution is standard. In a standard conceptual constitution:

(1) each concept is a self-sufficient unit or retains its identity in a conceptual scheme that in its entirety is the self-sufficient unit; i.e., either each concept itself or the conceptual scheme itself is capable of standing alone, apart, on its own two feet, and is not parasitic on, inextricably and dependently interwoven with other factors. Each concept or the conceptual scheme must be divorceable intact from our practices, from whatever constitutes the essential character of the plain, from elemental parts of human nature. . . .

(2) there are, fully separate from concepts, one or more domains of "items." Included among the concepts may be Dream, Hallucination, or others having reference to aspects of onself, these then being "items.". . .

(3) We, apart from "creating" concepts and providing their mental upkeep, are outsiders, standing back detached from concepts and items alike (even when items are aspects of ourselves), purely ascertaining observers who, usually by means of the senses, ascertain, when possible, whether items fulfil the conditions legislated by concepts.[21]

This is an intriguing account of the sceptic's ideas. Condition (1) states the sceptic's two-factor theory of justification, guaranteeing the separability of epistemic and practical considerations. Condition (2) is a version of realism, the demand that the world we want to know about is what it is independently of our opinions about it or ways of conceiving it. Finally, (3) explains why the sceptic sees nothing problematic in the idea of detachment from our natural attitude. We are, in a way, already detached. All that is required to convert ourselves into philosophers is to ignore practical limitations, which (1) assures us we can always coherently do. Clarke wants to argue that the sceptic's conception of philosophy stands or falls with this conception of a conceptual constitution. This looks like

an essay in theoretical diagnosis, the only strategy for breaking the intuitive deadlock. But I think the results are very mixed. Clarke has a sense
of the right way to go but ends up going the wrong way.

Clarke's argument focusses on (2) and (3). But (2) and (3) seem innocuous. Indeed, they seem innocuous because almost vacuous. What
could possibly be wrong with claiming that there is an "independent
domain of items" and that the aim of knowledge is to determine whether
these items "fulfill the conditions legislated by concepts"? All this means,
even in the case of dreaming, is that knowing that you are dreaming requires believing that you are dreaming when and only when you are dreaming. The condition "legislated" by the concept of dreaming is that one
not be awake. Where is the sceptical potential in that?

There isn't any. Scepticism does not arise simply from the highly abstract
model of knowing delineated by Clarke's sketch of a standard constitution.
It arises out of the thought that there ought to be some *non-trivial* account
of the "conditions" legislated by the concept of dreaming in terms of
features of experience. The crucial elision takes place in an unacknowledged move from "conditions legislated by concepts" to "marks and features" detectable without reference to the kind of knowledge expressed in
terms of the concepts in question. Applied to the contrast between dreaming and waking, this insistence on independently specifiable marks and
features has the effect of enforcing the sceptic's crucial doctrine: the priority
of experiential knowledge over knowledge of the world. For in this case,
"independently specifiable" has to mean "specifiable independently of all
knowledge of the world." So, if we are to know that we are awake, this
cannot be as a logical consequence of other worldly knowledge. It must
rather be on the basis of some kind of experiential index, and of course
there is no such thing. But there is no reason even to want such an account
of the "marks and features" that distinguish dreaming from waking unless
we are antecedently susceptible to foundationalism.

I think that Clarke's failure to identify what really generates the threat
of scepticism explains his urge to assert the inconceivability of the sceptic's
final version of the dream possibility. He would have no need to do so, if
he did not feel that it threatened plain knowledge of the world. But that
version of the dream possibility only illustrates what I have called the
neutrality of experience, which is no threat to worldly knowledge apart
from a commitment to the priority of experience. So again we see that it
is not the sceptic's abstract model of conceptual competence that moves
his argument but his specific views about the knowledge expressed with
particular concepts: views which, when examind closely, turn out to build
in foundationalism, hence epistemological realism.

How about clause (1)? Everything depends on what we take to con-
situte "the essential character of the plain". Clarke seems to think that,

for the sceptic, the step outside the plain involves a step outside "non-semantical practice." Thus:

> To philosophise, to step outside the circle of the plain, is to step outside the nonsemantical practice, then, speaking simple English, ask, affirm, assess, but, as a consequence, in unrestricted, untrammeled fashion. The peculiarly philosophical character of questions and propositions is their "purity." What we ask or affirm, is what the meanings do *per se*. Our commitments, implications, are dictated solely by meanings.[22]

This suggests that the essential character of plain is its immersion in nonsemantical practices. So, if our conceptual constitution is nonstandard in respect of clause (1) and we cannot prise our terms, meanings intact, from the matrix of our nonsemantical practices, we will not be able to philosophize.

I think that in this passage Clarke has caught a hint of the doctrine I call epistemological realism, for he has glimpsed the epistemological realist's idea that content alone is the final arbiter of epistemic status. He even hints at how the sceptic's conception of philosophical inquiry might be appealed to in defence of that idea. The sceptic can agree that, although content alone does not usually determine epistemological status, it does so in the context of pure philosophical inquiry, inquiry wholly free of economic constraints. For the sceptic, the nonsemantical equals the practical equals the epistemically extraneous. Thus, from the purely epistemological standpoint, constraints imposed by content alone are fundamental, just as the epistemological realist claims.

But, bearing in mind the crucial ambiguity in the idea of detachment, what is the purely epistemological standpoint? Even to ask this question is to see that, far from offering a defence of epistemological realism, the sceptic's account of philosophical inquiry presupposes that doctrine from the very outset. The proper contrast for the practical is the purely theoretical. But however purely theoretical, an inquiry will still be subject to whatever methodological necessities determine its direction. On the contextualist view of knowledge and justification, which is the real alternative to epistemological realism, constraints on justification are always determined by aspects of "nonsemantical practice." They are determined by topical, disciplinary and situational considerations that are always external to the content of whatever is to be justified. Abstracting from all "nonsemantical" aspects of practice leaves us only with whatever formal constraints are imposed by our epistemic concepts: e.g. that knowledge requires a "reasonable sufficiency" in the way of evidence. As we saw, this is not the line the sceptic wants to draw. He wants detachment to leave in place important substantive constraints on wordly knowledge. This will happen only if there are fundamental constraints, notably the priority of experiential knowledge over knowledge of the world, imposed by content alone: in other words, given epistemological realism. But the contextualist regards the priority of experience as only a methodological necessity of traditional epistemological inquiry, there being no constraints on knowledge of the world as such.

Once more, we see that the step outside "nonsemantical practice" cannot be equated with merely setting aside practical considerations. It must involve a step outside all directed inquiries, however theoretical. Thus the sceptic must suppose that there is a structure to knowledge of the world as such. But there is no immediate passage from setting aside all economic limitations to revealing such a structure. To put it another way, there is no reason why we should simply concede the sceptic's implicit equation of the purely theoretical with the purely epistemological. Our interests in a given belief may be purely epistemic, in the sense that we care only about whether it is true and what evidence can be brought to bear on it. But, again, there is no straightforward move from a purely epistemic interest in a problem to interest in a purely epistemic problem. There will not be any purely epistemic problems, of the sort the sceptic takes an interest in, unless there are substantive constraints on justification inherent in the very idea of knowledge of the world. We have seen repeatedly what these must be: they lie in the doctrine of the fully objective priority of experiential knowledge.

If epistemological status is never determined by content alone, detachment from all knowledge of the world leaves us nothing purely epistemological to reflect on. I think that, in so far as he hints at suspicion of the idea that we can reflect on "knowledge" in abstraction from everything that has to do with "nonsemantical practice," Clarke comes close to making this argument. But he fails to do so. Losing sight of the sceptic's epistemological preconceptions, Clarke connects the sceptic's vision of philosophy with an odd brand of semantic realism. The sceptic seems to think that "meanings" do things independently of what we mean by our words. Here Clarke is operating in very much the same territory as Cavell and, like Cavell, he ends up going down the wrong critical road. For if the nonsemantical is coextensive with the practical, why should meanings be changed by a simple decision to ignore practical considerations? And there is no reason to suppose that the sceptic's methodological purity consists in his having *no* intentions. But the whole issue of meaning is a red herring. The question is not whether propositions retain their meanings when divorced from "nonsemantical practices" but whether, when so divorced, they continue to impose constraints on justification, even with their meanings intact.

Why does Clarke take the wrong road? The obvious explanation is the continuing attraction of the mirage of definitive refutation. Clarke wants to do more than expose the sceptic's extensive theoretical commitments: he wants to convict him of incoherence or of trying to conceive the inconceivable. For this reason, although Clarke begins by asking the right question – What is the sceptic examining, our most fundamental beliefs or the product of a large piece of philosophizing? – he is not in the end a practitioner of theoretical diagnosis. The realization that our conceptual constitution is not standard is not the basis of his dissatisfaction with the sceptic. Rather it belongs to the *legacy* of scepticism: it is something that we learn by coming to appreciate, quite independently, the ultimate and intuitive incoherence of the sceptic's procedure.

By helping us understand how the sceptic sees things, Clarke makes it hard for us to convince ourselves that we cannot, even for the sake of argument, see things his way. Thus Clarke's difficulties illustrate once more the way that theoretical and therapeutic diagnosis work at cross purposes. Again, I conclude that we should not try to convince ourselves that we do not understand the sceptic. The objection to my argument left hanging at the end of chapter 4 – that in tracing scepticism to epistemological realism I have ignored the crucial role played by philosophical detachment in leading us to scepticism – has been turned aside, if I am right that the sceptic's preferred account of philosophical reflection assumes epistemological realism from the outset. But so far I have argued the point in rather general terms. If I am right, however, particular attempts to explain the essential nature of philosophizing in terms of prescinding from economic constraints should break down in ways that can only be repaired by importing, openly or covertly, foundationalist views. We shall find that they do.


## 5.6   ERROR AND ESTRANGEMENT

It is fatally easy to underestimate the amount of theory required to generate the problem of our knowledge of the external world, or indeed any form of radical scepticism. For example, there seems to be some temptation to think that, once we have taken up the appropriate reflective stance, the simple realization that we are prone to error is enough to set us on the road to radical doubt. This idea attracts both Cavell and McGinn in their efforts to capture the intuitiveness of the sceptic's starting point.

Recall Cavell's experience of detachment from the world, an experience that supposedly comes naturally to any creature complicated enough to possess language. The thought that possessing language induces a kind of estrangement from the world, that an ability to judge the world under-

mines the capacity for innocent, unselfconscious involvement, is both ancient and persistent. But there is no immediate reason to connect whatever
possibilities of estrangement are inherent in the possession of language
with susceptibility to radical scepticism. It may be, as Plato implies in the
*Phaedo*, that because of our capacity for judging the world, we are always
uncomfortably, if dimly, aware of the contingency and imperfection of
things and so, in that way, never quite at home. But there is no obvious
connection between this kind of estrangement from the world and the
threat of losing it altogether. Philosophical *unheimlichkeit* cannot be equated
with imprisonment in the circle of one's own ideas.

We need a more specific experience: as Cavell says, "an experience that
one may well know *nothing* about the real world." But, quite properly, this
only prompts him to ask "What kind of an experience is that? How or
when does it emerge?"[23] The answer he suggests is that it emerges out of
*particularly striking* experiences of error. It arises "as a response to your
having been wrong, in some obvious way, about something you are 'totally
convinced' or 'assured' of." Thus he reports having been left a telephone
message with the name of a hotel a friend was staying at, a telephone
number and a request to call. The way the note was written made it *obvious*
that the number was the number of the hotel though in fact, as subsequent
confusions eventually made clear, it wasn't. Familiar cases like this, Cavell
notes, "resemble the experience and conclusions of traditional epistemology." As we go over them, we come to see what we originally took
to be obvious truths as mere assumptions or as the conclusions of risky
inferences. A striking experience of error can seem to contain "a moral
about knowledge as a whole."[24]

But what moral? As Cavell concedes, not the one we are looking for.
Familiar experiences of error may contain "the moral that we human
beings are fallible" but, no matter how striking, not that "we suffer metaphysical ineptitude . . . , that we may know nothing about the real world."
Responses to our fallibility may include "probabilistic theories of confirmation" but not "radical or metaphysical skepticism, the idea that there
is no real confirmation at all."[25]

This is surely correct. The mere fact of error will not bridge the gap
between an initial decision to assume a reflective stance and the emergence of the problem of our knowledge of the external world, if that stance
involves no more than a setting aside of practical concerns and a consequent willingness to consider the possible falsity of even the most deeply
entrenched beliefs. As we have already noted, Descartes introduces the
dreaming problem precisely because the mere fact of perceptual error,
does not motivate a sufficiently radical doubt. The fact of perceptual error
suggests only that observational beliefs may have to be corrected in the
light of further knowledge about the world. It does not, by itself, so much

as hint at a radical estrangement from external reality. Hume puts the point succinctly. Familiar cases of perceptual error:

> are only sufficient to prove, that the senses alone are not to be im-
> plicitly depended on; but that we must correct their evidence by
> reason, and by considerations, derived from the nature of the me-
> dium, the distance of the object, and the disposition of the organ,
> in order to render them, within their sphere, the proper criteria of
> truth and falsehood.[26]

Cavell is therefore right: the sense of a possible loss of the world which prompts traditional epistemological inquiry demands "an experience of a different order."

What is this? According to Cavell, it is: "an experience that philos-ophers have characterised . . . as one of realizing that my sensations may not be of the world I take them to be of at all, or that I can only know how objects appear (to us) to be, never what they are."[27]

But now we are back on familiar territory. Cavell's originating experi-ence turns out to embody the entire case for scepticism, in the form of the standard transition from the neutrality of experience to the impossibility of wordly knowledge. Cavell seems not even to see that there is a tran-sition, his use of "or" implying that to admit the bare logical possibility that his sensations are not "of the world" is more or less equivalent to admitting that he may lack all worldly knowledge. But as I have argued at length, the inference from the neutrality of experience to scepticism depends on assuming the priority of experiential knowledge over knowl-edge of the world. Since there is no reason at all to concede that this epis-temological doctrine *forces* itself on any creature "complicated enough to possess language," there is no reason to concede that the experience Cavell describes is in any way natural. On the contrary, Cavell's own description reveals how much it is a reflection of one's having internalized a con-tentious theoretical view. Ironically, Cavell's search for an experience of a different order from any ordinary experience of error provides another instance of an unnoticed assumption and an unrecognized inference.

We find a similar problem in McGinn's account of how the decision to adopt a reflective attitude towards "our practice of making and accepting knowledge claims" seems to lead the epistemologist naturally to the ques-tion of "whether any among all his current beliefs can be regarded as pro-viding sure and genuine knowledge of reality." This question is supposedly prompted by his immediate realization that he has sometimes "through carelessness or oversight, or through misleading evidence, fallen into error about what is the case."[28] Again, this will not do: there is nothing in the fact of our fallibility to suggest radical scepticism. But even if there were, it would be a further step to a specific problem about our knowledge of the external world.

The attempt to link the problem of the external world with the fact of error fails in exactly the same way as the attempt to link it with the problem of the regress of justification. As we saw, taken in full generality, the regress applies to any attempt to claim knowledge about any fact whatsoever: "internal" or "external," "subjective" or "objective," it doesn't matter. Of course, regress considerations take on a different significance once certain kinds of knowledge are exempted from the scope of the argument. But this is just another way of bringing out how the ancient regress argument is not itself a sufficient basis for Cartesian scepticism. The same goes for the equally ancient argument from error. The liability to error that the sceptic starts from operates initially without restriction. Examples of error might include "I told the doctor it was a ringing sensation, but I now think that 'buzzing' would have been more accurate" or "I thought I was angry at John, but on reflection I see that I was embarrassed at my own behaviour" just as readily as "The tower looked round but was really square" or any other examples of what Hume calls "the trite topics, employed by sceptics in all ages, against the evidence of sense."[29] If there were an argument for radical scepticism in the mere fact of error, it would be for radical scepticism in a completely unrestricted form. In McGinn's version of the argument, the slide to the problem of our knowledge of the external world is accomplished entirely by the use of "reality," which straddles reality as whatever is the case and reality as the world "without the mind."

There is a further detail that deserves notice: the reference to "our practice" (singular) of making and accepting knowledge claims. If a contextualist view of justification is even an option, to talk this way is to take a lot for granted. It is to assume that "our knowledge claims" picks out a set of items with genuine theoretical integrity. The sceptic's attempt to reflect on our knowledge of the world would seem much more problematic if we took seriously the thought that knowledge claims are subject to a bewildering variety of contextual constraints, many of which depend on the way the world is. We might be left with no alternative to what Hume calls the "tedious, lingering method" and Descartes the "endless undertaking" of investigating much more specific examples of claims to knowledge, none of which will stand as representative of "our knowledge of the world." At no point in this endless undertaking will we be in a position to survey our knowledge of the world *as a whole*.

All this confirms my assessment of the sceptic's preferred account of philosophical reflection. A simple resolution to reflect on "our knowledge of the world" does not guarantee the existence of an appropriate object for reflective understanding. In this connection, the reminder that philosophical reflection is intended to be "purely theoretical" is beside the point. The question at issue is not the theoretical purity of the traditional epistemological project but its special kind of generality, which cannot, it now turns out, be generated from its purity alone. The traditional project takes it for granted that we can reflect on "how we come to have knowledge of the world" in abstraction from anything having to do with the world itself. The idea of what I called the "autonomy" of the epistemological is built into the very idea of reflecting on our knowledge of the world as such. The question of whether this is a plausible, never mind inevitable, way of thinking about epistemological matters is not even addressed by an account of philosophical reflection in terms of withdrawal from practical concerns.

## 5.7 PRACTICAL KNOWLEDGE AND RADICAL DOUBT

There is a compelling reason for being dissatisfied with the explanation of philosophical reflection in terms of detachment from practical concerns and limitations: the rationale it provides for the introduction of out of the way possibilities ties them far too closely to the quest for certainty. So closely, in fact, as to sever their connection with the threat of radical scepticism.

Consider the following anti-sceptical argument, discussed by Stroud. Someone makes the startling announcement that there are no physicians in New York. This claim seems to contradict what we all believe: that there are thousands. However, it turns out that by "physician" he means "anyone with a medical degree who can cure any conceivable illness in less than two minutes." Once this becomes clear, the announcement poses no threat to our original belief. The implied standard for being a physician is absurdly strict and in any case wildly different from our normal standard. But now compare the claim about the doctors with sceptical claims. We do not ordinarily insist that a person consider, much less that he rule out, bizarre sceptical hypotheses in order to know commonplace facts about the world. So isn't the epistemological sceptic like our imagined medical sceptic? Doesn't his conclusion depend on a similarly unreasonable redefinition of an ordinary concept? Stroud agrees that, if it did, "it would pose no threat to our everyday knowledge and beliefs." Our disquiet would be due to "nothing but illusion."[30]

The line of thought we are considering is that it is not unreasonable to consider sceptical hypotheses in the context of philosophical reflection. This is because, when we reflect philosophically, we step back from all practical concerns. But the trouble with this is that it tends to reinforce rather than to undermine the analogy between the philosophical sceptic's conclusion and the claim about the physicians. Suppose the medical sceptic said:

> Of course my standard for being a physician would be inappropriate if someone were to ask me right now whether he could obtain medical treatment in New York. Since current medical knowledge is far from perfect; since we are only starting to develop advanced diagnostic techniques; since computer-based analysis of symptomatic data is in its infancy; since many therapies are slow-acting and not all that effective, I will have to send him to one of our imperfect practitioners, whom I will happily call "a physician." Still, since medical technologies are susceptible of indefinite improvement, the shortcomings of current "physicians" reflect mere practical limitations. I was asking what would be a reasonable standard for being a physician, supposing all practical concerns to have been set aside. And it seems to me that being able to cure any conceivable illness in two minutes would be about right.

Setting all practicalities aside allows the medical "sceptic" to imagine what a "real physician" ought to be able to do, which may be very different from what, in present circumstances, it is practically reasonable to expect. (As Socrates said to Thrasymachus, a "doctor" isn't really being a doctor unless he is administering successful treatment.) Isn't the epistemological sceptic in the same business? Setting practicalities aside allows him to wonder whether we really have knowledge about the world, as opposed to knowledge for all practical purposes. Why isn't his negative conclusion as harmless as that of the medical "sceptic"? I think the answer can only be that "strictness," of the kind that varies with practical exigencies, was never the issue. Both the objection and the reply are beside the point. This entails that there must be something wrong with an account of philosophical detachment that proceeds purely in terms of abstraction from practicalities.

How does the 'strictness" of epistemological standards vary with practical concerns and limitations? One way is this: practical exigencies affect the *probability-threshold* that an error possibility must surpass for it to be reasonable to take it into account. If it would take a lot of time and effort to eliminate a given possibility, and if there is a premium on speedy decision-making, it will be reasonable to take it into account only when there is a significant likelihood of (and a significant cost attached to) our going wrong in the envisaged way. For practical purposes, therefore, we can justifiably ignore unlikely sources of error. But notice that, whether or not this compromises our claim to knowledge, it does not compromise our claim to justified belief (and not just in the sense of justified believing). If we ignore unlikely possibilities of error, then the decision we come to will not be certainly correct. But it may well be much more likely to be correct than not. So although prescinding from practical considerations may tie knowledge more closely to certainty, it will not take us a step towards radical scepticism, which rejects even the possibility of justified belief.

This is exactly the moral suggested by a closer look at the case of the aircraft spotters. The spotters never "know" that an aircraft is of type A because their identification procedure does not discriminate between aircraft of type A and those of type X. But type A planes are obsolete and rare. It is because of their rarity that, for practical purposes, it is not necessary to be able to recognize them. Still, the identification procedure, even if it does not yield knowledge, is able to yield justified true belief. To say that the spotters do not really know what they say they know is simply to say that they do not *know for certain*. So although the case of the spotters illustrates how epistemic standards interact with practicalities, it does so precisely because it does *not* provide an analogy for radical scepticism.[31]

This ties in with a criticism that has been made of Stroud's claim that it can be correct, in ordinary circumstances, to *say* that we know things that we might, on reflection, decide that we do not know after all. As we saw, Stroud takes this claim to neutralize certain ordinary language objections to scepticism. Austin asserts that we do ordinarily know various things, even though sceptical hypotheses never enter our heads, and he concludes from this that such hypotheses are not normally relevant to questions about knowledge. Stroud replies that Austin's examples only show that it is ordinarily alright to *say* that one knows this and that, which does not mean that one does know it. The trouble is, it is not ordinarily alright to say that one knows something after one has come to realize that one has no reason whatsoever for asserting it. It is not so easy to reconcile Austin's linguistic evidence with an acknowledgment of the truth of *radical* scepticism.

Notice that there is no problem applying Stroud's distinction to the spotters. But this is precisely because the example is not an analogy for radical scepticism. The reason why it is alright for a spotter to say that he knows a type A plane is approaching is because he has very good grounds for saying it, even if they are not absolutely conclusive. If the plane takes no hostile action, then it was most likely not a type A; and if it wasn't a type A, obviously he didn't know that it was. Still, it was reasonable, even correct, for him to say that he did. If he had said he was unsure, this would have been taken to imply that he had not been able to match the approaching plane with a particular checklist of features, which was not so.

So he was right to say that he knew even though, as things turned out, he didn't.

It can be alright for me to say that I know something when, although I have no good grounds for what I believe, I do not know this: for example, when my evidence is defective in ways that I could not possibly have been expected to foresee. But it is not alright for me to continue to claim knowledge after this has been pointed out to me. Again, the case of the spotters is different. It remains alright for them to claim knowledge even after they have been made aware of the limitations of their training. This is because they retain, and know that they retain, the capacity for justified belief. It is significant, then, that Stroud illustrates the distinction between knowing and having been correct to claim knowledge with an example which, like the case of the spotters, does not involve an absence of justification. The case he imagines is one in which a fellow guest asks me whether a mutual friend will be coming to the party. Having just spoken to him, knowing his trustworthiness, and being aware of his strong interest in attending, I reply that he will. Unfortunately, on his way over he meets with an utterly unforseeable accident, as a result of which I am reproached with not having known what I said I knew. We can agree with Stroud that the reproach is both true and completely outrageous. I didn't know, as things turned out, but I was entirely correct to claim that I did. However, this was because I had extremely good evidence that my friend would arrive. My knowledge failed only because my claim turned out be false, not because it was never justified.[32] The example gives no reason to think that it is alright to say that we know things about the world even after we have become aware of the truth of scepticism. If Austin's intuitions are sound, scepticism is false. They cannot be reconciled.

The sceptic's two-factor view of justification is no help here. We might think that the reason it would be alright to continue to claim knowledge is that we would retain knowledge for all practical purposes, even if we became aware that we lacked knowledge properly so-called. It is true, as we have seen, that practical factors can affect epistemic standards, tightening or loosening them as the case may be. But nothing in this conception of justification as having both an economic and an epistemic dimension suggests that practical justification can survive the *complete elimination* of epistemic support. Even knowledge for all practical purposes requires justified belief. Or at least, it does if justified believing depends on justified belief, as the sceptic requires.[33] Anyway, as we shall soon see, even allowing for the possibility of justified believing in the absence of justified belief, it would be wrong to assimilate such believing to knowing for all *practical* purposes.

We can bring out the defect in the analogy of the spotters by making a small change in it. Suppose that type A and type X aircraft fly over with equal frequency: we would not then say that a spotter ever *knew* that an aircraft was of type A, even for practical purposes. We would say rather that the spotters are trained to identify *possible* hostile intruders. For practical purposes, we might want a spotter to raise the alarm even when hostile aircraft are far *less* likely to appear than transport or reconnaissance planes. But a spotter would not know that a hostile plane was approaching. Nor would it be alright for him to *say* that he did. He would only know, and it would only be permissible for him to claim, that he had identified a possible intruder.

We must conclude that whatever makes it ordinarily permissible to say that we know various things about the world, even though we take no heed of sceptical hypotheses, it is not that such hypotheses are *unlikely* to be true. Nor, therefore, is it because our interests are ordinarily highly practical. Given my ordinary view of the world, it is not *unlikely* that I am a brain in a vat but *definitely false*. My ordinary way of looking at things entails that I am not a brain in a vat: it does not just make it improbable. It is therefore beside the point to argue that, when we suspend interest in practical concerns, it becomes reasonable to consider improbable hypotheses, for sceptical hypotheses, when relevant at all, are not improbable.

What is necessary before it becomes reasonable to consider sceptical hypotheses, then, is not detachment in the first, innocuous sense of suspension of interest in practicalities but detachment in the second, problematic sense of a step outside the ordinary way of looking at things. As I have already argued, a step outside cannot be a step into the void but must be a kind of retreat. It is impossible to see what this could be other than a retreat from beliefs about the world to what we know about our experience of the world. Once we make this retreat, and if we concede that experiential knowledge is generally and objectively prior to knowledge of the world, sceptical hypotheses become very relevant indeed. However, they are no longer unlikely. On the contrary, on the available evidence, they are as likely as anything else. This is why they raise the specter of radical scepticism. But, like the "detachment" that precedes their introduction, they do so only at the cost of introducing a substantial measure of epistemological doctrine.

We can make the same point by asking how the case of the spotters would have to be modified in order to make it truly analoguous to our epistemic situation as the radical sceptic conceives it. What we must do is insulate the spotters from any knowledge of the relative frequencies with which different types of aircraft fly over. Whereas Clarke's spotters are pilots flying hither and thither, we must imagine them confined to an observation post, using instruments perhaps, but at any rate given no feedback on their success rate. They must never be told and never observe whether an aircraft they have identified as hostile takes hostile action.

Suppose, for simplicity, that there are only two types of aircraft, type A and type X, and that the information that comes in to the spotters does not discriminate between them. In the imagined situation, the spotters can never have the slightest reason to think that a particular type of plane is approaching. Should they become aware of their position, the only reasonable attitude for them to take towards their "knowledge" of aircraft would be radical scepticism.

Notice, however, what we have done to make the analogy work. We have placed the spotters under a permanent epistemic limitation. Epistemologically speaking, we have cut their world in two. We have imposed an unbridgeable gulf between what they can detect from their observation post and what they would like to know about the outside world. By so doing, and only by so doing, we imagine them placed in a situation in which they cannot have the slightest reason, with respect to a certain body of possible claims, for accepting one rather than another. Equally, only if a generalized form of such an epistemic gulf is intrinsic to the human condition will there be a threat of radical scepticism with respect to our knowledge of the world. But the recognition of such a gulf is not forced on us simply by a willingness to look beyond the practical concerns of everyday life.

What we have come back to, yet again, is the ambiguity in the idea of detachment. Sticking with detachment as detachment from practical considerations gave us an interest in higher than normal standards of certainty but offered no route to radical scepticism. To get to radical scepticism, we needed detachment as respect for the totality condition on an explanation of knowledge of the world, for only this kind of detachment, by imposing a final order of epistemological priority, threatens to cut us off from the knowledge we want.

The example of the spotters thus reveals more about the sceptic's outlook than those who think of sceptical doubts as natural doubts can readily admit. On the one hand, it illustrates the sceptical epistemologist's conception of the demands on justification imposed by our ordinary concept of knowledge, in conjunction with certain aspects of the content of what we claim to know, as like an immeasurably powerful brake on rational belief. The practical concerns that inform everyday life are then seen as an auxiliary mechanism acting as a restraint on this brake and keeping it from being applied with full force. Take it away and the machine grinds to a halt. But this analogy, too, has its dangers. Abstracting from all ordinary constraints on the assessment of justifications does more than remove practical limitations: it involves removing the fixed points whose fixity (in context) gives specific inquiries their particular directions. For all that has been shown, then, to detach is not so much to apply a brake as to disconnect crucial linkages, leaving us with no machine at all, hence nothing to even try to understand. The sceptic heads off this possibility by postulating certain fundamental and ubiquitous constraints on justification. These constraints define our epistemic position: they are the linkages that remain when all others have been disconnected. Though we can disconnect auxiliary devices added for special purposes, the machine's innermost, essential workings can never be dismantled, so by dismantling whatever can be dismantled, we do no more than expose them to view. This ensures that when we take the step of radical detachment, setting aside not just practical concerns but all our beliefs about the world, there is still something relevant to knowledge for us to reflect on. This is demanded by the traditional epistemological project, but I see no reason to concede that it is implicit in either common sense or the human condition.

## 5.8  EPISTEMOLOGY AS PURE INQUIRY

The fatal ambiguity in the idea of detachment comes to the surface very clearly in Bernard Williams's account of Descartes's systematic doubt and its connection with what Williams calls Descartes's "project of pure enquiry." An examination of the idea of pure inquiry will reinforce the conclusion that the explanation of philosophical detachment in terms of a bracketing of practical concerns will not defend the thought that sceptical doubts are natural doubts. But Williams adds to the case for scepticism something that deserves separate consideration.

In the project of pure inquiry, Descartes's first rule of method, to "reject all merely probable knowledge, and only to trust to what is perfectly known and cannot be doubted," plays "a distinct and formative role." This already hints at a connection with scepticism. Williams hopes to make the connection by arguing that the notion of "pure enquiry" can explain how the search for truth can (reasonably) turn into the search for certainty, hence the reasonableness of the systematic doubt. But he also thinks that the systematic doubt provides the basis for a critique of all knowledge and so underwrites "a distinctively philosophical enquiry."[34] But as I have been arguing, the difficulty is to see the connection between the two.

The object of pure enquiry is "the truth and nothing but the truth."[35] In the first instance, this means that such enquiry is carried on in abstraction from all economic constraints, all limitations on time and resources. In particular, it takes no account of pressures on decision-making that result from practical needs and purposes. Descartes's "Doubt," his "instrument of reflective enquiry": "is not to be brought into practical matters: equally, no values drawn from those matters affect the enquiry.... [No] questions about what, in a general economic sense, is worth enquiring into or checking are, within the confines of the exercise, to count."[36] In daily life, "investment of effort into enquiry turns importantly on what is at stake."[37] Pure enquiry, by contrast, because it is completely non-instrumental, can reasonably be cost-indifferent. This is one obvious sense of aiming at "nothing but the truth." "Pure" enquiry does not aim at discovering truths in order to advance further aims. Truth itself is its sole aim.

When conducting such an investigation, Williams argues, there is no reason not to aim at basing one's researches on a method that is error-proof, a method that will exclude even the most far-fetched (hence normally unheeded) possibilities. This is how, in the context of pure inquiry, the search for truth turns into the quest for certainty. It does so because "the pursuit of certainty is the only possible road for the *pure* search for truth, the project of improving the truth ratio which is not constrained by any other limitations at all."[38] Systematic doubt, as a means for uncovering certainties, becomes the only proper basis for one's method.

This is all familiar enough and, in view of previous arguments, beside the point. What we must note, however, is how the idea of pure enquiry is starting to evolve. Originally, its purity consisted in its being utterly non-instrumental and consequently cost-indifferent. But now we are told that the aim of improving the truth ratio is not to be constrained by "any other limitations at all." What does this mean?

The pressure on the notion of pure inquiry to evolve comes from the thought that the method of doubt provides the basis for a *distinctively philosophical* project. At first, there seems to be no reason why this should be so. No doubt prescinding from practical constraints makes it reasonable to insist on a higher degree of certainty than would otherwise be proper: but why should it lead to a special and distinctive kind of investigation? There is no obvious connection between ignoring practical limitations and opening up a new subject, the "critique of all knowledge."

This point, already argued for in an abstract way, deserves elaboration. Consider, for example, experiments in physics. These never determine the values of the quantities we are interested in with absolute precision and accuracy. Moreover, the scope for improvement is subject to all sorts of practical and economic constraints: the sensitivity of currently available measuring instruments, the cost of running the experiments, the time, labour and money that would be required to develop new techniques, competition from other research projects, and so on. Perhaps if our resources were infinite, we could insist on a degree of precision and accuracy that would be wildly unreasonable in our actual circumstances. But would the project of improving our experimental techniques, in the interest of greater certainty, require us to worry about whether we are brains in vats? Not obviously. The cost of concerning ourselves with error possibilities that have no specific connection with any particular form of inquiry would not be measured in money or effort, for the cost would be suspending any interest in particular experiments. This is a different kind of cost altogether.

These considerations show that a change in the focus of inquiry cannot be equated with our interests having become less practical. An investigation can be of purely theoretical concern without having the slightest connection with the critique of all knowledge. We may be interested in getting precise values for certain physical quantities simply to test a cosmological hypothesis that has no instrumental significance whatsoever. We can just be *curious* about this or that historical episode: we do not have to be always looking for lessons. But since an interest in truth for its own sake is available to physicists and historians, as much as to philosophers, it follows that an explanation of pure inquiry *simply* in terms of non-instrumentality and cost-indifference will not explain how taking up the stance of the pure inquirer involves us in a new, distinctively philosophical project. This means that not being constrained by "any other limitations at all" has to go far beyond being freed from economic constraints. Since, within the special disciplines, there is indefinite scope for seeking out methods that "improve the truth-ratio," detachment from practical limitations may lead only to ultra-cautious disciplinary inquiry.[39] The detachment required by "the critique of all knowledge" is utterly distinct and amounts to a step outside all particular disciplines. The "limitations" that have to be lifted must include all the "hinge" propositions which, by lying apart from the route traveled by inquiry, give different forms of investigation their characteristic directions. This will indeed change the direction of inquiry. But it will involve more than making one's project purely theoretical.

The point applies beyond the special disciplines. Even if we are only concerned with our ordinary commonsense view of the world (supposing for the moment that we have *an* ordinary view), there is indefinite scope for taking an interest in matters that are less and less practical without ever stepping outside our ordinary view. The step outside our ordinary view is therefore one to be taken in addition to the step outside practical constraints. So we return to the question: suppose we unfix all the methodological necessities of the special sciences; and suppose we prescind from all the contextual constraints that seem to govern ordinary knowledge claims; is there any form of inquiry still open to us?

Williams sometimes seems to suggest that there is. Pure inquiry, it seems, is to be entirely presuppositionless. The pure inquirer searches for truth "from the very beginning," i.e. without taking anything at all for granted, certainly not any of the characteristic presuppositions of the special sciences. But how does one simply search for truth, without searching for an answer to any particular question? Williams considers an imaginary pure inquirer who wants "the truth on certain questions," missing the point that this desire has to lapse, or have its satisfaction indefinitely postponed, once radical doubt becomes the order of the day. A specific question cannot even be asked, much less answered, without exempting various things, temporarily or permanently, from doubt.

Since not even the most impractical inquirer can afford to be utterly directionless, no form of inquiry can be completely free of presuppositions. The Cartesian project is no exception. It is presuppositionless only in the sense of taking nothing for granted about the world. It must, therefore, be committed to some version of epistemological realism. Descartes assumes from the outset that there is an objective "order of reasons" underlying and cutting across ordinary subject-matter divisions, an autonomous epistemological structure that systematic doubt is supposed to bring to light. If there is no such structure, loosening the hinges of all topical investigations will leave nothing to investigate. But if there is, loosening them will offer a way into a distinctive and in some ways more fundamental kind of investigation, just as Williams says.

We see, then, that the original contrast between pure (= purely theoretical) and practical (= instrumental) inquiry undergoes a radical and essential transformation. Though "practical" starts out meaning "instrumental" it ends up meaning "directed towards the world *as opposed to* our knowledge of the world"; and though "pure" starts out meaning "not applied" it ends up meaning "presupposing no worldly facts." In this way, pure inquiry becomes inquiry into knowledge as such, rather than the knowledge we have on some particular topic or can acquire in certain circumstances. "Practical versus pure" comes to mean "worldly versus epistemological." But "theoretical versus practical" cannot be equated with "epistemological versus worldly." Not merely are the contrasts not the same, it is moot whether the second is a genuine *contrast* at all.

If, as I have argued repeatedly, what can and cannot be questioned is interest-relative, the exclusion of sceptical doubts from the concerns of common life is seriously misrepresented by assimilating it to matters of practicality. It is the characteristic focus or direction of scientific and historical investigations, as also of everyday inquiries, that requires them to tolerate some questions but not others. However, *any* form of inquiry is subject to this constraint: it need be no more "practical," in any normal sense, than the most *recherché* subject in philosophy. Determining which questions are relevant and which irrelevant is not a matter of practicality but of methodology.

Certainly, practical interests can force us to exempt certain propositions from doubt, but *simply because they are interests, not because they are practical*. In so far as practical pursuits force our inquiries to take certain directions, they require us to exempt from questioning propositions whose standing fast constitutes forms of inquiry with those directions. But, as I have said, pursuits that are in no ordinary sense "practical" do exactly the same. This is why the idea of "purity" or detachment is constrained to evolve. The purely negative account of detachment, in terms of the exclusion of economic concerns, determines no direction of inquiry whatsoever. The sceptic must suppose both that certain theoretical constraints remain, when practical interests have been set aside, *and* that these constraints presuppose nothing in the way of worldly knowledge.

I do not want to give a misleading impression. Williams himself makes it clear that the passage from assuming the stance of the pure inquirer to Cartesian doubt in its final, radical form is far from completely smooth. True, he continues to insist that the idea of pure inquiry as "the undertaking of someone setting aside all externalities or contingent limitations on the pursuit of truth . . . is itself enough to generate the doubt."[40] But he also argues that, at a crucial juncture, the radicalization of the doubt depends on supplementing the abstract, purely methodological idea of pure inquiry with definite philosophical views about knowledge. These are not, in his view, gratuitous assumptions, for they reflect something in our concept of knowledge "which offers a standing invitation to scepticism."[41] Williams is very much at one with those who think of sceptical doubts as natural doubts.

The problematic transition is from "distributive" to "collective" doubt, from "the universal possibility of illusion to the possibility of universal illusion."[42] Williams connects this move with the introduction of the Evil Deceiver who ensures that nothing in the world is as it appears to be, if there is any "world" at all. Williams regards this full-blown sceptical hypothesis as quite distinct from the other error-possibilities Descartes considers: not only ordinary perceptual illusion but dreaming too. These cases, he thinks, all involve "the use of some perceptions to correct others," so that "while we might be able to say, consistently with that, that we were not absolutely sure at any given moment that the present perception was veridical, we could not consistently say that no perceptions were."[43] The threat of universal illusion must depend on entirely new considerations.

We have returned to a topic we have already touched on: the failure of the argument from error to threaten us with a total loss of the world. This threat, as we saw in connection with Cavell, depends on the thought that our "sensations" may not be "of the world." Williams makes the same point. What makes the hypothesis of the Deceiver so threatening is "a certain picture of what veridical perception consists in." This picture, "the causal conception of perception," is "built into the hyperbolical doubt." According to the causal conception, "if I have veridical perceptions, then I have experiences which are caused by things outside me." So if the proposition that there are things outside oneself that cause one's experiences is doubtful, all perceptual judgments are doubtful, not "piecemeal" but "all at once."[44] The transition from distributive to collective doubt is accomplished.

I have already argued at length that this conception of "the senses" involves more than a causal story: it involves the crucial epistemological doctrine of the priority of experiential knowledge over knowledge of the world. Take away that doctrine and there will be no way to make the transition Williams is trying to explain. So, once more, we return to an illustration of the dependence of Cartesian doubt on foundationalist ideas. However, although Williams's account of the transition invites this diagnosis, an interesting feature of his view is that he expresses doubts about whether the transition really needs to be made. This is the new element in the case for scepticism that I alluded to above. There is a way, he thinks, in which the distributive doubt is quite sceptical enough. This suggests that there may be more in the argument from error than I have so far allowed. Indeed, if the distributive doubt is as radical as the collective, yet less theoretically loaded, there is a threat to my strategy of approaching scepticism by way of a diagnosis of the theoretical presuppositions of reflecting on our knowledge of the world *as a whole*.

Williams makes the argument by way of an analogy. Two men are in a forest in which there are various species of fungi. One believes that all are poisonous, the other that only some are but that he cannot tell which. However, both will avoid eating mushrooms. By parity of reasoning, when it comes to suspension of judgment, a distributive doubt is as effective as a collective doubt. I do not have to suppose that all my beliefs may be false in order to practice universal doubt. It is enough that any may be and that I have no way of telling which are.

The fungus analogy is also meant to illustrate "the central characteristic of Pure Enquiry," its insistence on applying epistemic standards in abstraction from all economic considerations.[45] If one were starving and there were nothing else to eat, it would not be so obviously reasonable to avoid eating the fungi: one might prefer the risk of poisoning to certain starvation. Similarly with beliefs: in a practical context, one would not prefer having no beliefs to risking having some false ones. But under conditions of pure inquiry one would. Under these conditions, the distributive and collective doubt enjoin the same course of action.

Our experience with the spotters should teach us to be wary of thinly described analogies. And I think that this analogy too, on closer examination, is more problematic than it first seems. For instance, what does it mean to say that the second man "cannot tell" which mushrooms are poisonous and which not? That he cannot tell at a glance? Or why does the first man think that *all* the mushrooms in the forest may be poisonous? It is not easy to answer such questions *while preserving the analogy with pure inquiry*. Pure inquirers, we may recall, are supposed to be freed from all practical and economic constraints. So what is to stop the would-be fungus eaters collecting all the mushrooms in the forest and sending them to a laboratory for analysis? This is to come back to the weakness of the argument from error. Perhaps the sort of superficial examination of the fungi that can be conducted in the forest will not determine which are poisonous. But errors that depend on recognizable contingencies do not suggest any general epistemological predicament. If this is how we imagine the fungus eaters, they cannot even get to an unqualified form of the "distributive" doubt, for there will be no doubt about which fungi are poisonous once the lab results are in. The second man will not believe in an unqualified way that he "cannot tell" which fungi are poisonous: he will believe that he cannot tell if he lacks the proper evidence. So we do not have an analogy for the *universal* possibility of illusion, much less the possibility of global error.

Clearly, we are meant to imagine the situation of the forest dwellers rather differently. We are to imagine that the features of the mushrooms that the men are able to recognize do not distinguish poisonous from non-poisonous fungi, we are not meant to think of this as a mere practical limitation that extra resources, such as a portable chemistry set, would remove. Such possibilities are foreign to the analogy. The forest and what can be learned in it are to be imagined as fixing the limits of a world. Thus what can be learned about the fungi in the forest – their shapes, colours, sizes and so on – is all that can ever be learned and, unfortunately, it will not separate the poisonous from the non-poisonous. In other words, if we are to have an analogy even for the universal possibility of illusion, we have to build in the idea of an inescapable epistemic disability, a disability that, within the confines of the analogy, is not to be treated as something that could be overcome by changed circumstances or increased material resources. In fact, what we have to build in is a structural analogue of the priority of experiential knowledge over knowledge of the world. For the foundationalist, though the course of experience does not determine the way the world is, or even that there is a world – experience is all we have to go on. This epistemic disability belongs to the human condition and cannot be overcome by time, money or technical expertise, which is why it remains with us even when all practical and economic constraints are set aside. So too for the forest dwellers, as we must imagine them. The observable features of mushrooms, which are all they will ever have to go on, do not determine which are safe to eat, or even that any are. They are like the radically sceptical spotters, locked in their observation post, epistemically disabled with respect to what they want to know.

The case of the spotters reminds us of Clarke's idea of a "standard" conceptual constitution. Williams's forest dwellers are certainly standard in Clarke's sense. They are "purely ascertaining observers" who apply "concepts" to "items" by noting "marks and features." But this aspect of them is not the source of their sceptical predicament. Their scepticism does not arise simply from their being purely ascertaining observers applying concepts by way of marks and features. Rather, it arises from the particular character of the "marks and features" that they are allowed to "ascertain." The only marks and features that, within the confines of the analogy, they are allowed to make use of have no known relation to the categories into which the mushrooms are to be sorted. Once more, it is not their conceptual constitution per se that lands them in scepticism but the epistemic disability that gets grafted on to it.

The analogy of the forest dwellers was supposed to explain how, under conditions of pure inquiry, the distributive doubt is as powerful as the collective doubt. This was supposed to show that, since Descartes can accomplish pretty much what he wants without the collective doubt, he does not *need* the *malin génie*, and so does not *need* the extra philosophical ideas this supreme source of error implies. However, thought through, the case of the forest dwellers, like the modified case of the spotters, is just the *malin génie* all over again. It is not surprising that the analogy tends to downplay the distinction between the distributive and the collective doubt since, if it contains the materials for the analogue of either, it will generate the analogues of both. But the crucial point is that there is no dispensing with the philosophical ideas that give such thought experiments their sceptical potential. Without the doctrine of a general, context invariant relation of epistemic priority – without a fixed and permanent division of propositions into the immediately verifiable and the inferential – the sort of radical doubt that Descartes aims at remains out of reach. Foundationalism remains the indispensable presupposition of Cartesian scepticism.

## 5.9  THE UNREALITY OF KNOWLEDGE

A recurrent theme of this chapter has been that a concern with certainty is neither necessary nor sufficient for opening oneself to Cartesian scepticism. What is necessary and sufficient is acceptance of foundationalism, which I identify with the doctrine of the priority of experiential knowledge. This is why I think it is absolutely essential to distinguish between the theoretical diagnosis of scepticism that I favor and that which traces it to the quest for certainty. If the distinction is not clearly made, we may think we are objecting to the one when we are only objecting to the other.

This is not just an abstract possibility. For example, I think that Barry Stroud falls into this trap and that this explains, at least in part, why he thinks that the diagnosis of scepticism that traces it to foundationalism is so superficial. Thus:

It is often said that traditional epistemology is generated by nothing more than a misguided "quest for certainty," or a fruitless quest for absolutely secure "foundations" for knowledge, and that once we abandon such a will-o'-the-wisp we will no longer be threatened by scepticism, or even much interested in it. But that diagnosis seems wrong to me – in fact, completely upside down. What some philosophers see as a poorly motivated demand for "foundations" of knowledge looks to me to be the natural consequence of seeking a certain intellectual goal, a certain kind of understanding of human knowledge in general.[46]

What I have argued, however, is not that scepticism arises out of disappointment in the quest for certainty but that the intellectual goal Stroud alludes to is coherent only if there exist fully objective relations of epistemological priority. Issues concerning absolute certainty are beside the point.

Stroud would resist all this because, for him, the idea of the priority of experiential knowledge falls naturally out of the demand for a properly general account of our knowledge of the world. But what we have seen in the last three chapters is that the idea of epistemic priority, as the sceptic needs to understand it, does not fall naturally out of bland methodological considerations. All we can get out of the methodological argument is that a certain kind of epistemological project, such as assessing all our knowledge of the external world, stands or falls with the existence of such kinds of knowledge. This does not establish their existence.

We must be careful, then, with the claim that the sceptic takes the priority of experiential knowledge over knowledge of the world to be "absolute." It is tempting to reply that he does no such thing. Stroud himself makes the point that all we need in order to press traditional epistemological questions are "levels of relative epistemic priority." But all this means is that experiential knowledge does not have to be incorrigible or indubitable to be prior to knowledge of the world. However, the objectivity and context-invariance of the "relative" priority of experiential knowledge cannot be in question. The claim that "relative" relations of priority are sufficient does not and cannot mean such relations hold only relative to a certain philosophical project. If that were so, the outcome of that project would have no implications for the status of knowledge claims in inquiries subject to different constraints. It would not amount to any kind of "assessment" of our knowledge of the world.

Given his identification of foundationalism with the quest for certainty, Stroud can claim very plausibly that we can press traditional epistemological questions without being foundationalists. Given, in addition, an account of philosophical reflection in terms of detachment from practical limitations, he can even go on to argue that, in so far as the traditional epistemologist takes an interest in certainty, this arises as a consequence of the unusual questions he asks, and the unusual context in which he asks them. So, he will conclude, an alleged obsession with certainty does nothing to explain, let alone invalidate, his asking them in the first place. However, I have no need to take issue with this since, in my view too, the quest for certainty explains very little about how the threat of radical scepticism arises out of the traditional epistemological project. My argument is that what matters about the goal of traditional epistemology is that it presupposes epistemological realism. Scepticism arises out of foundationalism in that the kinds of knowledge the sceptic examines depend for their theoretical integrity on the existence of fully objective relations of epistemic priority. The role of the quest for certainty in all this is moot. So while Stroud's argument is correct, as far as it goes, it frees scepticism from dependence on foundationalism only given his identification of foundationalism with commitment to incorrigibility at the level of basic belief. If I am right, this is far too narrow an understanding of foundationalism. It does not go anywhere near the heart of the matter.

If we do not appreciate where the contextualist and the foundationalist part company, we will be bound to feel that anti-foundationalist responses to scepticism are fundamentally unsatisfactory. Again, Stroud puts his finger on the source of the disquiet. He argues, quite correctly I think, that "once we accept the idea of one kind of knowledge being prior to another as an essential ingredient in the kind of philosophical inderstanding we seek, it immediately becomes difficult even to imagine ... anything that could satisfy us." This is because we face an insoluble dilemma. Thus:

> it seems that if we really were in the position the traditional account [of knowledge in a given domain] in terms of epistemic priority describes us as being in, scepticism would be correct. . . . But if we do not see ourselves in the position the traditional account says we are in, we might then manage not to fall into scepticism, but we will not have a satisfactorily general explanation of all our knowledge in a certain domain.[47]

Given the priority of experiential knowledge over knowledge of the world, we cannot explain, in a properly general way, how knowledge of the world is possible, for we cannot lay claim to knowledge of any links between experience and external reality without assuming that we do know something about the world after all. On the other hand, if we reject the doctrine of epistemic priority, we still cannot account for our knowledge of the world in the general way that we aim at in philosophy. For that general way demands that we trace knowledge of the world to something more fundamental, or at any rate different.

We first encountered a version of this dilemma as the claim that, as theorists of knowledge, we are doomed to dissatisfaction. There the argument was that, to see our way beyond scepticism, we must "look more carefully into the very sources of the epistemological quest." In particular, we need to see "how the almost effortlessly natural ways of thinking embodied in that traditional enterprise nevertheless distort or misrepresent, our position, if they do." But would this leave us with a satisfactory general explanation of how human knowledge is possible? It would not. At best, it would reveal, disappointingly, that we cannot have any such thing.

Our discussions of the aircraft spotters and the forest dwellers are relevant here. We saw that, to be analogies for radical scepticism, those examples have to be developed so that the imagined would-be knowers labour under some permanent epistemic disability. They have to be imagined, in other words, to have an unsatisfactory *epistemic position* that neither luck, effort nor ingenuity will enable them to transcend. This is precisely why an anti-foundationalist must find the analogies objectionable. However, his objection is not to the way the analogies portray our epistemic position but to the very idea that we have one. The burden of a contextualist's anti-foundationalism is not, or ought not to be, that the foundationalist distorts or misrepresent our epistemic position. His point is that we do not have "an epistemic position" of the sort that the foundationalist effortlessly attributes to us.

More than a verbal point is at stake here. Putting an anti-foundationalist response to scepticism in terms of our epistemic position's not being what the sceptic says it is invites Stroud's reaction: that our epistemic position is bound to be unsatisfactory, if not because it commits us to scepticism then because it precludes our attaining a reflective philosophical understanding of our knowledge of the world. But if we do not have any particular epistemic position, the absence of understanding that Stroud regrets will not amount to a lack. It *would* amount to a lack *if* we were antecedently committed to foundationalism and hence to the theoretical integrity of Stroud's domains. But it will not do so otherwise. The theoretical integrity of such domains stands or falls with our having an epistemic position, for the basis for classifying beliefs as, say, beliefs about the external world is, I have argued, ultimately epistemic. Such classifications, reflecting ineluctable epistemic facts, are what fix our epistemic position. It follows that lacking a fixed epistemic position is not to be equated with being in an unsatisfactory epistemic position. In abandoning the idea of our epistemic position, we abandon the kinds of knowledge that traditional epistemology demands we understand. It cannot be an objection to this kind of anti-foundationalism that it leaves us unable to understand, in a properly general way, such kinds of knowledge.

The idea that we have a fixed epistemic position, intrinsic to our human

condition, is simply one of the guises of epistemological realism. I have
suggested that one of the sources of this doctrine is an analogy between
epistemic and natural kind terms. Now we might wonder whether the
analogy between knowledge and, say, heat could ever really atract anyone.
In the case of heat, a theory of the nature of heat allows us to disqualify
some things ordinarily called "heat" while retaining a great many more.
The sceptic however has to defend a much more radical departure from
our ordinary classifications: nothing we ordinarily call "knowledge" really
deserves the name. The conditions we would have to meet to really know
the things we usually take ourselves to know are never ordinarily met
or applied, which makes them look much more like an imposition than
a discovery.

Though there is something to this, it is not conclusive if the sceptic's
preferred account of philosophical reflection is accepted uncritically. The
fact is that many "natural" phenomena do not occur naturally. The sort
of currents that permit experiments on electricity did not exist before bat-
teries; there were no samples of pure oxygen before Priestley and Lavoisier,
and so on. Lots of things can be studied in a pure state only under highly
artificial conditions. Perhaps knowledge is like that.

This is why I have pressed the question about the way in which the
conditions under which knowledge is viewed in the course of traditional
epistemological inquiry are controlled or artificial. The suggestion we have
been considering is that for the purposes of philosophical reflection all
normal practical constraints must be set aside. So it is not so much that
the standards we apply when assessing knowledge philosophically are
artificially strict: rather, everyday standards are deliberately relaxed. My
question, however, has been whether there are any topic-invariant, autonomous and fully objective epistemological standards, a question which is
begged by tracing the difference between standards applied in the course
of philosophical reflection and more ordinary standards to considerations
of practicality. There can be investigations, in theoretical physics say,
that are no more practical, in any straightforward sense, than attempts
to command a philosophical view of knowledge in general. This attempt to
trace the distinction between philosophical and other forms of inquiry to
the theoretical–practical distinction is therefore just a smokescreen. What
distinguishes traditional epistemology from other sorts of investigation is its
characteristic direction, the sorts of questions it asks and answers it will
accept. Its direction in turn depends on certain methodological necessities:
notably, as we have seen, certain relations of epistemic priority. The crucial
question, however, is whether these epistemological relations amount to
more than the methodological necessities of a peculiar project, whether
they correspond to constraints that "really" underlie all forms of factual
discourse, even those informed by different, indeed incompatible, meth-

odological necessities. To treat the constraints that give other forms of inquiry *their* characteristic directions as mere "practical" limitations is to misrepresent them. At least, because we cannot do physics or history while entertaining doubts about the existence of the external world or the past, we cannot immediately conclude that these disciplines are bound by *looser* constraints than general epistemology, rather than by constraints that are simply *different*. Strictness, as such, was never the issue. So one important reason why the diagnosis that traces scepticism to the quest for certainty goes badly wrong is that it suggests that it is. It invites the sort of replies that Stroud so forcefully presents.

In calling for us to look more closely at the sources of the traditional epistemological quest, Stroud means in part that we must look beyond the diagnosis that traces scepticism to foundationalism. If we respond to this call, then so far as I can see we will be forced to try to show that traditional philosophical questions about knowledge are not really fully intelligible, most likely by questioning the sceptic's conception of the objectivity of the world. But Stroud has done as much as anyone to bring out the difficulties of convincing ourselves that either the sceptic's questions or his conclusions are unintelligible or incoherent. The fact that we can see so clearly the barriers that stand in the way of a satisfying response is clear evidence that we understand them perfectly well. How can considerations that do not make sense push us so strongly in the direction of scepticism, or anywhere else?

However, I have not denied that the request for a completely general understanding of human knowledge *makes sense*. Or as I would prefer to say, I do not deny that we can make a certain amount of sense of it. We can make sense of it to the extent that we can follow certain crucial analogies: notably, that between epistemological classifications and natural kind terms. If we reject such analogies, thus discounting the idea of natural epistemological kinds and natural epistemological relations, we will not expect to be able to understand knowledge in general, knowledge of the external world, knowledge of other minds, the past, etc., and yet will not be disappointed at our failure. We will not be disappointed because there are *no such things*. There are no such things because these traditional kinds of knowledge lack theoretical integrity. Unless, of course, we are willing to commit ourselves to epistemological realism, which I see no reason to do. This is not scepticism by another name. I do not deny that we often know all sorts of things about "external" objects. The point is that, though the examples are genuine, the kind is artificial.

I want to conclude, then, that it is utterly misguided to *oppose* the demand for a more probing account of the sources of scepticism to the diagnosis that traces it to foundationalism. In trying to make sense of the distinctive generality of traditional epistemological questions, and of the kind of detachment that is required for the pursuit of such questions, we are consistently led back to foundationalism and to the epistemological realism it embodies. Going more deeply into foundationalism, and as a result being led to epistemological realism, proves to be a way of responding to the demand for a deeper diagnosis, not a rejection of it.

# 6

# Scepticism and Objectivity

## 6.1 REALISM AND SCEPTICISM

I have tried to bring out the theoretical commitments embedded in the idea of a detached assessment of the totality of our knowledge of the world. Now I must say something about the fourth element in the traditional or Cartesian examination of knowledge: that the knowledge to be assessed is knowledge of an objective world. Is there something about the very idea of objective knowledge that gives the sceptic the natural doubts he lays claim to?

All philosophers who see scepticism as a deep, intuitive problem are impressed by the importance of our aiming at objective knowledge. Thus though Bernard Williams tries to generate Cartesian doubt from a minimal and purely methodological conception of "pure inquiry," he does not in the end suppose that the idea of pure inquiry gets to the bottom of our concern with scepticism. To really understand scepticism we must recognize that "knowledge does have a problematic character, and does have something in it which offers a standing invitation to scepticism," something that cannot be fully accounted for in terms of "the relations between the concepts knowledge, doubt, certainty and so forth."[1] Since the most that we can expect from the idea of pure inquiry is that it will shed light on such relations, the conclusion must be that this idea does not get to the bottom of scepticism. This is just what I have claimed myself. However, this is where agreement ends.

According to Williams, the deep source of scepticism is to be found not in the quest for certainty but in the quest for objectivity. The standing invitation to scepticism that our concept of knowledge contains arises from:

the very basic thought, that if knowledge is what it claims to be, then it is knowledge of a reality that exists independently of that knowledge, and indeed (except for the special case where the reality known happens itself to be some psychological item) independently of any thought or experience. Knowledge is of what is there *anyway*.[2]

As Williams says, we might suppose this thought, which we can call "the presumption of realism" to be incontestable. The mere claim that the facts of the world are not bound to be what we think they are hardly seems to involve much in the way of sophisticated philosophical doctrine. Nevertheless, the consequences of this apparently incontestable thought can seem to be "both demanding and puzzling."[3]

We find a similar attitude in Nagel, who claims that: "The search for objective knowledge, because of its commitment to a realistic picture, is inescapably subject to skepticism and cannot refute it but must proceed under its shadow." Indeed, "Skepticism . . . is a problem only because of the realist claims of objectivity."[4] But he also speaks of "our natural realism." Not realism but its rejection – idealism – is the philosopher's view *par excellence*. Idealism is not a position that anyone takes naturally: those who adopt it feel driven by argument to do so by "philosophical reasons that seem to rule out the natural picture."[5]

Stroud too finds the presumption of realism deeply implicated in the case for scepticism, suggesting that "the source of the philosophical problem of the external world lies in [our] conception of an objective world or in our desire, expressed in terms of that conception, to gain a certain kind of understanding of our relation to the world." And, like Nagel, he is struck by the apparent naturalness of the realism the sceptic invokes. The relevant conception of an objective world can be explained in terms of "platitudes we would all accept." These platitudes do not involve detailed or sophisticated views about how the world actually is but simply "the general idea of what an objective world or an objective state of affairs would be."[6] We might say: if a conception of the world does not seem to threaten us with scepticism, it is not a *realistic* conception. Or as Colin McGinn has put it: "a prima facie vulnerability to . . . a [sceptical] challenge should be regarded as an adequacy condition which any form of realism should be required to meet."[7] Scepticism does not depend on any particular version of realism but only on what is common to all. As Nagel says, we become vulnerable to scepticism simply by virtue of aspiring to objective knowledge.

The pessimism of Nagel and Stroud about our prospects for coming up with a satisfying response to scepticism is the natural outcome of this combination of views. If realism is so natural and uncontroversial, and if scepticism grows ineluctably out of realism, scepticism too is natural and inevitable. But a tendency to stress the importance of realism is not confined to epistemological pessimists. It is shared by those who think that some form of verificationism is our best hope for an adequate response to scepticism. To suppose that the way to defeat radical scepticism is to link the concept of objective fact with that of evidence is to agree that the concept of objectivity – or if not the concept of objectivity itself, the claim of certain propositions to record objective facts – is the point at which battle must be joined. As we have seen, it is also, not coincidentally, to court the epistemologist's dilemma.

The claim, then, is this: that the concept of knowledge contains a standing invitation to scepticism simply by virtue of embodying the presumption of realism. I find it very difficult to see how this could be true. If the presumption of realism is as innocuous as it is said to be, it should be incapable of generating dramatic epistemological problems, such as scepticism about our knowledge of the external world. Either it is not so innocuous, understood as the sceptic must understand it, or while innocuous enough in itself, it becomes dangerous in conjunction with other, far less natural ideas.

This suspicion is reinforced by one of the most influential contemporary accounts of realism, that of Michael Dummett. Dummett's "preferred characterisation of a dispute between realists and anti-realists" is:

> one which represents it as relating ... to a class of *statements*, which may be, e.g., statements about the physical world, statements about mental events, processes or states, mathematical statements, statements in the past tense, statements in the future tense, etc. This class I shall term . . "the disputed class." Realism I characterise as the belief that statements of the disputed class possess an objective truth-value, independently of our means of knowing: they are true or false in virtue of a reality existing independently of us. The anti-realist opposes to this the view that statements of the disputed class are to be understood only by reference to the sort of thing which we count as evidence for a statement of that class.[8]

The obvious question to ask, of course, is how a disputed class comes to be disputed. Why suppose that a statement is in some special way disputable simply by virtue of being, say, about the physical world? The answer is equally obvious: Dummett's preferred characterization of realism simply builds in the whole panoply of foundationalist ideas: natural epistemological kinds, natural epistemological relations, our epistemic position, etc. There is no other way to make the right sense of phrases like "the sort of thing we count as evidence for a statement of that class" or "our means of knowing" whether statements in a given class are true. From a commonsense point of view, the sort of thing we count as evidence for a statement about the physical world is likely to be another statement about the physical world; not that we have any business assuming there is a genuine "sort" here in the first place. For statements about the physical world, as such, to constitute a disputed class, the sort of thing we count as evidence for them must be placed, in the end, in statements belonging to some other class entirely, a class which must exhibit some definite theoretical – which in this case means epistemological – integrity. Dummett's understanding of realism cannot be detached from a foundationalist conception of relations of epistemological priority.

Given the intimate connection between scepticism and foundationalism, it would not be surprising to find someone influenced by Dummett's account of realism claiming a close connection between realism and scepticism; and, in fact, it is Dummett's influence that explains McGinn's claim that opening the door to a sceptical challenge should be an adequacy condition on any formulation of realism. To follow Dummett in explaining realism in terms of commitment to "recognition transcendent facts" is to build foundationalism into the very definition of realism for, without the foundationalist's radically context-independent relations of epistemological priority, there would be no way of saying offhand whether a statement, simply in virtue of being "about the physical world," pretended to a potentially "recognition transcendent" truth value. But without this, there would be no way of assigning statements to the sort of broad classes McGinn envisages, for the purpose of taking up "realist" or "anti-realist" attitudes towards them. This whole way of thinking about realism simply takes it for granted that statements fall naturally into privileged and problematic classes, statements in the former giving the evidence on the basis of which the truth or falsity of statements in the latter can be "recognized", to whatever extent it is recognizable. So McGinn's confidence that realism opens the door to scepticism reinforces rather than undermines the thought that scepticism is inseparable from foundationalism.

If we are to hold that realism invites scepticism, but that scepticism is an intuitive problem, we shall have to look for a different argument.


## 6.2   TRUTH AND JUSTIFICATION

It is no accident that an account of realism that connects realism in an immediate and obvious way with scepticism should either build contentious epistemological ideas into the very definition of realism or, failing that, set some more platitudinous version of realism in the context of such ideas. The main reason why it is difficult to believe that the presumption of realism, in and of itself, contains a standing invitation to scepticism is that it is hard to see how any epistemological conclusion can be derived from logical or metaphysical premises alone. Suppose we agree that the world is an objective world, that however it may be with good and bad, when it comes to true and false, thinking does *not* make it so: why suppose that we have taken so much as a step in the direction of scepticism? Indeed, why should the mere fact that our world is an objective world suggest *anything* about our capacity for knowledge? Surely, conclusions about what we can and cannot know will depend essentially on further views about our epistemic relation to the world. If the mere fact that there is a world "out there" is to be an obstacle to knowledge, the presumption of realism must be in part an epistemological thought. However, if scepticism is to be an intuitive problem, it needs to be a very elementary one.

The obvious way to explain the core realist intuition – that when it comes to objective fact, thinking does not make it so – is in terms of a certain minimal thesis about the relation of truth to evidence: that our beliefs about the objective world, no matter how well supported evidentially, do not have to be true. This intuition about truth is most often rooted in a sense that objective truth, or truth about the objective world, is in some sense a matter of fitting the facts and not just a matter of living up to our standards of evidence. Thus, in the account of realism discussed earlier, Dummett moves easily between talk of a statement's possessing an "objective truth-value, independently of our means of knowing it" and its being "true or false in virtue of a reality existing independently of us."

It seems natural to many philosophers to conclude that if truth is a non-epistemic property of beliefs or propositions and thus, as Putnam says, a radically non-epistemic notion,[9] then truth about the objective world is always potentially evidence-transcendent. That a proposition is maximally well-supported by evidence never *means that* it is true, evidential support being one thing and truth another. Why, however, should the mere existence of a gap between truth and evidence threaten us with radical scepticism? At its most general, the answer is that realism seems to open the way to scepticism by making it impossible to account for the necessary truth-conduciveness of epistemic justification.

The intuitive thought here is that, whatever else he thinks, a realist must take the truth of a belief to consist in some kind of non-epistemic relation to the world, which we can think of under the general heading of "correspondence"; and the problem for the realist is to explain why this does not play into the sceptic's hands by decoupling justification and truth altogether. If truth is not to be analyzed in epistemic terms, there can be no internal or conceptual connection between attributing justification to a belief and attributing truth. But we cannot establish an empirical connection between the conditions under which we take beliefs to be justified and the conditions under which we take them to be true unless, *per impossible*, we have a way of grasping facts that operates independently of whatever beliefs we happen to find credible. This seems to mean that we cannot establish any connection between justification and truth. Yet it is surely an essential feature of epistemic justification that justifying a belief makes it more likely to be true, which is all that is meant by the claim that epistemic justification is necessarily truth-conducive. So it seems that, once we become realists, we will be unable to show that what we call "justification" really deserves the name.

There are of course trivial connections between justification and truth that any realist is entitled to assert. For example, to justify a claim that p is automatically to justify a claim that "p" is true. This much is guaranteed by the "equivalence thesis," that any proposition p is logically equivalent to the proposition that it is true that p. Or again, if justifying a proposition involves showing that it is likely to be true then, trivially, to justify p is to show that it is likely to be true that p. But such remarks do not point towards any connection between the truth of our beliefs and the specific facts on which their justification supervenes. The problem for the realist is to show how those factors are truth-conducive, given that they are supposed to be – hence why the epistemic property that supervenes on them is justification. The truth-conduciveness of justification sets the realist's problem: it does not solve it.

This problem arises in a particularly dramatic form for philosophers who think that justification is always, in the end, a matter of citing some things we believe in support of others and so, in this mimimal sense, a matter of coherence: for if justification is a matter of relations between beliefs and other beliefs, whereas truth concerns the relations between beliefs and the world, the way certainly seems to be open for the sceptic to challenge us to explain what the one has to do with the other. This is how Davidson sees things. According to Davidson, "truth is correspondence with the way things are," so that "a theory of knowledge that allows that we can know the truth must be a non-relativised, non-internal form of realism." A correct epistemology is one that allows us to be "realists in all departments." We want "objective truth conditions as they key to meaning, a realist view of truth, and . . . knowledge . . . of an objective world independent of our thought or language." The trouble is to explain how we can know that objective truth conditions are satisfied since, Davidson thinks, "this would appear to require a confrontation between what we believe and reality; and the idea of such a confrontation is absurd." But if rejecting the idea of such a confrontation leaves only coherence as the test of truth, how can we respond to the sceptic who asks "Why couldn't all my beliefs hang together and yet be comprehensively false about the actual world?" Only, it seems, by providing "a reason for supposing coherent beliefs are true." We need an argument to show that "coherence yields correspondence."[10]

This problem is important for me to consider and my full response to it will involve both this chapter and the next. One reason why the problem is important is that it seems to depend on so little in the way of epistemological theory. Perhaps it adds something to "the pure idea of realism," but apparently not much: just rejection of the not-very-promising notion of verification by confrontation. But what is even more significant is that, contrary to my claim that scepticism rests on foundationalism, we seem to have here a sceptical problem that arises out of the *rejection* of a traditional foundationalist idea. If we are driven to foundationalism by this problem, then, it must be because we prefer giving up the idea that justification is a matter of coherence to abandoning a realistic understanding of truth. This seems to support the very view I have been most concerned to oppose: that foundationalism emerges as a response to an initial encounter with a deeply intuitive form of scepticism and is not, as I want to claim, a presupposition of sceptical argument from the very beginning.

The position that Davidson stakes out has traditionally been thought untenable, which explains the opposition between foundational theories of *knowledge* and coherence theories of *truth*. At first, it is not clear why there should be a dilemma with an epistemological theory as one horn and a metaphysical or semantic theory as the other. But there is no doubt that one has been perceived. For example, Schlick makes his argument for a foundationalist epistemology turn on his criticism of the coherence theory of *truth*.[11] On the other side, his idealist contemporary, Blanshard, argues for his coherence theory of truth in part by arguing against notions central to foundationalist epistemology, such as Russell's "knowledge by acquaintance."[12] This leads a recent advocate of a coherence theory of knowledge to distance himself from the absolute idealists on the grounds that they "tended at times to conflate (or confuse) coherence theories of *justification* with coherence theories of *truth*."[13] But I am inclined to think that this "conflation" is more a matter of compulsion than confusion. Given a felt need to account for the truth-conduciveness of epistemic justification, we seem to face just the dilemma that seems initially so puzzling: either we explain knowledge in terms that connect directly with correspondence, hence with truth as the realist understands it, or we abandon realism and take truth to be some kind of epistemic notion. If neither strategy works, it will look as if we cannot account for the truth-conduciveness of justification at all and the result will be scepticism. So although we *can* distinguish coherence theories of justification from coherence theories of truth, leaving room for the possibility of adopting one without the other, the traditional thought has been that any attempt to do so will play into the hands of the sceptic.

Traditional foundational theories of knowledge take the first option. They do more than postulate epistemologically basic beliefs, from which the credibility of all other beliefs is supposed ultimately to derive, they offer a distinctive account of how those beliefs come to constitute knowledge. Thus Schlick takes such beliefs to involve a kind of "pointing to reality," so that merely having such a belief ensures or creates a strong logical presumption in favour of its truth. Theories of this kind are usually criticized for their dependence on the idea of verification by confrontation. Certain facts, objects or properties are thought of as simply "given." Beliefs that record them can thus simply be seen to be true. The very way in which we form or understand the propositions involved in basic beliefs ensures that those propositions will be true, or almost certainly true, so that, at the level of basic belief, the gap between believing with justification and believing truly becomes vanishingly small. This seems to Schlick the only way of holding on to the notion of truth as correspondence. If truth is correspondence with reality, it must be possible at some points to grasp this correspondence directly, without inferential or even conceptual mediation.

To reject the idea of verification by confrontation, or so it seems to many philosophers, is to settle for some kind of coherence theory of justification. As we have seen, Davidson is one. He claims:

> What distinguishes a coherence theory is simply the claim that nothing can count as a reason for holding a belief except another belief. Its partisans reject as unintelligible the request for a ground or source of justification of another ilk.[14]

The problem with the idea of verification by confrontation – "comparing" beliefs with reality – is that it seems vulnerable to a fatal dilemma. We need only ask whether or not the "direct" grasping of facts on which such comparison depends is supposed to be a cognitive state with propositional content. If it isn't, it can have no impact on verification. But if it is, all we have been given is another kind of belief.[15] A foundationalist like Schlick may still insist that beliefs of this kind are privileged in that all other beliefs must, in the end, be accommodated to them. But even so, justification remains a matter of accommodating beliefs to other beliefs and thus, it seems, a matter of coherence.

If this is right, we have no way of understanding justification except in terms of coherence, in Davidson's weak sense. But now the pressure is in the other direction. Analysing justification and truth in wholly disparate terms threatens to decouple them entirely: so if we do not explain knowledge and justification in terms that invoke the notion of correspondence, how are we to avoid explaining truth in terms of coherence? As much as anything, this has been the line of thought which, as Nagel says, makes philosophers feel compelled to abandon our natural realism. As Blanshard explains, if one holds that truth is tested for by coherence, but that the nature of truth is to be explained some other way, then:

> one cannot intelligibly hold either that it is tested by coherence or that there is any dependable test at all.... If you place the nature

of truth in one sort or character and its test in something quite different, you are pretty certain, sooner or later, to find the two falling apart. In the end, the only test of truth that is not misleading is the special nature or character that is itself constitutive of truth.[16]

On the other hand, how are we to analyze truth and justification in the same terms without seeming to concede the sceptic's point that knowledge is confined to appearances? Epistemic analyses of truth, because they make how things are depend on how, in certain circumstances, we would think they are, compromise the objectivity of worldly knowledge, which is no longer knowledge of what is there anyway. Once more, we face the epistemologist's dilemma.

Worse still, it is a short step from a coherence theory of truth to a fully fledged idealist metaphysics. To make the nature of truth consist in coherence is to hold that a proposition is true if it is included in some (better *the*) ideally coherent set of propositions. But the argument for coherence as the nature of truth depends on raising the spectre of radical scepticism. So, having raised it once, we can raise it again and ask what makes even an *ideally* coherent system of propositions true? Blanshard's answer is that what he calls the "immanent" and "transcendent" ends of thought must be one and the same. Thought's immanent goal is system and coherence: this is the inner drive that keeps thought moving. But the ultimate aim of thought is to encompass Reality and so, in the last analysis, the two are not to be distinguished. "Reality" and "the ideally coherent system of thought" are just two ways of talking about the same thing. "Unless they are accepted as one," Blanshard concludes, "we could see no alternative to scepticism."[17]

Contemporary philosophers such as Sellars, Rorty and Putnam, who are attracted to a similar view of truth, are under similar pressure. These philosophers defend (or have defended) variants of the Peircean notion of "true" as "incorporated in the ideally complete theory of everything" or "assertible at the end of inquiry" or "ideally justified."[18] The main problem with all such accounts of truth, it seems to me, is to make out what they mean. So far as I can see, we have little or no idea of what it would be for a theory to be ideally complete and comprehensive in the way required, or of what it would be for inquiry to have an end. But even if we had, it would still be tempting to ask what made our beliefs at the end of inquiry *true*? What stops the sceptic pressing Davidson's question: "why couldn't my beliefs about the world hang together and yet be comprehensively false?" Under pressure from this question, Sellars supplements his Peircean analysis of truth with a theory of "picturing" designed to explain the relationship between the basic terms of the ideal theory and the ultimate constituents of the world.[19] Understandably, Rorty and Putnam are not attracted by such a maneuver, so they prefer to argue that the "world" we lose when we reject the correspondence theory of truth was never more than a philosopher's fiction: that "internal" realism is all the realism we need. However, to intuitive realists like Williams, Stroud and Nagel, who see the presumption of realism as very deeply buried in our natural view of the world, this is unconvincing. Accordingly, they find views like those of Rorty and Putnam difficult to distinguish from out and out idealism.

That the presumption of realism is not easily jettisoned is shown by the fact that even coherence theorists are unwilling to abandon all the realist's intuitions about objectivity. Nobody wants to equate truth with justification by current standards. If we are to make any sense of objectivity, there must be some gap between something's being true and our happening, in our current situation, to find it credible. But this is enough to make us wonder whether the sceptical problem really depends on realism, supposing realism to commit us to a *radically* non-epistemic conception of truth. For example, it is clear that the objection Blanshard levels against combining a coherentist epistemology with a realistic understanding of truth can equally well be levelled at his own position, for he too makes the nature of truth consist in "one sort of character" and its test in "something quite different". This fact is obscured by his claim to have cast "coherence" for both roles. But suppose we ask either of coherence-as-test or coherence-as-nature "Coherence with *what?*" In the case of coherence-as-test, the answer is with "the present system of knowledge"; whereas for coherence-as-nature it is with "a system complete and all-inclusive,"[20] an inaccessible absolute which, for all we know, might be unimaginably different from anything we can now conceive. We have no guarantee that any of our beliefs will survive unaltered in the ideally completed system of thought, hence no reason to suppose that what we think of as justification is in any way truth-conducive.

Blanshard considers the objection that his theory of truth leads to scepticism. His reply is that:

> the coherence theory needs to be applied with some common sense. While the truth of a judgment does consist in the last resort in its relations to a completed system, no sensible person would claim to know these in detail, or deny the judgment any truth until he did know them.[21]

To its credit, the coherence theory "upholds the scepticism that is a mainspring of progress," but "in practice it is not sceptical at all."[22] However, the question is not about what the ordinary person would do in practice but about the sceptical potential of the coherence theory of truth. Everybody agrees that radical scepticism has no place in common life: the problem is to explain why this is so and, in particular, whether our natural non-sceptical attitude reflects an everyday blindness to a deep truth about the human condition. Blanshard's objection to the correspondence theorist who admits coherence as the test of truth is that locating the nature of truth in something external to its test precludes the possibility of showing that test to be in any way reliable; and his problem is that his own account of truth faces the same difficulty. He writes as though "practical" justification were simply a matter of not being overly concerned with details, whereas in fact we have been given no reason to think that a judgment's fitting in with "our present system of knowledge" tells us *anything* about "its relations to a completed system."

One way of meeting the difficulty would be to introduce an extra postulate to the effect that inquiry conducted according to our present and future canons is fated to converge on some unique, ideally coherent body of belief. This is more or less what Blanshard does, for he claims that "thought is related to reality as the partial to the perfect fulfilment of a purpose."[23] But the leap of faith involved in the introduction of such a teleological postulate is just as available to the most dyed-in-the-wool realist.[24]

The problems that beset a traditional idealist like Blanshard arise equally acutely for latter-day coherence theorists like Putnam and Rorty. Rorty's response has been an increasing willingness to dispense with the notion of truth in any sense that a realist would find congenial. The sort of philosopher Rorty identifies with holds that:

> great scientists invent descriptions of the world which are useful for purposes of predicting and controlling what happens, just as poets and political thinkers invent other descriptions of it for other purposes. But there is no sense in which any of these descriptions is an accurate representation of the way the world is in itself.[25]

Putnam, by contrast, has been tempted by Blanshard's solution: hence his willingness to argue that in "mature" sciences theories tend to converge, as if a recent lack of dramatic change indicated proximity to the end of inquiry.[26] This traditional idealist theme recurs even in Bonjour's defence of the coherence theory, though in conjunction with a correspondence theory of truth. Bonjour hopes that our system of beliefs will "gradually converge on some definite view of the world, and thereafter remain relatively stable, reflecting only those changes ... which are allowed or even required by the general picture of the world thus presented"; and he finds an *a priori* connection between this kind of stable coherence and the likelihood of objective truth.[27] He does not explain, however, what would justify our holding such convergence to be more than a passing phase. Those who see scepticism as rooted in realism are likely to be persuaded by Nagel's point that there have been enough cases where "what was once thought to be a maximally objective conception of reality" has been explained away by "a still more objective conception" that "we would be foolish not to expect [this process] to go on."[28]

So the conclusion seems to be that if all the sceptic needs is some kind of gap between truth and (what we think of as) justification, then idealist or epistemic accounts of truth contain just as much of a standing invitation to scepticism as their realistic competitors. But I am not sure that this is really the conclusion we ought to draw. It could just as well be argued that epistemic accounts of truth offer only illusory alternatives to realism.

I said earlier that the main problem with epistemic accounts of truth is to understand them. The point was to suggest that it is far from clear how much sense, if any, we can make of notions like "ideal justification." But I think we can now see that this is no accident. Since accounts of truth like Putnam's or Blanshard's are *designed* to decouple truth conceptually from anything we currently recognize as justification, thus doing justice to the realist's best intuition, they actively prevent our giving any further explanation of ideal justification. As soon as we try to be specific about what ideal justification involves, we will be able to say of any belief that meets those specific standards that it still might not be true, which is to say not ideally justified. The whole point of the notion of ideal justification is to make it possible for us to think of ourselves as capable of transcending our current ideas about the world, no matter how far they have advanced. This means that if we understand anything by "ideal justification," it is in virtue of our prior grasp of the notion of truth. Ideally justified beliefs are beliefs formed under conditions in which all relevant sources of error are either absent of have been allowed for, which is as good as to say under conditions in which there are no obstacles to determining the truth. We cannot give an informative analysis of truth in terms of "ideal justification" because the latter phrase is either empty or understood in terms of truth.

To put the point another way, we can say that the epistemic theorist of truth is caught in a dilemma. To the extent that he thinks of ideal justification as something that we, or beings with ways of thinking recognizably like ours, are capable of , his identification of truth with ideal justification will seem implausible to anyone who feels the force of the realist's claim that the world simply does not have to be the way we think it is: grasping this horn, the epistemic theorist will not salvage enough of our ordinary conception of objectivity. But to the extent that he severs ideal justification from our abilities, knowledge and situation in the world, not only is he no better placed than the realist when it comes to answering the sceptic, his understanding of his central theoretical notion, ideal justification, be-comes parasitic on an unacknowledged allegiance to commonsense realism.

One result is that Putnam is wrong to differentiate himself from the metaphysical realist on the grounds that such a realist must hold that even beliefs in an ideally justified system could all be false. Provided he reverses the direction of explanation, the realist can agree that they could not. If our understanding of ideal justification, to the extent that we have any, depends on our grasp of the notion of truth, there may well be a concep-tual connection between truth and ideal justification, but not because truth is an epistemic notion in disguise.

It is doubtful, then, whether epistemic accounts of truth are genuine alternatives to realistic accounts. But even if they were, they would offer no solution to our sceptical problem.

## 6.3 SCEPTICISM WITHOUT TRUTH

One possible reaction to the argument under consideration is to question its implicit essentialism. The argument derives much of its force from an implicit suggestion that there is one essential something (correspondence) that constitutes truth, another essential something (coherence) that con-stitutes justification, and no essential connection between them. Or so it seems. However, I think that if the charge of misplaced essentialism is to be made to stick, our best strategy will be to look further at the argu-ment's epistemological presuppositions, which are much richer than at first they seem. In my view, and contrary to first appearances, the chal-lenge to the realist to explain the truth conduciveness of justification does not turn on any particular understanding of truth as "correspondence." This means that Rorty, for example, is wrong to suppose that his polemics against the correspondence theory of truth are the way to break scepti-cism's grip on our philosophical imagination.[29]

The argument under review seems to take us from realism to scepticism by way of realism's connection with a certain conception of truth, a con-nection that has been questioned. Among contemporary realists, Michael Devitt is notable for his insistence that realism is "a metaphysical (onto-logical) doctrine" and that "correspondence truth is not in any way con-stitutive of it."[30] Devitt holds that "we should settle the metaphysical issue before any semantic one."[31]

At first sight, Devitt's claim seems implausible. Consider his statement of commonsense realism: "Tokens of most current observable common-sense, and scientific, physical types objectively exist independently of the mental."[32] What sort of independence is at issue here? Not causal: realists and their critics are not divided over whether the existence or character of

worldly objects depends causally on our thoughts about them, for to assert
such dependence is either truistic or absurd. It is a truism that our thoughts
and intentions affect how we act on, thus modify, the objective world: in
this sense the world is certainly not confined to what is there anyway.
Equally, it is absurd to suggest that objects spring into being or change
their characters as a result of psychic influences: critics of realism are not
advocates of magic. The independence that is relevant to the question of
realism, then, is not causal but epistemological and it is hard to imagine
how to express the idea of epistemological independence, which is a relation between propositions (or beliefs or at any rate entities that are in
some essential way sentence-like), except in terms of views about truth
and evidence. To think of the world as "what is there anyway" is to hold
that whether one's beliefs about the world are true depends in the end on
the way the world is. One's beliefs can be entirely rational, supported by
the best evidence at one's disposal, and so on: but if the world is an objective world, this does not make them true. So, whatever else it involves,
realism is committed to a view of truth that blocks the collapse of what *is*
true into what we *think* (or even under certain conditions would think)
is true.

The idea of reality's being "independent of thought" introduces into
realism an essentially epistemological component, and it is in virtue of
this component that realism is involved with issues about truth. We had
already reached this conclusion by questioning the relation between realism and scepticism. I suggested that if realism had no epistemological
component whatsoever, it would have no immediate connection with any
epistemological issues: certainly, there would be no question of its containing a standing invitation to scepticism. What we must stress now,
however, is that the epistemological dimension of realism is not only very
minimal but entirely negative. All that is involved in the idea of the objective world as "what is there anyway" is that an objective proposition's
being true is one thing and our believing it to be true, or being justified
in believing it to be true, something else again. In other words, whatever
"true" does mean, it does not mean "assertible by our current standards,"
or anything like that. We may, of course, have various ideas as to how
this fact is best explained, but none ought to change the epistemological
picture. The idea of reality as what is there anyway may go very naturally
with talk of truth as fitting the facts: but so far as sceptical problems go,
this kind of metaphorical talk need not be fleshed out with a detailed articulation of the notion of truth as correspondence or as anything else.

I think, then, that Devitt goes too far if he means to imply that questions about realism can be completely disentangled from questions about
truth. Nevertheless, I agree with what I take to be his essential point: that
realism can be stated without invoking any *explanatory* or *substantial* notion

of truth. I conclude from this that not only do the epistemological questions that realism is thought to invite not depend on any particular account of the nature of truth, they do not even depend on the thought that truth *has* a "nature." Anyone convinced that scepticism is a natural or intuitive problem should welcome this conclusion. From the standpoint of someone committed to minimizing the theoretical underpinnings of sceptical argument, dependence on a richly theoretical notion of truth is as bad as dependence on any contentious epistemological doctrine. But the sceptic requires no such notion of truth. So to this extent, I agree with Stroud and others that the sceptic's realism can be stated in terms of platitudes we would all accept. Where we part company is over whether the platitudes alone contain a standing invitation to scepticism.

We can best make the point with the aid of an example of a non-explanatory or deflationary notion of truth, so-called "disquotational truth." Disquotational "true" ("Tr") is a predicate (of sentences) obeying Tarski's Convention T:

"p" is true (in language L) if and only if p,

no matter what sentence of L is substituted for p. It is arguable that treating truth as an attribute of sentences is a departure from our ordinary conception: that, as we ordinarily conceive it, truth is attributed to some thing much more like propositions. But the essential idea of the disquotational theory – that our understanding of truth is exhausted by our grasp of the relevant biconditionals – can readily be put in terms of a proposition-based view.[33] So although, for convenience, I shall stick mainly to disquotational truth, nothing in what follows turns on the thought that "true" is predicated of sentences. My argument is meant to apply to deflationary views generally.

The truth-predicate, as the disquotationalist sees it, is a useful expressive device, enabling us for example to assert or endorse all the sentences in a given set, S, without stating them one by one. Since " 'p' is Tr" and 'p' are always interdeducible, we assert all the sentences in S by constructing the sentence:

(X) (x∈S → Tr(x))

As a device for semantic ascent, the truth-predicate allows us to go in for generalized assertion or denial by way of generalization over sentences. This is in effect what we do in natural language when we say things like "Everything he said is true."

If we think that disquotational truth is all the truth there is (or at least all the truth we need), we opt for a view that falls short of what is usually thought of as realistic. Obviously, such a view of truth is highly deflationary compared with any theory that explains truth in terms of some specific word-world (or thought-world) relationship: for example, a theory that explains truth in terms of a causal-physical relation of reference.[34] But it also needs to be sharply distinguished from a theory like Davidson's which, though it has nothing to say about what truth consists in, is a genuine correspondence theory for all that. True, Davidson himself now thinks that it was a mistake for him to have called his theory of truth "a correspondence theory." But his reason for this is that "Correspondence theories have always been conceived as providing an *explanation or analysis* of truth, and this, a Tarski-style theory of truth, certainly does not do."[35] We must therefore distinguish two ways in which we might come to think that there might not be much to say about truth. One is Quine's: "true" is a device for semantic ascent, not the name of a substantive, explanatorily significant property: whatever it is that all true sentences have in common. The other is Davidson's: though truth is such a property, it is primitive and unanalyzable. Davidson may sometimes sound like a deflationist, but his attitude to truth is, in fact, rather like Moore's to goodness: anti-naturalist and anti-reductionist, rather than deflationary.[36]

Davidson thinks that truth is "beautifully transparent" compared with epistemological notions like "belief" and "coherence" on the grounds that "Truth, as applied to sentences or utterances, shows the disquotational feature enshrined in Tarski's Convention T, and that is sufficient to fix its domain of application." However, this does not mean that he thinks Convention T captures everything essential about truth. Convention T fixes the domain of application of the truth-predicate, but only "relative to a language or speaker". Thus:

> there is more to truth than Convention T; there is whatever carries over from language to language or speaker to speaker. What Convention T reveals is that the truth of an utterance depends on just two things: what the words mean, and how the world is arranged. There is no further relativism to a conceptual scheme, a way of viewing things, a perspective.[37]

However, this is inconclusive since, even on a purely disquotational view of truth, there is something that "carries over from language to language," namely the advantages, for any language, of containing such a logical device.[38] This means that we cannot go straight from the fact that something carries over from language to language to the conclusion that there is more to truth than Convention T, never mind the view that the something more is a kind of correspondence. As Stephen Leeds, a leading advocate of a purely disquotational view of truth, notes: "to explain the utility of disquotation, we need say nothing about the relations between language and the world; we do not have to give a natural definition – indeed any definition – of "true in L" for arbitrary L."[39]

We do not have to choose between taking truth as primitive, as having, so to say, an ineffable nature, and offering a detailed explanation of the "truth-making" connection between language and reality. The deflationary approach to truth represented by pure disquotationalism (and related views) is based on the thought that there is no compelling need to think of truth as having a nature at all, hence no need for concern over whether that nature can usefully be further analyzed. But to take this line is not to make concessions to idealism. To reject the idea of truth's having a nature is not to suppose that its nature is covertly epistemological. We can, therefore, hold on to the negative core of the realism that Davidson and others put forward. Davidson's view of truth is "realistic" in that it refuses to analyse truth in epistemic terms: this is the point of his insistence that his view involves no "relativization." But pure disquotationalism is just as resistant to epistemic accounts of truth: "p" is true if and only if p, not if and only if "p" is well-supported by evidence, or anything like that. If "realistic" means no more than "non-idealistic," a deflationary view of truth is as "realistic" as any version of the correspondence theory. So if correspondence theories of truth open the door to scepticism simply by virtue of refusing to analyze truth in epistemic terms, so should radically deflationary theories.

This has been denied. Putnam, for example, thinks that accepting a deflationary view of truth involves rejecting the very idea of "objective rightness." This leads to self-refuting relativism and, in the end, to a denial that our assertions and thoughts are assertions and thoughts (as opposed to mere noises or subvocalizations), which he calls "a kind of mental suicide."[40] This is no doubt a kind of sceptical outcome too, but very different from the kind that depends on accepting some notion of objective truth, which is what those who think that realism threatens us with scepticism have in mind.

The disquotational theory of truth says that we understand "true," not by associating the word with a property like correspondence or ideal assertibility, but simply by coming to accept all sentences ("T-sentences") of the form:

"Snow is white" is true if and only if snow is white.

Someone might object that this is circular, since our understanding of the logical connective, "If and only if," presupposes the notions of truth and falsity. The reply, as Putnam notes, is that the disquotational theory does not claim that we understand "true" by learning that " 'Snow is white' is true" is true if and only if it is true that snow is white, but rather "by being trained to *assert* " 'Snow is white' is true" when (and only when) we are prepared to *assert* ("Snow is white". But asserting is more than noise-making, for it is "guided by the notions of correctness and incorrectness"; and "the problem of truth reappears when we ask for an account of what it is for an assertion to be correct and incorrect."

Putnam considers, and finds inadequate, the obvious reply: that "correct" is just a synonym for "true," the use of which has already been explained. An assertibility condition for the ordinary scientific sentence, "There is an electric current flowing through his wire," is that the needle of a suitably connected voltmeter is deflected; and just as describing such assertibility conditions for this and similar sentences does not pre-empt the question "What is electricity," describing assertibility conditions for "Such and such sentence is true" does not pre-empt the question "What is the nature of truth". To say that truth is different from electricity in this way must, therefore, be to claim that there is no room for a theory of truth: that there is *no* property of truth, "not just in the realist sense but in *any* sense." This is to deny that our thoughts and assertions are thoughts and assertions.[41]

It should be clear right away that Putnam is not entitled to the conclusion that, for a deflationist, there is no property of truth in *any* sense. If we are willing to see a property wherever there is a predicate with a proper use, we can perfectly well say that "true" stands for a property. Of course, if we think that the appropriate T-sentences give a complete theory of that property, we will not be moved by requests for further information about what it is that all true sentences have in common. Putnam is therefore simply repeating the central claim of all who take a deflationary approach to truth: that truth is not a substantial property. But it does not follow from the claim that truth is not a substantial property that there are no objective *truths*. It is no part of any deflationary view of truth that snow is white because I believe that snow is white, hence no part of any such view that the truth of what I believe is somehow constituted by the fact of my believing it. So far as I can see, the move from a deflationary conception of truth to mental suicide is achieved by sliding from "There is no 'property' of truth" to "Nothing is really true" to "There are no objective truths," and none of these transitions is in the least warranted.

I think that the reason Putnam feels free to argue this way is that he never really takes seriously the thought that truth might not have a "nature." If truth does not consist either in ideal assertibility or some kind of correspondence with reality, then it must consist in assertibility by current standards.[42] His thought, as we have seen, is that a deflationary approach to truth pushes us towards an "assertibility" or "proper use" conception of meaning. So if, as we may agree, asserting is more than noise-making, because it is something we do correctly or incorrectly, and if we have rejected both the idea of truth as idealized assertibility and as correspondence to reality, the only form of correctness that remains is conformity with current standards (or the standards of a particular community). If this is the argument, it simply assumes that we must mean to identify truth with some substantial property, the only problem being to see what remains when traditional candidates have been set aside. But going beyond this quick rejoinder, the truism that we can only assess assertions on the basis of standards currently in force and evidence currently available is no reason to think that rejecting traditional accounts of the nature of truth forces us to identify truth with current assertibility. It would do so only if a deflationary view of truth committed us to a use theory of meaning *and* if any theory of this kind required us to think that a sentence s means the same as "s is assertible." Clearly, it does not: s and "s is assertible" may have, and generally will have, quite different assertibility conditions. Take, for example, ordinary observation reports. We have noted from time to time that, in making them, we presuppose that conditions are more or less normal: if they aren't normal, we have to think again about what we claim to have seen or heard, perhaps even concluding that our claim was not properly made at all. But it is also important to correctly entering observation reports that we concentrate on what we are supposed to be observing and not, while observing, on the conditions of observation. The procedure for correctly entering a particular claim can thus be quite different from the procedure for determining whether the claim was correctly entered, since the two procedures can require attention to entirely disparate circumstances. In general, to suppose that a sentence is meaningful if it can be used to make moves in a rule-governed practice is not to suppose that every sentence is comment on the practice that sanctions it. Since, therefore, there is no reason to equate "s is true" with "s is assertible," unless there is reason to equate "s is assertible" with s itself, the attempt to identify a deflationary account of truth with a crude epistemic account is blocked. To repeat, a deflationary approach to truth involves resisting identifying truth with *any* epistemic property, including assertibility by current standards. Truths thus remain objective, even if there is no substantial property of truth.

Putnam thinks – though does not succeed in arguing – that a deflationary view of truth will close the essential gap between truth and current assertibility, and he takes this to support his own view that truth is *idealized* assertibility. But a similar attack on deflationary views can be made on behalf of the correspondence theory. For example, Michael Friedman has argued explicitly that deflationary views ought to be rejected because only a certain kind of correspondence theory "allows our over-all theory of the world to have general self-critical power and, therefore, genuine potential for self-justification as well." Such a theory allows for highly general self-criticism because "it leaves open the possibility that most (or all) of our beliefs are false." Presumably, Friedman thinks this is a possibility that deflationary views preclude. They dispose of sceptical problems *too* easily: the possibility of self-justification goes hand in hand with the possibility of asking sceptical questions.[43]

I see no reason to concede that deflationary views of truth make it impossible to *ask* sceptical questions. There may perhaps be reasons for denying that all our *beliefs* could be false and there might be some anti-sceptical potential in such a denial; but I am sure that no such conclusion is sustained by a deflationary view of truth alone. To explain our understanding of truth in terms of our acceptance of the relevant T-sentences is to say nothing about how many *truths*, if any, we have to be thought to accept. If there are reasons for thinking that most of our beliefs have to be true, if we are to have beliefs at all, they will have to be found in our further views about belief and meaning and not, if they are deflationary, in our views about truth.

If this is right, Friedman's reason for associating lack of self-critical power with an overly effortless rejection of the sceptical challenge looks quite peculiar. His conception of a project of self-justification involves using our "over-all theory of the world" in conjunction with our theory of truth to show that "our inductive methods" tend to produce truths. He agrees that this procedure is, in a way, circular, since we will be relying on views underwritten by the methods we are trying to validate. However, building on the ideas of Putnam and Quine, he thinks that the circularity need not be vicious. We will return to this particular anti-sceptical strategy in due course. For now, however, I want to stay with Friedman's reason for opposing a disquotional account of truth, which is that the only kind of self-justification such a theory allows for is not only circular but viciously so. As he says, "On the basis of such a theory, together with the rest of our theory of the world, we can easily prove that each sentence of our theory of the world is true." That is, assuming everything I already accept, and granted a disquotational theory of truth, I can prove, for each sentence I accept, that it is true, which obviously does nothing to meet any sceptical problem. But if a deflationary view of truth leaves me with no way of arguing against scepticism that is not viciously circular, the conclusion ought to be that such a view is more conducive to scepticism than a full-blooded correspondence theory, not less. The problem with such a disquotational view will be that it offers us too much self-critical power rather than too little.

Of course, this supposes that a deflationary theory of truth does not, by itself, make it impossible to ask sceptical questions. But I have already suggested that it does not. What we must bear in mind, once more, is the distinction between our understanding of *truth* and our commitment to various bodies of *truths*. As I see things, the latter, rather than the former, is what scepticism is ultimately all about. What the sceptic wants to know is whether we have any reason to think that the evidence at our disposal really justifies our accepting (what we take to be) the truths that it is supposedly evidence for; or in the case of certain alleged truths, such as the presupposition that there is *some* kind of external world, whether there is or even could be *any* evidence that bears on them. This is certainly what is at issue when the question is raised of how the supposedly ultimate evidence furnished by experience underwrites conclusions about the external objects. What matters here is not how, in general, we understand truth, or even, except in a limited, negative way, how we understand truth for sentences in the problematic class, but the evidential relations, or lack of them, between two bodies of truths, or candidate truths. I fully agree with Quine: 'We understand what it is for the sentence "Snow is white" to be true as clearly as we understand what it is for snow to be white. Evidently, one who puzzles over the adjective "true" should puzzle rather over the sentences to which he ascribes it.' But I think that this is what the sceptic does: he puzzles over our right to assert certain bodies of alleged truths. Questions about correspondence versus epistemic versus deflationary analyses of truth do not really come into it.

What happens, I think, is that questions about how to understand truth *seem* to be tied up with sceptical questions because substantial theories of truth tolerate a certain obvious reading of the sceptical problem about justification and truth (as Blanshard for example formulates it) in a way that deflationary theories do not. If, like Davidson, we treat truth as a primitive but substantial non-epistemic property of beliefs, we are well on the way to placing the nature of truth in "one sort of character" and its test in "something quite different," and this does add color to the challenge to connect justification with truth. It is, accordingly, tempting to think that, if we do not place the nature of truth in any sort of character, the problem of forging an essential connection between disparate natures lapses. But even to mention this temptation is to reveal how little in the case for scepticism turns on our understanding of truth. The sceptic's intention is to ask certain very general questions about knowledge and justification: he wants to know, with respect to various propositions p, q. r, ... that we accept, why p's being confirmed (by our standards) makes it likely that p, why q's being confirmed makes it likely that q, why r's being confirmed makes it likely that r, and so on? This question can be raised without even broaching any detailed questions about the analysis of truth. This remains so even when we put the problem of objective knowledge in terms of the relation between truth and coherence. Suppose that justification is always a matter of accommodating beliefs to other beliefs; and suppose that our beliefs that snow is white, grass is green, bananas are yellow, and so on fit together beautifully: we can still ask why this makes it likely that snow is white, grass green and bananas yellow? Or, using the truth-predicate as a handy way of putting the question in a neat, general from, we can ask why a belief's fitting in with other beliefs makes it likely to be true. In other words, to ask a sceptical question, all we need from the truth-predicate is the generalizing device that disquotational truth provides. It may be second nature to formulate the problem of objective knowledge in terms of the relation between coherence and correspondence, but the metaphor is not essential. Still less do we need a worked-out theory.

If the metaphor is not essential, criticisms of scepticism based on criticism of the metaphor are inconclusive. Consider the charge that anything short of a strongly foundational theory of knowledge – the sort incorporating a notion like "pointing to reality" or "comparing beliefs with facts" – inevitably "cuts justification off from the world."[44] It is tempting to reply that this charge involves a notion of "the world," the world as thing-in-itself, that is so empty as to leave no way of saying either what it would be to be in contact or what it would be to be cut off.[45] At best, we will have in mind a vague picture: that our belief-system might float away from reality like a balloon cut from its moorings. So we face a dilemma. On the one hand, if we are allowed to think of the world as our familiar world of people and things, it is not true that a non-foundational conception of justification automatically cuts justification off from the world: on the contrary, our ordinary conception of the world includes views about how our encounters with the world lead to belief. On the other hand, if we are allowed no way of saying what it is we are cut off from, the charge that justification get cut off from the world is unintelligible: this is the world that Rorty thinks is "well lost." But I think that such arguments are beside the point. The sceptic does not need a metaphysical view of "the world" any more than he needs one of truth. All he needs is the legitimacy of his project of total assessment. In the context of this project, it is beside the point even to bring up our ordinary views about how our interactions with worldly objects leads to belief, since these belong to the convictions under scrutiny.

I say that all we need from the truth-predicate is a generalizing device. But the qualification "from the truth-predicate" must not be forgotten. On the epistemological side, as I have already argued, we need a great deal more. The sceptic has to take for granted all sorts of ideas about evidence, about our "epistemic position" and about the theoretical integrity of the classes of propositions he generalizes about. He needs, as I have argued, foundationalism and epistemological realism. This discussion of truth contributes to defusing scepticism only by focussing the debate on what I think it should be focussed on: the sceptic's contentious epistemological ideas. When we see that the sceptic's truth talk is really a way of asking his characteristically *general* questions about knowledge and justification, we see that the totality condition on a philosophical understanding of knowledge, and the controversial and implausible ideas it embodies, is the proper target for the theoretical diagnostician. A bland commonsense presumption of realism contributes little or nothing to the sceptic's case.

Let me now further the argument by looking at some particular attempts to connect realism with scepticism. Then we can return to the question of whether a "coherence" conception of knowledge and justification can be used to pose sceptical problems in a way that sidesteps foundationalist commitments.

## 6.4  OBJECTIVITY AND PROGRESS

There is something undeniably seductive, as well as seemingly intuitive, about the thought that scepticism follows ineluctably from the objectivity of the world. But I think that this seductiveness and apparent intuitiveness can be traced to two factors: making the case for scepticism so that the crucial foundationalist commitments do all their work behind the scenes and failing to make a clear distinction between radical scepticism and something far less threatening.

The traditional case for idealism, as we saw Blanchard put it, is that if we place the nature of truth in one sort of character and its test in something quite different, we are sure, sooner or later, to find the two falling apart. As Arthur Fine, who rejects both realism and its standard alternatives, has put it: "when one sees that the realist conception of truth creates a gap that keeps the epistemic access one wants always just beyond reach, it may be tempting to try to refashion the idea of truth in epistemic terms in order, literally, to make truth accessible."[46]

Unfortunately, if our ordinary concept of knowledge embodies the presumption of realism, no such refashioning of the idea of truth will be satisfying. We will remain caught in the epistemologist's dilemma, forced to choose between agreeing with the sceptic directly and modifying our prephilosophical ideas in ways that exactly match his reservations about them. The choice, it seems, is between scepticism and abandoning the quest for objective knowledge.

This whole line of thought is suspicious. The "gap" Fine refers to amounts to no more than the possibility of even the most strongly justified belief's failing to be true. But why should we suppose that, simply by allowing for corrigibility, we incur the risk of radical scepticism? On the face of it, to say that we can always go wrong is one thing: to conclude that we never know anything is another. This looks suspiciously like the argument from error which, as we have seen repeatedly, is not an argument for radical scepticism.

Or recall Blanshard's thought that his idealism preserves "the scepticism that is the mainspring of progress" while preventing this salutary scepticism from degenerating into radical scepticism, which he thinks must happen if we do not explain the nature of truth in epistemic terms. The proper reaction is that there is no connection between these two forms of "scepticism," hence no need for an account of truth designed to block the move from the one to the other.

More promising at first is Friedman's argument that because only a full-blooded correspondence theory of truth allows for the possibility that *all* our beliefs about the world are false, only such a theory allows for a radically sceptical challenge to our knowledge of the world. Since he thinks that to make room for such a challenge is also to make room for a genuine project of self-justification, Friedman welcomes what Blanshard fears. Even so, his argument invites a similar response: what licenses the move from the *mere logical possibility* even of wholesale error to the danger of radical scepticism? Such a possibility is at best a necessary condition for there being a threat of scepticism with respect to our knowledge of the world. But fulfilling a necessary condition is hardly the same as offering a standing invitation. There is no immediate inference from the premise that all our beliefs about the world might be false to the conclusion that there is never the slightest reason for holding any proposition about the world to be true, no move from the possibility of error to the impossibility of justification.

Here too we return to a familiar problem. We first encountered it in connection with sceptical hypotheses, such as that we are brains in vats with our experiences artificially stimulated so as to replicate the experiences we would have if our ordinary beliefs about the world were true. I argued then that the mere existence of a "logical gap" between appearance and reality has no tendency to show that knowledge of reality is impossible, unless we cleave to the doctrine of the priority of experiential knowledge over knowledge of the world. The most that such thought-experiments establish, I argued, is the neutrality and perhaps the autonomy of experience; and there is no passage from either thesis to radical scepticism except via a foundationalist doctrine of epistemological priority. What I want to suggest now is that, as an argument for radical scepticism, the worry that our beliefs might "hang together" and yet be comprehensively false is a variant on these familiar themes. The difference is that, whereas in connection with the dreaming hypothesis or the brain-in-a-vat possibility, appearances tend to be identified with sensory appearances, the challenge to connect coherence with truth, thereby explaining the truth-conduciveness of epistemic justification, involves generalizing the notion of "appearance" to cover everything we are inclined to think: all our beliefs about the world, our entire "notional world." The challenge is:

given only knowledge of what we believe about the world, and how our beliefs fit together, how can we show that those beliefs are likely to be true?

This emerges quite clearly in Nagel's account of the passage from objectivity to scepticism. Objectivity and scepticism, he argues:

> are closely related: both develop from the idea that there is a real world in which we are contained, and that appearances result from our interaction with the rest of it. We cannot accept those appearances uncritically but must try to understand what our consitution contributes to them. To do this we try to develop . . . an account of both ourselves and the world that includes an explanation of why it initially appears as it does . . . If the initial appearances cannot be relied on because they depend on our constitution in ways that we do not fully understand, this more complicated idea should be subject to the same doubts, for whatever we use to understand certain interactions between ourselves and the world is not itself the object of that understanding.[47]

But although, on the surface, there might seem to be a direct passage from the idea of objectivity to scepticism, the real work is all done by Nagel's determination to treat any views we form about our interactions with the world as further elements in a web of belief whose relation to reality is thought to be problematic. None of this is very clearly explained: what connects dependence on "our constitution" with any *general* unreliability? But in any case, the connection revealed is not between scepticism and objectivity as such but between scepticism and the demand that we "explain," in the sense of "validate," our knowledge of the world *as a whole*. In the context of this project, it is tempting to suppose that realism demands that we treat all our beliefs as "appearances" to be set against "reality". The point of this, in turn, is to suggest that all we ever unquestionably know is how we believe the world to be – how it *appears* (to us) to be – which presents us with the insurmountable problem of getting from this island of privileged knowledge to an appreciation of how things really are.

Foundationalism insists on the priority of experiential knowledge over knowledge of the world. This priority is thought to be absolute, in the sense of completely context-independent. Nagel's argument is no objection to the thesis that all sceptical arguments turn on this doctrine, hence on the epistemological realism it presupposes. As we suspected, it turns out to differ from more familiar sceptical arguments only in invoking a generalized notion of experiential knowledge, in which everything we believe, rather than just sensory experience, falls under the heading of "appearances." Without this tacit foundationalism, there is no argument for scepticism. If "understand" means only "explain," then at most we have an argument for the inevitability of unexplained explainers, explanatory principles for which, at the moment, we have no explanation. This may show that the quest for objective knowledge will never terminate – that each explanatory advance will bring new questions to pursue – but it will not show that the idea of objectivity undermines itself, that objective knowledge is impossible. To get to that conclusion, we must take "understand" to mean "validate." However, failure to "explain" in this sense how appearances relate to reality will not undermine our knowledge of the world, any more than success will validate it, unless our knowledge of appearances is epistemologically prior to all objective knowledge.

We can conclude that to get to the impasse Nagel describes we need far more than the mere idea of an objective world. The epistemological asymmetry Nagel reads into his version of the "appearance/reality" distinction is not a demand imposed by "objectivity" but *a methodological necessity of philosophical reflection* as Nagel understands it. As we have seen, to convert this methodological necessity into a truth about the human condition, as Nagel implicitly does, we must fall in with epistemological realism.

Interestingly, Nagel himself concedes what I take to be the crucial point when he notes that "The pure idea of realism – the idea that there is a world in which we are contained – implies nothing specific about the relation between the appearances and reality." Exactly: the priority of knowledge of appearances over knowledge of the world is an indispensable extra ingredient in the argument linking realism with scepticism. This being so, however, it is seriously misleading for Nagel to go on to claim that "The search for objective knowledge, *because of its commitment to a realistic picture*, is inescapably subject to scepticism"?[48]

A further way to see this is to notice that subtracting the implicit foundationalism from Nagel's argument leaves him too with the sort of argument from error that we have repeatedly found, and which philosophers from Descartes on have generally acknowledged, to be incapable of grounding a radically sceptical conclusion. Without supplementation, all that follows from the observation that "there is a real world in which we are contained, and that appearances result from our interaction with the rest of it" is that we must be prepared to correct our beliefs in the light of further discoveries about the way they were acquired, not that we suffer from some permanent and drastic epistemic disability. Nagel himself remarks that although the "ambitions of knowledge and some of its achievments are heroic, . . . a pervasive skepticism or at least provisionality of commitment is suitable in light of our evident limitations."[49] But there is all the difference in the world between openness to correction and radical scepticism; and the former is the *most*, not the least, that he has argued for.

We have come to the second factor in the seductiveness of the claim that realism invites scepticism: a tendency to conflate anti-dogmatism, the uncontroversial "scepticism" which arises from common experiences of error, with radical scepticism, which arises out of contentious epistemological theory. This tendency, which as much as anything accounts for the feeling that radical scepticism is implicit in "platitudes we all accept," can take subtle forms.

Williams and Nagel both connect scepticism with the quest for objective knowledge. In turn, they connect the quest for objectivity with the thought that an attempt to understand the world must involve an attempt to understand our place in it, hence why the world appears to us as it does. If we are to get a grip on reality as "what is there anyway," we must overcome:

> any systematic bias or distortion or partiality in our outlook as a whole, in our representation of the world . . . in the sense of gaining a standpoint (the absolute standpoint) from which it can be understood in relation to reality, and comprehensibly related to other conceivable representations.[50]

The example that most impresses Williams and Nagel involves the distinction between secondary and primary qualities: the colors, sounds, tastes, and smells that we experience versus the underlying physical processes that cause us to experience them. To draw this distinction is to allow that physical objects may not have all the qualities we naively attribute to them. Under pressure from scientific inquiry, a naive conception of such objects as characterized by continuous, colored surfaces, gives way to a conception in which they are characterized by a complex, gappy microstructure, their perceived colors depending on a complicated and variable array of factors involving both object and observer. Since beings with sensory systems very different from our own would not experience colors as we experience them, colors as we experience them are not part of "what is there anyway": only certain interactions between light and electrons, which can give rise to color experiences in appropriately constituted perceivers, qualify for that status. For a certain class of phenomena, then, the distinction between primary and secondary qualities is a program for sorting out what, in our experience of the world, belongs to the world and what belongs to us. This is why to appreciate the distinction is to make a gain in objectivity, to get closer to what Williams calls "an absolute conception of reality."

Thinking along similar lines, Nagel sees the quest for objective knowledge as an exercise in "self-transcendence," an attempt on the part of limited beings to overcome their limitations by altering their conception of the world so that:

it is no longer just the view from where they are but in a sense a view from nowhere, which includes and comprehends the fact that the world contains beings which possess it, explains why the world appears to them as it does prior to the formation of that conception, and explains how they can arrive at the conception itself.[51]

Physical theories of light and color, special relativity, quantum physics: all involve advances in objectivity because each forces us to rethink the relation between the physical world and particular observers' perceptions of it.

Both Williams and Nagel see this drive towards objectivity as built into our ordinary concept of knowledge, and both identify it as the source of that concept's sceptical potential. But there is no connection between the quest for greater and greater objectivity in our view of the world and the threat of radical scepticism. Radical scepticism arises out of a challenge to show how any knowledge of the world is even possible, an epistemological question that is not so much addressed by the quest for objectivity as just described. To be open to the sorts of conceptual advances mentioned above is simply to be non-dogmatic: to be willing to rethink both one's views of the world and the particular sorts of experiences that seem to support them. This has nothing to do with worries about whether "experience" in some generic sense can provide grounds for beliefs about the world as such.

One way to see this is to notice that the objectivity of the objective or absolute view consists in its being *self-explaining*. We have an objective view of things to the extent that we have, in addition to views about the world, explanations of how those views arise. But seeking a view of the world that is in this sense self-explaining has nothing to do with seeking a view that is somehow self-validating, still less one that is final and unrevisable. There is nothing absurd in the idea of a succession of (improved) views, all equally "absolute" in Williams's sense. The *explanatory* task that Williams and Nagel think the concept of knowledge sets for us has nothing to do with the *epistemological* task of grounding the totality of our beliefs about the world. We could complete the one without making any progress in the other.[52] For suppose we achieve an absolute view, of the sort Williams thinks we should strive for: nothing stops us making Nagel's move and treating all the beliefs involved in that view as "appearances," which need to be related to "reality." The self-explaining character of the view will not speak to any concerns that this move generates. The explanatory relations involved in an absolute view will only add to the ways in which our beliefs hang together: they will not explain, if this really does need to be explained, why hanging together is in any way indicative of truth.

Let us recall Nagel's argument linking realism with scepticism. A key

move in that argument involves the claim that "whatever we use to understand certain interactions between ourselves and the world is not itself
the object of that understanding." What sort of understanding is at issue
here? If it is a matter of explaining how beings like us form the sorts of
beliefs we form then, as Quine insists, there is no barrier in principle to
procedures that lead to explanations of themselves. There is nothing con-
tradictory in, say, the idea of scientific investigations into the psychology
of scientific theorizing. Nagel's stricture makes sense only if "understand"
carries overtones of "ground" or "justify," and if what is to be grounded
is our entire "view of the world." Then, indeed, anything we use to ground
it will itself either remain ungrounded or be justified only in an unaccept-
ably circular way. However, this does not show, as Nagel thinks, that "the
idea of objectivity ... seems to undermine itself": it only illustrates the
close connection between scepticism and the presuppositions that inform
the attempt to assess the totality of our knowledge of the world.

Nagel himself reveals a sense of the gap between his explanatory and
epistemological concerns when he notes that:

> the fact that objective reality is our goal does not guarantee our
> pursuit of it succeeds in being anything more than an exploration
> and reorganisation of the insides of our own minds. On a realist view
> this is always a possibility ... A less radical point is that whatever
> we may have achieved we are only at a passing stage of intellectual
> development, and much of what we now believe will be overthrown
> by later discoveries and later theories.[53]

But this way of assessing the situation is deeply misleading. With the
doctrine of the priority of experiential knowledge over knowledge of the
world firmly in place, we have no possibility, not no guarantee, of reaching
our goal of objective knowledge. It must, therefore, be wrong to suggest
that the same line of thought leads both to the less and the more radical
point. If progress is supposed to be something we can recognize, the idea
of objectivity cannot both "give meaning to the idea of intellectual progress" and make radical scepticism immediately and obviously irrefutable.
Nagel is simply playing back and forth between anti-dogmatism, Blanshard's "scepticism that is a mainspring of progress," and radical scepticism, thereby making it look as if the common experiences that justify the
one lead automatically to the other.

What enables him to connect the two is an ambiguous notion of "reduction to appearance." We are supposed to see how only objectivity can
give meaning to the idea of progress by considering well-known examples
of objective advance and asking:

Could a theory which ascribed intrinsic colours, tastes, smells, feels and sounds to things account for the appearance that these are to be explained as the effects on our senses of primary qualities? Could a theory of absolute space and time explain the appearance that we occupy relativistic space-time? In both cases the answer is no. An objective advance may be superseded by a further objective advance, which in turn reduces it to appearance. But it is not on the same level as its predecessors.[54]

Advances in objectivity thus involve explanatory asymmetries. This is why they reduce their predecessors to "appearance." But compare the sense of "appearance" in play here with that involved in the sceptical challenge to connect appearances with objective facts. In the one instance, appearances are simply ways that we were once inclined to think the world is but which, in the light of further inquiry, we now believe it isn't. In the other, "appearances" are ultimate epistemological data. In the first sense, "appearances" applies only to some of our experiences and beliefs (or former beliefs); in the second it applies to all of them: for given the priority of knowledge of "the insides of our own minds," even our best current candidates for objectively true beliefs are, from the "objective" standpoint, only "appearances." Only by glossing over the difference, is Nagel able to connect the experience of self-correction with the threat of radical scepticism.

I conclude that the connection between "objectivity" and radical scepticism arises not through our trying to "understand objective knowledge" but rather our trying to "understand knowledge objectively," i.e. from the "detached," philosophical perspective. But to think that this is even a possible project, we have to assume that "our knowledge of the world" picks out an autonomous object of theory. In other words, epistemological rather than metaphysical realism remains the indispensable presupposition of the case for scepticism.

## 6.5 EPISTEMOLOGY NATURALIZED

As we have seen, one important way in which it is easy to miss the theoretical burden carried by arguments for radical scepticism is to treat familiar considerations relating to the possibility of error, which at most support a willingness to accept correction, as if they made the case for some far more dramatic sceptical conclusion. Just how tempting a fallacy this is can be gauged from the way it appeals to philosophers with quite disparate philosophical temperaments. At first sight, Quine's conception of philosophy seems very different from, say, Nagel's. But his treatment of scepticism is misleading in more or less the same way.

A recurrent theme in discussions of philosophical scepticism is scepticism's intimate connection with a special and unusual form of inquiry, hence with the unusual context or conditions in which that inquiry is conducted. Nagel, Stroud and Williams belong very much to this central tradition. Whatever their differences elsewhere, they agree in connecting the threat of scepticism with the attempt to understand human knowledge in a distinctively *philosophical* way; and each in his own way sees this distinctively philosophical project as intimately involved with the the idea of our taking up a special, detached attitude towards all more ordinary pursuits. I think that this view of scepticism is essentially correct. My disagreement with these philosophers is over the extent and the character of the theoretical presuppositions of this conception of philosophical understanding.

Now, certain of Quine's characteristic remarks on the topic of scepticism might lead us to suppose that he too favours a diagnostic approach. Quine emphatically rejects the idea of a "view from nowhere": there is, he states categorically, no "cosmic exile."[55] If Quine is right, the standpoint from which philosophers glimpse the threat, or even the truth, of scepticism does not exist. If scepticism emerges as a problem only when we take up a distinctively detached, reflective stance, then for Quine it should never emerge.

I have argued that the idea of detachment is inseparable from foundationalism and epistemological realism. If I am right about this connection, we should expect Quine's lack of sympathy for the idea of a special philosophical standpoint, to go with a distaste for foundational projects. This is what we find. Quine dismisses the idea of a general validation of empirical knowledge, "science" in his broad sense. The "Cartesian quest for certainty" is "a lost cause" and so we should stop "dreaming of deducing science from sense data."[56] So again, if the threat of scepticism arises out of failure to provide what is, from the very outset, an illusory, indeed impossible, kind of validation, that threat should be equally illusory.

Given this diagnosis, there should be no question of Quine's responding to scepticism in any direct way. On the other hand, Quine does not seem to be sympathetic to a purely diagnostic approach to sceptical problems. He refers dismissively to "Wittgenstein and his followers [who] found a residual philosophical vocation in therapy: in curing philosophers of the delusion that there were epistemological problems." For his own part, he finds it "more useful to say . . . that epistemology goes on, though in a new setting and a clarified status."[57] This continuing attachment to the idea of a theory of knowledge explains Quine's unwillingness to dismiss scepticism

out of hand. The thought that "Doubt [is] ... the mother of philosophy ...
has a true ring for those of us who look upon philosophy primarily as the
theory of knowledge." This is because "the theory of knowledge has its
origin in doubt, in scepticism."[58]

Given this connection between scepticism and the theory of knowledge,
Quine's attachment to the theory of knowledge clearly prevents his linking
the threat of scepticism with the attempt to go into cosmic exile. Thus
scepticism, according to Quine, arises from within science, rather than in
attempts to reflect on science from without. Sceptical doubts are scientific
doubts. Since science represents the quest for objective knowledge in its
most self-conscious form, if Quine's account of how sceptical doubts arise
were correct it would support the thought that the quest for objective
knowledge undermines itself, while freeing that thought from any dependence on the urge to get outside all our beliefs about the world. And since
Quine's arguments do not depend on any particular substantive notion of
truth, his own attitude towards truth being notably deflationary, it would
also free it from dependence on a strong correspondence theory of truth.
We would have the sort of intuitive argument we are looking for.

However, Quine's attitude to scepticism, at first seemingly straightforward, proves on further examination to be curiously ambivalent. Though
he sometimes takes the position that, because sceptical doubts are scientific doubts, they can be allayed by straightforward scientific means, at
other times he hints that the sceptic may perhaps be right after all: "The
Humean predicament is the human predicament."[59] The explanation for
this ambivalence is to be found in the fact that his account of how sceptical
doubts arise is badly confused. On the one hand, the "sceptical" doubts
prompted by "science" are indeed easily resolved, but have no connection
with the radical scepticism that informs the Humean predicament; and on
the other, though genuine radical scepticism cannot be resolved "scientifically," the possibility of such radical doubts was never a scientific discovery in the first place. Quine's ambivalence stems from his failure to
observe the relevant distinctions.

How does science lead to scepticism? According to Quine, "The basis
for scepticism is the awareness of illusion, the discovery that we must not
always believe our eyes." Sceptical arguments exploit phenomena like
"seemingly bent sticks in water ..., double images, dreams." However,
since "Illusions are illusions only relative to a prior acceptance of genuine
bodies with which to contrast them", "Rudimentary physical science, that
is, common sense about bodies is ... needed as a springboard for scepticism. It contributes the needed notion of a distinction between reality
and illusion."[60]

But Quine does not mean to imply that no general sceptical conclusion can be
reached. He is not arguing that, since we have to accept "common

sense about bodies" even to make the distinctions that are crucial to the sceptic's argument, there is no question of our casting doubt on everything we believe about the external world, all at once. On the contrary, the sceptic is: "quite within his rights in assuming science to refute science; this if carried out would be a straightforward argument by *reductio ad absurdum*. I am only making the point that sceptical doubts are scientific doubts."[61]

Quine thinks that the point that sceptical doubts are scientific doubts is important because a proper understanding of how sceptical doubts arise reveals how they can be quelled. The "crucial logical point" is that since "the epistemologist is confronting a challenge to natural science that arises from within natural science," he may "in confronting this challenge . . . make free use of all scientific theory."[62] This account of how sceptical doubts arise explains epistemology's "clarified status" and "new setting." Epistemology, or (a significant qualification) "something like it," now "falls into place as a chapter of psychology and hence of natural science."[63] It does so because of the "free use" that the epistemologist is allowed to make of scientific theory.

Stroud objects to this.[64] He argues that the mere fact that the sceptic's argument falls within the general *reductio* pattern by no means entitles the anti-sceptic to make free use of all the knowledge the sceptic has called in question. This is surely correct. But it seems at first that Quine has a reply. This is that Stroud's objection assumes that Quine means to concede that the sceptic's argument is a successful *reductio*, which Quine does not say. On the contrary, Quine seems to imply that the sceptic's argument, though perhaps *prima facie* plausible, is *not* successful. The sceptic's strategy is unexceptionable and "if carried out" would amount to a *reductio ad absurdum* of our pretensions to knowledge of the world. But presumably Quine's point is that it cannot really be carried out. Thus he remarks in reply to Stroud that his "only criticism" of the sceptic for repudiating science entirely, having discovered that science is "vulnerable to illusion on its own showing," is that he is "over-reacting."[65] Presumably, a more comprehensive look at what science has discovered mandates a more measured response. But over-reacting is not the same as following an evidently self-defeating strategy.

The point of this reply is to concede enough to the sceptic to leave room for a theoretically interesting, scientific response to his doubts. But if the point that the sceptic is "over-reacting" is really Quine's "only criticism," his approach to scepticism is much more diagnostic than he appears to want to admit. It is true that, if the sceptic were arguing as Quine suggests, he would be over-reacting. But seeing this requires no comprehensive view of science and nothing in the way of positive epistemological theory. All that is required is to ask how the sceptic's intended *reductio* proceeds. How, exactly, does the discovery that straight sticks look bent in water, together with similar discoveries, "refute science"? It doesn't. At most, it refutes the naive assumption that things are always exactly as they appear to be, to the most casual glance. But common sense about bodies allows for the fact that things are not always the way they seem; and it also tells us something about the circumstances in which this is so. So if the "rudimentary science" at issue is just "common sense about bodies," there is no question of its being refuted. Certainly, there is no threat of radical scepticism here. The fact that "we must not always believe our eyes" does nothing to support the conclusion that perhaps we never should. This is the (fallacious) argument from error all over again. So if we follow up Quine's claim that his "only criticism" of the sceptic is that he is over-reacting, all we find is the thought that the sceptic goes wrong by inferring a radically sceptical conclusion from the mere fact of error. This is at best a purely diagnostic point. But it is not satisfactory even as a diagnosis; for though, as we have seen, it is possible to go wrong this way, the fallacy has been generally recognized. Commonsense points about perceptual illusion have never, in the end, been regarded as sufficient to establish radical scepticism.

This strongly suggests that Quine himself is confused about which arguments support radical scepticism and which do not. Science is supposed to lead to scepticism by contributing the distinction between reality and illusion. However, the question is not whether science contributes *a* distinction between reality and illusion but whether it contributes the right one. I think that it is clear that it does not. The distinction Quine alludes to is one that our commonsense views about the world allow for. This is not the fully general distinction between appearance and reality that the sceptic needs. So it is not suprising that, when Quine traces scepticism to science, he really has in mind a "scientific" discovery of a quite different order. This is the discovery that "our only source of information about the external world is through the impact of light rays and molecules upon our sensory surfaces."[66] Unlike the commonsense distinction between reality and illusion, this is not a contrast between some observations (those that can safely be taken at face value) and others (those that can't): it is a contrast between everything we believe about the external world and something more primitive. We are moving back in the direction of foundationalism, here in the guise of a "scientific" discovery.

Quine's discovery echoes Descartes's pre-philosophical conviction that everything he believes has come to him through the senses. Thus the same criticism applies. No doubt retinal irradiation is a causal pre-condition of forming beliefs about the world; but it does not follow from this that all beliefs about the world, in so far as they amount to knowledge, must be seen as inferences from experiential data. So how does Quine intend us to think of "stimulations" or "retinal irradiations": as physical causes or epistemologically basic data? Are the data the surface irritations themselves, or the information (which presumably falls short of information about the physical world) those irritations supply? There is no answer to this question.

If the "scientific" discovery Quine alludes to is to have any bearing on radical scepticism it must be taken to imply that we labour under an irremediable epistemic disability. What we know by way of our stimulations must amount to less than knowledge of the external world, even though we have no other way of access to external facts. This is how Quine often talks. Thus he tells us that our data are "meagre" compared with the theoretical edifice we erect on their basis. And here "theory" encompasses even our most commonsense talk about objects. Though one is of recent vintage, whereas the other is "shrouded in prehistory," there is no functional difference between "the hypothesis of molecules" and the "hypothesis of ordinary physical objects."[67] This is the traditional doctrine of the absolute priority of experiential over knowledge of the world.

With this doctrine in place, radical scepticism is indeed unavoidable. There is, of course, a kind of argument from error here, but not the commonsensical sort of error that Quine alludes to elsewhere. The error possibilities that now emerge reflect the underdetermination of "theory" by "evidence": the fact that all our data could be what they are even if the world were not at all the way we take it to be. No doubt this is the line of thought that tempts Quine to conclude that the Humean predicament is the human predicament. It is also what Stroud has in mind when he questions our right to appeal to science to defuse the sceptical doubts that arise within science. His conclusion is unquestionably correct: if science leads us to accept the priority of experiential knowledge, then the sceptic's *reductio* is indeed successful; and once all our knowledge of the world has been shown to be hopelessly underdetermined by the only data we can ever have, there can be no question of confidently appealing to that knowledge to rebut the sceptic's argument.

We must, however, stress a point that Stroud notices but does not emphasize. This is that the epistemological doctrine on which radical scepticism depends was never a scientific discovery. Science tells us about the physiology of perception: it does not tell us about the structure of empirical knowledge. The crucial doctrine concerning that structure – the doctrine of the priority of experiential knowledge of the world – is something we impose on our knowledge of the world when we try to assess it in its totality: in other words, when we take up the very position of cosmic exile that Quine thinks we cannot take up.

Quine's uncertainty on this matter creates intolerable tensions in his outlook. Indeed, strictly speaking his position is incoherent. Since retinal irradiations are themselves events in the external world, we cannot claim to have discovered that all we ever really know about are retinal irradiations and not external events. No scientific discovery about retinal irradiations suggests any epistemological moral. Quine does not need knowledge of retinal irradiations, but the information, whatever it is, he supposes them to contain. He also needs this information to be epistemologically basic.

Intermittently, Quine recognizes this. He realizes that once we abandon attempts to go into cosmic exile, and so concentrate on the causal explanation of our talk about objects rather than its wholesale validation, the traditional doctrine of epistemological priority has nothing to recommend it. We can, he says, "just talk explicitly in terms of causal proximity to sensory receptors and drop the talk of epistemological priority."[68] What he does not recognize, however, is that if we drop the talk of epistemological priority, we ought also to drop the talk of ordinary claims about objects as embodying a "theory" that "transcends" the data on which it is based. But he does offer another account of observational data. An observation sentence, according to Quine, is "one on which all speakers of the language give the same verdict when given the same concurrent stimulation," that is "one that is not sensitive to differences in past experience within the speech community." Given this definition, there will generally be "no subjectivity in the phrasing of observation sentences . . . ; they will usually be about bodies."[69] Unfortunately, this is inconsistent with the claim, essential to representing scepticism as a scientific problem, that there is no functional difference between the hypothesis of molecules and the "hypothesis" of ordinary physical objects, for there is at least the functional difference between observation sentences and the rest. Theoretical sentences, according to Quine, can never be verified one at a time, but only in the context of a large body of further theoretical commitments. Such sentences "have no empirical consequences they can call their own: they confront the tribunal of sensory evidence only in more or less inclusive aggregates." By contrast, the observation sentence is "the minimal verifiable aggregate; it has an empirical content all its own and wears it on its sleeve."[70]

Of course, this is the sort of distinction between observation and theory that emerges when we "view the matter unreservedly in the context of the external world."[71] But this is just another way of making the point that the sort of observation/theory distinction that is suggested by an empirical or "scientific" approach to the practice of scientific theorizing is not the one that is relevant to the sceptical problem about our knowledge of the external world. That distinction must have its roots elsewhere and it must put all our beliefs about the world on the side of "theory," something it can do only by making the content of "observation" fall short of information about objects. Put it this way: Quine's account of obervation sentences sets no limits to what, given suitable abilities and training, might be observationally reported. It is therefore hostile to the idea that we occupy some fixed epistemic position, and so labour under some chronic epistemic disability. Since the threat of scepticism is inseparable from the idea that such an epistemic position belongs to the human condition, this means that Quine's later account of observation sentences is not just not relevant but is actually opposed to the ideas that make that threat seem so real. Quine takes scepticism seriously only because he has a competing conception of observation: that which takes "stimulations" to be our only "source of information" concerning the external world, and which reduces even the most commonsensical remarks to theoretical claims involving various "posits." This competing conception of obervation is just the myth of our epistemic position in science fiction guise.

Ironically, the point that the sceptic's way of drawing the appearance/ reality distinction, which is what Quine's observation/theory distinction comes to in the form that connects it with scepticism, stands or falls with the project of assessing the totality of our knowledge of the world is one that Quine himself often makes. Thus he remarks that "The old tendency to associate observation sentences with a subjective sensory subject matter ... was due to the drive to base science on something firmer and prior in the subject's experience." And he adds, "we dropped that project." However, what he does not do is draw the inevitable conclusion: that since the sceptical problem about our knowledge of the world, which lies at the heart of the Humean predicament, depends crucially, and on Quine's own showing, on the tendency just decried, dropping that project leaves no reason for maintaining that the Humean predicament is the human predicament. It leaves no reason for supposing that there is a sceptical problem that demands even a theoretical solution, much less a scientific one. What there is room for is a deeper theoretical *diagnosis* than Quine has put forward.

So the position is this: there are discoveries about the possibility of illusion that can be regarded as discoveries of rudimentary science but which do nothing to support radical scepticism. Equally, there is an epistemological doctrine that leads to radical scepticism but which is in no sense a scientific discovery. Quine conflates the two because of the loose way he talks about stimulations as "data." The result of this conflation is the view that radical scepticism is a "scientific" problem, amenable to scientific solution.

Just as Quine is in two minds about the notion of "data," so he is in two minds about the goal of naturalized epistemology. As we have seen,

Quine appears to reject a purely diagnostic approach to epistemological problems. He does so because he thinks that epistemology, or something like it, goes on, though with a clarified status. But whether there is real disagreement here depends on what epistemology comes to after its status has been clarified. The new "naturalized" epistemology, Quine tells us:

> studies a natural phenomenon, viz, a physical human subject. This human subject is accorded a certain experimentally controlled input – certain patterns of irradiation in assorted frequencies, for instance – and in the fullness of time the subject delivers as output a description of the three dimensional external world and its history. The relation between the meager input and the torrential output is a relation that we are prompted to study for somewhat the same reasons that always prompted epistemology; namely in order to see how evidence relates to theory, and in what ways one's theory of nature transcends any available evidence.[72]

But notice that this equates the distinction between evidence and theory with that between input and output, and so incorporates the confusion over the notion of data that vitiates Quine's attempt to represent scepticism as a problem that arises from within science itself. What, if anything, remains once this confusion is cleared away?

One way to understand this project is to see it as attempting an explanation of how our interactions with the world, as we currently understand it, lead us to understand the world in just that way. This will be a causal explanation: a scientific account of how scientific views arise. This does not render naturalized epistemology automatically devoid of all epistemological significance, and so epistemology in name only. But it does mean that, if it connects with any disinction between appearance and reality, or evidence and theory, it will not be the distinction that animates arguments for radical scepticism. It may, for example, trace the process by which classifications based on "our immediate animal sense of similarity" give way to those reflecting "the remoter objectivity of a similarity determined by scientific theory."[73] In this way, it will reveal some of our ways of seeing the world as "superficial," responsive to and evolving in the light of primitive needs, such as food gathering, but poor guides to the ultimate character of physical reality. Thus we find that "Color is king in our innate quality space, but undistinguished in cosmic circles."[74] It looms large for animals that evolved wondering which vegetables to eat; but these same animals have to forget about it when they turn to theoretical physics. Science itself has taught us to rethink the significance of some of the observations that set us on the road to science. We have learned that there is no reason to suppose that "our subjective spacing of qualities" must have "a special purchase on nature and a lien on the future." Natural selection has given us both "a color-slanted quality space and the ingenuity to rise above it."[75]

This is very much in the same spirit as Nagel's conception of the way advances in science constitute advances in objectivity. As we change our views about the world, we make increasingly sophisticated allowances for our perceptual and cultural idiosyncrasies. By so doing, we flesh out one idea of the world as "what is there anyway." Quine's idea of a naturalized epistemology is thus a very close relative of Williams's "absolute conception of reality" and Nagel's "objective view."

This account of naturalized epistemology, and of how it ties up with questions about appearance and reality, fits in well with Quine's acceptance of the circularity that his project seems to involve. There is, he says, "reciprocal containment . . . : epistemology in natural science and natural science in epistemology."[76] He agrees that "If the epistemologist's goal is validation of the grounds of empirical science, he defeats his purpose by using psychology or other empirical science in its validation." But no such objection applies once we have "stopped dreaming of deducing science from sense data." For then we are "after an understanding of science as an institution or process in the world, and we do not intend that understanding to be any better than the science that is its object."[77] But again, in so far as there is a real project here, it is one that has nothing to do with scepticism. As I argued in connection with Nagel, the sort of "reduction to appearance" that goes with the kind of advance in objectivity that a naturalized epistemology might describe does not lead to the distinction between appearance and reality that the sceptic requires.

"Science" does indeed constantly teach us to distinguish "appearance" from "reality." It teaches us how some observations can be relied on and some cannot; it teaches us to allow for factors in our biological or psychological makeup that can lead to various kinds of error, and so on: it alerts us to Bacon's Idols of the Tribe and the Cave. The time of a celestial event recorded by a given competent observer may diverge, in initially unpredictable ways, from the time recorded by other observers. This suggests observer error. Taking into account the different reaction times of different observers, their "personal equations," allows us to reconcile these discrepant observations. Learning to make corrections of this kind, we learn more about what "our constitution" contributes to how we see the world. This is a more sophisticated, more recognizably "scientific" example than learning to allow for a straight stick's looking bent in water. But no matter how far we push inquiries of this sort, we will always be in the position of using some things we think about the world to correct others. As we saw, this is what Nagel balks at: he finds his aspirations blocked by the fact that "whatever we use to understand certain interactions between ourselves and the world is not itself the object of that understanding." But this shows that, for Nagel, who connects dependence on "our constitution" with the sceptical potential of our natural realism, more is at stake than a piecemeal, though indefinitely expandable, investigation of how our constitution affects "appearances." Using some of our views about the world to correct others becomes objectionable when, and only when, our aim is to secure all our knowledge of the world, all at once, which is the very project Quine is supposed to have dropped.

Here we return to Quine's original, and ineffective, sceptical argument from illusion. The advances in objectivity Quine and Nagel describe do encourage a certain modesty: the recognition that observations can be prone to systematic distortion and that none of our theoretical views have "a lien on the future." But we should not slip back and forth between the modesty that advances in objectivity do promote and the chronic vulnerability to radical scepticism that has another source entirely. Nagel, as we saw, is prone to do just this. Though Quine is cagier, or more ambivalent, about the status of scepticism, his writings allow us to trace a similar configuration of ideas.

A final point: the reason for not fearing circularity in connection with the explanatory project of naturalized epistemology has to be distinguished from the rejection of the "needless logical timidity" that led the old epistemologist to eschew meeting the sceptic with scientific arguments. In the one case, we are told not to fear circularity because the new epistemological project has nothing to do with the validation of science. In the other, we are told that since scepticism – the challenge to validate science – is itself a scientific problem, we are entitled to appeal to scientific knowledge in solving it, traditional scruples about circularity notwithstanding. The first reason for not fearing circularity tells us nothing about how scepticism is to be answered since it applies to a project that has no connection with radical scepticism. As for the second, we found it to be confused, pointing either to a fallacy that could be diagnosed without the aid of elaborate scientific knowledge, or else to an epistemological problem which, because of its extra-scientific source, cannot be resolved scientifically at all, once its legitimacy is admitted. Unfortunately, Quine does not distinguish the two reasons for not fearing circularity. If he did, he would not be tempted to make any connection between responding to scepticism and his conception of a naturalized epistemology.

Quine's attempt to represent scepticism as a scientific problem, then, gives us no reason to think that science, as the quest for objective knowledge, or even as incorporating the quest for objective self-understanding, is self-defeating. The only thing that threatens to defeat our aspirations to objective knowledge is an epistemological doctrine whose force can be appreciated only from the position of cosmic exile that Quine, a shade dogmatically perhaps, refuses to assume.

## 6.6 TRUTH AND CONTEXT

In conclusion, let me return briefly to some questions about truth. I argued earlier that adopting a deflationary attitude towards truth does not necessarily put any serious obstacles in the sceptic's way. His question about the relation of justification to truth can be posed without reliance on any particular account of what, if anything, truth consists in. He simply asks why, for any belief that p, p's being confirmed according to our standards makes it likely that p? Whether such questions are legitimate, I have argued, turns on the acceptability of epistemological rather than metaphysical realism. No matter what we say about metaphysical realism, epistemological realism creates the logical space for sceptical problems.

So suppose, conversely, we reject epistemological realism while holding on to metaphysical realism, minimal or otherwise. Are we equally open to sceptical challenge?

I think not, for a reason implicit in an argument already given: epistemological problems cannot be erected on a purely metaphysical basis. But this general consideration may fail to carry conviction in this particular case. In fact, we might well suppose that combining a contextualist view of justification with a realist view of truth raises the sceptical problem about the relation between truth and justification in an even more acute form. For if justification strategies vary with context, but truth remains always the same, a context-insensitive property of beliefs, or belief-world relation, won't it be miraculous if these heterogeneous procedures all tend to produce truth. It will certainly take some explaining.[78]

Plausible as it seems at first, I do not find this line of argument convincing. It assumes that the contextualist is worse off than the typical coherence theorist because he has many sets of epistemic criteria to connect with truth instead of just one. But this misrepresents the contrast between them. In particular, the objection overlooks the externalist element in contextualism. For a contextualist, the direction of inquiry holds certain propositions contextually fixed. But since knowledge may require that those propositions actually be true, the contextualist does more than insist that justification procedures are diverse and context sensitive: he denies that justification is always a matter of satisfying purely epistemic criteria. Accordingly, he feels under no compulsion to show, in some general way, how satisfying diverse collections of such criteria will tend always to ensure the presence of some non-epistemic relation between our beliefs and the world. Questions about the truth-conduciveness of justification procedures will have to be asked case by case and, when they are so asked, they will be answerable empirically. The criterial conception of justification belongs to the traditional coherence theorist, who insists on looking for justification at the level of "our total view." We shall return to the contextualist's rejection of this conception of justification in the next chapter.

By way of illustration, suppose we have adopted a rich, theoretical form of realism, conceiving truth in terms of a causal-physical relation of reference; and suppose we now ask about the value of some particular kind of evidence, for example why the readings given by a particular piece of apparatus should be taken as reliable indicators of the truth of certain statements about the occurrence of a given kind of physical event: then in this and similar contexts, we will be able to connect evidence with truth, understood in causal terms, provided we are allowed to appeal to knowledge of the relevant causal relations. We will run into a serious sceptical problem only if the appeal to such knowledge is ruled out of court. Such a ruling will in turn depend on the legitimacy of following the traditional sceptical procedure and collecting our beliefs into broad, context-independent epistemological classes and insisting that we assess the epistemic standing of all the beliefs in some such class all at once. But we have now come right back to what I have been calling epistemological realism. We no longer have even a prima facie sceptical problem resting on metaphysical realism alone.

I conclude that epistemological realism is the crucial presupposition of sceptical questions, indeed that metaphysical realism has no particular connection with any sceptical problems or answers to them. This is not to say that we might as well be metaphysical realists. On the contrary, once the question of how we should understand truth has been disconnected from the project of responding to scepticism, there are no reasons for not being a deflationist. But that is another argument entirely.[79]

# Coherence and Truth

## 7.1 WHAT IS A COHERENCE THEORY?

Let us return to the problem of connecting "coherence" with truth. This problem arises out of two apparently compelling thoughts: first, that if we are to have knowledge of an objective world, the truth of what we believe about the world must be independent of our believing it; and second, that justification is inevitably a matter of supporting beliefs by other beliefs, hence in this minimal sense a matter of coherence. These thoughts seem to imply that there is no accounting for the truth-conduciveness of (what we like to think of as) epistemic justification, for why does the fact that our beliefs hang together, supposing they do, give the least indication that they are true?

As I said, the availability of a route to scepticism that apparently involves little or nothing in the way of contentious epistemological theory, taking for granted only the very minimum that must be involved in any concept of objective truth, lends considerable plausibility to the thought that we invite scepticism merely by aspiring to knowledge of an objective world. Add to this the fact that the vestigial epistemological ideas it does exploit seem decidedly *anti*-foundationalist and what becomes of my claim that foundationalism is an essential presupposition of sceptical argument?

My strategy for meeting this objection has been to argue that the standing invitation to scepticism supposedly contained in the very idea of knowledge of an objective world has its real source, not in any particular understanding of truth, but in the attempt to assess our knowledge of the world as a whole, a project that stands or falls with a foundationalist conception of justification. Examining attempts to argue that scepticism, or at least a *prima facie* threat of scepticism, is immanent in the quest for objective knowledge, we found that the crucial move consists in treating all our beliefs about the world as "appearances." So, I suggested, the challenge to connect coherence with truth is just a variant of the familiar sceptical challenge to show how knowledge is possible, given

that "appearances" could be just what they are even if the world were not
at all what we take it to be, a challenge that depends essentially on
foundationalist ideas about epistemological priority. The only difference lies
in an extension or generalization of the notion of "appearances" from
sensory appearances ("experience") to the subject's entire "notional world."
Putting the argument in terms of coherence may obscure the sceptic's
foundationalist preconceptions but will not eliminate them.

If this is right, there must be something wrong with the familiar contrast
between foundationalist and coherentist theories of justification. And I
think there is. In my view, there is no stable doctrine that deserves to be
called "the coherence theory of justification." As we shall see, the price the
coherence theorist pays for avoiding fatal concessions to contextualism is
seeing his theory collapse into a variant form of foundationalism. Or in the
case of Davidson's theory, which may not in the end be best thought of as a
coherence theory at all, we shall find an uneasy mixture of theoretical
diagnosis and would-be direct refutation.

It is not easy to discuss "the" coherence theory of justification, since
agreement as to what form a coherence theory theory should take is far
from complete. However, two fundamental points will guide my discussion.

The first is that what I am referring to as "coherence theories" are
intended by their proponents to offer *direct answers* to scepticism. Such theories are not offered as contributions to the diagnosis, theoretical or therapeutic, of sceptical questions. Their advocates see nothing wrong with the
attempt to assess all our knowledge of the world, all at once. They think
that the question "Why suppose that any of our beliefs about the world are
the least bit justified?" can be answered in terms of the coherence of our
belief system. Or if they entertain doubts about the possibility of giving a
conclusive answer along these lines, their conception of the epistemological
task commits them to conceding that the sceptic *cannot* finally be answered.

Clearly, this must be the attitude of any coherence theorist inclined to
recast the notion of truth in epistemic terms. No one who intended his
account of justification as a contribution to a theoretical diagnosis of
scepticism would feel the need to refashion the concept of truth. The point
of this refashioning is to provide an *a priori* link between the nature and test
of truth. But the demand for such a connection arises only in connection
with attempts to assess the totality of our beliefs about the world. To
answer questions about particular, highly specific justification procedures,
raised in contexts where our entire knowledge of the world is *not* up for
assessment, empirical links will do.

What about those more recent coherence theorists, such as Davidson and
Bonjour, who would like to combine a coherence theory of justification with
a correspondence theory of truth? They too hold that scepticism requires a
direct answer. As for Davidson, recall his aim of providing "a reason for

supposing coherent beliefs are true." Because he concedes that explaining justification in terms of coherence invites the question "how can coherence alone supply grounds for belief?", Davidson thinks that this aim imposes itself on the proponent of even the most "mild" coherence theory. But to accept this aim is to forgo a diagnostic approach to scepticism. This is why, though Davidson registers his agreement with Richard Rorty's remark that "nothing counts as justification unless by reference to what we already accept, and there is no way to get outside our beliefs and our language so as to find some test other than coherence," he adds that, whereas Rorty thinks that this somehow undercuts the threat of scepticism, his (Davidson's) view is "there remains a question how . . . we nevertheless can have knowledge of, and talk about, an objective public world which is not of our own making."[1] Nor is it surprising that the reason Davidson eventually offers for supposing coherent beliefs true – namely, that our concepts of belief and meaning exclude the possibility of our beliefs being mostly false – is entirely *a priori*: no other sort of answer is available, once the totality of our knowledge of the world has been called in question. This is scepticism taken at face value.

We find a similar attitude behind Bonjour's defence of a coherence theory of justification. Bonjour criticizes Rorty and myself for allegedly suggesting that "skepticism should be disregarded entirely." In Bonjour's eyes, "if skeptics did not exist, . . . the serious epistemologist would have to invent them." This is because the serious epistemologist must offer both "an account of the standards of epistemic justification" and "a *metajustification* [emphasis in original] for the proposed account by showing the proposed standards to be adequately truth conducive." Since Bonjour rejects epistemic analyses of truth, he takes this to require showing *a priori* that "achieving coherence in one's system of beliefs is . . . at least likely to yield correspondence."[2]

I think that Davidson and Bonjour are right to take this attitude, given their understanding of what a coherence theory of justification involves. Rorty is wrong to think that scepticism can be undercut *merely* by claiming that "there is no way to get outside our beliefs and our language so as to find some test other than coherence." In fact Rorty's attitude is incoherent. To see this, suppose we said to Rorty that of course we can "get outside" our beliefs and our language: we do it all the time. For one thing, we do more than talk about objects, we handle them too. But even the use of language points beyond language: to the things we talk about. So why should we think of "our beliefs" and "our language" as a kind of prison that we can't "get outside"? This way of talking is altogether too reminiscent of "our epistemic situation," the difference being that, whereas the sceptic laments our imprisonment, Rorty tells us not to worry about what could not be otherwise.

Such reflections can make us wonder whether it is really so obvious that there is no such thing as verification by confrontation, hence no test of truth other than coherence. If someone says that there is a robin on the fence, and I look out of the window to see for myself, why isn't this a case of verifying a claim by checking it against the facts? The reply will be that such questions miss the point. What is ordinarily called "checking the facts" is in reality a matter of acquiring further beliefs, e.g. perceptual beliefs. But even so, if these beliefs *are* true, if they do record facts, why aren't some claims ultimately accepted or rejected by reference to facts, and not *just* other beliefs? Ordinarily, to say that I accepted a claim simply because it accorded with my beliefs would be to imply that I did not really know it to be true, which is not what the coherentist critic of scepticism intends.

Of course, Rorty means to make a philosophical point, not deny a truism. However, the point in question implies commitments that do not fit with a diagnostic approach to scepticism, which is why his attitude is incoherent. What my imagined exchange reveals is that the rejection of attempts to "get outside our beliefs," as much as the attempts themselves, carries its intended meaning only in the context of a call for an assessment of the totality of our beliefs about the world, for only in this context is it plausible to offer a *dilemma* between committing oneself to "getting outside language" and conceding that there is "no test other than coherence." To generate Rorty's stark contrast, we must disqualify all ordinary involvements with objects from counting as "getting outside," which makes sense only if our goal is to validate the totality of our beliefs about the world. If Rorty rejects the traditional epistemological project, he has no business claiming that we cannot get outside language. But if he does not, the admission that we cannot get outside language, though it will make its intended point, will be a concession to scepticism, not a refutation of it. We can conclude that a consistent theoretical diagnostician should be suspicious of the dichotomy between foundationalism (of the Schlick type) and the so-called coherence theory, seeing both positions as responses to a question that ought not to be taken at face value. Equally, by accepting this dilemma and taking one horn, Rorty shows that he is not such a diagnostician, or anyway not consistently. Davidson's sense that, when things have got this far, sceptical questions have been placed decisively on the table is entirely correct.

So much for the first feature of coherence theories, that they are intended as direct answers to scepticism. The second feature I want to emphasize is that they are intended to be alternatives to foundational theories. Though we might think this goes without saying, in practice the gap between foundational and coherence theories often turns out to be narrower than we might expect. If I am right in my diagnosis of scepticism, this is not surprising. If scepticism presupposes foundationalism, there is an essential tension in a conception of justification which is intended to offer a direct answer to the sceptic while steering clear of foundationalist presuppositions. This connects with certain disagreements over what makes for a coherence theory: different suggestions reflect different responses to this tension.

Let us recall the standard foundationalist claim that the coherence theory, though the only alternative to foundationalism, makes it possible to believe with justification anything whatsoever. Philosophers who have taken this thought seriously have tended to see it not only as establishing the need to recognize epistemologically basic beliefs, but also as showing that a certain kind of account must be given of how those beliefs come to constitute knowledge. The idea has been that unless there are points at which our web of belief is tied to the facts, by a kind of "direct," non-conceptual grasping of reality, then no matter how complex its internal relations of justification, the whole thing may be an elaborate delusion.[3] It is therefore essential that we grasp some truths by comparing beliefs with facts: and since, in the light of sceptical possibilities, these generally turn out to be experiential facts, we are led to foundationalism in its most familiar form. It is against the background of this tradition that Davidson, like Rorty, defines a coherence theory of knowledge as one that rejects the idea of verification by confrontation. While admitting that it is "natural to distinguish coherence theories from others by reference to the question of whether or not justification comes to an end," he argues that, since there are "coherence theorists who hold that some beliefs can serve as a basis for the rest," this "does not define the position." He concludes that "What distinguishes a coherence theory is simply the claim that nothing can count as a reason for holding a belief except another belief."[4]

This is a bold and not immediately plausible claim. Even if there are philosophers calling themselves "coherence theorists" willing to admit that "some beliefs can serve as a basis for the rest," coherentism's most typical advocates do just what Davidson objects to: define the theory in terms of its characteristic account of the structure of epistemic justification. However, there may be less disagreement here than meets the eye. As we shall see, even philosophers who stress the coherence theory's "nonlinear" conception of justification cannot avoid conceding that justification comes to an end somewhere. But this does not mean that we can conclude, without further argument, that there is no distinction between foundationalism and the coherence theory. As always, we must distinguish formal from substantive foundationalism, so that what matters need not be *whether* justification comes to an end but, as Davidson suggests, where, why and how.

This said, however, I don't see that Davidson's negative thesis does any better than the suggestion he rejects at defining the coherentist position. Just as, in the theory of truth, the negative thesis that truth is not an epistemic notion fails to distinguish Davidson's minimal but substantive conception of truth theory from deflationary conceptions, so in epistemology the rejection of verification by confrontation – which we might call the "No Acquaintance Principle" – does not distinguish the coherence theory from a contextualist view. A contextualist may well agree that nothing *counts as a reason* for holding a belief except another belief. But he may deny that knowledge and justification always derive exclusively from reasons, perhaps by allowing them to depend in certain cases on features of epistemic contexts that are not even represented in the knower's beliefs, much less *known* to be present.

We must remember that this "externalist" position is available to a contextualist only because his conception of justification is hostile to the sceptic's demand for a total assessment of our knowledge of the world. I have agreed with critics of externalism that this is a demand that no externalist view of knowledge can meet head on. Thus I hold that a contextualist conception of justification can be advanced only in conjunction with a theoretical diagnosis of scepticism: it cannot amount to a direct answer. It follows that, since Davidson (like coherence theorists generally) clearly *does* intend his theory to leave room for a direct answer to scepticism, he cannot be a contextualist. Furthermore, since his No Acquaintance Principle does not distinguish coherentists from contextualists, there must be more to the coherence theory, even in Davidson's mild version, than is captured by this negative thesis. The question is: what more?

## 7.2   RADICAL HOLISM

Like Davidson, Bonjour defines the coherence theory negatively, in terms of its rejection of a key foundationalist idea. But whereas Davidson stresses verification by confrontation, Bonjour fastens on foundationalism's "linear" conception of justification. On this conception, inferential justification is transmitted along chains of reasoning as truth is transmitted across logical consequence or nobility by descent. This picture of justification apparently mandates foundationalism. There can be no infinite regress of premises for premises for premises . . . ; circular reasoning is inadmissible; and no justifying inference can start from mere assumptions. It follows that some justification must be absolutely non-inferential. Some beliefs or propositions must be intrinsically credible, hence epistemologically basic.

This argument – Agrippa's trilemma – lies behind Schlick's classic attack on the coherence theory. The only way to avoid the absurdity that any system of belief is as good as any other is: "not to allow that any statements whatever can be abandoned or altered, but rather to specify those that are to be maintained, to which the remainder are to be accommodated."[5] In effect, Schlick sees the coherence theorist as willing to settle for circular justification, in the guise of mutual consistency. Since he regards this as evidently unsatisfactory, and since he assumes more or less without discussion that there can be no infinite regress of justification, he concludes that there must be terminating beliefs that are not mere assumptions. And if they are not mere assumptions, this must be because they possess some kind of intrinsic epistemic privilege. This is not so much a refutation of scepticism as a dogmatic claim that since scepticism must be false, and since there is no viable competitor to foundationalism, foundationalism must be true.

Schlick's key thought is that, for a coherence theorist, any belief can be justified simply by embedding it in a network of suitable (mutually) supporting beliefs, even though they may be as absurd and unwarranted as the original belief itself. Thus we find him claiming that:

> If one is to take coherence seriously as a general criterion of truth, then one must consider arbitrary fairy stories to be as true as a historical report, or as statements in a textbook of chemistry, provided the story is constructed in such a way that no contradiction ever arises[6].

As a result, the coherence theory: "fails altogether to give an unambiguous criterion of truth, for by means of it I can arrive at any number of consistent systems of statements which are incompatible with one another."[7] This shows that the coherence theory is "logically impossible".

An obvious objection is that Schlick has failed to distinguish theories of truth from theories of justification. The claim that the coherence theory is "logically impossible" goes through only if the theory is taken to be a theory of truth, and even then only if the coherence theorist concedes that any consistent system is true. On the other hand, if the topic is justification, the demand for an "unambiguous criterion of truth" – i.e. for a criterion that always selects a unique justified system – is surely too strong, and not even a strict foundationalist like Schlick can hope to meet it. Schlick takes his argument to show that the only way to avoid the absurdity that there are indefinitely many systems of belief with equal claims to be "true" is to identify a privileged class of basic statements, "confirmations," that "are to be maintained" and to which "the remainder are to be accommodated"; and no matter how we specify the beliefs that are to be maintained, there is no reason to suppose that there will invariably be a unique, best way of "accommodating" the remainder to them.[8]

Does clearing up these confusions dispose of Schlick's argument? Clearly not. The heart of his objection to the coherence theory is not that, at any time, there must be a unique system of justified beliefs but that there cannot be endlessly many. Somewhere there must be a limit to what can be

justifiably believed. It must be possible to identify some systems of belief as
superior to others even if, at a given stage of inquiry, there may be several
more or less as good. At the very least, a critic can insist, the coherence
theory must make it clear why "standard" systems of beliefs are preferable
to sceptical alternatives. But if the coherence theory is committed to the
tenability of any arbitrary fairy story, it cannot hope to meet even this
modest requirement.

This "many systems" objection is a dramatic version of the sceptical
argument that has been the central topic of this chapter and the last: the
argument that explaining justification in terms of coherence decouples
justification and truth. Typically, the coherence theorist replies by rejecting
the equation of coherence with mere logical consistency. In assuming that
statements cohere whenever "no contradictions exist between them,"[9]
Schlick misrepresents the mainstream coherentist tradition. As Bonjour
put it, coherence theorists do not take coherence to consist merely in "the
absence of conflict" but insist on "some sort of positive connection . . .
among beliefs."[10] However, focussing too closely on the denial that consistency is sufficient for coherence may lead us to miss what is really at
issue. On first hearing, an insistence on "positive connections" sounds like
a demand for an expanded stock of epistemologically significant relations.
Perhaps coherence will involve mutual entailment, or if this is too much to
expect, quasi-logical relations – say of confirmation or probability – weaker
than entailment but stronger than consistency. However, if this were the
point, it is not clear that Schlick's argument would be met, for what would
prevent our surrounding our arbitrary fairy story with logically appropriate
confirming statements? It is therefore important to realize that more is at
issue here than what sorts of epistemologically significant relations between
statements we should recognize. In rejecting the equation of coherence with
consistency, the coherence theorist is not simply or even primarily advocating a richer conception of relations between individual statements. His
intention is rather to direct our attention away from relations between
particular statements to certain features of belief-systems taken as a whole.
He therefore sees himself as having a different theory of the structure of
justification, one in which the ultimate unit is not the individual statement
or belief but rather the entire system. Of course, relations between particular beliefs will be important, but not so much in themselves as for their
contribution to the coherence of some "total view."

The great vice of the "linear" conception of justification, the argument
goes, is to obscure the fact that justification is "essentially systematic or
holistic in character."[11] In effect, Schlick argues that if justification does
not depend on consistency with certain privileged beliefs, it must reduce to
consistency *simpliciter*, and all this shows is Schlick's inability to break with
the linear conception. Bradley put the coherentist view succinctly when he

remarked that "my experience is solid, not so far as it is a superstructure but so far as it is a system."[12] Contemporary coherence theorists like Sellars have something similar in mind when they identify coherence with *explanatory* coherence.[13] Once we are alive to the importance of systematic features of our belief-system as a whole, we realize immediately that not just any consistent set of beliefs, even one to which we add a few "positive connections," will be a serious system.

Historically, the emphasis on system is as important to the coherence theory as the rejection of verification by confrontation. When Bonjour tells us that "beliefs are justified by being inferentially related to other beliefs *in the overall context of a coherent system*" he places himself squarely in the tradition of Bradley and Blanshard.[14] The same goes for Gilbert Harman, who argues that justification depends on inference and that inference is a process by which we modify what we currently believe so as to produce a new "total resulting view." So understood, inference is not a simple linear process of deriving new beliefs from given premises (or deleting old ones to resolve contradictions) but is guided by large-scale systematic considerations. The aim of inference is to "increase the explanatory coherence of our view, making it more complete, less *ad hoc*, more plausible."[15] We will be justified in adding a given belief to our overall system if doing so (perhaps along with other modifications) leads to an increase in overall explanatory coherence: i.e. an increase in the explanatory coherence of our *total* view, our entire system of beliefs. I call the doctrine that epistemic justification supervenes on features of our belief system taken as a whole "radical holism."

Explanatory coherence is a complex, multi-criterial notion and theorists have differed over how it is to be understood. But two aspects of coherence are absolutely fundamental and are thus emphasized by virtually everyone. One is what Bradley called "comprehensiveness." The goal of inquiry is to understand as much as possible and so, other things being equal, a system is more coherent the more it encompasses. But if out goal is understanding, mere comprehensiveness is insufficient: equally important is interconnectedness or systematicity. As Bonjour puts it, the coherence of a system of beliefs is "increased by the presence of inferential connections between its component members" and "diminished to the extent to which it is divided into subsystems of beliefs which are relatively unconnected to each other by inferential connections."[16]

Clearly, these twin requirements of comprehensiveness and systematicity must work in tandem, neither having much merit on its own. Though we could achieve a high degree of explanatory integration by minimizing the number of fundamental theoretical views to which we are committed, this does not entitle us to ignore or even deny facts that we cannot explain: we should not pursue explanatory integration at the cost of unduly impoverishing our system of beliefs. Equally, we could be as comprehensive as we liked if systematic considerations meant nothing to us. But what we want is to take in as much as we can while preserving a high degree of logical interconnectedness among our beliefs.

Now although radical holism is a very strong thesis, it can appear deceptively weak. Recall Harman's claim that inference is a passage from one total view to another. In one way, this is trivially true: if I acquire a new belief or abandon an old one the sum total of my beliefs changes, and so I can be said to have modified my total view. But in this sense, inference can be a passage from one total view to another without its being the case that all my beliefs are essentially involved in every inference. This more or less innocuous talk of transitions between total views must therefore be distinguished from the claim that, in any example of inference, all my beliefs are simultaneously at stake, so that in the passage from one total view to another all *are* essentially involved. This latter, far-from-trivial view is what Harman's account of inference implies and what I understand by radical holism. It is the view that, in any inference, all beliefs are up for grabs, so that inference consists in comparing the total views that result from various modifications to our existing system, with a view to selecting the most coherent.

Commitment to radical holism is also apt to be obscured by a tendency on the part of coherence theorists to think of "coherence" in two different ways. Although officially "coherence" designates a property of our belief system taken as a whole, it often gets treated as the name of a relation that a candidate belief may or may not bear to some antecedently given system, usually the system of beliefs that one actually has. Thus Davidson tells us that, to defeat scepticism, a coherence theorist must show that "most of the beliefs in a coherent total set are true,"[17] here taking coherence as a property of "total sets" of beliefs. But he also claims to establish that "there is a legitimate presumption that any one [of a person's beliefs], *if it coheres with the rest*, is true," treating coherence as a matter of a given belief's fitting in with an existing body of beliefs.[18] Even Bonjour, who lays particular stress on the holistic character of coherentist justification, can be found claiming that according to the coherence theory, "the epistemic status of an empirical belief derives entirely from its coherence with the believer's overall system of empirical beliefs."[19] But both Davidson and Bonjour are following precedent. "What really tests a judgment," Blanshard writes, "is the extent of our accepted world that is implicated with it and would be carried down with it if it fell." "That," he concludes, "is the test of coherence."[20] We may call the two versions of coherence "systematic" and "relational."

I do not say that all philosophers who think of themselves as coherence theorists use "coherence" ambiguously. Lehrer, for one, opts unequivocally for relational coherence. According to Lehrer, I am justified in accepting a given proposition at a particular time if and only if it coheres with my "acceptance system" at that time. My acceptance system consists of all those propositions I accept for the purpose of obtaining truth and avoiding error with respect to the specific things accepted; and a proposition coheres with this system if and only if all its competitors are either beaten or neutralized, on the basis of the propositions the system contains. I will not go into the details of such notions as neutralization: the point I want to make is simply that this version of the coherence theory finds no use for anything like Bonjour's conception of "global" coherence. There is, however, reason to doubt whether a theory like this should be thought of as a coherence theory. More than a verbal point is at stake. However we decide to use the phrase "coherence theory," we should be clear about the theoretical distance separating Lehrer's "coherence theory" from more typical examples.

First of all, it is not clear that coherence with one's acceptance system involves coherence with one's total system in anything other than the trivial sense noted above. Nothing in Lehrer's theory suggests that all elements in the system are essentially involved in defeating or neutralizing any given proposition's competitors. Accordingly, Lehrer's theory may not be radically holistic and could even be compatible with contextualism,[21] But since we have connected radical holism with the coherence theorist's response to scepticism, the question naturally arises of whether a theory of Lehrer's type offers a direct answer to the sceptic. It is not clear that Lehrer even intends it to. Coherence with one's acceptance system only establishes "personal justification," which is not objective justification.

True, Lehrer does argue that each of us is justified in accepting, as a kind of first principle:

T. I am a trustworthy evaluator of truth.

This is because, if I accept T, my acceptance system will see to it that sceptical competitors for T are either beaten or neutralized. But again, the justification is only personal. T's sceptical competitors are excluded by things I actually accept and these could be false, T included. It seems plausible that T would be false if I were a brain in a vat or the victim of Descartes's *malin genie*. So even if I remained personally justified in accepting T, I would lack knowledge.

On this point, Lehrer agrees with the sceptic. But he thinks that it is important to clear up an ambiguity in the notion of justification. Given suitable input, a brain in a vat might be justified in holding the same beliefs as you and I, for "When such a person accepts that he sees a hand before him, he has exactly the same reasons for thinking what he accepts is true as any person in the actual world."[22] Still, his justification is defeated by an error on which it rests. Accordingly, complete justification, which is objective, requires coherence with one's "verific system," i.e. the system derived by eliminating all falsehoods from one's acceptance system. And knowledge, according to Lehrer, requires even more: undefeated justification. This is defined in terms of coherence with a person's "ultrasystem." This comprises not just one's verific system but all acceptance systems derived from one's actual system by the logically consistent addition of truths or elimination of falsehoods. The thought here is that one should not lose any knowledge by coming to accept more truths. A knowledge-yielding justification should survive all "verific" modifications to the acceptance system on which it depends.

There is much that is attractive about Lehrer's position. The point to note, however, is that when it comes to objective justification, which is the sceptic's concern, Lehrer's theory goes externalist. Since I cannot distinguish between the propositions I currently accept and those that are actually true, I cannot know whether I am more than personally justified in accepting a particular proposition; though if I do accept it, my acceptance might amount to knowledge. Lehrer is not, of course, under any illusions about this, and he even calls his theory "doxastic reliabilism." As he says, "Undefeated objective justification that does not rest on any error depends on the truth of T, that is on our actually being trustworthy evaluators of truth."[23] Anyway, not only is Lehrer's theory not clearly committed to radical holism, in so far as it bears on objective justification it is a form of externalism. These are reasons for not considering it a true coherence theory.[24] It is certainly atypical.

But to return to the main theme, even when a theorist uses "coherence" ambiguously, applying it both to relational and systematic coherence, the ambiguity need not be fatal. As Blanshard's remark on the test of coherence makes clear, to decide whether a given candidate belief coheres with our existing system of beliefs we must determine what damage rejecting that candidate would do to our existing system taken as a whole. Perhaps Lehrer too has something like this in mind, for his account of acceptance gives enormous epistemic weight to propositions we actually accept. Competitors to given proposition are ruled out by clashing in various ways with a person's acceptance system: it is not subverted because it clashes with *them*. Relational coherence is thus determined by a given candidate-belief's contribution to systematic coherence. This is as it should be, since explaining justification in terms of merely relational coherence would imply no serious break with the "linear" model of justification. If the remark just quoted were Blanshard's last word on the test of coherence, he and Schlick might be at odds over how to specify the beliefs to be maintained, to which others are to be accommodated, but they would not be in disagreement as to the structure of epistemic justification. Radical holism requires subordinating relational to systematic coherence; and even Lehrer with his highly atypical coherence theory seems inclined to do this.

We must never forget that coherence theories are intended to offer direct answers to the sceptic. Advocates of such theories are thus committed to taking the question of the truth-conduciveness of epistemic justification at face value. So again we see that relational coherence cannot be fundamental. Fitting in with our accepted world will not be indicative of truth, and so will not be relevant to justification, unless our antecedent view, in virtue of its systematic coherence, is likely to be largely true. Lehrer acknowledges this point when he makes objective justification depend on the actual truth of T. Davidson too is very clear about the matter: a belief gains credibility through cohering with a person's existing system of beliefs because, Davidson thinks, the beliefs in a coherent overall system must be mainly true. But whereas Lehrer transforms his coherence theory into a kind of externalist reliabilism, if Davidson is right we can show that our actual acceptance system always approximates Lehrer's verific system, assuring us (some measure of) objective as well as personal justification.

However, although a coherence theorist can treat coherence relationally without violating his commitment to radical holism, the ambiguity in the notion of coherence is a potential source of serious confusion in that it is apt to blur the distinction between coherence theories proper and contextualist views of knowledge and justification. We noticed this in our passing glance at Lehrer's theory. What we have now seen is that, for a coherence theorist, systematic coherence must be fundamental. But systematic coherence implies radical holism and it is over radical holism that coherence and contextualist theories divide, no matter how extensive their common ground when it comes to the defects in traditional versions of foundationalism.

We now have the beginnings of an answer to our initial question "What is a coherence theory": it is a theory of justification distinguished from foundationalism both negatively, by its rejection of the doctrine of intrinsically credible basic beliefs, and positively, by its embrace of radical holism. What we must now ask is whether these commitments define a stable position.

## 7.3   COHERENCE AND EXPLANATION

Let us take a closer look at the concept of systematic or "global" coherence. As we noted, this concept of coherence has often been linked with the concept of explanation. It is not hard to see the intuitive appeal of this idea. For the coherence theorist, justification is a matter of balancing the demands of scope against those of theoretical integration. Since the goal of explanation is also to account for a lot on as economical a theoretical basis as possible, so there is something attractive about identifying coherence with explanatory coherence. But the identification is not entirely straight-forward. The coherence theorist's distinctive thought is that the virtues of an explanatory theory can be looked for at the level of our "total view" or entire system of beliefs. Can we think of total views as explanatory?

Someone might object that doing so will lead us straight back to founda-tionalism. Explanation presupposes things to be explained, so that if jus-tifying inference is inference to the best available explanatory view, there must be justified beliefs that are not the result of inference. But the reply will be that this misses the point of explaining justification in terms of the virtues of *total* belief-systems. Such systems will include things to be ex-plained and other things that do the explaining. A belief will be justified to the extent that it can be incorporated in some such system, either as explanatory hypothesis or as something explained. We do not have to think of the whole system as explanatory but of nothing in particular; on the other hand, neither do we have to attribute intrinsic credibility to facts that get explained.

Still, how are we to think of the "explanatory connections" whose presence enhances the coherence of our total view? Ascending to the level of our entire system of beliefs, we abstract from all particular questions and contexts of inquiry. This means that explanatory relations between beliefs must hold in virtue of content: explanation must be a content-based relation. In effect, if we are to think of total views as possessing differing degrees of explanatory coherence, explanatory connections have to be more or less identified with logical connections. Some of these connections will be strictly deductive, though if we are sympathetic to "logical" theories of probability, we may recognize non-deductive connections too. We may also put restrictions on the propositions that can figure in explanations: e.g. that at least some of them be "lawlike." Nevertheless, explanatory connections will remain a subclass of logical relations. Bonjour is quite explicit about this, telling us that explanatory connections are just "inferential connec-tions of a particularly pervasive kind." Here Bonjour takes for granted the "deductive-nomological" account, according to which a fact is explained when it is deducible from scientific laws together with further statements of particular fact. Taking this view of explanation for granted, Bonjour notes, the claim that the coherence of a system is enhanced by the presence of explanatory relations among its members is just a corollary of the point that co-herence depends on inferential connectedness.

The problem with this is that attempts to characterize explanation in more or less formal terms, say as involving deducibility from laws and initial conditions, are a failure. And the reason they fail is that explanation is not a purely content-based relation. On the contrary, it is a paradigm of an epistemologically significant relation that is interest-relative, hence context sensitive. I am in my office at exactly two o'clock one afternoon. This can be deduced from the fact that I was here a fraction of an instant before together with the impossibility of my exceeding the speed of light. But does this deduction explain my presence in my office? We are inclined to say not, because it is hard to see how the deduction could respond to any question anyone would normally ask. But strictly speaking, the question has no answer when put so baldly. Whether a deduction gives an explanation depends on our interests and background knowledge: it depends on what we don't know already and what, in particular, we want to know about the fact in question. An explanation is a response to a definite "why question."[25] These contextual considerations are not just pragmatic extras. Take them away and there is no fact of the matter as to whether one proposition explains another.

I shall not pursue detailed questions about explanation. For if what I have just said is even roughly right, there is something very suspicious in talking about the explanatory coherence of our total view. The problem is that, although explanatory relations involve more than logical relations, when we ascend to the level of our belief system as a whole, thus abstracting from all specific questions and contexts of inquiry, logical relations between beliefs are all that remain.

There is an analogous problem in the way that coherence theorists talk about inference. As we saw, Bonjour treats explanatory connections as a subclass of inferential connections. The thought here is that our web of belief is held together by "inferential relations." But it isn't. If we have a web of belief at all, it is at best held together by logical relations, and logical relations are not "inferential."

This has been made very clear by Gilbert Harman. Harman shows that if rules of inference are rules for acquiring or discarding beliefs, the rules of deductive logic cannot be thought of as rules of inference. For example, it would be a mistake to think of Modus Ponens as the rule that, if we believe that P and also believe that P entails Q, we should believe Q. Perhaps Q is so implausible that we should rethink our premises. Deductive logic, though it puts constraints on belief systems, does not tell us what to believe, even given an initial set of beliefs. But even these constraints are less than absolute, for it is not the case that the rules of deductive logic are absolutely unrevisable. If we could get our view of the world to work better by revising our ideas about logic, it would be reasonable to do so.[26]

Harman takes this argument to establish radical holism: if the rules of logic are not rules of inference, inference must be inference to the best explanation, which Harman identifies with inference to the most coherent total view. But as Harman develops it, the argument ignores both foundationalist and contextualist views of justification. Harman's argument would not apply with complete generality if, by their very nature, some beliefs were "premises" and others "conclusions." Nor would it work so straight-forwardly against a contextualist, who will hold that some beliefs are fixed-in-context. Still, I think that the argument shows something important: what may be inferred from what is never determined by logical relations alone. This means that logical relations ground inferential relations only relative to a particular context of justification, which determines what is fixed and what isn't. At the level of our total view, though there will still be logical relations, there will be no inferential relations *unless foundationalism is true.* For only if foundationalism is true are there constraints on justification, hence on inference, that hold independently of all contextual considerations.

This all ties in with the question of whether coherence, as more than consistency, involves "positive connections" between beliefs. Though this is often said, it seems too weak a requirement if the positive connections are simply more logical connections, whether in the form of entailments or relations of logical probability. Schlick's objection to consistency as the criterion of coherence would hardly be met simply by adding that coherent systems should be thought of as closed under logical consequence. This is why it is tempting to look for other than purely logical relations: explana-tory or inferential relations. But the coherence theorist, since he rejects both contextualism and foundationalism, is not going to find them where he needs them: at the level of our total view.

There are echoes of this problem in Bonjour's attempt to explain co-herence. Having suggested that coherence requires positive connections between beliefs, he raises the question of what sort of connection is re-quired. The obvious answer, he claims, is that: "the connections in question are *inference relations*: namely, any sort of relation of content which would allow one belief or set of beliefs, if justified, to count as the premise(s) of a cogent epistemic-justificatory argument for a further belief."[27] But when is a particular belief justified? When it is a member of a suitably coherent system of beliefs. What makes a system coherent? Inferential relations between its members. And what are inferential relations? Content-based connections that take us from one justified belief to others. We seem to be going round a rather small circle.

We need to backtrack and ask how radical holism really functions in the coherence theorist's response to the argument from fairy stories: the many systems objection. Looking at the notion of explanatory coherence as it applies to belief-systems taken as a whole, we can see right away that the twin goals of comprehensiveness and systematicity are potentially rich in implications. As we noted, the requirement of simplicity or theoretical economy flows naturally from that of systematicity. But there are also important requirements that flow from the goal of comprehensiveness, notably that of conservatism. We caught a hint of this in Blanshard and (perhaps) Lehrer, who more or less identify the test of coherence with the principle of doing least damage to our "accepted world." More recently, Quine and Harman lay particular stress on the rationality of making the least change in our antecedent view that will maximize explanatory coherence. Though it may sound objectionable at first, there is nothing mindless about this kind of conservatism. The point is rather that comprehensiveness has a certain priority over systematicity, in that our aim is systematicity in complexity, not just systematicity per se. Given the goal of taking in as much as possible, only the greatest gains in theoretical insight justify eliminating large bodies of beliefs. Sceptical hypotheses fail this test. Their acceptance would do immeasurable damage to our "accepted world" for no gain and arguably some loss in theoretical integration.

I think, however, that there is more to the coherence theory than this. To see what more, we need to take a closer look at the way in which coherentist justification is conservative. It is important to the coherence theorist that conservatism be derived from the fundamental goal of comprehensiveness. As such, it will point to a general tendency in justification rather than an independent constraint. Indeed, to recognize it as an independent constraint would amount to abandoning the coherence theory's essential holism. What we would have, instead of a true coherence theory, would be a variant of foundationalism in which epistemic privilege was given to actual beliefs, the fundamental kind of coherence now being relational rather than systematic. Again, we see how easy it is to confuse the coherence theory with other things. We saw earlier that it is easy to lose sight of the implications of radical holism because of the trivial sense in which inference might be said to involve a transition from one total view to another. Now we see that, in the usual run of things, such transitions will leave the vast majority of our antecedent beliefs in place. This means that, generally speaking, the expected outcome will be the same whether we think of ourselves as choosing between competing total views in the light of a conception of coherence that includes the comprehensiveness requirement or as privileging our existing beliefs and adopting only such beliefs as can be accommodated to them. But these two ways of thinking of justification cannot be equated. To take only the most obvious reason, the ways in which they confront the problem of connecting justification with truth are likely to be very different.

Even so, there is something problematic about conservatism. Conservatism supposedly results from the rationality of rejecting candidate beliefs that would do widespread damage to our existing system of beliefs, except when they provide either enormous gains in theoretical integration or compensating increases in scope elsewhere in the system, or where their rejection would do even more damage. But doesn't this still grant too much epistemic weight to existing beliefs? For consider any example of what would normally be judged compelling observational evidence for the falsity of some deeply entrenched theory: abandoning the theory will do serious damage to the way our system of beliefs hangs together, whereas rejecting a few observations will not do that much to decrease the scope of our total view. Does this mean that the coherence theory offers an indefinite license to hang on to what would generally be regarded as discredited opinions?

Long ago I argued that there is scant justification for thinking of "our system of beliefs" as a unified theory of everything. Our beliefs are not, I argued, topically integrated. If I am right, there is reason to be sceptical about the idea of extending the virtues of theories to "our belief system as a whole," treating "our beliefs" as if they added up to a "total theory of the world." This connects with the problem about observation. By coherentist standards, it would be wrong to reject particular observational beliefs if doing so would be more damaging to our system of beliefs than uprooting the theory that they threaten to refute. The difficulty is to see how this could ever happen, given the apparent lack of topical integration in our "view of the world." Because the rejection of beliefs about particular matters of fact whose acceptance would imperil an existing theory, need have no implications for the rest of our beliefs, we are free to keep the theory at the expense of the facts.

This way of stating the problem suggests the solution. Faced with a lack of topical integration in his object of investigation, the epistemologist intent on evaluating the totality of our beliefs about the world must see them as epistemologically integrated. For the coherence theorist, this means in part (though only in part) that total views cannot be conceived as containing only 'first order" beliefs about the world but must contain in addition *epistemic beliefs*: for example, beliefs about the conditions under which beliefs of various kinds – say certain observational beliefs – are likely to be true, or beliefs about the ways in which initially compelling beliefs might nevertheless be subject to error. Such beliefs are essential components of total views because they allow the rejection of particular observational beliefs to have widespread systematic implications. Once we set things up so that rejecting otherwise irreproachable observations amounts to abandoning epistemic beliefs that are crucially important for our system of beliefs at large, observational beliefs will no longer stand alone against and so be automatically overwhelmed by entrenched theories.

The result that total views essentially involve epistemic beliefs could also be derived directly from the requirement of comprehensiveness. A model of justification governed by such a requirement, we might argue, is dynamic rather than static. Explanatory coherence is the ideal by which we regulate the input to our system of beliefs. This input will take the form of what Bonjour calls "spontaneous beliefs." And surely there must be some such input if the goal of increasing comprehensiveness is to have any serious application. But this input must also be rationalized in the sense that our system of beliefs must contain beliefs that attribute a high degree of truth-reliability to certain spontaneous beliefs. Otherwise, we would be able – or if not always able, at least rationally entitled – to declare the goal of comprehensiveness realized by deciding to reject any future spontaneous beliefs that threatened existing theories. Bonjour calls this need for rationalized input "the Observation Requirement."[28]

This conception of how belief-systems work has deep roots in the coherentist tradition.[29] Belief-systems are subject to input that they themselves certify as reliable. The input is therefore not basic, since it is backed up by general beliefs. On the other hand neither is it guaranteed to accord with our pre-existing beliefs about the world. The result is that justification is a matter of finding an optimum mix of beliefs – including epistemic beliefs – in light of the overall criteria of explanatory coherence. There will be plenty of room for adjustment since our array of epistemic beliefs is certainly very complicated.

Notice that our epistemic beliefs are not unchangeable. Epistemic beliefs, on this view, are a subclass of beliefs about the world: they are beliefs about the conditions in the world under which truth-reliable beliefs are apt to be acquired. Accordingly, observations may turn up that tend to undermine, directly or indirectly, the epistemic beliefs that underwrite their reliability. But since the relation of dependence is reciprocal – epistemic beliefs certify observational beliefs which in turn confirm epistemic beliefs – our response may be to preserve coherence by modifying our epistemic beliefs. But as long as we are able to preserve harmony on the epistemic front, our system of beliefs will be able to account for its own reliability and so may be said to be *epistemologically coherent*. It seems to me that, to the extent that our beliefs fall short of amounting to a single unified theory of everything, at the level of our belief-system taken as a whole, epistemological coherence is the most important aspect of explanatory coherence.

We see from this that explanatory coherence amounts to more than a structural constraint; for in mandating the inclusion of epistemic beliefs it also imposes requirements on the content of coherent total views. Thus when the coherence theorist rejects the equation of coherence with mere logical consistency, he does more than require "positive connections." The kind of interconnectedness he requires depends on the presence of certain kinds of beliefs and so is more than purely a logical affair. Indeed, recognizing this weakens the demand for positive connections, since consistency alone may be a strong constraint when epistemic beliefs are taken into account.

We can tie epistemological coherence to the interest relativity of explanation: the factors that make for epistemological coherence are precisely those that are relevant when the question on the table is simply whether a candidate for acceptance is true. When truth is all that is at issue, epistemological coherence becomes the most salient aspect of explanatory coherence.

Once we see how the coherence theorist understands the idea of a total view, we see also why he is unlikely to be impressed by Schlick's argument. The problem is not so much that, in equating coherence with consistency, Schlick takes too narrow a view of the epistemologically significant relations between beliefs. Rather, because he ignores the coherence theorist's radically holistic conception of justification, he fails to consider what would have to be involved in anything a coherence theorist could recognize as a coherent total view. In particular, he completely ignores the central role of epistemological coherence. His argument derives whatever plausibility it commands from getting us to consider rather localized stories or theories. Evidently, such theories are not total views. They exclude beliefs about acceptable epistemic practices and make no provision for rationalized input. Schlick does not even consider what it would be like to hold a total view of the world that allowed for the truth of any arbitrary fairy story. Still less does he show that such a view would hang together as well as our actual view, for he does not even show that it would be consistent.

Could the "many systems" objection be modified to cope with this objection? An attempt has been made by John Pollock, who argues that a coherence theory would make it possible for someone to believe with justification that all his senses mislead him all of the time. Since this is clearly absurd, the coherence theory cannot be correct.[30]

At first glance, Pollock's argument seems more sophisticated than Schlick's in virtue of making some allowance for epistemic beliefs. Pollock's man has "positive beliefs concerning how exactly his senses mislead him." But these are only to the effect that "whatever looks tall is really short, whatever looks red is really blue," and so on. Pollock does not say what epistemic beliefs his man would have to hold in order to think that he knows that his senses were misleading in these ways: beliefs about how he had discovered this, for example. Pollock misses this objection, I think, because he holds that, according to the coherence theory, "a person is justified in holding a belief P whenever he holds an infinite (possibly circular) sequence of beliefs $Q_1$, $Q_2$, . . . such that P is supported by some beliefs in the sequence and each belief in turn is supported by later beliefs in the sequence."[31] If this were all there were to the theory Pollock's objection would go through. But we conceded this point, when we noticed that a mere insistence on positive connections is not enough to dispose of the many systems problem. However, once we recognize the importance of epistemic beliefs, we also realize that we cannot characterize coherence in the purely formal terms that Pollock favors.

The result is that, from the point of view of the coherence theorist, Pollock's sample system is seriously underdescribed. In spite of his claim that, given a coherence theory of justification, "we could well imagine a person whose beliefs were such as to justify him in rejecting all the evidence of his senses," he has not really shown us how to do this. Principally, this is because he has not told us what epistemic beliefs such a person would have to hold; and here, I think, Pollock's own intuitions tell against him. For why is he so sure that it is absurd to suppose that someone could be justified in believing that all of his senses mislead him all of the time? The reason can only be that he can think of no way of fleshing out the example in such a way as to give such a person a coherent story about his epistemic position. If such a story could be told, it would not be so obvious that the supposition in question is absurd, and again the argument would fail.

## 7.4  LOCAL AND GLOBAL

I have characterized the coherence theory in terms of two commitments: negatively, by the theory's rejection of epistemologically basic beliefs, and positively by its embrace of radical holism. It is important to realize that these commitments are distinct and that there is no immediate inference from the one commitment to the other. Rejecting foundationalism does not lead automatically to radical holism.

The foundationalist doctrine of intrinsically credible basic beliefs offers a strongly atomistic conception of justification. (To say that certain privileged beliefs are intrinsically credible is to say that each such belief is credible all by itself, irrespective of what else is believed.) Clearly, a contextualist conception of justification is hostile to this doctrine, since it makes justification depend on a context of background beliefs and even on situational factors that are entirely extra-doxastic. A contextualist account of justification may be, so to say, *locally holistic*, in that a context of justification always involves a significant array of beliefs. Nevertheless, to say that no belief, considered in isolation, has any particular epistemic status is not to say that the epistemic status of every belief is a function of features of our belief system as a whole. Indeed, nothing has yet been done to suggest that we have a useful or even a tolerably clear notion of "our belief system as a whole." But wherever we come down on this issue, this much is evident: there is no direct move from anti-atomism to radical holism.

Now, in the previous section, we connected explanatory coherence with epistemological coherence via the essential role played by epistemic beliefs. But in light of what has just been said – in particular, the point that a contextualist conception of justification may be locally holistic – it is clear that we must separate two strands in this argument: the linking of justification with explanation and the move to radical holism implicit in looking for epistemological coherence at the level of our total view. That there is a close connection between explanation and justification is plausible enough. Perhaps we should think of epistemic justification as a species of explanation: justifying means explaining why a given belief is likely to be true, or more likely to be true than certain specified competitors. But there is nothing in this idea to suggest that, whenever a question of justification arises, it must be answered in a way that involves all one's beliefs essentially.

It often seems to me that coherence theorists are hardly aware of there even being an inference here. In part, this is because the transition to radical holism is helped along by their tendency to focus on notably vague and general epistemic beliefs: that "one's senses are not systematically misleading" or, the most extreme example, Lehrer's principle T, "I am a trustworthy evaluator of truth." Such commitments are vague and general enough to be regarded as presuppositions of just about any way of coming to believe anything. So by involving them in all justificatory questions, the coherence theorist creates the impression that everything we believe is at stake in any context of justification, even if only indirectly, by way of their credibility's connection with fundamental epistemic beliefs. But there is scant reason to believe either that we have any such commitments or that, even if we do, they are potentially at risk in every context of justification. Faced with the choice between holding on to a well-entrenched theory and accepting apparently impeccable counter-evidence, what is at stake will not be "the reliability of the senses" but the reliability of evidence collected under certain specific conditions. Such a choice may implicate significant bodies of belief on both sides of the question, but will not automatically implicate "our total view" on either.

At first glance, then, radical holism is far from plausible. It does not seem that, when ordinary questions of justification arise, all our beliefs are in question. Ordinary justification seems more a matter of evaluating some beliefs on the basis of others, which are taken to be more or less in order, if they are thought of at all. Accordingly, inference does not seem to be a passage from one total view to another in anything other than the trivial sense noted earlier. Harman's talk of assessing total views seems more at home in the context of the traditional epistemological project of assessing all our beliefs about the world, all at once. It is as though Harman builds the totality condition into his account of everyday justification. (But this is a condition on a distinctively philosophical understanding of our knowledge of the world rather than a constraint on common or garden justification.)

The same could be said of radical holists generally. We saw how such theorists smooth the path to holism by suggesting that all justification implicitly involves highly general epistemic beliefs. But though it is less than obvious that such beliefs are ever involved in ordinary contexts of justification, they can seem relevant when highly general epistemological questions, that is to say sceptical questions, are on the table. This is precisely the function of Lehrer's principle T: to ensure that our acceptance system leaves us at least subjectively justified in ignoring sceptical alternatives to our ordinary views. But to follow this line is to take it for granted that sceptical hypotheses are relevant in all contexts of justification, which is plausible only if content alone determines epistemological status.

To head off the objection that appearances do not favour radical holism, Bonjour distinguishes two levels of justification, local and global. At the local level, we are concerned with "the justification of a single empirical, or small set of beliefs, within the context of a cognitive system whose overall justification is (more or less) taken for granted." However, "it is also possible at least in principle, to raise the issue of the overall justification of the entire system of empirical beliefs," which takes us to the global level. This distinction can be aligned in an obvious way with that between relational and systematic coherence.

The local/global distinction allows Bonjour to trace radical holism's initial implausibility to the fact that ordinarily questions of justification arise only at the local level. At this level:

> A given justificandum belief is shown to be justified by citing other premise-beliefs from which it correctly follows via some acceptable pattern of inference. Such beliefs can themselves be challenged . . . [but] there is no serious danger of an infinite regress at this level . . . , since . . . [one] quickly reaches premise beliefs that are dialectially acceptable in that context and which can thus function there rather like the foundationalist's basic beliefs.[32]

However, we must not be misled by this functional similarity. As Bonjour notes, contextually basic beliefs are not confined to "those which would be classified as basic by any plausible version of foundationalism."[33] Still, we might want to say, they do, in context, serve as terminating points for chains of justification, so that, if we do not look beyond the local level, justification will sometimes proceed linearly. Interestingly, this amounts to an admission that one does not become a foundationalist simply by countenancing linear justification. This is as it should be. Foundationalism proper – substantive foundationalism – is more than a doctrine concerning the formal structure of justifying inference. A contextualist can allow that justification often proceeds linearly. But this formal similarity does not make contextualism a variant of foundationalism.

Can a coherence theorist proper accept linear justification at the local level? Not according to Bonjour, who refuses to countenance linear justification at all. His view is not that local justification *is* linear but rather that "at the local level justification *appears* linear."[34] The reason for its not being truly linear is that local justification takes for granted the non-linear justification of an "overall cognitive system." Thus the appearance of linearity that attaches to local justification derives from its incompleteness. If we tried to give a full justification for even a single empirical proposition, we should have to justify the cognitive system in which it is locally embedded, which would require a move to the global level and a consequent departure from linearity. Bonjour is absolutely right to take this line: if local justification is genuinely linear, the coherence theory collapses into either foundationalism or contextualism. The coherence theory may allow for an appearance of linearity in everyday justification but, to stake out a distinctive position, must remain radically holistic.

We can see from this that we must not let talk of different "levels" of justification mislead us into thinking that the coherence theory admits two different *kinds* of justification. If it did, we should be able immediately to press the question with which the contextualist confronts the traditional epistemologist: why suppose that failure in a distinctive investigative project, structured by its own, characteristic methodological necessities, casts doubt on the legitimacy of epistemic evaluation entered in quite different contexts, hence subject to different constraints? But the coherence theory does not recognize distinct kinds of justification: the distinction between local and global is simply that between partial and complete. This is why, for the coherence theory, "the issue of justification as it arises at the . . . global level . . . is in the final analysis decisive for the determination of empirical justification in general."[35] A coherence theorist must hold that, without an adequate global justification in the background, local justifications are illusory.

Interestingly, Bonjour recognizes that in all likelihood "completely global issues are never in fact raised outside the context of explicitly epistemological discussion," adding that this does not show that there is anything "illegitimate" about them.[36] Note again the familiar dilemma: either the sceptic asks a straightforward, naively intelligible question, or his question is "illegitimate," which is to say not really coherent. No room is allowed for the possibility that isolating the theoretical presuppositions that give the question its sense puts the impossibility of returning a direct answer in a new light. It does not even occur to Bonjour that the relation between questions of justification arising in radically different contexts might be problematic. Yet this possibility goes to the heart of the contrast between a coherentist and a contextualist approach to justification. As I argued in chapter 3, when we move from "local" to "global" questions of justification we do not, as we do for Bonjour, push local questions farther, or to a new "level," *we change the subject entirely*, from physics, or history, say, to epistemology. On this view, because traditional epistemology is just one more disciplinary inquiry guided by its own, distinctive disciplinary constraints, a failure to return a satisfactory answer to the traditional request for an assessment of the totality of our knowledge of the world need not imply that local justifications are in any way defective or incomplete. For a contextualist, local justification does *not* presuppose global. Local justification not only *appears* linear, it may sometimes *be* linear. Of course, it does not have to be. Since a contextualist, as much as a coherence theorist, is likely to deprecate unnecessary contractions in his beliefs, he might, as local holist, hold that an appearance of linearity is always in part the result of deeper constraints: e.g. the conservatism implicit in the goal of comprehensiveness. But he still will not think that all his beliefs are essentially involved in every epistemic decision. The key question, therefore, is not whether the quest for global justification is (or, better, can be made) intelligible but how it is related to local justification.

One lesson to learn from this is that the terminology of "local" and "global" needs to be handled with care. A contextualist who blithely falls in with it is likely to find himself in trouble.

We might be tempted to think just the opposite, for if we ask how a contextualist view of justification works to defuse the problem of connecting justification with truth, the most obvious suggestion appeals to precisely the contrast between local and global. For a contextualist, we might say, only demands for local justification are admissible, so that the global question goes by the board. Challenged on the truth of a given belief, I can appeal to my own experience, to the testimony of others, to whatever tests, experiments or investigations I or other people have carried out, and so on. Should the evidential value — the truth conduciveness — of whatever I cite itself come under suspicion, we have a further matter for empirical investigation. How reliable an observer am I in the relevant circumstances? Is my friend's testimony generally trustworthy? How accurate are these instruments? How often does this test produce false positives? And so on. So long as questions about evidential value remain at this level of specificity, we will feel no temptation to suppose that we can justify a given belief by appeal to something other than further beliefs. Neither will we be moved to reconstrue truth in epistemic terms or to feel that the evidential value of our justificational strategies must have some kind of *a priori* basis. Such temptations arise only if we admit the sceptic's demands for some kind of global account of the truth-conduciveness of "the test of coherence," precisely what a contextualist view of justification says we need not do. But however attractively simple, a blunt appeal to the contrast between local and global demands for justification leaves too many questions hanging to be a satisfying explanation of how the sceptic goes wrong.[37]

Firstly, at what point do demands for justification become too general?

How local must they be to remain admissible? Lacking an index of im-proper generality that is independent of our becoming vulnerable to scep-ticism, we have a dismissal of sceptical questions but no real account of what is wrong with them.

Secondly, how does a contextualist view of justification go beyond a point any sceptic will readily concede: that to get on with ordinary in-quiries, we have to rely on all sorts of assumptions? No one denies that, for everyday practical (and even theoretical) purposes, we have to ignore fundamental epistemological questions. But this does not mean either that such questions are badly posed or that sceptical answers to them are incorrect. I have admitted as much myself.

Thirdly, sceptical questions can be very general without being global. Even the challenge to connect coherence with truth concedes, for the sake of argument, that we know what we believe and how our beliefs hang together. So it does not violate the contextualist stricture on attempts to validate everything we believe, all at once. The sceptical problem that results from failure to meet this challenge is not therefore going to be defused by ruling out global demands for justification.

These points would be well taken if the contextualist intended simply to rule out "global" questions. But this is not his intention. At issue is the very distinction between local and global. In drawing this distinction, Bonjour and any who think like him hint that their "global" questions are simply more general than the "local" questions that typically con-cern us in everyday life. This is what I deny. The "global" question that animates traditional epistemology derives its content from its own charac-teristic presuppositions which are different from but not obviously more fundamental than those that fix the content of questions belonging to other areas of inquiry. This is why the key question is not whether de-mands for global justification can be made intelligible but whether local justification presupposes global. In my view, the claim that it does reflects commitment to foundationalism, or more generally, epistemological re-alism, and these are the real objects of the contextualist's suspicion. But if I am right about this, and if a coherence theorist must hold that local jus-tification presupposes global, the coherence theory must be foundationalism in disguise. And so it is.


## 7.5  INTERNALISM AND EPISTEMIC PRIORITY

I argued long ago that traditional epistemology is intrinsically foundational simply in virtue of treating "knowledge" as some kind of surveyable whole. So I find particularly revealing Bonjour's remark that "in the final analysis" global justification is decisive for justification in general. This implies that the justificational issues that arise at the global level are in a completely general and objective way *epistemologically prior to all local issues*. How could this be?

Global justification depends on our checking our system of beliefs for how well it hangs together. Clearly, to apply this test at all, I need some fairly clear conception of what my beliefs are and how they hang together. But it is not enough for me just to have (meta) beliefs about my (first-order) beliefs. Those meta beliefs must themselves amount to knowledge, or at least be justified. If they are not justified, appealing to them will do nothing towards providing a global justification of my beliefs about the world. We come back to the point I have insisted on all along. Compared with traditional foundationalism, the coherence theory extends the concept of appearances. Appearances are not confined to sensory appearances but cover the entire way we take the world to be: our "accepted world," as Blanshard would say. But the metabeliefs that capture our knowledge of appearances, in this extended sense, must still be privileged. They must be in some general and fully objective way epistemologically prior to knowledge of the world. If they are not, grounding knowledge of the world on them will do nothing to improve its epistemological status. Equally, not even a proof that no such grounding can be given will detract from it. Without the doctrine of the epistemological priority of knowledge of appearances over knowledge of the world, we are left with an innocuous point about the logical relations between two kinds of proposition, from which no epistemological morals can be drawn. Compared with traditional foundationalism, then, the coherence theory expands the content of our (allegedly) epistemologically basic beliefs. But it does not dispense with the idea of context-independent relations of epistemological priority. It remains committed to epistemological realism in a specifically foundationalist form.

Someone might object that this conclusion has been reached too quickly. Even granting that our metabeliefs must be both justified and epistemologically prior to our beliefs about the world, we can still inquire into the source of their credibility. Must their credibility be intrinsic, as traditional foundationalists claim, or can it be explained in terms of coherence?

It is tempting to argue that the credibility that the coherence theorist attaches to his basic metabeliefs *cannot* be explained in coherentist terms and so, given his project of global justification, *must* be intrinsic. His metabeliefs cannot derive their credibility from their coherence with his system of (first-order) beliefs since, apart from appealing to the very metabeliefs in question, he has no reason at all for supposing that he has *that* system of first-order beliefs. This point is made with admirable clarity by Bonjour, who regards it as a serious objection to the sort of radically holistic coherence theory he favours. It is, as he says, "beyond any doubt viciously circular to claim that the metabeliefs which constitute the believer's grasp of his system of beliefs are themselves justified by virtue of their coherence with that system."[38] Accordingly, since the coherence theorist is unable to justify his metabeliefs by appealing to their coherence with his beliefs about the world, he must appeal to their coherence with each other. But he cannot. Doing so would require him to formulate a set of meta-metabeliefs, detailing his metabeliefs and how they hang together; and at this meta-meta-level, the same problem would arise all over again.[39] Once we embark on a project of global justification, the only alternatives to intrinsic credibility are vicious circularity and infinite regress, just as the foundationalist has always maintained.

I think that this argument is correct, as far as it goes. But someone might reply that it simply assumes, without justification, that a coherence theory is committed to an absolutely uncompromising form of internalism. Let us recall that externalism is not to be equated with pure reliabilism.[40] Rather, a theory of knowledge (or justification) is externalist if it allows us knowledge (or justified belief) provided that certain conditions on knowledge are in fact met, rather than known (or justifiably believed) to be met. To count as externalist, a theory need not claim (as do pure reliabilist theories) that all conditions on knowledge or justification are of this character, only that some are. If we now stipulate that a theory is internalist if and only if it is not externalist, we get a distinction that is exclusive and exhaustive: externalist theories allow some "external" constraints on knowledge or justification; internalist theories do not allow any.

This way of drawing the distinction makes internalism a very strong view. On this account, internalism demands "cognitive access" to everything that is relevant to knowledge or justification, with the consequence that knowledge (or justified belief) can arise *only* out of further knowledge (or justified belief). Clearly, it was its assumed commitment to internalism, in the strong sense just defined, that forced what we were thinking of as "the coherence theory" to collapse into foundationalism. True, if we submit to the demand for total cognitive access, we will find ourselves driven into either a regress or vicious circularity, unless we recognize a class of intrinsically credible, basic beliefs. But if we resist this demand, we will be under no such pressure. So why not resist it? After all, if "externalism" is defined broadly, so that it is by no means co-extensive with pure reliabilism, it is not immediately obvious why there could not be an externalist version of the coherence theory: and if such a position is even possible, the attempt to saddle the coherence theorist with the foundationalist's doctrine of intrinsic credibility is a failure.

This reply would be effective if the coherence theory's commitment to internalism were optional. So to complete the argument we must show that it is not. To do this, we must recall a result from the previous section: that a coherence theorist *must* hold that local justification presupposes global justification. A coherence theorist must hold that local justifications are *essentially incomplete*: for if it is allowed that local justifications can be perfectly in order without global justifications to back them up, the coherence theory gives way to contextualism. It follows from this that no coherence theorist can take on board views that undermine the essential dependence of local upon global justification. But this is just what externalism does: *externalism breaks the essential link between local and global justification.*

The reason for this should be obvious: local justification is essentially incomplete only if justification requires (in "the last analysis" anyway) cognitive access to everything on which it in any way depends. If such access is not required, the possibility opens up that local justifications can be perfectly in order without reinforcement from a global justification. For example, the practice of historical research may be perfectly in order provided that its "presuppositions," relating to the age of the Earth and so on, are *true*, whether or not we have any idea of how they themselves might be justified. This is to say that we will see local justification as essentially *incomplete* only given a prior commitment to internalism.

This conclusion reinforces my claim that the very terminology of "local versus global" is tendentious: indeed, that it is a reflection of internalist, hence foundationalist, commitments. The situation here is closely related to that encountered when we examined the idea of the "detached" standpoint from which the sceptic delivers his negative verdict on our putative knowledge of the world. This special viewpoint is generally explained in terms of a contrast between the sceptic's purely theoretical investigations and the more or less practical inquiries characteristic of everyday life. But I argued that the commonsense theoretical/practical distinction will not serve the sceptic's purposes, so that this explanation obscures his real commitments. The distinction he really needs, and in practice takes for granted, is that between topical questions, having to do with various worldly matters, though quite possibly devoid of practical import, and *purely epistemological* questions: i.e. questions about knowledge that can be pursued in abstraction from any and all factual presuppositions. Similarly here: the local/global distinction seems only to be a matter of scope and thus to carry little or no theoretical freight; but in fact it is another mask for the loaded constrast between questions about the world and questions about our knowledge of the world. That more than scope is at issue is clear, for from the standpoint of a philosopher like Bonjour, even a theory that had to do with (say) the entire physical universe would raise only a "local" issue. In fact, there is only one "global" issue: the purely epistemological question of the possibility of knowledge of the world *as such*. Behind the innocent-seeming "local/global" distinction lies the topical/epistemological distinction, in the tendentious form in which it is drawn by epistemological realists.

This must be so. If we agree that "local" justifications are *not* always essentially incomplete, the distinctive constraints on global justification become irrelevant to local justification. This means that they can *only* be seen as methodological necessities informing a particular, distinctive intellectual project, so that what seems to be merely a distinction of scope (local versus global) is really a distinction of subject matter.

The conclusion, then, is this: to keep his distance from the contextualist, the coherence theorist must hold to internalism, in which case his theory collapses into foundationalism. That the coherence theorist is indeed trapped in this fatal dilemma emerges very clearly in Bonjour's attempt to respond to the charge that the coherence theory is just foundationalism all over again, the subject's beliefs about his belief-system playing the role of ultimate basis. It is greatly to Bonjour's credit that he is acutely aware of the problem. Most coherence theorists, he notes, either take for granted the believer's grasp of his own system of beliefs or else simply ignore the question of whether coherentist justification, which demands this grasp, is accessible to the believer himself. The "obvious conclusion" he suggests is that "even an intended coherence theory must involve an irreducibly foundationalist element, that one's grasp of one's own system of beliefs must be justified in a foundationalist manner, even if everything else depends on coherence."[41] But there is a way to block this obvious conclusion. This is to recognize that, when a given belief is subjected to a demand for justification:

> the existence of the justificandum belief is *presupposed* by the very raising of the issue of justification, so that the metabelief in question is not in need of justification. . . . The normal justificatory issue, on this view, is whether the believer is justified in holding a certain belief *which he does in fact hold*, not whether such a belief would be justified in the abstract, independently of whether he holds it.[42]

Applying this general point to the coherence theory, for which the unit of justification is an entire system of beliefs, we are led to conclude that "the raising on an issue of empirical justification *presupposes* the existence of some specifiable system of empirical beliefs." Accordingly, "the primary justificatory issue is whether or not, under the presumption that I do indeed hold approximately the system of beliefs which I believe myself to hold, those beliefs are justified."[43] Coherentist justification is justification under the *Doxastic Presumption*.

This maneuver represents an attempt to occupy a middle ground that simply does not exist. On closer examination, the Doxastic Presumption proves to be Janus-faced, looking in one direction towards foundationalism and in the other towards contextualism.

Justification under the Doxastic Presumption is supposed not to be foundationalist because, when it comes to beliefs about my belief-system, "no claim is being made that these metabeliefs possess any sort of intrinsic or independent justification or warrant of any kind."[44] Indeed, Bonjour holds the strong view that it is impossible for there to be basic beliefs of the kind postulated by foundationalism. The reason is that, for a belief to be justified, there must be a reason, grasped by the believer, why it is likely to be true. But since no justifying argument for an empirical belief can proceed from entirely *a priori* premises, any justified empirical belief will rest in part on further empirical grounds, and so will not be basic.[45] Obviously, this argument presupposes internalism: for a belief to be justified, the believer must have a cognitive grasp of anything that is relevant to its justification. But, as we have seen, for a philosopher of Bonjour's persuasion internalism is not a gratuitous assumption, and this makes it difficult to see why he thinks that justification under the Doxastic Presumption does *anything* to disarm the sceptic.

Bonjour wants to say that coherentist justification takes us a long way towards answering the sceptic, though not quite all the way. His view, which sounds reasonable at first, is that it is possible to make headway with one sceptical problem without claiming to have solved them all. If the sceptic chooses to target our knowledge of what we believe, we will simply have to admit that, since coherentist justification operates under the Doxastic Presumption, "a coherence theory cannot in principle answer this form of scepticism."[46] It would be desirable to answer it, but we will have made great progress against the sceptic if we can vindicate knowledge of the world relying on nothing but the Doxastic Presumption. However, this simply will not do. If the metabeliefs the coherence theorist takes as his starting point can be justified in neither a foundational nor a coherentist fashion, then from Bonjour's internalist standpoint they cannot be justified at all. Seen in this light, the term, "Doxastic Presumption," seems to indicate a desire to have things both ways. While, officially, the metabeliefs the coherence theorist must take for granted do not possess *any kind* of intrinsic warrant, talk of a "presumption" in favor of their truth is surely suggestive of some measure of intrinsic credibility, albeit defeasible. It would be clearer to say that coherentist justification is justification under the Doxastic *Assumption*. But since no internalist can allow justification to arise out of a brute assumption, putting things this way would simply underline the impossibility of being an internalist without being a foundationalist.

In point of fact, the very idea of partial success against the sceptic requires adopting the foundationalist conception of rock-bottom relations of epistemic priority. Presumably, justification under the Doxastic Presumption constitutes progress towards answering the sceptic because it does not presuppose true beliefs about the world but only true beliefs about beliefs.

But why should giving an account of empirical justification which presumes nothing about the world be thought of as progress? Suppose that I succeed in showing that my beliefs about the world are justified under the Doxastic Presumption, or that I show that this cannot be done: what have I gained, or what have I lost? If my beliefs about my belief-system are in some general and objective way more certain or more secure than any of my beliefs about the world, or if the former are in the nature of things the ultimate ground of the latter, success will secure my worldly beliefs against the ravages of scepticism, just as failure will lay them waste. But if no such grounding is required, if our grasp of the "inner" has no intrinsic superiority over our grasp of the "outer," there is nothing to gain and nothing to lose. This is so even if the Doxastic Presumption is true and I do have a more or less accurate conception of what my beliefs are and how thay hang together.

The result is that something has to give: either the coherence theory must admit a foundationalist component or internalism must be abandoned. The metabeliefs which provide the starting point for coherentist justification can themselves be justified neither in a foundationalist nor a coherentist fashion. Thus if "justification" under the Doxastic Presumption confers *any* genuine warrant on our beliefs about the world, it must be able to do so provided only that these metabeliefs are *true* (for the most part, or approximately: the qualifications do not matter here). But no coherence theorist could admit this, least of all Bonjour. Not only would he deprive himself of his chief argument against foundationalism but, as we have seen, he would lose his defence against contextualism too, being no longer in a position to claim that local justification is essentially incomplete. Nevertheless, just as the term "Doxastic Presumption" is strongly, if illicitly, suggestive of intrinsic credibility, so much of what he says *about* the Doxastic Presumption is suggestive of externalism, indeed of contextualism.

Consider the claim that, in connection with my beliefs about the world, the "normal justificatory question" concerns my right to claim a particular epistemic status for beliefs that I *in fact* have. Clearly, similar points could be made in connection with more "local" questions. If I ask you to back up your claims about Napoleon's strategy at Waterloo, "the normal justificatory question" concerns your warrant for certain claims about the man who *in fact* fought a battle a hundred and eighty-five years ago. That there was such a person, never mind whether the Earth even existed back then, is not "normally" in question, belonging rather to the background against which the normal question is posed. Closely examined, Bonjour's defence of the Doxastic Presumption turns on the claim that asking (and answering) the sceptical question he especially wants to ask depends on setting aside other possible questions, such as why we think we know what we believe; and since this is true of *all* questions, his argument fails to reveal anything special about the *Doxastic* Presumption, as opposed to whatever presumptions give other inquiries their particular directions. But there would be something special to reveal only if the presuppositions of other forms of inquiry were somehow intrinsically more ambitious, which no radical anti-foundationalist can claim. Once more we see that the slightest movement away from internalism leaves the coherence theorist with no defence against the contextualist.

Eliminating the foundationalist undertones from Bonjour's discussion makes it clear that assigning a quasi-foundational role to the relevant metabeliefs is no more than a methodological necessity of epistemological inquiry as he conceives it. Again, this undercuts the claim that "local" justifications, though subject to different presumptions, are nevertheless contingent on global justification. Thus Bonjour teeters on the brink of a fatal concession when he notes that, if it is to speak to the problem of avoiding a regression to foundationalism, the Doxastic Presumption cannot "function like a premise" in the coherentist's global justification of our knowledge of the world but must rather constitute "a basic and unavoidable feature of cognitive *practice*." This is mildly misleading in that Bonjour has a very special "cognitive practice" in mind, namely "epistemic reflection." By his own showing, "local" justifications presuppose first and foremost the truth of other beliefs about the world, rather than the extensive array of metabeliefs falling under the Doxastic Presumption, and so the presumption underlies cognitive practice generally only on the condition, mandated by internalism, that "local" justification presupposes global. Still, he is right to this extent: the sort of reflection he has in mind must exempt from question my grasp of my system of beliefs, and so his idea of an unavoidable feature of cognitive practice is close to that of a methodological necessity of traditional epistemological inquiry. But this move towards contextualism creates irresistible pressure to abandon internalism. This is why we find Bonjour telling us that the Doxastic Presumption formulates "from the outside" something I inevitably do when engaged in epistemic reflection. What is this, if not externalism?

Lehrer, we saw, goes explicity externalist when he addresses questions of objective as opposed to personal justification. Bonjour would like to have it both ways. But in Bonjour's defence, this may be because he recognizes, more clearly than Lehrer, that once a philosopher is willing to be any kind of an externalist, he has no good reason for holding on to the complicated justificational apparatus required by radical holism.[47] Anyway, the conclusion remains: if the coherence theory demands internalism, it collapses into a variant form of foundationalism; and if it doesn't, it collapses into contextualism. There is no escaping this dilemma.

## 7.6   CRITERIAL JUSTIFICATION

In light of our discussion, we need to re-examine the grounds for the coherence theory's claim to a distinct identity. In particular, we must look at its claim to articulate a distinctively "nonlinear" conception of justification.

Foundational theories of knowledge and justification recognize more than one locus of epistemic privilege. Since not everything we believe is basic, there must be principles conveying warrant from beliefs that are intrinsically credible to beliefs that are not. And if we are to avoid embarking on a new regress, at least some such principles must themselves be intrinsically credible.

Now, as first enountered, the suggestion that justification might proceed nonlinearly appeared as a radical rejection of the foundationalist doctrine of basic beliefs. But everything we have seen, in this chapter and the last, suggests that this cannot be right. The coherence theorist must assign a privileged status to certain "metabeliefs," as Bonjour calls them. So, as I have argued, he differs from the more familiar type of foundationalist, not by refusing to grant a privileged status to knowledge of appearances, but rather by extending the notion of appearances from experience, narrowly conceived, to a subject's entire notional world. But still, surely *something* important is captured by the idea of "nonlinear" justification. For though the coherence theorist remains committed to the universal objective priority of knowledge of appearances, he does not countenance discrete evidential relations between particular items of knowledge belonging to the privileged stratum and particular beliefs about the world. This is the burden of his radical holism. Particular beliefs about the world are justified by being incorporated into some suitably coherent total view.

But how radical can holism be, consistent with the coherence theorist's aim of providing a direct answer to scepticism? It is not easy for the coherence theorist to return a satisfactory answer to this question.

To make our discussion more concrete, let us consider Harman's defence of the claim that all inference is inference to the best available total explanatory view. As we noted in passing, Harman argues that it is a mistake to suppose that there are two sorts of inference, inductive and deductive. If inference is the process by which beliefs are acquired or discarded, the rules of deductive logic are not rules of inference at all. Equally, inductive inference, as inference to the best explanation, is holistic and so not a matter of following rules which, like the rules of deductive logic, link some particular propositions with their consequences. There is neither deductive inference nor inductive logic.

But is there really a clear contrast here? True, if inductive inference is inference to a total explanatory view, it will not be rule-governed in the sense that it will not depend on mechanically following procedures which take us from particular premises to particular conclusions. It will, however, be guided by the criteria for selecting the most coherent total view and the question is: why are such criteria better suited to controlling belief than, say, Modus Ponens? Given that epistemic justification is meant to be truth-conducive, to accept a particular set of criteria amounts to believing that belief-systems satisfying those criteria are likely to be true, or at least more likely to be true than systems that do not. But if everything is up for grabs at once, nothing being held in place by inalienable epistemic privilege, then it seems that as soon as we articulate the criteria of coherence, they become merely additional components of a particular total view, or range of views, and the question then becomes why we infer a view embodying these standards of coherence rather than some possible competitor. Perhaps this is why Harman once concluded that "the principles of induction are not even known."[48] The principles that govern transitions between total views cannot be known, if they necessarily escape articulation.

Considerations like these lie behind Dummett's charge, levelled against Quine, that thoroughgoing holism makes "the principles which govern change undecipherable."[49] However, this conclusion is too strong. Nothing argued so far precludes our understanding wholesale change of belief retrospectively, by coming to see ourselves as having inferred in accordance with certain criteria. What is precluded is our having been self-consciously guided by them, so that for truly radical holists the owl of Minerva flies at night, if it flies at all. Anyway, the question for the coherentist now becomes: are the beliefs that result from the unguided formation of a total view ever justified? If the answer is no, there is no possibility of our justifying our current total view on the basis of considerations that the coherence theorist agrees are available. But if the answer is yes, the result is a kind of externalism. We are allowed justified beliefs, even though certain factors that are crucial to their being justified are quite unknown to us. In particular, we get justified beliefs when we form our total view in accordance with principles that are in fact truth-conducive, even though those principles remain, at the time, necessarily unarticulated. Clearly, this is unsatisfactory as a direct answer to the sceptic. But even as a form of externalism, it is peculiarly unmotivated, for once we allow justification to supervene on unrecognized truths, why restrict those truths to a narrow class of epistemic principles?

What is the alternative? I think there is only one: the coherence theorist must settle for a purely criterial theory of justification. That is to say, to maintain his holistic conception of justification when it comes to belief about the world, while holding on to the internalism demanded by a direct answer to the sceptic, he must assign a privileged position to the fundamental criteria of explanatory coherence.

Again, we can bring out what such a view involves by contrasting it with contextualism. For a contextualist, a given context of inquiry or justification takes its characteristic direction from a background of beliefs that are *not* in question, or more generally questions that are not at issue. This means that justification may supervene on the possession of a background of true beliefs about the world, or even on truths that are not actually believed. In other words, a contextualist need never suppose that justification *depends exclusively on intra-systematic features* of our "web of belief." But if justification depends on the possibility of integrating a given belief into the most coherent available total system, so that inference is non-trivially a matter of the comparative assessment of total views, this is exactly what must be supposed. To accept holism with respect to beliefs about the world is to hold that in any context of justification all such beliefs are effectively in question, in which case justification can only consist in measuring competing total systems against the criteria of coherence.

It is essential to such a view that these criteria enjoy a privileged status. Judging in accordance with particular criteria – in the sense of using those criteria to regulate all one's beliefs about the world – is reasonable only if the principles asserting the truth-reliability of those criteria are intrinsically more secure than, hence epistemologically prior to, all beliefs about the world. Thus we see that, although the coherence theorist differs with the foundationalist over the fine structure of justification, he too accepts the need for two loci of epistemic privilege: basic "metabeliefs" and principles taking us from basic beliefs to non-basic. There is no escaping the conclusion: the coherence theory is a variant form of foundationalism and shares foundationalism's commitment to epistemological realism.

Clearly, the coherence theorist's position is uncomfortable. Though his predilection for holism is rooted in suspicion of all forms of epistemic privilege, it now appears that epistemic privilege is what his holism leads him back to. If coherence theorists do not always feel discomfort, it is because this point is easy to miss. As we have seen, if a view is really total, it will include various epistemic as well as non-epistemic beliefs, and since these beliefs are empirical, the coherence theorist may suppose he can treat all epistemic beliefs empirically. But the principles we accept as regulating our acceptance of a total view cannot coherently be identified with internal epistemic beliefs. These beliefs indeed enjoy no special privilege, for they are accepted only for their contribution to the coherence of a total system of beliefs. For that reason, they do not provide the basis for preferring that total system to its rivals. The principles that do provide it are the ones that demand a privileged status; and if they have no right to it, a purely criterial view of justification has nothing to recommend it.[50]

Now we have seen repeatedly that the traditional epistemological project, in virtue of the foundationalist conception of justification implicit in it, confronts us with the epistemologist's dilemma. If we are to validate our knowledge of the world as a whole, we must ground it on knowledge belonging to some more primitive and privileged level: experiential knowledge. But our principles of inference or evidential connection must link this more privileged knowledge with knowledge of the world. It seems, then, that they must themselves have to do with the world. Perhaps, for example, they assert that certain kinds of experiences are generally reliable guides to how things objectively are. But of course they cannot be like this if we are to succeed in validating the totality of our knowledge of the world, for to invoke such principles would merely be to base some beliefs about the world on others. This is why bridge principles must be *a priori*. But not only is it hard to see, in the face of sceptical thought experiments, how they can be *a priori*, if they were *a priori* the objectivity of the world would be compromised. To preserve our sense of the objectivity of the world, we must accept the neutrality of experience, which given a foundational view of knowledge and justification, is an insurmountable obstacle to validating our knowledge of the world. If we abandon the neutrality of experience, we may improve our chances of validating our knowledge of the world, but at the cost of weakening our sense of its objectivity. But if I am right and the coherence theory is a variant form of foundationalism, it should face a version of the same dilemma. This should mean in turn that the problem of the truth-connection is insoluble for those coherence theorists who want to hold on to even a minimally realistic notion of truth; that is, theorists who want to resist explicating truth in terms of our (supposedly) current criteria of coherence.

The problem emerges very clearly in Bonjour's attempt to show that under certain conditions coherence is indicative of truth: in particular, that our ordinary view of the world is more likely to be true than any sceptical hypothesis. His argument makes use of what he calls "the Observation Requirement," the demand that a system of belief, if it is even to be a candidate for empirical justification, must "contain laws attributing a high degree of reliability to a reasonable variety of cognitively spontaneous beliefs."[51] He then asks: suppose that a system of beliefs subject to the Observation Requirement remains coherent and stable over the long run, how is this best accounted for? He concludes that our normal view of the world, according to which our cognitively spontaneous beliefs are caused by and convey generally reliable information about happenings in the external world offers a better explanation than any competing sceptical hypothesis.

Bonjour's arguments are very detailed and involve distinguishing different kinds of sceptical hypothesis. But it seems to me that the details do not really matter, for they concern the question of whether sceptical alternatives can really be made as coherent as our ordinary view. Whatever the details, then, his basic strategy is fatally flawed. For what the claim that our normal view offers the best explanation of long run stability amounts to is that the system of beliefs that results from combining our cognitively spontaneous beliefs with a normal view of the world is *more coherent* than any that results from combining them with some sceptical hypothesis. But this point counts against scepticism only if we have already assured ourselves that coherence is indicative of truth.

Bonjour places particular emphasis on what I have called "epistemological coherence," noting that "there is available a complicated albeit schematic account in terms of biological and to some extent also cultural and conceptual evolution which explains how cognitive beings whose spontaneous beliefs are connected with the world in the right way could come to exist." By comparison, he thinks, even the most elaborate sceptical hypotheses look both underdescribed and *ad hoc*. If we ask why Descartes's demon deceives him, we may be able to flesh out the story with an account of the demon's desires. But it will just be tacked on since "there is and can be nothing about the demon considered merely as a producer which makes any such account more likely to be true that any other."[52] He may be right here: sceptical stories do look thin when divorced from the challenge to base knowledge of the world on sensory experience and are examined instead as potential components in a total system of beliefs. But he has not spoken to the question at issue, which is not whether sceptical systems are more or less coherent but why we should take coherence to be connected with truth.

When this is the question, no reply along Bonjour's lines can hope to succeed. If inference to the best explanation is understood in terms of maximizing the explanatory coherence of our total view, as it must be when the legitimacy of our total view is in question, any attempt to explain the connection between coherence and truth via an inference to the best explanation is inevitably question-begging. If there is a problem of connecting coherence with truth, at the level of the totality of our beliefs about the world, it cannot be addressed by any form of abductive inference, for the truth-conduciveness of all such inferences is the very question at issue. The necessary truth-conduciveness of the factors relevant to justification demands some kind of *a priori* connection between them and truth. But even the most minimal realism with respect to truth seems to rule out the possibility of any such connection, which means that the problem of the truth-connection, as the coherence theorist must pose it, is insoluble.

However, this is not quite the end of the matter, for there is one more argument I need to consider. The argument is developed by Michael Friedman in the course of a discussion of how to validate inductive methods but it is suggestive of a general approach to scepticism. The interest in Friedman's approach lies in the fact that, though strategically it has close affinities with that just considered, he not only recognizes its inherent circularity but tries to make a virtue of it. Central to his argument is a subtle question: even if an empirical response to scepticism will always be circular, must the circularity be *vicious*?

According to Friedman, an empirical answer to inductive scepticism will involve deriving "the reliability of our inductive methods from our psychological and physical theories, our theories about how the human mind arrives at beliefs through interaction with the environment."[53] More specifically, it will aim at establishing statistical laws of the form:

For all $S$, the probability that $S$ is true, given that $S$ is accepted (rejected) by method $M$ is $r$.

This will allow us to say that method is reliable if:

For all $S$ and $R$, if $M$ rejects $R$ in favor of $S$, then the probability that $S$ is true is greater than the probability that $R$ is true.[54]

There is no other reasonable procedure, since there is "no inductive method that is more reliable in every possible world than every other method." Inevitably, then, "the reliability of our inductive methods, if they are reliable, depends on general facts relating the process of belief acquisition to events in the world" and so, "in appealing to general facts about the actual world, confirmation theory has to depend on the very methods it is attempting to justify." But although this procedure is unquestionably circular, it is not vicious because its success is by no means *guaranteed*: "for all we know, the theories produced by our inductive methods will eventually undermine the reliability of those very methods."[55]

This approach owes a great deal to Quine's understanding of the task of epistemology as that of "defend[ing] science from within, against its self-doubts."[56] As we saw, Quine thinks that sceptical doubts are the offspring of scientific inquiry, for it is through such inquiry that the sceptic's stock examples of error — sensory "illusions" and so on — come to light. Recognizing this, we are supposed to see that the epistemologist's traditional "fear of circularity is a case of needless logical timidity."[57] The sceptic casts doubt on the reliability of our methods of belief-acquisition by focussing on a few facts that inquiry has brought to light. But it may be that, on a more comprehensive view of our epistemic situation, these methods can be seen not to undermine their own reliability. We have no guarantee that this is so, but if we can show it we will have made real progress. We will have shown that the sceptic is "over-reacting."[58]

I argued in the previous chapter that the problem with this account of "sceptical" reasoning is that it is not clear why the kind of "self-undermining," or undermining of the evidential base for our beliefs, that it alludes to should be thought to raise a genuinely sceptical problem at all. This kind of self-undermining, which leads us to modify beliefs or methods in response to it, looks like what goes on when we *correct* our outlook in the light of experience. It does not look like the kind of reasoning that would lead us to think that nothing we believe is ever so much as justified.

This response to Quine applies equally well to the project described by Friedman. Friedman quotes a well-known argument from Russell to illustrate how science might undermine itself: "Naive realism leads to physics, and physics, if true, shows that naive realism is false. Therefore naive realism, if true, is false; therefore it is false." And he notes that "Russell neglects to add that this would cast doubt on physics as well as naive realism, since physics is itself inferred from naive realist perceptual beliefs." [59] Had Russell pointed this out he would indeed have been over-reacting. For the passage from simpler to more refined conceptions of the world by no means automatically puts us under pressure to reject everything we believed when we held to some simpler conception. All we are required to do is to reassess and if need be correct former beliefs in the light of what we have since come to believe. All we have been given is an example of conceptual or theoretical change: a sceptical argument is not yet in sight. If the circularity in Quine's approach is not vicious, this is because no genuine sceptical problem is ever addressed.

None of this is surprising. Sceptical problems arise, not from scientific facts, or not from such facts alone, but from challenges to legitimate beliefs belonging to certain very broad and purely epistemological kinds. So can the Quinean strategy envisaged by Friedman be brought to bear on a genuinely sceptical problem? In particular, can it be brought to bear on the problem of connecting, in full generality, our methods of justification with the truth of our beliefs?

I think that it is clear that it cannot. An epistemologically coherent system of beliefs allows for the explanation of its own reliability. Friedman's "sceptic" is simply one who claims that our beliefs may not even be epistemologically coherent, that they may not even hang together in the way we would like them to. I have already suggested that, even if this were so, it would not have to be seen as establishing a sceptical conclusion, since this kind of failure of full explanatory coherence would not automatically amount to a radical epistemological breakdown. But now the point is that, even if the breakdown could be repaired, or shown never to have occurred, the fundamental problem of relating justification, understood as turning on belief-belief relations, to truth, understood realistically, would not even have been touched. Friedman's argument, like Bonjour's, calls attention to what is an important dimension of coherence. But it tells us nothing about what coherence has to do with truth. This would go for any empirical theorizing of the sort Friedman or Bonjour envisage.

## 7.7 SCEPTICISM AND CHARITY

It seems from the argument of the previous section that nothing less than an *a priori* connection between coherence and truth will satisfy the coherence theorist bent on providing a direct answer to scepticism. Does this mean that up-to-date coherence theorists, as much as their idealist precursors, are committed in the end to an epistemic conception of truth?

It is at this point in my argument that Davidson's "mild" version of the coherence theory becomes especially significant. If Davidson is right, the pressure on coherence theorists to adopt an epistemic conception of truth comes from the assumption that an *a priori* connection between coherence and truth requires a direct connection between truth and the criteria of coherence. This is a mistake. The connection is mediated by the notion of belief. Coherence is a feature of systems of beliefs, not systems of propositions, and massive falsity in one's beliefs is simply impossible. This insight gives us an *a priori* connection between coherence and truth without requiring us to think that truth can be analyzed or defined in terms of epistemic criteria.

The link between belief and truth goes through the notion of meaning. More precisely, it emerges out of the ineliminability of charity as a constraint on interpretation, that is, out of the absolute necessity for seeing anyone's beliefs, including one's own, as more or less consistent and for the most part true. Where we cannot find truth (for the most part), we cannot find belief either. So there is no question of anyone's beliefs being entirely or even mostly false.

Davidson's approach to scepticism contrasts sharply with the naturalistic strategy advocated by Friedman. Friedman thinks that if his envisaged self-justification is to avoid having its success guaranteed in advance, truth must be understood in terms of a causal-physical theory of reference. A causal theory of reference is "the only kind of theory that can figure in a justification of inductive inference which is not *viciously* circular."[60] A charity-based theory, such as Davidson's, assigns referents to the terms of a theory in such a way that "we maximise (roughly) the number of *true* sentences of the theory" and a disquotational theory is simply "the optimal charity-based theory for one's *own* language." Approaching reference this way, "we can easily prove in our semantics that most of the theory to be 'justified' is in fact true."[61] The empirical facts relating the process of belief acquisition to the success of its outcome will play no role in our validation of our methods. A causal theory of reference, by contrast, does not by itself guarantee that we are reliable in the beliefs we form about the world. For such a theory "looks 'backward' to features of the environment that bear the 'right sort' of causal relation to the use of the expression" and so "specifies the referents of terms by considerations that are independent of the truth or falsehood of the sentences we happen to accept."[62]

Surely, however, there are no such considerations. Or rather, to make sense of the thought that there might be, we will have to revert to a confrontationalist epistemology. We will have to suppose that, in some

cases, reference relations can be grasped "directly," through something like
Russellian acquaintance. Short of this, we are fated to derive our understanding of reference from unproblematic cases of referring, and when we
do this we become subject to charity as a methodological constraint. It is
true that a causal theory will not analyze reference in terms that allude to
the truth of our beliefs. But this means only that charity belongs to the
methodology of the theory, rather than to the theory itself. When we try to
determine what sort of causal relation counts as "the right sort," we have
no choice but to work from clear cases of successful reference, and this will
involve taking ourselves to have all kinds of true beliefs. In this sense,
charity represents a constraint on all theories, not a distinctive kind of
theory. This means, in turn, that a charity-based theory like Davidson's is
not precluded from recognizing that causation may have something to do
with reference. And in fact, causation is crucial to his argument.

So far, so good. But will recognizing the role of charity in the theory of
reference allow us to make headway with the problem of relating coherence
to truth? And, if so, how? Let us look more closely at Davidson's argument.

The inevitability of charity results from the interdependence of belief and
meaning. Thus:

> What a sentence means depends partly on the external circumstances
> that cause it to win some degree of conviction; and partly on the
> relations, grammatical, logical or less, that the sentence has to other
> sentences held true with varying degrees of conviction.[63]

Meaning, in other words, is something to be recovered from the relationships sentences held true bear to each other, in the speaker's system of
beliefs, and to the world. In the face of wild inconsistency or massive error,
we could detect no such stable relationships. Better, there would be no such
relationships to detect. So a person's beliefs are open to interpretation –
indeed, have content, hence are genuinely *beliefs* – only on condition that
the possibility of widespread inconsistency or massive error is excluded.
Belief is "in its nature veridical."[64] This welcome conclusion allows
Davidson to combine his coherence theory of knowledge with a correspondence theory of truth because it detaches the "realistic" conception
of truth from the thought that truth is a *radically* non-epistemic notion.
Davidson writes:

> Truth emerges not as wholly detached from belief (as a correspon-
> dence theory would make it) nor as dependent on human methods
> and powers of discovery (as epistemic theories of truth would make
> it). What saves truth from being "radically non-epistemic" (in
> Putnam's words) is not that truth is epistemic but that belief, through
> its ties with meaning, is intrinsically veridical.[65]

Though Davidson's result amounts to a transcendental deduction of the conservatism that coherence theorists typically put forward as one aspect of coherentist justification, it can make us wonder whether Davidson subscribes to the coherence theory as I have characterized it. To be sure, he agrees with coherence theorists in rejecting verification by confrontation. But if we are guaranteed a permanent hard core of true beliefs, he can also agree with Schlick that justifying is always a matter of accommodating some beliefs to others: and if he can show that beliefs about external objects inevitably belong to that hard core, he can refute the sceptic as well. Unlike foundationalists, however, he is not committed to specifying a particular class of privileged beliefs; and yet, at the same time and in contrast to traditional coherence theorists, he apparently has no need of an elaborate notion of coherence. As he says, "Coherence is nothing but consistency."[66] He can both meet the many systems objection without recourse to an obscure notion of global explanatory coherence and secure the general truthfulness of a coherent body of beliefs without recourse to Bonjour's question-begging abductive inference. Whatever we choose to call Davidson's theory, it opens up an attractive prospect.

I think, however, that on examination Davidson's position proves to be an unstable combination of conflicting elements. He certainly seems to understand his problem as a radically holistic coherence theorist would understand it, for his argument, he tells us, is meant to show that "coherence yields correspondence," that hanging together on the part of our beliefs is indicative of their truth. On the other hand what he seems really to argue is that coherence and correspondence are *both* products of charity. The main dimensions of coherence, according to Davidson's "mild" theory, are consistency and reasonable scope. If beliefs derive their significance from the way they are embedded in a wider system, there will be no question of anyone's having only one or two beliefs or being wildly inconsistent. Without a system of reasonably wide scope, there will be nothing in which a particular belief might be embedded; and without consistency, there will be no stable embedding. So charity demands coherence. But since it also demands discernible relations to objective circumstances, it demands truth as well.

Davidson attempts to recover his intended conclusion by making it look as if the enforcement by charity of both coherence and truth (for the most part) is a lemma from which he can infer that "there is a legitimate presumption that any one [of our beliefs], if it coheres with most of the rest, is true."[67] This makes it look as if truth is contingent on coherence. But the appearance is misleading, for it is not as though, on Davidson's view, beliefs could fail to cohere. In general, though not invariably, we are bound to find that any one of a given person's beliefs coheres with "most of the rest," on pain of being unable to attribute to him any beliefs at all. Failure to cohere is necessarily exceptional.

   The interdependence of belief and meaning and the consequent inevitability of charity emerge most clearly in the case of radical interpretation,
where we try to gain access to a speaker's meanings given only an ability to
identify prompted assent. According to Davidson, it is evident that, in such
a situation, an interpreter must:

> interpret so as to read some of his own standards of truth into the
> pattern of sentences held true by the speaker. The point of the
> principle is to make the speaker intelligible, since too great deviations
> from consistency and correctness leave no common ground on which
> to judge either conformity or difference. From a formal point of view,
> the principle of charity helps solve the problem of the interaction of
> meaning and belief by restraining the degrees of freedom allowed
> belief while determining how to interpret words.[68]

But does it restrain them enough? Doesn't this way with the sceptic threaten
to be too quick to amount to any kind of answer? For the sceptic's question
just is: couldn't a system of beliefs, our own included, conform to our
"standards of truth" and still be wildly out of step with how things objectively are?

   This brings us to another way charity works to reduce the sceptic's room
for maneuver. Davidson tells us:

> Something like charity operates in the interpretation of those sentences
> whose causes of assent come and go with time and place: when the
> interpreter finds a sentence of the speaker the speaker assents to
> regularly under conditions he recognises, he takes those conditions to
> be the truth conditions of the speaker's sentence.[69]

This leads straight to the refutation of scepticism. Thus:

> What stands in the way of global scepticism of the senses is ... the
> fact that we must, in the plainest and methodologically most basic
> cases, take the objects of a belief to be the causes of that belief. And
> what we, as interpreters, must take them to be is what they in fact
> are. Communication begins where causes converge: your belief means
> what mine does if belief in its truth is systematically caused by the
> same events and objects.[70]

Here we see that Davidson's approach to interpretation is not simply to let
reference fall out where it may, subject to the contraint of maximizing the
number of truths in the speaker's belief-system. Charity in this sense is not
enough of a constraint. This is obvious when we reflect that if, with

Davidson, we think that our logic (which we must attribute to any speaker) is first-order quantification theory, we are guaranteed a way of interpreting his beliefs – his total "theory" – so that they all come out true: for charity demands consistency and every consistent first-order theory has a model. But since even the most minimal realist wants more than "truth in a model," there must be some constraint on interpretation that connects reference with something "external," with how things objectively are. This is where the appeal to causation comes in. As Davidson himself remarks, it is only the distinction between "sentences whose causes to assent come and go with observable circumstances and those a speaker clings to through change" that "offers the possibility of interpreting the words and sentences beyond the logical."[71]

Thus although Davidson's approach to interpretation remains broadly holistic, hypotheses about the causes of assent being subject to revision as we gain understanding of the alien's beliefs, occasion sentences possess an ineliminable element of methodological primacy: there are limits to how far we can suppose ourselves liable to error in their case without losing our grip on the possibility of interpreting a speaker at all. So we see how the external and internal determinants of reference are made to work together: there are privileged cases in which the external determinants serve to establish a base from which to work our way into the interior of the alien's belief-system, a region where belief-belief relations play an increasingly dominant role in the determination of meaning. In working our way inward, we appeal to charity to "favour interpretations that as far as possible preserve truth,"[72] which is to say, preserve truth in the light of whatever reference relations we have already established in the methodologically basic cases. In fixing the meanings of less accessible beliefs, we must be responsive to whatever we have found in the plainer cases, where reference is more immediately tied to causation.

At this point in his argument, Davidson's allegedly mild version of the coherence theory is no longer clearly different from more standard versions. If the basic evidence provided by the interpretation of observation sentences is to give us any purchase on the interpretation of standing sentences, assent and dissent to such sentences must be connected, at least epistemically, with the more theoretical beliefs that standing sentences express. The traditional conception of coherence, we saw, demands rich logical connections between beliefs and, partly as a way of ensuring sufficient connectedness, epistemic beliefs providing for rationalized input. Davidson is committed to the same demands, if his methodology is to provide scope for interpretation beyond the observational.

Be that as it may, however, from the standpoint of explaining how we must proceed with radical interpretation, assigning methodological primacy to observation sentences is the right move for Davidson to make. But in making it, he reveals how little help we can expect from the theory of interpretation in our confrontation with the sceptic. The workings of charity are clear enough when the problem is to interpret someone else's beliefs, from the "outside" so to speak. To interpret another, we use our knowledge of the observable features of the world, taken as unproblematic, as the basis for determining referents for the alien speaker's terms; and we can determine causal relations because we have independent access to cause and effect: prompted assent and the circumstances that prompt it. But when we adopt the first-person standpoint, for the purpose of assessing the totality of our beliefs about the world, the idea of independent access ceases to make sense. We cannot determine what we are inclined to say or think and, independently, the circumstances that prompt us to say or think it.

I take it that Davidson does not mean to lapse into foundationalism. Observation sentences are methodologically primary for a radical interpreter but not thereby epistemologically basic for the person whose beliefs are being interpreted. What is not clear, however, is that such a distinction could be made if we were willing to extend the idea of radical interpretation to ourselves. However, although pressed in this direction, the way to traditional foundationalism is closed to Davidson. Traditional foundationalists try to explain the connection between justification and truth by making sensation the point of contact between belief and the world. Davidson rejects this on the grounds that sensation must either be understood as itself involving belief, in which case we still face the problem of connecting coherence in our beliefs with objective truth, or understood as a non-propositional event standing in a causal relation to belief, in which case sensation has nothing to do with justification. Thus:

> The relation between a sensation and a belief cannot be logical, since sensations are not beliefs.... [The] relation is causal. Sensations cause some beliefs and in *this* sense are the basis or ground of those beliefs. But a causal explanation does not show how or why the belief is justified.[73]

This is so only if one is a radical holist, hence an internalist. If one is neither, causal factors can be epistemologically relevant, though they need not always be. Thus that Davidson gives this argument is further confirmation of his affinity for the traditional type of coherence theory. But this only makes Davidson's own appeal to the causation all the more puzzling. True, Davidson eschews tying beliefs to sensations or Quinean "stimulations," preferring a direct connection with external, publicly accessible objects. But why should this make a difference, so long as the link remains causal and "a causal explanation does not show how or why a belief is justified?" If reference turns on causation and causation has nothing to do with justification, the conclusion ought to be that reference has nothing to do with justification either.

Now we see the importance of the subtle shift in direction we noted earlier. Davidson's announced intention was to argue that "coherence yields correspondence." This is the form that a direct answer to the sceptical problem must take. For if we concede the legitimacy of calling in question all our beliefs about the world, and all at once, then, the most we can suppose ourselves to have in the way of a basis on which to construct our answer to the sceptic is knowledge of relations between our beliefs, coherence. This is why, if truth is not defined in terms of coherence, it is hard to see why our beliefs should have the slightest tendency to be true. Under pressure from this difficulty, Davidson shifts to an argument that derives both coherence and correspondence from charity. But the appeal to charity turns out to involve the idea of unproblematic access to certain causal relations between speakers and objects in the world. If, in the context of the sceptic's question, we grant ourselves this access, the game is over before it begins.

There is, however a final development, the idea of an omniscient interpreter.[74] Davidson invites us to:

> imagine for a moment an interpreter who is omniscient about the world, and about what does and would cause a speaker to assent to any sentence in his (potentially unlimited) repertoire. The omniscient interpreter, using the same method as the fallible interpreter, finds that fallible interpreter largely consistent and correct. By his own standards, of course, but since these are objectively correct, the fallible interpreter is seen to be largely consistent and correct by objective standards.[75]

Since we can see that an omniscient interpreter, whose beliefs were true, would have to find most of our beliefs true as well, we can assure ourselves that most of them are true. We can see this even from the detached, radically first-person standpoint forced on us by the project of assessing the totality of our beliefs about the world.[76]

One thing in this passage strikes the eye immediately: an enormous expansion of the scope accorded the causal factor in meaning. This factor was first introduced as the key to interpreting occasion sentences, whose "causes to assent come and go with observable circumstances."[77] Fixing the reference of terms that occur in occasion sentences gives us something against which to test our interpretations of standing sentences, which have no readily identifiable "causes to assent." But the omniscient interpreter's knowledge extends to "what does and would cause a speaker to assent to *any* sentence in [the speaker's] (potentially unlimited) repertoire."

Given such knowledge, it becomes unclear why the omniscient interpreter is bound to use the same method as the fallible interpreter, a method forced on the latter by his lack of access to the causes of assent to standing sentences. So it is not obvious that Davidson's thought-experiment is even consistently described.

Secondly, if interpretation turns on knowledge of the causes of assent, then to suppose that there could be an omniscient "interpreter" is simply to take for granted the existence of systematic, external causes of belief, thus begging the question against the sceptic. For unless we already have some way of connecting coherence with truth, thus assuring ourselves of the existence of an objective world, we will have no way of knowing that our beliefs are interpretable, in this sense of "interpret."[78]

Finally, once we see the causes of assent as something external to our entire system of beliefs, what possible reason could we have for supposing that the interpretation available to the omniscient interpreter, through his knowledge of the real causes of our beliefs, matches the self-understanding that we generate through exploring the inferential relationships between beliefs in our system from the "inside." For example, if we were brains in vats, kept ignorant of our fate and hooked up to some kind of speaking apparatus, the omniscient interpreter would take our utterances to be about events in the computer that controls our simulated sensory input, though presumably we would not. So even if the omniscient interpreter argument were able to assure us that we have some knowledge, it would leave us unable to be sure about what knowledge we had. If reference has to be recovered from the causes of assent then, in the context of the sceptic's challenge to the totality of our knowledge of the world, in which no knowledge of causal relations to objective circumstances can be treated as unproblematic, reference becomes inscrutable. At most, the sceptic is forced to recast his question about how we justify our beliefs in terms of a question about how we know what those beliefs, even when mostly true, are really about. But why should I be comforted by the thought that, if I were a brain in a vat, I should not have mostly false beliefs about the world as I now conceive it but mostly true beliefs about the vat-environment? Once we embrace views that commit us to answering the sceptic directly, our claim to knowledge of the world will have to rest on faith and hope, not charity.

The problem that has emerged is quite general. A direct answer to the sceptic's question about justification and truth accepts the legitimacy of inquiring into the epistemological status of the totality of our beliefs about the world. In consequence, it accepts internalism, agreeing that we can meet the sceptic's challenge, thus understand how knowledge in general is possible, only by appealing to things that even the sceptic allows we must know. For the particular problem we have been discussing, we need an argument to show that coherence yields correspondence. But the desired link cannot be forged on the basis of our knowledge of how beliefs are interpreted and understood. If the meaning of our beliefs, or the reference of their terms, is responsive only to relations between beliefs, we will be unable to appeal to meaning and reference to defeat a sceptic who thinks that our beliefs could hang together and still be comprehensively false. To be of use, meaning and reference must be responsive to something external and objective: causal relations to objective circumstances. But now the internalist constraint makes itself felt. We need more than the existence of the appropriate causal relations: we need at least some such relations to be known. So while, on the one hand, we cannot suppose they are known and still respond to the sceptic's challenge at its intended level of generality, on the other, if we do not suppose them known, we will be able to show neither that we have knowledge nor even what knowledge we would have if we had it.

The combination of holism and internalism is therefore fatal even to Davidson's somewhat residual realist aspirations. Realism demands that we connect our beliefs with something external and objective. If we establish the connection in a way that requires awareness of the external, objective something, we will be accused of begging the question, or of failure to explain how the *totality* of our beliefs is grounded. But if we drop the awareness requirement, we violate the internalist constraint and fail to explain to ourselves how it is that we really have knowledge. We point to conditions such that, if they are fulfilled, we have knowledge, but have no way of showing that they are fulfilled.[79]

However, these latest reflections suggest a way of salvaging Davidson's argument. Perhaps the tensions we have been exploring are not internal to Davidson's conception of the relations between belief, truth and meaning, but exist rather between that conception and his apparent wish to meet the sceptic with a direct answer. Perhaps the way to save the argument is to treat it as a diagnostic response to the problem. To read Davidson this way is to see him as claiming to have identified an unacknowledged presupposition of Cartesian thought-experiments: namely, that the content of our beliefs remains invariant even under massive change of truth-values. So whereas the sceptic assumes that, even if our beliefs were all false, they would still be the same beliefs, Davidson shows that they could not be, because of the interdependence of truth and meaning. If a Cartesian nightmare were to come true, we would have beliefs with different content, but still mostly true.

This is a possible way of interpreting Davidson's argument. I would not myself wish to argue in quite this way because I think that doing so implicitly concedes too much that should not be conceded. To feel obliged to rule out even the bare logical possibility of global falsity is to agree that, if such massive error were possible, the sceptic would be in a strong position. But as I have argued repeatedly, there is no valid move from this bare logical possibility to radical scepticism. Also, and relatedly, Davidson's argument, even when interpreted diagnostically, involves far too uncritical an attitude towards the sceptic's totality condition on a properly philosophical understanding of our knowledge of the world. And, as have just seen, if we take at face value the sceptic's attempt to assess our knowledge of the world as a whole, the sceptic's problem concerning the justifiability of beliefs tends less to be solved than transformed into a problem about the inscrutability of reference. To deal with this, we still need a diagnosis of the sceptic's totality condition on a philosophical understanding of our knowledge of the world. So, in sum, I think that without such a diagnosis, Davidson's argument will be ineffective while, with one, it will be unnecessary.

But does Davidson provide the required diagnosis, though in a version of his own? Could we see him as arguing that we cannot take up the position of radical interpreters with respect to ourselves? I do not see how, since his entire argument turns on getting us to imagine how an interpreter would have to interpret us. This is his version of the detached, reflective stance that goes with the quest for philosophical understanding. But for the sceptic, Davidson's stance is not detached enough. Davidson glosses over the problem of the inscrutability of reference by assuming that the radical interpreter, omniscient or otherwise, has unproblematic access to the world. With this assumption in place, I can assure myself that my beliefs are both true and about what I normally take them to be about by reflecting on how such an interpreter would have to interpret me. However, when I reflect that he is in the same epistemic predicament as I – that the reference of his terms is inscrutable too – I have no such source of reassurance. It is as if Davidson only recognizes Clarke's "plain" or "epistemic" sceptical possibilities. I try to imagine that all of my beliefs are false or, if not false, caused in some highly deviant way. But in so doing, I still hold on to the idea that the facts of the matter, including the facts of reference, are knowable, if not immediately by me then by someone else. If this is so, Davidson never really confronts the sceptic's thought-experiments as the sceptic intends them. But neither does he show that they are incoherent.

I do not claim that Davidson has nothing important to say. But I think it is best to see him as offering a way of thinking about belief and meaning that comes into its own after we have seen our way beyond traditional sceptical worries. If we abandon "our knowledge of the world" as an object of theory, and therewith cease to be threatened with a loss of all wordly knowledge, we will lack all temptation to try to take up the stance of the radical interpreter with respect to ourselves. We will then be able to appeal to charity to show that we could never have any reason to treat anyone else as a radical sceptic. But if we are to understand the source of traditional sceptical problems, there is no dispensing with the kind of epistemologically centered diagnosis I have tried to develop.

# 8

---

# The Instability of Knowledge

## 8.1 CLOSURE AGAIN

From time to time we have touched on the thought that the key to scepticism is to be found in the plausible but allegedly false principle that knowledge is closed under known logical implication: that if someone knows that p, and knows that p entails q, then he knows that q. I have already given reasons for thinking that no criticism of the sceptic based on rejection of this principle is likely to succeed, if the sceptic is granted his conception of philosophical inquiry and its relation to everyday epistemic practices. Now I want to examine the issue of closure in more detail.

One reason for my taking an interest in this approach to scepticism is that it is a competitor to the sort of theoretical diagnosis that I favor. Those who dissolve scepticism by denying closure do not charge the sceptic with speaking unintelligibly but rather with relying on an epistemic principle that our ordinary concept of knowledge neither does nor need conform to. At the same time, they allow that the principle of closure is *prima facie* very plausible; if I know that p, and that p entails q, then surely I know that q. How could I fail to, for surely deduction from knowledge antecedently possessed is a source of knowledge, if anything is? So even if finally unacceptable, the principle of closure looks initially enough like a platitude that it takes a subtle analysis of the concept of knowledge to shake our faith in it. Those who reject closure, then, do not accuse the sceptic of making an obvious mistake. On the contrary, they do justice to the apparent naturalness of his reasoning, and this is one of the strengths of their approach.

There is, however, a further reason why I particularly need to address the issue of closure. Rejecting epistemological realism, I see constraints on knowledge and justification as subject to contextual variation: whether I count as knowing something or other depends on the kind of investigation or discipline my putative knowledge belongs to, my worldly circumstances, and so on. But though the relevant contextual constraints must *be* met, they need not always be *known* to be met. Thus, as I have said, my contextual view of knowledge and justification involves a substantial element of externalism; and since externalist theories of knowledge are widely believed to require nonclosure, my own approach to scepticism might be thought to require this too.

However, I want to make two things clear from the outset. The first is that, whether or not the externalist component in my view of knowledge and justification requires me to deny closure, I have no wish to make a denial of closure the basis of my response to scepticism. Indeed, it has never been my intention to rest my case against the sceptic on a direct appeal to externalism itself, still less on one of its more problematic alleged consequences. The aim of my essay is theoretical diagnosis: to bring to light the sceptic's essential commitment to an undefended, and I think indefensible, epistemological realism. The idea is to put sceptical doubts in a wholly new light: to make them appear, not as natural doubts, but as an unwanted consequence of dispensable theoretical ideas. But even if dispensing with these ideas leads us to look more sympathetically on externalism, theoretical diagnosis still comes first. We are in no position to look favorably on externalism so long as we agree that there is a naively intelligible question as to how it is possible for us to know anything whatsoever about the world; and that there is no such question is exactly what my theoretical diagnosis is meant to show. So far as I am sympathetic to externalism, then, it is as a consequence of my theoretical diagnosis of the traditional epistemological project.

The second is that I find the arguments that have been taken to establish nonclosure inconclusive, to say the least. They are not, however, uninteresting or unimportant. Not only are there lessons to be learned from their failure but, as we shall see, philosophers attracted by them are responding to a real feature of our experience of scepticism. So I still think it is worth asking whether nonclosure is an automatic consequence of an externalist understanding of knowledge, or of a contextualist understanding in so far as it is externalist. At the very least, we will learn something about the consequences of contextualism. But I think that, in fact, we will learn more than this.

## 8.2  KNOWLEDGE AND RELIABILITY

Denials of closure are often based on pure reliabilist theories of knowledge. The guiding intuition behind such theories is that knowledge is belief that is *non-accidentally* true. The hallmark of such belief is that, in some important way, it depends on and so covaries with the facts. But for a *pure* reliabilist, this belief-fact link need have nothing to do with justification. So, for example, Alvin Goldman explains it in terms of causation: I know that P if my belief that P is, in some appropriate way, caused by the fact that P. In a similar spirit, D. M. Armstrong makes knowledge turn on a "law-like connection" between someone's believing that P and the state of affairs that makes it true that P. Robert Nozick argues that, to count as knowledge, beliefs must "track the truth." According to Colin McGinn, to know that p I must come to believe that p *via* a "way of telling" that p: this is his "discriminative capacity" analysis of knowing. Fred Dretske (now) explains knowledge in terms of "information flow": to amount to knowledge, my belief that s is F msut be caused, or causally sustained, by the information that s is F. The differences between these theories are not insignificant. But they are all variations on a common theme: knowledge is non-accidentally true belief, belief formed in such a way as to be truth-reliable.[1]

For these theorists, the great virtue of explaining knowledge as non-accidentally true belief is that so doing lets us sever the traditional connection between knowledge and justification. This makes knowledge a more primitive accomplishment than justified belief: animals can have discriminative capacities, hence knowledge, even if their lack of language or inability to perform sophisticated inferences disqualifies them from being justified believers.[2] Many contemporary externalists hold that, once we recognize that the long-standing connection between knowledge and justification can and should be severed, not only do we open the way for a simpler and more adequate analysis of the concept of knowledge, we also see how arguments for scepticism go wrong.

However, although denials of closure are frequenly associated with pure reliabilism, they do not depend on it. If such views lead to nonclosure, it is because they are externalist and not because they detach knowledge from justification. When Dretske first brought the issue of closure clearly into focus, he did so in the context of a "relevant alternatives" view of knowledge. This view of knowledge, inspired by Austin, is much more "justificationist" than those just mentioned. It is still, however, externalist. As I have argued, it would be a mistake to equate externalism with pure reliabilism. The essence of externalism, let us recall, is to allow knowledge when a person in fact meets certain conditions, whether or not he knows he meets them. These conditions may be "external," not just in not being represented in the person's knowledge or beliefs, but in having to do with his actual situation. The capacity for knowledge is thus like any other capacity: it depends partly on the powers of the individual and partly on the circumstances in which he is required to exercise them. But to acknowledge this similarity is to drive a wedge between knowing something and knowing that one knows it. For me to know that p, certain conditions – which I may or may not know anything about – will have to be met; whereas to know that I know that p, I will need to know that those conditions are fulfilled. My knowing that p neither guarantees nor requires my knowing that I do. Given this account of externalism, a view of knowledge like Dretske's will be both justificationist and externalist if it holds (1) that knowing depends on being able to rule out all relevant alternatives (this is the justificationist part) and (2) the person does not have to *know* that the alternatives he is able to rule out are all that are relevant, the range of relevant alternatives being fixed in part by external factors. In Austin's example, what I need to do to identify a bird as a goldfinch may depend on what other similar birds are *in fact* present in my locality.

So to repeat: the distinction between internalism and externalism cannot be identified with that between justificationism and pure reliabilism. True, the strict internalism advocated by Bonjour is equivalent to foundationalism. So if we were to stipulate that a genuinely justificationist account of knowledge exclude all external factors (beyond the truth condition), we would identify justificationism with internalism and thus with foundationalism. This would give us an opposition with justificationism and internalism on one side and reliabilism and externalism on the other. But even then, "reliabilism" would cover more than pure reliabilism, for thus defined the term applies to contextualist views of justification.

These considerations suggest that we should apply to reliabilism a distinction analogous to that between substantive and merely formal foundationalism. We can take the (vague) intuition that knowledge involves non-accidentally true belief to establish formal reliabilism, much as the fact that justification comes to an end sooner or later establishes formal foundationalism. But in my book, formal foundationalism is not necessarily foundationalism, for we can agree that justification always comes to an end somewhere or other without supposing that there need be any general theory – or any (purely epistemological) fact of the matter – as to how or where it comes to an end. This applies to externalist versions of foundationalism as well. If they are only formally foundationalist, they are not really foundationalist at all. Applying a similar distinction to reliabilism, we can agree that knowledge requires reliably formed, hence non-accidentally true belief, without supposing that we need or can get a uniform account of the basis of the required reliability. On the contrary, we should expect the basis to vary contextually with the precise content of what is believed and the circumstances in which the belief is acquired. In some cases, the basis of our reliability may be causal, as when proper training makes us reliable reporters on a particular range of facts. In others, it may involve more or less elaborate inference.

This will not satisfy pure reliabilists, who feel the pull of their own version of epistemological realism. These theorists want to identify a single, ubiquitous belief-world relation on which knowledge supervenes. So, as much as traditional foundationalists, they want a theory of knowledge, not just a theory of the concept of knowledge. The trouble is that, if knowledge is not to collapse into true belief, truth-reliability must be taken to hold with respect to kinds of beliefs, kinds that cannot be defined so narrowly that they have each only one member: a particular belief that I happen to get right in some particular, never-to-be-precisely repeated circumstances. So my capacity for knowing that P will depend on my reliability in relevantly similar cases, where relevant similarity will involve both other beliefs and other circumstances. What is hard to believe, however, is that relevant similarity, rather than being at least in part interest-relative, is simply fixed by the propositions to be known, or by the (worldly? epistemological?) facts. For this to happen, our beliefs themselves will have to fall into natural epistemological kinds, such that the beliefs themselves determine what abilities we have to have if those beliefs are to amount to knowledge. So it seems to me that, though certain pure reliabilists may have more in common with the traditional foundationalist than they like to think, the thrust of reliabilism is (epistemologically speaking) anti-realist. Whether our reliabilism is substantive (pure) or merely formal, we ought to be suspicious of epistemological realism. Reliability presupposes assignment to a reference class, which is something *we do* with our beliefs (in the light of our interests etc.), not something they do for themselves. Once we reject traditional foundationalism, we commit ourselves to letting knowledge depend in part on factors other than further knowledge. This is the sense in which there is an unavoidable choice between foundationalism and externalism. But there is not an inevitable choice between foundationalism and pure reliabilism.

In light of this, it is not surprising to find intimations of nonclosure in Wittgenstein. Propositions that, as Wittgenstein says, "stand fast" may be known to be entailed by known propositions, but this does not mean that they can themselves be thought of as known. If indeed we have a special "non-epistemic" relation to such propositions they should not, and perhaps even cannot, be. Here, it seems to me, Wittgenstein is responding to the fundamental intuition behind denials of closure, which is that we cannot bootstrap our presuppositions into items of knowledge. Historical research would not yield knowledge if the Earth came into existence five minutes ago complete with misleading evidence of great antiquity. But let us suppose that it will yield knowledge provided that (among other things) the Earth has *in fact* existed for many years past. Still, we will not want to say that, having come to know various particular historical facts, we can convert the presupposition of the Earth's past existence into an item of knowledge by inferring it from the particular facts that, relying on this very pre-supposition, we have come to know. Even in its contextualist variant, it seems, externalism requires nonclosure.

One way to react to this argument is to say "So much the worse for externalism." If nonclosure really is a consequence of a contextualist or any other externalist approach to knowledge, we should rethink whatever arguments led us to favour that approach. I sympathize with this. It is not easy to dispel the air of paradox that surrounds denials of closure. Can it really be true to say that I know Napoleon was victorious at Austerlitz but do *not* know that the Earth existed at the time?

We could argue that this air of paradox is illusory, for on reflection there is nothing particularly surprising in the fact that a proposition can differ in epistemological status from its logical consequences. For example, any necessary truth is a logical consequence of any empirical proposition. So too with propositions that stand fast: they may not state necessary truths, but they are not exactly straightforward empirical propositions either. Perhaps "not everything that has the form of an empirical proposition is one."[3]

Although such reflections may attenuate our sense of paradox, I doubt they eliminate it entirely. Wittgenstein would tell us that knowledge stands or falls with our ability to give evidence, which is why the proposition that the Earth has existed for many years past cannot be seen as stating something that we know. The very fact that puts this proposition beyond question – that it is built into the very nature of what we understand as historical inquiry makes it incapable of evidential support, hence not properly thought of as either known or not known. But as I have remarked more than once, the difficulty with this line of thought is to see how, in the end, it differs from scepticism. Even philosophers strongly influenced by Wittgenstein can be haunted by the thought that there may be no final difference, hence Cavell's sense of "the truth of scepticism" and "the human disappointment with human knowledge." This suggests that closure is not easily abandoned. It is not easy to resist the thought that, if we do not know what we know our ordinary beliefs to entail, those beliefs do not amount to knowledge, or what we used to think of as knowledge.

## 8.3 CONTEXT AND CLOSURE

It is important to distinguish the different ways in which closure might fail. Perhaps knowledge fails always to be transmitted across known logical entailment because belief is not always so transmitted. Suppose that right now I know that I am sitting at my desk in my office; suppose also that I know that, if I am sitting at my desk, I am not a brain in a vat: do I therefore know that I am not a brain in a vat? Perhaps I don't even believe that I am not. Unless I have scepticism on my mind, I have no opinions one way or the other. I do not *reject* the thought that I am really just a brain in a vat, because this possibility never crosses my mind. Even if I believe things that I know to entail that I am not a brain in a vat, ordinarily I fail to put two and two together. Some of Wittgenstein's examples may work like this. In the normal course of events, the axial propositions around which our various investigative practices turn are never even formulated. To identify them at all takes effort and amounts to a philosophical discovery. Perhaps, then, we do not know them to be true because ordinarily we do not even believe them, in any straightforward sense. Perhaps this remains so even after we have come to realize that they are entailed by all sorts of ordinary beliefs.

This is not the sort of failure philosophers who deny closure have in mind. They argue for a *radical* failure of closure. Their view is that even when I do put two and two together, my knowledge of particular matters of fact remains intact. Even when fully aware that I do not and cannot know that I am not a brain in a vat, I still know all sorts of particular facts about the world. We see, then, that we would be underestimating the concession that these philosophers make to the sceptic if we were to remark only on their allowing that the case for scepticism is *prima facie* plausible. According to them, what the sceptic claims is not just plausible but in large measure correct. I never know that sceptical hypotheses do not obtain; I never know that I am not always dreaming or not a brain in a vat: nevertheless, I do know that I am sitting at my desk right now. Offhand, it is not easy to see how this could be.

The answer is supposed to lie in the externalist approach to knowledge. But what could motivate an externalist to deny closure is far from obvious. What I find especially puzzling is the way nonclosure links externalism with concessions to the sceptic. For I have argued that scepticism depends on foundationalism and that foundationalism and internalism are two names for the same thing.

There are general reasons for thinking that externalists should hesitate before making such concessions. Since any externalist will hold that my capacity for knowledge depends in part on the conditions that obtain in the actual world, he should be open to the possibility that, if I am not a brain in a vat, I know that I am not, even though, if I were, I would not know much of anything.[4] There are two ways for this to happen. One is that the process that leads me to think that I am not a brain in a vat is truth-reliable in the actual world but would not be in the vat-world. The other is that the way of knowing that is available to me in this world would not be available to me there. What makes this second option appealing is that, for an externalist, there is no reason why ways of knowing should be individuated by purely "internal" criteria. So even if my situation and that of a brain in a vat are indistinguishable "from the inside", it does not follow that we are restricted to the same ways of knowing. There is of course the further question as to how far I can defend whatever knowledge-claims happen to be true by externalist standards. Can I *know that I know* that I am not a brain in a vat? However, one of the central externalist points is that this *is* a further question. Knowing that P does not require knowing that you know that P.

   This argument needs elaboration, and since they are generally taken to imply nonclosure we can focus on pure reliabilist theories of knowledge. Though the knowledge-constituting link between belief and the facts has been variously characterized, a common theme runs through all such analyses: the relation to the facts that distinguishes between knowledge and true belief is one that has to hold in the actual world, not in any imaginable circumstances. This means that a person's capacity for knowledge depends on his environment, not just his cognitive faculties. A subject capable of gathering knowledge in one environment might be incapable of it in another. Cues that are reliable bases for certain kinds of judgments in the world as it is could cease to be such if the world were different. Such a change need not be reflected by any cues available to the erstwhile knower: there need be nothing in his internal representation of the world that indicates his unreliability.

   To point this out is simply to stress the fact that such theories of knowledge are externalist: whether a person's beliefs amount to knowledge is not solely, perhaps not at all, a function of what goes on (or can be detected from) "inside." Nevertheless, the point is sufficient to reinforce our puzzlement at the tendency on the part of certain philosophers, not just to deny closure, but to do so on the basis of sceptical thought-experiments. Those who take this route to the denial of closure want to agree with the sceptic that I cannot know that I am not a brain in a vat, while resisting his inference that, if this is so, I cannot know anything about the external world. But as I have argued again and again in tracing scepticism to foundationalism, classic sceptical puzzle cases challenge us to explain how we can tell *from the inside* that we are not in the sceptic's imagined situation. What is puzzling, therefore, is that any externalist should feel bound even to react to this challenge, much less concede defeat in the face of it. On any externalist account of knowledge, never mind a pure reliabilist account, someone may have knowledge or lack it without there being any detectable difference in his inner state. What matters for knowledge is having a true belief that is not accidentally true, and it is surely not *accidental* that a person who is not a brain in a vat believes that he is not.

   The brain in a vat is not so lucky. As standardly imagined, its beliefs depend less on natural laws, or any other reliable belief-forming processes, than on the whims of the experimenters. Since they are experimenting with the control of beliefs and experience and can make radical changes in both, any time they wish, it is arguable that the brain in a vat cannot know that it is a brain in a vat even if they decide to let it in on the secret. Anyway, depending on how we fill in the details – of both the example and the non-accidentality condition – it is perfectly possible: (1) that a person's believing that he is not a brain in a vat, when he is not, is not at all accidental, and so amounts to knowledge, even though his inner states are just what they would be if he *were* a brain in a vat; and (2) that a brain in a vat, with the very same inner states that it would have if it were not a brain in a vat, cannot know anything about its situation because, even if its beliefs happened to be true, this would be in some crucial respects accidental.

The conclusion seems to be that no externalist can be compelled to deny closure. If the details of his account of knowledge *do* point in that direction, this is good reason to revise the details. For the situations of the ordinary person and the brain in a vat seem to be symmetrical. The ordinary person knows lots of particular facts about his environment and also knows something they all imply: that he is not a brain in a vat. The unfortunate brain cannot know whether it is in a vat or not, but then it can't know anything else about its environment either. There is no threat to closure here.

Nor should there be. Truth-reliability (in the actual world) is transmitted across logical consequence, hence *a fortiori* across known logical consequence. If closure fails, therefore, it should do so only where we fail to believe the known logical consequences of our beliefs. Arguments for radical failures of closure should prove either to be fallacious or to involve significant concessions to internalism. Indeed, if my understanding of internalism, not to say my general diagnosis of scepticism, is correct, they will involve concessions to foundationalism, concessions that no externalist ought to make.

We saw in the previous section that we do not have to choose between internalism and pure reliabilism. Now we see that it would be wrong even with respect to externalist theories of knowledge to insist on an exclusive distinction between pure reliabilism and contextualism. For if the capacity for knowledge is like any other capacity, dependent partly on the person and partly on his circumstances, even pure reliabilist theories have a residual, contextualist element. But it would be easy for a reliabilist to find himself pulled in contrary directions. As we saw, if he wants an invariant knowledge-making relation, and if he wants the range of circumstances under which that relation has to hold to be fixed simply by the contents of our beliefs, he is pulled in the direction of epistemological realism. At the same time, however, in so far as his theory treats knowledge as the outcome of a circumstantially effective capacity, he is pulled in the direction of contextualism. We might even expect to find the source of denials of closure in this very tension.

However, this is all extremely abstract. The next step is to examine in detail some representative arguments for nonclosure to see if in fact they go wrong in the way I suggest they must.

## 8.4  KNOWING AND TELLING

I want to begin by considering a very straightforward argument: the "intuitive" case for nonclosure offered by Colin McGinn. McGinn thinks that it would be a mistake to rest the case for nonclosure on the details of some particular analysis of knowledge; for as he says, "those wedded to closure might want to object that this consequence of the . . . analysis is sufficient to show its untenability."[5]

McGinn explains knowledge in terms of the exercise of "discriminative capacities." To know that P, I have to have the capacity to tell whether propositions like P are true. It belongs to the notion of such a capacity that it only operates within certain environmental limits (like the capacity of a key to open a lock, which depends on the lock as well as the key). So I can know that there is a hawk in front of me because I can discriminate between hawks and handsaws (and other real-world alternatives). But I cannot discriminate between my situation and that of a brain in a vat. Thus I can know that there is a hawk on the fencepost, know that this entails that I am not a brain in a vat, and yet not know that I am not a brain in a vat. Closure fails.

This argument is not supposed to depend on the details of McGinn's analysis of knowledge. It rests, he claims, only on the "intuitively correct principle" that "one can *know* that P only if one can *tell whether* P."[6] But whether or not his argument is really more "intuitive" than those of other philosophers, it simply begs the question by assuming that deduction from known premises is not to count as a way of "telling whether" a given proposition is true.

Consider: can I tell whether there is a table in front of me, when there is? According to McGinn:

> in the ordinary sense of "tell whether," what this requires is that I can distinguish there being a table from there being a chair or a dog or some such. So, granted that conditions are normal – there is a table there, my eyes are functioning normally, etc. – I *can* tell whether there is a table there. But can I tell whether I am a brain in a vat? Again, assume conditions are normal: I am not a brain in a vat, there is a table there, my eyes are functioning normally, etc. Then what is required for telling whether I am a brain in a vat is that I be able to distinguish my being a brain in a vat from my not being a brain in a vat. But it seems clear that I lack this ability – I cannot tell whether I am a brain in a vat because I have no means of distinguishing being in that condition from not being in that condition.[7]

Clearly, this argument works only if all "telling whether" depends on a capacity for direct perceptual discrimination. If there is such a thing as inferential knowledge, I may be able to know, by inference from just about any proposition I know about a particular external object, that I am not a brain in a vat: nothing has been said that excludes this. Admittedly, this way of "telling whether" may be available only if I am not in fact a brain in a vat. But the same is true for my knowing that there is a table in front of me. The "discriminate capacity" that gives rise to such knowledge is present or operative only if conditions are normal. In highly abnormal conditions – for example, if I were a brain in a vat – I would lack that capacity. But whenever that capacity does yield knowledge, deduction from the knowledge it yields produces a non-accidentally true belief that I am not a brain in a vat. So why doesn't it yield knowledge too?

This response does highlight something peculiar about sceptical hypotheses: that I have a way of telling that they do not obtain only if they do not obtain. But there is no obvious route from this point to the failure of closure. We have returned to the point that, for an externalist, a "way of telling" does not have to work in any possible world but only in the actual world (and perhaps worlds sufficiently like it); and in the actual world, the way of telling McGinn excludes out of hand does work. The apparent failure of closure results from McGinn's insisting, when it comes to my knowing that I am not a brain in a vat, on a way of telling that would work *even if I were a brain in a vat*, and then finding that there is no such way. But why should there be? He would not insist that my knowing that there is a table in the room result from a way of telling that would work under such conditions. The standards for "telling" get switched, with the effect that McGinn's argument is both fallacious, through equivocation, and involves a departure from externalism. The equivocation consists in being externalist when it comes to knowledge of particular matters of fact while going internalist when it comes to ruling out sceptical counter-possibilities: for the "way of telling" that is insisted upon when it comes to my knowing that I am not a brain in a vat is *thoroughly internalist*. This is why it is a way of telling that would have to work even if I were a brain in a vat. The only way in which I can't tell that I am not a brain in a vat is that my experience could be just the way it is even if I were. My situation and the brain's would be just the same "from the inside." But, if we stick to externalism, knowledge does not stand or fall with such internal factors. If it did, I wouldn't know that there is a table in front of me, because by internalist standards of telling, I can't "tell" real tables from vat-image tables.

How does McGinn get himself into this position? Not by making any simple mistake. What leads McGinn to switch standards, hence to deny closure, is his assumption that "different propositions carry with them different requirements as to the discriminative capacities necessary for knowledge of them," so that "knowledge of logically weaker propositions can require greater discriminative power than knowledge of logically stronger propositions."[8] Propositional content fixes the requirements on discriminative power. We are moving back into familiar territory.

Now, even granting the point about content determining the required discriminative capacity, it is not clear that the argument goes through. For it appears to trade on an ambiguity in the scope of "telling whether." I can tell (narrow scope) of what is in fact an object in front of me whether it is a table. This does not mean that I can tell (broad scope) whether there is an object in front of me which is a (real, non-vat-image) table, any more than I can tell whether I am a brain in a vat. So McGinn goes from a narrow scope premise to a broad scope conclusion. And we can't say that, in the actual non-vat world, I can properly, because reliably, make the broad scope claim (since in such a world I do not need discriminative capacities adequate to directly ruling out sceptical counter-possibilities in order to be reliable in my other beliefs). For, in the actual world, my beliefs will be just as reliable if I go on to draw their logical consequences. If the rationale for McGinn's theory is what he says it is, that ways of telling have to be answerable to a reliability condition, there is no reason to exclude deduction from known premises from our "ways of telling."

But, independently of all this, there is no reason at all for an externalist to grant the point about content and discriminative capacity. It is no doubt true that the content of a proposition makes some contribution to determining the sort of "discriminative capacity" necessary for telling whether it is true. But no externalist should hold that the content of the proposition *alone* determines this. Rather, the strength of discriminative capacity required also depends on what the actual world requires us to discriminate between. The more hawk-like non-hawks the world contains (and the more hawk-like they are), the greater the discriminative power required for knowing that a given bird is a hawk. If all birds except hawks died out, it would be possible to know that a bird is a hawk simply by way of noticing that it is a bird. Similarly, if I am not a brain in a vat, I can know that I am not by way of any simple fact I know about the external world.

What we find in McGinn's argument, then, is further confirmation of my claim that, in the end, arguments for scepticism always turn out to depend on epistemological realism. The thought that *the propositions themselves* determine what "discriminative capacities" we must possess if true beliefs involving those propositions are to count as knowledge is another form of the central doctrine of epistemological realism, the myth of intrinsic epistemological status. But in McGinn's concession to the sceptic, there is a foundationalist element too. As it turns out, the way of "telling whether" demanded by the proposition that I am not a brain in a vat is one that would work even if I were a brain a vat. That is to say, if I could know that

I am not a brain in a vat, it would have to be on the basis of experiential knowledge alone, just as foundationalists say. However, McGinn's commitment to foundationalism is not fully general. Only *some* propositions – e.g. those that refer to sceptical alternatives – demand to be judged by foundationalist standards. This is why the sceptic is importantly wrong as well as importantly right: in other words, why closure fails.

I have already noted that externalist theories, in virtue of their contextualist elements, are at odds with epistemological realism. So it should not be surprising that McGinn finds it difficult to stick to the idea that the content of the proposition known alone determines the strength of the discriminative capacity required for knowing it. Go back to the case of the table. I have to be able to distinguish tables from chairs, dogs etc. This is because chairs and dogs share the real world with tables. In a world where human beings were, as a matter of fact, liable to be captured and whisked off to Alpha Centauri to take part in experience-simulation experiments, I would have to be able to distinguish tables from vat-image tables. If I couldn't, I could not know that there is a table in front of me. This shows that, even in McGinn's eyes, the discriminative capacity required for knowing that there is a table in front of me does not depend solely on the content of what I know. But if we abandon the idea that the requirements on discriminative capacities are fixed this way, the case for denying closure collapses.

We should conclude from this that no externalist should hold that what is required to "tell whether" P is a function solely of the content of P. If we explain knowledge in terms of truth-reliability, the environment is bound to play a part. And once we recognize this, there is no longer any reason to deny closure.

This reinforces our result that any broadly reliabilist account of knowledge is inevitably to some degree contextualist. We cannot be simply "reliable": we can only be reliable about certain things *under certain conditions*. If conditions change, our discriminative powers may change with them, even though we ourselves remain the same. To attribute a discriminative power, therefore, is always to presuppose a certain reliability context.

Once we realize this, it becomes clear, I think, that though it will be difficult to display genuine failures of closure, apparent failures will be very easy to come by. All that is necessary to produce one is to effect a tacit shift in contextual presuppositions when moving from a given proposition to one of its known logical consequences. But we cannot demonstrate genuine nonclosure this way. So long as the original presuppositions are in force and fulfilled, we will know to be true both the proposition in question and its known logical consequences. When those presuppositions shift, we will cease to know the truth of one or more of those consequences, but we will cease to know the truth of our starting proposition as well.

## 8.5   RELEVANT ALTERNATIVES

Let us now turn to Dretske's attempt to show that nonclosure follows from a "relevant alternatives" account of knowledge.

Unlike McGinn, Dretske steers clear of full-blown sceptical possibilities. True, the examples he appeals to are structurally analogous to such cases, but in other ways they are more commonsensical. There may be some advantage in this, if his examples suggest how to deal with sceptical cases while remaining, in themselves, less controversial.

Here is a typical Dretske example. I take my son to the zoo, see several zebras and, when questioned by him, tell him that they are zebras. Dretske thinks we will all agree that I know that they are zebras: they look like zebras, they are in a pen clearly marked "Zebras," and this *is* the city zoo. But I also know, let us suppose, that if they are zebras, they are not mules cleverly disguised to look like zebras. However, according to Dretske, I do *not* know that they are not this kind of clever fake. Closure fails.

How is it possible that I should know that they are zebras yet fail to know that they are not cleverly disguised mules? *Pace* McGinn, I do not think that intuition can carry the day. Even if we agree that closure seems to fail in a case like this, we need a further explanation of what is going on in the example before we conclude that the apparent failure is genuine. As we saw in the previous section, there are subtle ways in which closure can seem to fail while not really failing at all.

At the most abstract level, Dretske's explanation has two parts: (1) that some of the logical consequences of propositions that we know have the status of *presuppositions*; and (2) that "epistemic operators" like "S knows that . . ." do not "penetrate" to presuppositions. A statement's presuppositions, "although their truth is entailed by the truth of the statement, are not part of what is *operated on* when we operate on the statement with one of our epistemic operators."[9] But *what* fails to penetrate to a known statement's presuppositions? What is it about knowledge that is not automatically transmitted across (known) logical entailment? The answer, for Dretske, is (or was) a certain kind of justification: justification based on "special precautionary checks."

Consider a case where I know, perceptually, that a certain wall is red. If it is red, it is not a white wall cleverly illuminated to look red. More generally, acquiring perceptual knowledge depends on the conditions of perception – lighting and so forth – being normal. But do we always know that they are normal? According to Dretske:

> Normally we never take the trouble to check the lighting. We seldom acquire any *special* reasons for believing the lighting normal although we can talk vaguely about there being no reason to think it unusual.

The fact is that we habitually take such matters for granted, and although we normally have *good* reasons for making such routine assumptions, I do not think these reasons are sufficiently good, not without special precautionary checks in the particular case, to say of the particular case we are in that we *know* conditions are normal.[10]

Knowledge, then, requires special checks. In the zebra case, which Dretske says "illustrates" the point made in the passage just quoted, I do take special checks to determine that the animals are zebras (and not gnus, giraffes, or whatever); but I take no special steps to rule out the possibility that they are a clever hoax. So I know the one thing but not the other.

I think that this argument sounds very plausible when one first hears it. On examination, however, it proves to trade on at least four fatal confusions.

First a reminder. Whether a relevant alternative account of knowledge is externalist or not depends on what makes a relevant alternative relevant and on whether someone who knows P, by having ruled out the relevant alternatives, has to know that the alternatives he has ruled out are all the relevant ones. If it is sufficient that they *be* all the relevant ones, the relevant alternatives account of knowledge is externalist. And the same will be true if relevance depends, at least in part, on what might *in fact* be the case in the knower's environment, whether or not he knows this. Understood this way, the "relevant alternatives" approach to knowledge is closely related to the "discrimination" approach, favored by McGinn. To be able to rule out the relevant alternatives to P is, precisely, to have a "way of telling" whether P. Or, to put it the other way round, to have the necessary "discriminative capacity" is just to be able to rule out what are, in my actual environment, P's competitors: that is, the relevant (= real world) alternatives to P.

We can see right away that Dretske's treatment of his examples commits him to externalism. Which alternatives I need to rule out to know that the animals are zebras depends on the facts of the situation (respectable zoos don't go in for hoaxes), not on what I know. This must be so. Which alternatives are relevant is a function of what the presuppositions of my statement exclude as *irrelevant*; and we have just seen that these presuppositions only have to *be* true for me to know whatever presupposes them. They do not have to be, and indeed generally are not, *known* to be true. If they had to be known to be true, Dretske could not deny closure.

However, when we notice this we also notice that we must be careful not to confuse two questions. One is: must I *first* know that the relevant presuppositions hold in order to come to know that P? An internalist will want to answer "yes", but the whole point of externalism is to defend the plausibility of answering "no." In this sense, Dretske is quite right that knowing that P doesn't generally require knowing that Q, even when one knows that P entails Q: this is what any externalist must hold. Put it this way: for an externalist, something may have to be true for me to come to know that P without its being *epistemologically prior* to P.

The issue of epistemological priority goes to the heart of the division between internalists and externalists: internalists hold that any thing that is presupposed by my coming to know that P must be known by me independently of my knowing that P. Externalists deny this: presupposition does not translate into epistemological priority. But rejection of the internalist's doctrine of epistemological priority should not be equated with a denial of closure. For there is a quite different question to ask, which is: if I do come to know that P, do I *thereby* also come to know that Q (supposing that I know that P entails Q)? It is far from obvious that Dretske's, or any other, externalist account of knowledge requires answering "no" to this question. Yet only a negative answer here supports a denial of closure. This is the first of the four confusions I mentioned above.

But what exactly are the "presuppositions" that my knowledge fails to penetrate to? This brings us to Dretske's second and perhaps most significant confusion, which is that Dretske conflates the presuppositions of a proposition P with the presuppositions of my knowing that P. As a result, he treats as my failure to know that P what is in fact only my failure to know that I know. Once we pay attention to what is, for any externalist, an absolutely crucial distinction, the case for nonclosure collapses.

Consider the two examples, the lighting example and the case of the zebras. Although supposed to make the same point, they prove on closer examination to be entirely different. In the first example, the knowledge in question is my knowledge that the wall is red and my "presupposition" is that the conditions of illumination are normal. But we must be absolutely clear that if the failure of my knowledge to penetrate to my "presuppositions" is to support nonclosure, my presuppositions must be found among *the known logical consequences of the proposition that I know to be true*. However, that the conditions of illumination are normal is not entailed by, and so is not in the relevant sense presupposed by, the proposition that the wall is red. What presupposes normal conditions of perception is my coming to know (through perception ) that the wall is red. So suppose Dretske is right and I do not know that conditions are normal – which, for an externalist, I do not have to know – there is still no threat to closure. For what we have here is a case in which I fail to know that Q even though, let us suppose, I do know that my knowing P entails that Q. We do *not* have a case in which I know that P, know that P entails Q and yet do fail to know that Q. True, I do not know that Q. But equally, I do not know that P entails Q, because in this instance P does *not* entail Q. Q (conditions are normal) is entailed by knowing that P (my knowing that the wall is red), not by P itself (the wall is red).

By running together the lighting and zebra examples, Dretske is able to make it look as if I don't ever have to know what I presuppose (the lighting example), even though what I presuppose is evidently entailed by what I know (the zebra example). But the appearance is entirely illusory. In the lighting example, the presuppositions in question are indeed not known to hold, but since they concern my knowing that P, and not P itself, they are not entailed by what I admittedly do know. In the second case, the situation is reversed. The presuppositions in question are entailed by what I know, the proposition P, but, when the first confusion we noted has been allowed for – when, that is, we distinguish between closure and epistemic priority, there is no reason to concede that we do not know them to hold.

Notice that in saying this I am not offending against the thought that we cannot bootstrap ourselves into knowledge that the reliability conditions on a given belief are fulfilled, hence into knowing that we know. The analogue in the zebra example of the presupposition that lighting conditions are normal would be that I am not in a hoaxing zoo, or that respectable zoos generally do not go in for such hoaxes; for only under some such conditions is the evidence that leads me to think the animals are zebras reliable. But the proposition that the animals in some particular pen are not disguised mules does not entail that any such condition is fulfilled. So we can allow that knowledge is closed under known entailment without falling foul of the anti-bootstrapping proviso.

Granted, closure would come under threat from examples like the lighting example if my knowing that P entailed my knowing that I know that P. In the lighting example, I fail to know what I know to be entailed by my knowing that the wall is red. But I do know that the wall is red. If, therefore, I *know that I know* that the wall is red, just in virtue of knowing that the wall is red, I fail to know things I know to be entailed by something that I know: I know that I know that the wall is red, while failing to know to be the case what must be the case if I am to know that the wall is red. However, an immediate consequence of any externalist analysis of knowledge is that the automatic move from knowing that P to knowing that one knows that P is blocked. The whole point of externalism is to allow that I can know things without knowing anything about the conditions that make it possible for me to know them. Knowledge of these conditions is relevant to knowing that one knows that P, but not to knowing that P itself. To know that I know that the wall is red, I *do* have to know that the lighting is normal. But simply to know that the wall is red I do not have to know this.

With this in mind, let us look further at the thought that knowledge requires "special precautionary checks." One obvious reaction to this is that such checks are required for knowing that Q only when it is still an open question whether Q. It would be absurd to insist on special checks when the possibility that not-Q has already been conclusively ruled out. But if this is so, Dretske's argument for nonclosure is simply question-begging in much the same way as McGinn's. In assuming that special checks are required to rule out fraud on the part of the zoo authorities, he is assuming that my knowing that the animals are zebras leaves open the question of whether they are fake zebras. But if knowledge is closed under known entailment, it doesn't.

Again, what we see here is the legacy of Dretske's having confused the presuppositions of a given proposition with the presuppositions of my knowing that proposition. Investigations into the possibility of fraud are relevant to the question of whether conditions in this zoo are normal: that is to say, they are relevant to the question of whether I know that I know that the animals in the pen are zebras. They are just like investigations of the conditions of illumination in Dretske's other example. In a way, Dretske is quite right: that conditions are normal is not entailed by the proposition I know, assuming they are normal. So this is an open question and special checks are in order. But this does nothing to show that they are in order with respect to propositions that I know to be true so that, if I have not carried them out, I fail to know evident logical consequences of things that I do know.

Of course, this is all taking externalism for granted. "Know" is to be taken to mean "know by externalist standards," so that knowing does not entail knowing that one knows. But the question at issue is whether an *externalist* ought to deny closure; and, as we have seen, Dretske's account of relevant alternatives commits him to externalism. However, I think that his externalism, like McGinn's, is equivocal. We can see this in the zebra example. My evidence for the animals' in the pen being zebras is conclusive only in the context of certain presuppositions which, as we have seen, I do not have to know to hold. In order for me to come to know that the animals are zebras, it is enough that they do hold. That is to say, the facts I rely on only have to be reliable in the world as it is, where respectable zoos do not go in for elaborate hoaxes. But for me to know that the animals are not disguised mules, Dretske insists on my acquiring evidence that would be reliable even in a world where such hoaxes were commonplace. He gets closure to seem to fail by raising the standards whenever sceptical counterpossibilities make an appearance. This is reasonable only if the relevant alternatives to a given proposition, hence the special checks required to determine whether that proposition is true, are determined *entirely by the content of that proposition.* As we saw in connection with McGinn, this is not something an externalist should hold. For an externalist, what I need to exclude must be in part determined by what happens in my environment.

Here we come to a further confusion. On the question of how the content of what we believe determines which alternatives are relevant, Dretske differs from McGinn. Dretske thinks that the presuppositions of a statement, hence the relevant alternatives to it, are determined, not by the statement's semantic content, considered in abstraction from all particular occasions of use, but by what the speaker means in making it. Thus:

> in saying that the coffee is boiling I assert that the coffee is boiling, but in assserting this I do not assert that *it is* coffee that is boiling. Rather, this is taken for granted, assumed, presupposed. . . . [To] have a reason to believe the coffee is boiling is not, thereby, to have a reason to believe it is coffee which is boiling.[11]

In this respect, knowing is like having a reason. (In fact, knowing depends on having a special kind of reason.) However, though all this may be true, it has nothing to do with closure. Dretske is trying to explain why epistemic operators fail to "penetrate" to the logical consequences of the propositions they operate on. But the effect of his explanation is to introduce scope distinctions for his operators. Epistemic operators that appear to operate on the entire content of a statement turn out, on analysis, only to operate on some of its components. This means that counterexamples to closure will only be apparent, exploiting scope distinctions that, in ordinary language, are not marked by surface grammar. It may well be that I know that the coffee is boiling without knowing that it is coffee which is boiling. It may even be that I know that the animals in the pen are zebras without knowing that they are animals (rather than vat-image animals, say). However, these examples pose no threat to closure unless the whole content of the proposition known to be true falls within the scope of the epistemic operator. If all that is meant by saying I know that the coffee is boiling is that the liquid I am talking about is in fact coffee and I know, of it, that it is boiling, of course I can fail to know that it is coffee. But in this situation, what I *do* know no longer entails what I don't. What we have is:

(1)  Fa & K(Ga)
(2)  K(Fa & Ga → Fa)
(3)  −K(Fa)

which is not a counterexample to closure.

To sum up, Dretske's case against closure rests on four confusions: not distinguishing what I need to know to come to know a given proposition from what I know when I do know it (equating a rejection of epistemological priority with a denial of closure); conflating the presuppositions of P with those of my knowing that P; using examples that work against closure only if my knowing that P entails my knowing that I know that P, which no externalist is in a position to assert; and introducing, but then ignoring, scope distinctions in connection with epistemic operations. His arguments are more complicated than McGinn's, who only inherits some of his confusions. But when these confusions are cleared away, nothing remains of Dretske's case for nonclosure.[12]

## 8.6 TRACKING THE TRUTH

For my final example of an attempt to argue for nonclosure, I turn to Robert Nozick. Nozick claims that his analysis of knowledge demands nonclosure; for since it backs up the sceptic's claim that we do not know that sceptical possibilities do not obtain, while allowing us knowledge of various mundane facts, either closure fails or the analysis is incoherent. However, if Nozick means to imply that his basic ideas about knowledge demand nonclosure, he is wrong. Far from *demanding* nonclosure, without *ad hoc* supplementation they will not even sustain it.

According to Nozick, S knows that P if his belief that P "tracks the truth." There are thus four conditions on knowing: the uncontroversial requirements:

    (1)   P is true
    (2)   S believes that P

and the "tracking" conditions,

    (3)   not-P=>not-(S believes that P)
    (4)   P=>(S believes that P).

where "__=> . . ." represents the "subjunctive" conditional ("if it were—it would be . . .").[13] Once more, the guiding intuition is that knowledge is a kind of non-accidentally true belief, belief that covaries with the facts. A belief amounts to knowledge if it would be held if the relevant fact held and would lapse otherwise, hence Nozick's calling (4) an "adherence" and (3) a "variation" condition. This is not Nozick's full analysis, but setting the complications temporarily aside, it seems to be thoroughly externalist. Knowing is made to depend entirely on standing in a certain "subjunctive relation to the truth" and not at all on awareness, still less knowledge, of so doing.

The burden of the case against closure is apparently borne by condition (3). To appreciate the force of (3), consider some ordinary proposition, P, that one might claim to know: Nozick's example is that he is sitting on a chair in Jerusalem. And consider some sceptical possibility, SK: for example, that one is a brain in a vat on Alpha Centauri, stimulated so as to have all the beliefs and experiences that one has in the actual world. Since SK describes a situation in which the subject, S, continues to believe that P, even though not-P, it may seem that Nozick's belief that P fails to meet (3) and so fails to amount to knowledge. But this is not so, for (3) does not say that S must fail to believe P in any *logically possible* situation in which not-P. Rather, it requires us to consider what *would* happen if not-P, and what *would* happen is constrained by the facts of the actual world. If Nozick were not sitting down in Jerusalem, he would be standing up, or lying down; or he would be somewhere else on the globe, Cambridge perhaps. But he wouldn't be on Alpha Centauri and so we do not have to consider what would happen to his beliefs if he were. In terms of possible worlds, evaluating the subjunctive conditional in (3) requires us to look at worlds in which it is not the case that P, but which are otherwise as close as possible to the actual world. Nozick calls this range of worlds "the not-P neighborhood" of the actual world. To track the truth, a belief must covary with the facts over a certain appropriate range of possibilities. It does not have to follow them no matter what.

It should be clear that Nozick's views are very close to those of Dretske.[14] Dretske's claim that knowledge requires that we be *able* to distinguish the state of affairs that we believe to hold from certain alternative possibilities in effect imposes a subjunctive condition on knowledge. Indeed, we can think of Nozick's conditions as one way of spelling out what is involved in such a discriminative ability: we are able to distinguish a situation from alternatives if, other things being equal, had that situation not obtained, we should not have believed that it did. Also, for Dretske, the sort of discriminative ability required for knowledge that P need not be powerful enough to discriminate situations where P obtains from all logically possible situations in which it does not: it is sufficient that we be able to distinguish its being the case that P from certain *relevant* alternatives. Nozick's talk of the "not-P neighborhood" of the actual world is another way of making the same point. Given the closeness of their views, it would be surprising if Nozick were able to add anything really new to Dretske's case against closure.

Nozick's discussion of knowledge has notably realistic overtones. He insists that knowledge involves a belief's standing in a *real* subjunctive relation to the world.[15] But is the tracking relation really so straightforwardly factual?

The first point to notice is that, though he does not *define* knowledge as true belief formed by a reliable method, Nozick's analysis is nevertheless strongly dependent on reliabilist intuitions. Accordingly, that a given belief tracks the truth is not a *brute* fact. Some beliefs track the truth because we have belief-forming methods and procedures that are truth-reliable. This is implicit in Nozick's examples. Nozick would not believe that he is in Jerusalem, if in fact he were somewhere else, because he has the ability to keep track of his location. As McGinn would say, he has ways of "telling whether" he is in Jerusalem or not.

A second point is that tracking is not, in general, a property that belongs to beliefs considered in isolation. For humans anyway, the ability to keep track of one's location depends on having lots of other true beliefs. Beliefs, therefore, do not in general function as *solo trackers*, if indeed they ever do. Accordingly, if we had to consider what would happen to a given belief if it were embedded in a network of mostly false beliefs, it is doubtful whether any factual belief would track.

Dependence, in point of truth-reliability, on collateral true beliefs is just one way in which truth-reliability is necessarily relative to a certain range of circumstances, circumstances that include, but need not be restricted to, those about which we have beliefs. Methods of belief formation that are highly, or even perfectly, reliable in our actual circumstances may not be reliable at all in circumstances far removed from them. But how far is too far? How reliable is reliable enough? It is natural to ask: reliable enough for what? To ask such a question, however, is to confront once more the pervasive interest-relativity of epistemological assessment. And once again, it is not easy to believe that there is a fully objective answer, an answer reflecting the epistemic facts, to the question "How outlandish are the possibilities we have to consider in order to determine whether a given belief covaries with the truth in such a way as to count as knowledge?" If we insist on saying that knowledge depends on a real subjunctive relation to the truth, we must remember that "real," as Wittgenstein remarked of "know," does not tolerate a metaphysical emphasis.

With these considerations in mind, let us look at Nozick's case for nonclosure. We have already seen that, as a mere logical possibility, SK does not threaten knowledge of mundane facts. However, that Nozick is in Jerusalem evidently entails that he is not on Alpha Centauri and so entails not-SK. So what about knowledge that not-SK? Here, Nozick says, the sceptic is right: we don't know that not-SK. Sceptical possibilities are *designed* to violate the variation condition (3): they are set up so that, if SK, you would still believe that not-SK. But to get from failure to know that not-SK to failure to know that P, we need closure and, given a subjunctive condition on knowledge, closure fails. To assess what would be the case if not-P we have to examine the not-P neighborhood of the actual world; to assess what would be the case if not-Q, the not-Q neighborhood. These may be very different, even though P entails Q. Where Q is not-SK, they will be wildly different.

We can see right away that Nozick's denial of closure is not guided simply by the reliabilist intuitions that underpin the tracking analysis.

Rather, it depends essentially on the thought that the range of possibilities over which a belief must covary with the truth, if it is to count as knowledge, is determined entirely by the content of the proposition believed. As Nozick puts it, the content of the proposition believed determines *how far out* from the actual world we have to look in order to evaluate the relevant subjunctive conditionals. Beliefs about relatively particular facts keep us close to the actual world. In fact, they keep us so close that most of our other true beliefs are preserved and, in part as a consequence, our methods of belief formation remain reliable. Covariation with the truth, tracking, is thus ensured. By contrast, any reference to sceptical possibilities takes us so far afield that we end up considering situations in which most of our collateral beliefs are false. As a result, tracking fails and, with it, closure.

This gives us at least as much reason to modify the details of the tracking analysis as it does to accept nonclosure. There is nothing in the intuition that knowledge involves belief that covaries with the truth across an appropriate range of possibilities that requires us to treat appropriateness as exclusively a function of the content of the propositions believed, so that in the case of certain propositions, the demands on our capacity for truth-reliability, hence tracking, become cut loose from factual limitations, particular problem situations, interest-relativity, and all the other factors emphasized by the contextualist conception of knowledge and justification. Nozick too, it turns out, accepts the epistemological-realist view that content determines status. The propositions we believe determine exclusively what we must be able to do, if we are to know them to be true. We have no say in the matter. What counts as an appropriate range of possibilities is not something that we – for example, through our interests – are allowed to influence.

If we do not treat appropriateness this way, we shall have to apply the variation condition with more discrimination. But, I think we want to do this anyway. Recall the tracking analysis's kinship with Dretske's relevant alternatives view: it would be strange to insist that, when it comes to situations to which there are no relevant alternatives, we cannot know that such situations obtain, because we cannot rule out the relevant alternatives. Yet this is what a blanket insistence on applying a variation condition amounts to. However, Nozick is quite open to the suggestion that condition (3) needs to be applied discriminatingly. Notably, he does not apply it to knowledge of necessary truths. When a proposition we believe is true in all possible worlds, we cannot ask whether we would still believe it if it were false.

Of course, it is not a necessary truth that not-SK. Nevertheless, it is true in the actual world that Robert Nozick, the person sitting down in Jerusalem, *could not be a brain in a vat on Alpha Centauri*. All sorts of things *might* have been true of him: he might have been standing up in Jerusalem, sitting down in Cambridge, and so on, the extent of what might have been being given by the worlds that lie in the not-P neighborhood of the actual world. But in none of these worlds is Nozick a brain in a vat. In general, propositions we know to be true will have among their logical consequences various things that just have to be the case: some because they are strictly necessary, others because their negations take us so far from the actual world that they describe things that couldn't happen. Or, their negations project us into circumstances in which none of our available methods of belief formation are truth-reliable and which thus make tracking impossible. But we are not compelled to say that we do not know such circumstances not to obtain unless we hold that the demands on truth-reliability are rigidly fixed by the contents of what we believe. Consistently with the spirit of the tracking analysis, we can allow that we know that P if and only if either the belief that P itself tracks the truth or is known to be entailed by some belief that does. (Since entailments are logical necessities, knowledge that they hold will be exempted from the variation condition.) This is the analogue of the suggestion we made in connection with McGinn: that if truth-reliability is what matters, "telling whether" need not always be a matter of direct perception. If we do not apply (3) with more discrimination, we commit ourselves to thinking that, when it comes to things that couldn't be the case, we never know that they aren't.

Applying (3) more discriminatingly, I can say that, if I were a brain in a vat, I wouldn't know anything, even though, in my actual circumstances, I know all sorts of things, including that I am not a brain in a vat. For if my beliefs and experiences were controlled by the experimenters, they would not covary with the facts, even within ranges of worlds close to (what would then be) the actual world. It may also be, for anything that has been said so far, that though I know that I am not a brain in a vat, I do not know that I know this. However, no externalist can object to distinguishing knowing from knowing that one knows.

I must stress that Nozick himself is acutely aware of condition (3)'s problematic character. Not merely does he not apply it to knowledge of necessary truths, he is the first to point out that, in its original form, it is too strong even for ordinary factual knowledge. So we need to move on from Nozick's first approximation analysis of knowledge to his more considered account.

To bring out the problem with (3), Nozick offers the case of a grandmother who comes to believe that her grandson is alive and well by seeing him when he comes to visit her. However, if he had been ill or dead, to spare her anxiety the family would have told her he was in good health. Since, even if he were not alive and well, she would still have believed that he was, according to (3) she doesn't know that he is, in spite of the fact that she can *see* that he is. This seems wrong.

The crucial feature of the case is that the grandmother's way of coming to believe that her grandson is well covaries with his state of health. If he were dead, she would not come to her false belief in the way that she comes to here true belief. It seems, then, that a full analysis must take note of how beliefs are formed. However, we can see right away that the matter will require careful handling, if the case against closure is to be maintained. The problem is that, from an externalist standpoint, classic sceptical puzzle cases build in a similar dependence of ways of forming beliefs on the truth of what is believed. If I were a brain in a vat, so that my beliefs about the world were mostly false, I would not form those beliefs in the way that I would form them if they were mostly true. An envatted brain's beliefs would be controlled by the experimenters, as an embodied being's beliefs would not be. Clearly, this creates real difficulty for Nozick. He wants to allow that the grandmother knows that her grandson is well, even though, because of an unavoidable change in her method of belief formation, she would believe him to be well even if he were not. At the same time, he does not want to allow that I know that I am not a brain in a vat when I am not though, because of a similarly unavoidable change of method, I would believe that I am not even if I were.

This danger notwithstanding, Nozick incorporates into his full account of knowledge the idea of a way or method of believing. S knows, via method (or way of believing) M, that P if and only if:

(1*)   P is true

(2*)   S believes, via method or way of coming to believe M, that P.

(3*)   If P weren't true and S were to use M to arrive at a belief whether (or not) P, then S wouldn't believe, via M, that P.

(4*)   If P were true and S were to use M to arrive at a belief whether (or not) P, then S would believe, via M, that P.[16]

Then, having said what it is for one method to outweigh another (the details don't matter here), he can say that S knows that P (*simpliciter*) if and only if (a) S knows that P via some method M and (b) all other methods $M_i$ via which he believes that P that do not satisfy conditions (1*)–(4*) are outweighed by M. In the grandmother case, belief based on family testimony does not track, for the family would tell her the same thing no matter what. But that method is outweighed by her actual method, seeing for herself, in that if she saw her grandson dead, she wouldn't accept her family's assurances. (If she would, it is reasonable to wonder whether she knows anything about his state of health in the first place).

This way of dealing with the case of the grandmother runs straight into the problem we anticipated. The full account of knowledge allows that S can come to know that P via method M though, if P were false, M would not be available and S would have to rely on some other method, $M_1$, which would lead him (in this case mistakenly) still to believe that P. It therefore appears to allow S to know that not-SK. Given my actual situation, I can come to know, by using my eyes etc., all sorts of particular facts about the world; and I can deduce from any such facts that I am not a brain in a vat. But if I were a brain in a vat, this route to knowledge would not be available to me. I wouldn't be moving around and I wouldn't be using my eyes and ears: I would be relying, whether I knew it or not, on input controlled by the experimenters, so that any conclusions I deduced from my seeming perceptual knowledge of the world would be as ill-founded as that seeming knowledge itself. For an externalist, there can be no compelling reason to distinguish this case from that of the grandmother. If not-SK, I know not-SK (by the method indicated); though if SK were the case, that method would be unavailable and I would rely on a different way of forming beliefs that would lead me (mistakenly) to believe that not-SK.

If this sounds familiar, it is because Nozick's example of the grandmother is a close relative of Dretske's zebra case. In Nozick's example, if the grandmother's belief were false, her available "ways of knowing" would also change. Similarly in Dretske's example: in a normal, non-hoaxing zoo, the general appearance of an animal, or the sign over its pen, is a reliable guide to what kind of animal it is. That is why I can come to know that the animals my son asks me about are zebras by taking note of their stripes, the sign on their enclosure and the like. But in a hoaxing zoo, this way of forming beliefs would not be reliable and my path to knowledge would be foreclosed. The example is set up so that, for my belief to be false, the zebras would have to be fakes; and if they were, my usual ways of knowing what animals are in what pens would no longer be available.

We saw that the zebra case does not support a denial of closure, though it will seem to do so if we conflate the presuppositions of what we know with the presuppositions of our knowing it. True, this will not be a conflation if knowing requires knowing what one knows. However, to insist on this requirement is not to modify one's externalism but to abandon it altogether. Given how close they are, what goes for Dretske ought to go for Nozick.

Nozick protects ordinary perceptual knowledge by having the contents of the particular propositions known restrict the range of possible worlds we need to consult when determining whether the tracking conditions are met. By contrast, the content of a belief that not-SK forces us to look much farther out from the actual world, with the result that our belief that not-SK fails to track and closure fails. But once knowledge is made to depend on ways or methods of knowing, so that whether we do or even can follow a given method depends on the facts of the actual world, the ranges of worlds we need to consider in assessing *our* claims to knowledge will always lie close to the actual world. The grandmother knows that her grandson is well even though, if he were not well, she would be deprived of her actual way of knowing.

It is clear that if the cases are treated uniformly, *our* knowledge in *this* world that not-SK will not turn on what we would believe if SK. If knowledge is knowledge gained by methods available to us, it cannot matter what we would believe in situations where those methods were unavailable and in which we would have to rely on methods that would lead us to form beliefs that are not appropriately related to the facts.

There is only one way for Nozick to avoid this conclusion: ensure that the methods of knowing available to us in this world are the same as those that would be available if various sceptical possibilities were to hold, for example if we were brains in vats. This means fixing the identity conditions for methods in the manner of a thoroughgoing internalist. Thus he tells us:

> A person can use a method . . . without knowledge or awareness of what method he is using. Usually, a method will have a final upshot in experience on which the belief is based, such as visual experience, and then (a) no method without this upshot is the same method and (b) any method experientially the same, the same "from the inside," will count as the same method. Basing our beliefs on experiences, you and I and the person floating in the tank are using the same method.[17]

But though this is the only way of distinguishing the case of the grandmother from that of the brain in a vat, hence of salvaging the case for nonclosure, it wears its *ad hoc* character on its sleeve. If I can use a method without awareness of what method I am using, why should experiential factors be decisive in fixing its identity? Above all, why should an externalist treat them this way? Whether my beliefs track the truth is not determined by "internal" factors, so why should the method I am using be individuated in such terms? Of course, if two methods are "internally" indistinguishable, there may be a question about how, if at all, I can tell what method I am using. But, for any kind of externalist, knowing what method I am following should be relevant to my knowing that I know that P, not necessarily to my simply knowing that P.

Nozick notes that his analysis of knowledge, while externalist when compared with traditional accounts, nevertheless treats the method a person uses as "identified from the inside, to the extent it is guided by internal cues and appearances."[18] But his attempts to justify this mixture of externalism and internalism are not impressive.

One argument is that, if we allow methods to be externally differentiated, deduction from known premises could count as a distinct method. However: "The problem is that the method of inferring Q from known P is indistinguishable by the person from the method of inferring Q from (believed) P."[19]

However, my problem is to see why an externalist should see this as a problem. It would be a problem if we were trying to prove that we *know that we know* Q. But Nozick isn't: he is only trying to show that knowledge is possible. After all, it is essential to Nozick's case for nonclosure that my method of forming the belief that I am sitting on a chair be "indistinguishable" from that of a brain in a vat. This does not prejudice my knowledge that I am sitting on a chair. So why should the fact that deduction from actual knowledge, as my way of coming to believe that I am not a brain in a vat, is indistinguishable from deduction from false belief prejudice my knowledge that I am not a brain in a vat? Again, this fact might prejudice my knowing that I know that I am not a brain in a vat. But if this is what Nozick has in mind, we have returned to the recurrent flaw in arguments for nonclosure: representing something as relevant to knowing that P when, in fact, it is relevant to knowing that one knows. If I am to know that I know someting or other, then indeed I may well have to know something about how I came to know it. But this gives no reason for thinking that I have to know this simply in order to have knowledge of some fact about the world.

Another argument is that "The method used must be specified as having a certain generality, if it is to play the appropriate role in subjunctives."[20] This too gets us nowhere: externalist criteria for individuating methods can have enough generality to play a role in subjunctives. The role they play will be "inappropriate" only in that it will not advance the case for nonclosure. What we need is a reason for thinking that the generality must be "set by differences the person would notice" that does not grow out of the requirement that knowing entail knowing that one knows. A theory of knowledge that builds in this requirement involves more than a peripheral concession to internalism: it has ceased to be externalist at all.

In my judgment, there is no such reason to be had. Certainly Nozick offers none. All he tells us is that, if methods of knowing can be individuated externally:

> you needn't reach to inference to establish your knowledge that you are not floating in the tank on Alpha Centauri. You see that you are not on Alpha Centauri, and via this method, externally specified, you track the fact that you are not – even though if you were it would seem perceptually the same to you as it does now. That perceptual seeming, though indistinguishable internally from your actual current seeing, is distinguishable externally as a distinct method, if such external individuation of methods is allowed to count. Would even

Doctor Johnson have said, "How do I know that I am not dreaming? By seeing what is in front of me"?[21]

Presumably, we are meant to think that this response would be too naive even for Johnson. But is it naive at all, once we are alive to the distinction between internalist and externalist analyses of knowledge? Johnson might well be claiming that, when he is not dreaming, he knows that he is not by seeing what is in front of him, though when he is dreaming this way of knowing is not available to him. This doesn't strike me as especially naive. And, in any case, opening the way for such distinctions is characteristic of externalist epistemologies.

So far as I can see, there are only two ways in which Johnson's response might be considered naive. One is to take him to be trying to *prove that he knows* that he is not dreaming now and not simply stating the conditions under which he does in fact know it. But this just takes us back to the tendency, on the part of those who argue against closure, to slip from considering whether you know that P to whether you know that you know.

The other way Johnson's response might seem naive is if we are set on an internalist answer to "How do you know . . . ?" questions. It would be naive to answer "By seeing that P" to the question "What internal cues lead you to know that P?" For if you can be in the same internal state even if not-P, internal cues alone can never be sufficient for knowledge. But if this is what it means to ask "How do you know . . . ?", how does Nozick know that he is sitting at a desk in Jerusalem? By tracking the truth? This would be as bad as Johnson's imagined answer to the question about how he knows he is not dreaming. And of course, if Nozick traffics in internalism to this extent, his case for nonclosure is threatened from another direction. The sort of answer to "How do you know . . . ?" that must be insisted on, if Johnson's imagined reply is to seem hopelessly naive, puts in jeopardy all knowledge of the external world. By Nozick's internalist standards, I can't say "how I know" that I am not a brain in a vat on Alpha Centauri; but in this sense, I can't say "how I know" that I am in Oxford. And if I don't have to be able to say "how I know," in that sense of "how I know," in order to know that I am in Oxford, why do I have to be able to be aware of how I know in order to know that I am not on Alpha Centauri?

The fact is, Nozick's argument turns on helping himself to rhetorical questions to which, if he wants to remain *any* kind of externalist, he is not entitled. If "How do you know . . . ?" means "How do internal cues ensure that the beliefs induced track the truth?" the answer is that they don't. You know if you track, otherwise not. There need be no answer to "How do you know. . . ?" that lives up to internalist (which, as we have seen, means foundationalist) standards. If Nozick's considerations have any force, it can only be as an expression of completely general doubts about the plausibility of externalist analyses of knowledge, in which case he cannot be so sure that we know the mundane facts he takes it for granted we do know.

In sum the situation is this: the case for nonclosure depends on treating certain beliefs as demanding to be judged by foundationalist standards. This requires holding that propositional content determines epistemological status. This is the way in which nonclosure depends on epistemological realism: it requires that beliefs have an intrinsic epistemological status, independent of the circumstances in which they are acquired. However, any account of knowledge that makes essential reference to ways of acquiring beliefs threatens this commitment. The only way to deflect the threat is to individuate methods so that our ways of forming beliefs become invariant across normal worlds and sceptical alternatives. If this is to be more than an *ad hoc* attempt to salvage a conclusion that one's analysis threatens to disallow, it will need independent defence. But all the reasons for taking this view of methods of belief formation come from a conception of knowledge that is hostile to the fundamental intuitions behind the tracking analysis.

Though Nozick arguably avoids some of Dretske's outright errors, he adds nothing really new to the case for nonclosure. To the extent that his account of knowledge avoids looking hopelessly *ad hoc*, it trades on the same confusions.

## 8.7  CLOSURE REGAINED

What should we make of all this?

We have taken note of the deep intuition underlying denials of closure: that no piece of knowledge can guarantee the fulfillment of its own reliability conditions. If it could, we could bootstrap ourselves into knowing that we know certain propositions to be true. But all externalists agree that no such bootstrapping technique is even available. Thus even if I know both that P and that P entails Q, I will not know that Q *if Q states a reliability condition on my believing that P*.

This is the intuition that prompts Wittgestein's reluctance to think of himself as knowing the propositions that stand fast for him. If Napoleon was victorious at Austerlitz in 1805, the Earth and all it contains did not come into being five minutes ago complete with misleading indications of antiquity. Had it done so, historical evidence would be worthless: the conditions under which that kind of evidence is reliable would not hold. But surely I cannot argue that since I *do* know all sorts of historical facts, for example that Napoleon was victorious at Austerlitz, these conditions must hold. As Dretske says, certain general facts about the past history of the Earth are "channel conditions" for my acquiring information about

Napoleon, and no knowledge I gain subject to those conditions confers knowledge of their fulfillment.[22] If the gauge is in working order, I learn from the needle's pointing to "F" that my car's gasoline tank is full. But I do not thereby also learn that the gauge is in working order: that the needle is not, say, simply stuck on "F."

I think that all this is true, but that none of it has anything to do with closure. The lesson to learn from the arguments we have considered is that the reliability conditions for a given item of knowledge do not generally number among the entailments of what is known. Conversely, propositions that are to be found among the entailments of something that we know do not state reliability conditions on our knowing it.

The gasoline tank example illustrates the first point. It is perfectly true that I do not learn that the gauge is working properly simply by learning that the tank is full. But what I do learn, that the tank is full, does not entail what I don't, that the gauge is working properly. If the needle is stuck on "F," the tank may or may not be full. What is true is that, in particular circumstances, I may have no way of distinguishing the case in which my belief that the tank is full amounts to knowledge from that in which, even if it happens to be true, it does not. But all this means is that knowing does not guarantee knowing that one knows, though of course it does not preclude it either. I *can* know something without knowing that I do: this is a consequence of any externalist account of knowledge.

Wittgenstein's historical example illustrates the second point. What I know – that Napoleon was victorious at Austerlitz – does entail that the Earth has existed for more than five minutes. But this proposition, though entailed by propositions that state reliability conditions on my knowledge of Bonaparte's career, is itself too weak to be thought to state such a condition. The Earth could have existed for many years past and my beliefs about Napoleon still be *completely* unreliable.

Arguments from traditional sceptical possibilities can go either way. Some of the things we know do not entail that we are not brains in vats. That Robert Nozick is in Jerusalem does not entail that he is not a brain in a vat. (It entails that he is not a brain in a vat on Alpha Centauri, but not that he is not a brain in a vat in Jerusalem). Others arguably do entail this: that Nozick is sitting on a chair in Jerusalem does entail that he is not a brain in a vat, assuming that having one's vat balanced on a chair doesn't count as sitting. But *simply* not being a brain in a vat is not a reliability condition on such knowledge. One could meet this condition and still be subject to bizarre illusions with respect to the position of one's limbs. One could be a normally embodied person and yet competely unable to keep track of one's geographical location.

Propositions stating reliability conditions on knowledge that a given proposition is true are thus not to be found among that proposition's entailments. If they are strong enough to state reliability conditions, they will not be entailed; and if they are entailed, they will be too weak to amount to reliability conditions. This is why we found arguments for nonclosure playing back and forth between the presuppositions of whatever proposition P we are supposed to know and the presuppositions of our knowing that P. This is the only way to make certain "presuppositions" appear both to be entailed by what we know and, at the same time, to state conditions on our knowing it. True, this playing back and forth will be entirely legitimate if we insist that knowing requires knowing that one knows, but only internalists – that is to say, only foundationalists – are in a position to make this stipulation. Of course, they are also in no position to deny closure, even if tempted. True, they can argue that a given belief does not amount to knowledge unless we know that the reliability conditions on beliefs of that kind are met. But this will preclude their insulating beliefs about mundane matters of fact from sceptical undermining, for it amounts to conceding that the sceptic is right to insist that we cannot know that the reliability conditions on beliefs about particular matters of fact are met if we cannot exclude the possibilities of sytematic deception he puts forward. Denials of closure, therefore, result from attempts to have a foot in both camps: sometimes denying that knowing requires knowing that one knows while, at other times, tacitly affirming that it does.

Someone might reply that the existence of the Earth for many years past is *a* reliability condition on historical knowledge, even though not a complete one. The same would apply to my not being a brain in a vat: this is a necessary though not a sufficient condition for knowing particular facts about my environment. So if I can find an item of knowledge that entails that I am not a brain in a vat, I can produce a counterexample to closure. Perhaps, but it is far from obvious.

Suppose that Q is both a known logical consequence of P and, in the weak sense just noted, *a* reliability condition on knowing that P: does the intuition that we cannot bootstrap ourselves into knowing that we know prevent knowledge that P bringing in its wake knowledge that Q? I see no reason to suppose that it does. I agree that no item of knowledge guarantees full knowledge of its own reliability conditions: indeed, this is just another way of stating the externalist point that knowing does not guarantee knowing that one knows. But this is not to say that nothing we know brings with it, *via* a known entailment, any knowledge that is so much as relevant to the fulfilment of those conditions. Consider the example of the gasoline gauge again. Both the proposition that the gasoline tank is full and the proposition that the gauge is in working order entail that my car is not just a figment of my imagination. Is it so obvious that, though I do know particular facts about my car, I do not know that the car exists? Or again, if I know that Napoleon was the victor at Austerlitz, don't I also know that the battlefield, hence Austria, hence Europe, hence the Earth existed at that time? Or if I don't know that the Earth existed, what do I know? Do I know that Austerlitz existed? Where does closure not fail?

To say this is not to say that I must first and independently establish my car's or the Earth's existence in order to know particular facts about them, only that knowledge of particular matters of fact brings with it knowledge of whatever they evidently entail: the issue is closure, not epistemological priority. Nor is it to offend against the anti-bootstrapping intuition. Knowing that my car exists does not mean knowing that my gasoline gauge is not defective; knowing that the Earth existed in 1805 does not mean knowing that my information about Napoleon comes from reliable sources; and knowing that I am not a brain in a vat does not mean knowing that I generally know where I am on the surface of the Earth. So even when Q is relevant to my reliability in my belief that P, knowing that Q doesn't amount to knowing that I am reliable with respect to P.

Not that the matter has to rest on a clash of intuitions. There remains the important point that any philosopher in the least sympathetic to externalist accounts of knowledge ought to be suspicious of talk about "the" reliability conditions for a particular belief, or for beliefs of a particular kind. For an externalist, whether we can reliably form true beliefs on a given topic must depend on circumstances as well as on the content of the beliefs in question. This opens up the possibility that, in the actual world, I know that I am not a brain in a vat, know that the Earth has existed time out of mind, and so on, even though in a "sceptical" world I would know none of those things. But in such a world, I should not know any particular facts either.

This is why those who deny closure must hold that the relevant alternatives to be eliminated, or the power of the discriminative capacity to be exercised, if a given proposition is to be known to be true, is determined by the content of the proposition in question. As I have remarked more than once, this doctrine is a variant of one of traditional foundationalisms's most basic ideas, an idea that commits foundationalism to epistemological realism. This is the idea of intrinsic epistemological status, the thought that propositions themselves determine, in virtue of their content alone, the conditions that must be met if our believing them is to count as knowing. The contextualist rejection of epistemological realism is, in large measure, a rejection of this very doctrine. If the demands on knowledge are fixed by circumstances, as well as by content, no proposition or belief has an intrinsic epistemological status.

Since, as we have seen, there is a contextual element in all externalist accounts of knowledge, this points to the theoretical incoherence of the case for nonclosure. Arguments for our never knowing that sceptical alternatives do not obtain, regardless of the facts of the world, depend essentially on granting sceptical hypotheses a permanent, intrinsic epistemological status. Without this concession to epistemological realism, externalist theories of knowledge lead straight to the conclusion that, in worlds where such hypotheses do not hold, we may know that they do not, even if in worlds where they did hold we would be incapable of such knowledge. Because it requires that epistemic status be detached from worldly circumstances, the anticlosure theorist's concession to the sceptic involves tacit acceptance of the epistemological realist doctrine that status is determined by content. At the same time, the externalist case for granting us knowledge of mundane facts depends on an explicit rejection of this very same doctrine. My view is therefore the opposite of many externalists: externalists ought *not* to deny closure. More than this: it is by holding on to closure, not by rejecting it, that we learn something about how the sceptic goes wrong. What the sceptic discovers is the instability of knowledge, not the impossibility.

## 8.8   THE INSTABILITY OF KNOWLEDGE

Let us examine the "argument from clairvoyance," which Bonjour regards as a decisive refutation of externalist theories of knowledge.[23] Since Bonjour's interest is in justification, he is not concerned with, and indeed finds it hard to take seriously, accounts of knowledge that detach knowing from being justified. His externalist is therefore someone who thinks that *de facto* reliability is sufficient for justification. That he is wrong, Bonjour thinks, can be shown by example. For instance, imagine someone who is in some repects a completely reliable clairvoyant but who has good reasons for distrusting his clairvoyant powers. Bonjour claims that such a persons's clairvoyant beliefs would not be justified, so would not amount to knowledge, even if in fact they were formed in a completely reliable way.

I find schematic cases like this difficult to evaluate. In some circumstances I might be inclined to agree that possession of evidence against one's reliability undermines knowledge; but in others I might prefer to say that someone has knowledge he has good reason to think he does not have. *Pace* Bonjour, I do not find this a *contradictio in adjecto*. But there is no need to dispute intuitions, for even if we share Bonjour's, cases like this do not refute externalism. At most, they show that knowledge (sometimes) requires more than reliability, not that it turns on "internal" factors alone. In other words, Bonjour's argument is at best a refutation of pure reliabilism, not of externalism generally.

Bonjour recognizes that a reliabilist might allow that, in the face of contrary evidence, a reliably formed belief might fail to count as knowledge. Accordingly, his crucial example involves a clairvoyant who "possesses no evidence or reasons of any kind for or against the general possibility of such a cognitive power or for or against the thesis that he possesses it." Now suppose that this person's clairvoyant power leads him to believe, without a shred of evidence, that the President is in New York City: is this an instance of knowledge, or are there "sufficient grounds for a charge of subjective irrationality" to prevent his being epistemically justified?[24] Suppose first that the clairvoyant believes himself to be clairvoyant and that this influences his "acceptance of the belief" as to the President's whereabouts: "is it not obviously irrational, from an epistemic standpoint," Bonjour asks, "for [him] to hold such a belief when he has no reasons at all for thinking that it is true or even for thinking that such a power is possible?" Suppose, then, that he holds no such belief: but now, why isn't "the mere fact that there is no way for him to have obtained [information about the President's whereabouts] a sufficient reason for classifying [his belief that the President is in New York] as an unfounded hunch and ceasing to accept it?" If he doesn't, isn't he being "epistemically irrational and irresponsible"?[25]

I think that this example illustrates something, but not what Bonjour thinks. First of all, it is significant that Bonjour refers to his clairvoyant's acceptance of a *belief* about the President's location, rather than acceptance of a proposition. One would have thought that coming to believe just was coming to accept a proposition. Why this talk of accepting a belief?

Our recent discussions of arguments for nonclosure should put us on the alert. We found in those arguments a recurrent tendency to confuse the conditions for knowing something or other with those for knowing that one knows it. I think that something similar is going on here. The effect of Bonjour's odd locution is to take us out of an ordinary practical context, where the clairvoyant comes to believe (reliably) that the President is in New York and so, let us imagine, makes plans to catch a glimpse of him, into a reflective, epistemological context in which he asks himself whether this belief of his is really an item of knowledge or just a hunch. We no longer imagine him as forming, by a reliable method, an otherwise unrationalized belief. Rather we think of him as going over his beliefs, assessing their epistemological status. So we are willing to say that he becomes irrational if he *refuses* to say "hunch" and *continues* to believe that the President is in New York. He could neither refuse nor continue if the epistemological question had never come up.

Once we see that this is how the example works, the externalist's reply is clear. The clairvoyant's lack of evidence for his clairvoyance is not directly relevant to the question of whether he knows where the President is but only to whether he knows that he knows. His irrationality consists in his carrying on as if he knew – in effect, deciding that he does know – when he has no basis, internalist or externalist, for such a decision. He may in fact know, but he has no business simply deciding that he does.

However, although not directly relevant to knowing, failure to know that one knows may still be relevant indirectly. It is consistent with the externalist's insistence that knowing does not require knowing that one knows that there be cases in which deciding that one does *not* know undemines knowledge that one previously had. As Gilbert Harman points out, once we abandon a strictly foundational view of inferential justification, we must recognize that the epistemic status of a belief can change, even though its original grounds remain as good as they ever were. Thus a belief may be acquired in such a way as to amount to knowledge but, once in place, may acquire new inferential relations to other beliefs, which either strengthen its position or weaken it.[26]

If this is so, Bonjour's example, though it does not refute externalism or even pure reliabilism, illustrates something potentially significant: the instability of knowledge. This instability reflects the sensitivity of knowledge to context, where context includes features of the doxastic as well as the external environment. More precisely, Bonjour's example hints at the capacity of epistemological reflection to destroy, or temporarily occlude, one's erstwhile knowledge, without damaging one's general reliability. If he had never reflected, Bonjour's clairvoyant (let us suppose anyway) would have known where to find the President. But once his continuing to believe that the President is in New York comes to depend on the groundless and (again let us suppose) unreliably formed conviction that he is reliable in these matters, he contaminates his original unselfconscious belief by making its continuance partially dependent on a defective inference. He ceases to know what he would have known if he hadn't asked himself so many questions. As Bernard Williams has remarked in another connection, reflection destroys knowledge.[27]

We can link this possibility with the intuitions that have led some philosophers to deny closure, for I think that what apparent failures of closure may really exploit is just this potential instability. If this can be shown, it will strengthen my case considerably, for I expect that my defence of closure will have left many readers unsatisfied. Can I really claim to know that I am not a brain in a vat, on the grounds that I am at present sitting in my office? Isn't this Moore's "proof" all over again? But I didn't say that I could *claim to know* that I am not a brain in a vat. In fact, I didn't even say that I could *claim* not to be a brain in a vat. All I said was that I do know all sorts of mundane facts; and that for as long as I know them, I know that various sceptical possibilities do not obtain. Claiming is another matter.

In Bonjour's example, the source of instability lay in the possibility of further reflection's undermining knowledge that one previously had by way of connecting it with certain more problematic beliefs. Now we can add, somewhat speculatively, another way in which this undermining might come about. Suppose that in certain cases, or in certain special circumstances, the explicit drawing of logical consequences that are normally left tacit is sufficient to induce a decisive presupposition shift: this would give rise to apparent failures of closure that are really rather subtle. It would also open up the possibility that some knowledge is necessarily tacit because vulnerable to undermining *simply* by being made explicit. This is something to consider: that I know that I am not a brain in a vat so long as I do not worry about whether I am one or not. Knowledge in the street and scepticism in the study.

My recognizing this even as a possibility is enough to show that, in defending closure, I am not necessarily claiming that Moore was right after all: that the way to refute the sceptic is to hold up one's hand, thereby demonstrating that one is not a brain in a vat. To hold that knowledge is closed under known logical entailment is not necessarily to hold that closure can always be directly exploited for anti-sceptical purposes. There are subtle confusions to guard against here. Even if I can argue that I am not a brain in a vat, because brains in vats do not have arms to hold up, this does not mean that I can show that *I know* that I am not a brain in a vat simply by repeating Moore's performance. This argument needs the premise that I know that I am holding up my hand, and so requires me to know that I know I am holding up my hand. This is not guaranteed by what I know, even if I do know it.

But there is also the more interesting possibility that I cannot ever *argue* that I am not a brain in a vat, at least by appeal to mundane facts. This, I suspect, is at least in part what Wittgenstein has in mind. In a context where that possibility is a serious issue, my knowledge of those facts may waver, or become temporarily unavailable, so that I will no longer be able to appeal to what I ordinarily know, still less to my knowing it. It may even be that by explicitly drawing out the logical consequences of ordinary mundane knowledge, I place myself in such a context. But even this will not mean that closure fails, only that knowledge of certain facts is inevitably tacit. It will mean that there are things that I normally know but which I cannot claim to know without ceasing to know them. If I claim to know them, I change the contextual presuppositions in a way that makes it impossible to make good on my claim. Even so, all we will have is an instance of the instability of knowledge, not an instance of nonclosure.

I do not insist that this is so. I do not know whether simply making a piece of tacit knowledge explicit is ever enough to effect a decisive shift in contextual presuppositions. I do not even know whether there is a fact of the matter. I shall say a little more about this below. But I find something appealing in the idea of the instability of knowledge, for it ties in well with the Humean perception that *scepticism* is unstable.

We have seen that the concessions made to the sceptic on the part of those who deny closure depend on taking on board many of the sceptic's own theoretical commitments. Nonclosure depends on a kind of partial foundationalism. Whereas the sceptic thinks that all beliefs demand to be judged by foundationalist standards, the critic of closure thinks that only some do. Both think that the beliefs set the standards. I have argued for a quite different view: foundationalist standards do not reflect ineluctable epistemological facts; they are inescapable only in that they are a methodological necessity of the traditional project of assessing the totality of our knowledge of the world.

This view of foundationalism can explain why the sceptic's standards might seem to have an intrinsic connection with certain beliefs. The only context in which I have any reason to take seriously the possibility that I am a brain in a vat is that provided by the traditional epistemological project. Thus, that hypothesis is a live option only when foundationalist standards are in play. Accordingly, the belief that I am not a brain in a vat seems to demand to be judged by foundationalist standards because I bring those standards into play by taking sceptical possibilities seriously. But if I do not bring up such possibilities, foundationalist constraints on knowledge of the world remain dormant – in fact, contextually inappropriate – in which case I know what I know, including that sceptical possibilities do not obtain. This seems to me a much better account of how foundationalist standards come to be in force: they are not brought into play just by the content of certain beliefs, as the critics of closure suppose, but by the demands of a particular philosophical project. If they seem to be brought in by certain beliefs, it is because, outside of that project, there is no reason for taking certain possibilities seriously.

Given that closure holds, when a shift in the direction of inquiry brings foundationalist standards into play, not only do I not know that I am not a brain in a vat, I do not know *anything* about the external world. But I have never denied that the sceptic is conditionally correct, in the sense that, by the standards he insists on applying, we never know anything about the world. My point has always been that these standards are something *we* apply. They are not built into the human condition but into a particular intellectual project, itself far from theory free, and standards that are brought into play by a particular project have no claim on us outside it. Accordingly, since foundationalist standards are not in play in the course of common life, my knowledge ordinarily extends to the tacit knowledge that I am not a brain in a vat.

This *could* be represented as a kind of failure of closure. Someone who thinks that drawing out a logical consequence can itself effect a decisive shift in the context of inquiry, hence of contextually appropriate epistemological standards, and who also dislikes the idea of tacit knowledge, might prefer to say that I know that I am sitting on a chair as long as I do not draw the conclusion that I am therefore not a brain in a vat. However, this would be the uninteresting kind of failure that results from failure to put two and two together; and though it is possible to connect the instability of knowledge with this mild kind of nonclosure, I see no particular virtue in so doing.

To return to the main theme, then, suppose that we uphold closure but allow that explicit mention of sceptical alternatives, whether by way of assertion or denial, is apt to change the context of inquiry, suspending whatever ordinary topic we were pursuing and projecting us into a context in which any and all knowledge of the external world comes into question: it will follow that, though we ordinarily do know that sceptical alternatives do not obtain, this knowledge is necessarily tacit, in that any attempt to make it explicit will undermine it. So in a way, Wittgenstein will be right: propositions that stand fast cannot be entered into conversation as claims to knowledge, for if they are so entered they will fail. Still less can we enter them prefaced by "I know that . . ." so as to claim to know that we know. But to say that certain propositions cannot be made the object of explicit knowledge-claims is not to say that they assert things that we can never know to be true. If knowledge can be undermined by reflection, and if bringing certain propositions to the fore is apt to project us into a reflective context, we will have a peculiar epistemic relation to those propositions, knowing them to be true so long as we let them go unmentioned. But a peculiar epistemic relation is not a non-epistemic relation.

We see, then, that it is as important to the theoretical diagnostician as it is to the sceptic to distinguish between constraints on knowing and constraints on claiming to know. Stroud appeals to this distinction to neutralize evidence that the sceptic distorts the meaning of ordinary epistemic terms. Since the facts of ordinary usage, assembled by Austin, all have to do with when it would ordinarily be appropriate to say "I know," there is no necessary incoherence in suggesting that we do not in fact know the things that we ordinarily and quite appropriately claim to know. However, this distinction cuts both ways. Stroud argues that we can be entitled to claim to know things that, as it turns out, we do not know after all. But the combination of abandoning epistemological realism and allowing that the explicit entering of certain propositions can change the contextually appropriate epistemological constraints opens up the possibility of undermining tacit knowledge by making it explicit. This means there can be things that we cannot *claim* to know but which, ordinarily, we *do* know, for all that.

## 8.9   THE HUMEAN CONDITION

So I end as I began, with Hume.

Hume discovered that scepticism triumphs in the study but is impotent in the street. This is the central, paradoxical feature of scepticism: it seems to be both irrefutable and incredible. It is an undeniable philosophical truth, yet strictly limited in its powers to penetrate common life.

I think, however, that if we look closely at Hume's discovery, we detect a standing ambiguity in his understanding of scepticism. On the one hand, scepticism appears in "academic" guise as a theoretical insight, the recognition that our ordinary beliefs never really amount to knowledge. This discovery may be disappointing but need not be threatening. If acknowledging the sceptic's theoretical point leaves vital certainties unaffected, it will not be. Thus understood, scepticism is an epistemological thesis, not a state of mind.

When Hume has his eyes fixed on this academic thesis, as is mostly the case in the *Enquiry*, he can treat scepticism lightly, as revealing the "whimsical" condition of mankind. We may be doomed to groundless believing but we are not thereby doomed to insecurity. However, there is another, more "Pyrrhonian" side to scepticism which makes itself strongly felt in the *Treatise*, accounting in large measure for the difference in emotional tone between the earlier and the later work. In its Pyrrhonian guise, scepticism involves a real, if temporary breakdown of belief, hence a transient loss of knowledge. In the study, ordinary certainties waver; they seem to come loose from their moorings; we are not just convinced that our beliefs amount to something less than knowledge, we are no longer sure what to believe. For Hume, then, scepticism manifests itself as both a surprising epistemological thesis and a disturbing *epoche*. If Hume is more relaxed in the *Enquiry*, this is because academic scepticism is in the ascendant and it is easier to be ironic about an epistemological thesis than about chronic instability in one's beliefs.

Let me now recall some of the results of my essay in diagnosis. Contemporary Humeans connect scepticism with our desire to assess the totality of our knowledge of the world from a detached, external standpoint. I have argued that these two conditions are really one. If we are to assess our knowledge of the world as a whole, we must try to ground that knowledge on something other than knowledge of the world. This can only be experiential knowledge, which turns out to be inadequate to the task. Foundationalism is a presupposition of scepticism, not a by-product.

But what is foundationalism? Following up this question led me to the doctrine I call "epistemological realism." This is not realism about the things we claim to know about but realism about the typical objects of epistemological inquiry. So the traditional project's dependence on foundationalist ideas about knowledge and justification turned out to imply an essential commitment to epistemological realism. In the first instance, unless experiential knowledge is in some completely general and fully objective way epistemologically prior to knowledge of the world, the project of tracing knowledge of the world to experiential knowledge will not amount to an assessment. Our knowledge of the world will neither be secured by our success nor undermined by our failure. But does this mean that we can never hope to understand, in a properly general way, how knowledge of the world is possible, so that there is a gap in our understanding that we will never be able to fill? Pursuing this question revealed an even deeper level at which the traditional project depends on epistemological realism: "our knowledge of the external world" derives its theoretical integrity and thus owes its existence as a genuine kind of knowledge to the doctrine of the priority of experience. Thus, only given epistemological realism do we have something to assess; and only if there is something for us to assess does the impossibility of assessing it point to a gap in our understanding.

One consequence of this proved to be that the idea of philosophical detachment, the idea of taking an "objective" attitude towards our knowledge of the world, cannot be fully explained in terms of formal constraints. The traditional epistemologist's version of philosophical detachment is not fully captured by talk of taking up a "reflective" stance or suspending "practical" interests, for such descriptions of his procedure do not guarantee an object for his distinctive reflections. The key questions, therefore, do not concern his urge to reflect so much as the things he tries to reflect on. The crucial feature of his project is not that it is purely theoretical but, in the sense I explained, purely epistemological. Scepticism arises, Hume tells us, when reason acts alone. But one question never crosses Hume's mind: why suppose that when reason acts alone, when we suspend all topical inquiries, that anything remains for us to reason about?

Not only is it misleading to describe the detached outlook in terms of a suspension of practical interests, it is wrong to represent it as "objective," the outlook entailed by involvement in ordinary projects being thus "subjective." There is nothing especially objective in focussing on one's (supposed) epistemic relation to the world rather than on the world itself. Indeed, we could with some justice think of Nagel's "objective" view as representing the extreme of self-involvement, hence the extreme of subjectivity. There is, therefore, no need to think of epistemological lessons that arise as artifacts of attempts to assume this position as indicative of the deep truth about our epistemic position. The deep truth about our epistemic position is that we do not have one.

Detachment, then, is just another way of insisting that, if we are to attain a properly philosophical understanding of our knowledge of the world, we must set our knowledge of the world aside and try to ground it on something more primitive. Detachment is not a dramatic psychological achievement but simply the recognition of a methodological necessity of the traditional epistemological project. Or is it? What I just said about the subjectivity of the philosophical outlook suggests that perhaps we should not forget the psychological aspects of detachment entirely. Retreating to the study for the purposes of philosophical reflection does involve a kind of withdrawal from the world, for it involves attenuating or suspending the interactive relations with our environment that, for an externalist, are crucial to much ordinary knowledge. "*In normal circumstances*, that I have two hands is as certain as anything I could adduce as evidence for it." But under conditions of philosophical reflection, circumstances are not normal and what is ordinarily completely certain can cease to be so.

If this is possible, when we enter the study several factors may conspire to undermine our ordinary certainties and hence, perhaps, our ordinary knowledge. The methodological constraints of our epistemological inves- tigation may lead us to link ordinary items of knowledge with extraordinary demands: finding a purely experiential basis for them, or insisting that we know something only if we know that we know it. In this way, we can undermine our knowledge, either by causing our beliefs to waver or by exchanging the usual basis for something visibly insecure. Perhaps the latter is a result of the former and that is how we move from Academic scepticism to Pyrrhonian. We act like Bonjour's clairvoyant, as I described him: ceasing to know things by way of asking ourselves how we know them. True, the methodological constraints that inform Cartesian epistemological reflection depend on a false – or at the very least completely unsupported – metaphysical doctrine: epistemological realism. But it is perfectly possible to undermine one's knowledge by tying it up with inferences involving false beliefs.

However, it is certainly possible to be sceptical of all this. Does Hume really undermine his ordinary knowledge of the world when he enters the study? Or does he simply find himself unable to solve a problem that we can now see to be an artifact of prior metaphysical commitments? It is hard to say. Still – and here is where the non-methodological aspects of detach- ment come in – the conditions of philosophical reflection are certainly not normal. As I said, philosophical detachment involves more than a decision not to appeal to worldly beliefs in an account of how knowledge of the world is possible: it also involves a potentially significant change of cir- cumstances. Hume himself, I believe, hints at this point when he stresses the vividness and immediacy of the experiences he has the moment he quits the gloom of the study. So perhaps philosophical reflection can be seen as inducing a temporary loss of knowledge.

For my purposes, it is not important to reach a final decision here. My point is that such a temporary loss of knowledge is the *most* that sceptical reflections can accomplish. The fact, if it is a fact, that we can undermine our ordinary knowledge by subjecting ourselves to the exigencies of the Cartesian project does not mean that we lack that knowledge in ordinary circumstances, in which knowledge is subject to quite different substantive constraints. The sceptic's fallacy is that he takes the discovery that, in the study, knowledge of the world is impossible for the discovery, in the study, that knowledge is impossible generally. He infers the impossibility of knowledge from what is, at best, its instability. Hume got half way there. He was keenly aware of the instability of scepticism. But if I am right, the instability of scepticism and the instability of knowledge are two sides of the same coin, so that scepticism is not the final truth about "our epistemic position" that epistemological pessimists take it to be.

Of course, given epistemological realism the sceptic's inference is not a fallacy at all. The epistemological realist will see philosophical reflection as a device for bringing into relief the permanent, underlying features of our epistemic position that are normally obscured by our involvement in particular "practical" pursuits. But nothing short of this will save the sceptic's conclusion. He is therefore inevitably vulnerable to theoretical diagnosis. His reflections do not reveal an undeniable truth about the human condition but only the consequence of theoretical ideas that are far from evidently correct. The Humean condition and the human condition are not the same. We will be pessimists in epistemology only if we mistake the one for the other.

# Notes

## PREFACE

1 Barry Stroud, *The Significance of Philosophical Scepticism* (Oxford: Oxford University Press, 1984); Thomas Nagel, *The View from Nowhere* (Oxford: Oxford University Press, 1986), p. 88; P. F. Strawson, *Skepticism and Naturalism: Some Varieties* (London: Methuen, 1985).
2 W. V. Quine, "Epistemology Naturalised" in W. V. Quine, ed., *Ontological Relativity and Other Essays* (New York: Columbia University Press, 1969), p. 72. Stanley Cavell, *The Claim of Reason* (Oxford: Oxford University Press, 1979), p. 241.
3 Bernard Williams, *Descartes: the Project of Pure Enquiry* (Harmondsworth: Pelican, 1978), p. 64.
4 Barry Stroud, "Understanding Human Knowledge in General" in Marjorie Clay and Keith Lehrer, eds, *Knowledge and Skepticism* (Boulder, CO: Westview Press, 1989), p. 32.
5 Michael Williams, *Groundless Belief* (Oxford: Blackwell, 1977).

## CHAPTER 1   PESSIMISM IN EPISTEMOLOGY

1 Thompson Clarke, "The Legacy of Skepticism," *Journal of Philosophy* (1972), p. 754. Subsequent citations given by "Legacy" and page number. But although I fully agree with Clarke both that this is the right question to ask and that the object of the sceptic's reflection is the product of a large piece of prior philosophizing, I have rather different ideas about the essential character of the piece of philosophizing in question.
2 This view is developed by Myles Burnyeat, in his important paper "Idealism and Greek Philosophy: What Descartes Saw and Berkeley Missed," *Philosophical Review* (1982). See also my "Descartes and the Metaphysics of Doubt" in Amelie O. Rorty, ed., *Essays on Descartes' "Meditations"* (Berkeley: University of California Press, 1986) which offers a rather different view. I discuss the issue further in "Scepticism without Theory," *Review of Metaphysics* (1988).
3 David Hume, *A Treatise of Human Nature*, ed. L. A. Selby-Bigge, 2nd edn, rev. P. H. Nidditch (Oxford: Oxford University Press, 1978), p. 183; *Enquiry*

*Concerning Human Understanding* in *Enquiries Concerning Human Understanding and Concerning the Principles of Morals*, ed. L. A. Selby-Bigge, 3rd edn, rev. P. H. Nidditch (Oxford: Oxford University Press, 1975), p. 160. Subsequent references given by *THN* or *EHU* and page number. For the best recent account of the role of scepticism in Hume's thought see Robert Fogelin, *Hume's Skepticism in the "Treatise of Human Nature"* (London: Routledge, 1985).

4 *EHU*, p. 155 n.
5 *EHU*, pp. 159–60.
6 *THN*, p. 183.
7 Ludwig Wittgenstein, *On Certainty* (Oxford: Blackwell, 1969), ¶166. Subsequent references given by *OC* and paragraph number.
8 *THN*, p. 183.
9 *THN*, pp. 268–9; "affrighted and confounded," p. 264.
10 *EHU*, p. 160.
11 *THN*, pp. 267–8.
12 *THN*, p. 268.
13 *THN*, p. 218.
14 *THN*, p. 218.
15 *OC*, 481.
16 *THN*, p. 269.
17 *THN*, p. 185.
18 *THN*, p. 218; "scepticism as strained," e.g. *THN*, pp. 185, 268: "the slightest philosophy," *EHU*, p. 152.
19 Both quotations, *THN*, p. 218.
20 Stanley Cavell in *The Claim of Reason: Wittgenstein, Scepticism, Morality and Tragedy* (Oxford: Oxford University Press, 1979), pp. 129ff; quotations p. 165. Henceforth cited as *Claim*.
21 Whether Hume thinks this could be questioned. At *THN* pp. 187–231, Hume describes the natural progression from naive realism to total scepticism without exactly endorsing the position reached at any point. But this is not a retreat from scepticism: it is Hume at his *most* sceptical. Like the Pyrrhonian sceptic of antiquity, and unlike the academic, he declines to affirm dogmatically that knowledge is impossible. He does not know whether knowledge is possible, though there are moods in which he is powerfully inclined to feel that it isn't. Note, however, that Hume's naturalism – the thought that the best we can do by way of explaining why we believe the sorts of things we do is to give causal-psychological accounts – presupposes the truth of scepticism. Scepticism clears the way for naturalism by destroying our self-image as *animal ratione*, or even *animal rationis capax*.
22 *THN*, pp. 222–3, emphasis mine.
23 I do not say that the elements of Hume's account of scepticism are all original. In fact, some are very ancient: Hume's affinities with the classical sceptics are worth further exploration.
24 P. F. Strawson, *Skepticism and Naturalism: Some Varieties* (London: Methuen, 1985), ch. 1. Cited below as *Varieties*.
25 P. F. Strawson, *Individuals* (London: Methuen, 1959), p. 35: "Thus [the sceptic's] doubts are unreal, not simply because they are logically irresoluble

doubts, but because they amount to the rejection of the whole conceptual scheme within which alone such doubts make sense." In *Varieties* Strawson agrees with his critics that transcendental arguments only show how our way of seeing the world hangs together, not that sceptical questioning of the entire package is incoherent.

26 *Varieties*, p. 20.

27 That we can never simply invoke commonsense certainty against the results of philosophical reflection is a main theme in Marie McGinn's *Sense and Certainty* (Oxford: Blackwell, 1989).

28 The thought that the sceptic does not set out to be sceptical goes back at least to Sextus Empiricus. See *Outlines of Pyrrhonism* bk 1 lines 12ff, in *Sextus Empiricus*, vol. 1, tr. R. G. Bury (London: Heinemann, 1933).

29 *Varieties*, pp. 19–20, emphasis in original.

30 *OC*, 94, 103.

31 *THN*, p. 187.

32 *OC*, 135.

33 This is the burden of Stroud's *The Significance of Philosophical Scepticism* (Oxford: Oxford University Press, 1984). Henceforth cited as *Significance*.

34 See "Skepticism and the Possibility of Knowledge," *Journal of Philosophy* (1984), and "Understanding Human in Knowledge in General," in Marjorie Clay and Keith Lehrer, eds, *Knowledge and Skepticism* (Boulder: Westview Press, 1989). Henceforth cited, respectively, as *Possibility* and *Understanding*.

35 For Nagel's ideas about scepticism see his *The View from Nowhere* (Oxford: Oxford University Press, 1986), ch. V. Cited below as *View*.

36 *View*, p. 231.

37 Cf. Strawson (*Varieties*, pp. 37–8) on the detached versus the involved outlook: "error lies not one side or the other of these two contrasting positions, but in the attempt to force the choice between them. . . . [T]he appearance of contradiction arises only if we assume the existence of some metaphysically absolute standpoint."

38 I was tempted to add Richard Rorty to my list of new Humeans, with the proviso that, if Nagel approximates to the Hume of the *Treatise*, environed in the deepest darkness, Rorty is closer to the Hume of the *Enquiry*, who found our groundless believing less depressing than ironically amusing. But Rorty's relation to mainstream epistemology is deeply equivocal, so that he doesn't fit cleanly into the picture.

On the one hand, Rorty presents himself as a "post-philosophical" intellectual, more specifically a liberal ironist. As he sees it, problems like scepticism, central to what philosophers like Stroud think of as "the quest of traditional epistemology," are artifacts of ideas about knowledge and truth – particularly truth – that we would do well to abandon. This is not because we can show that the terms in which such problems are couched are incoherent. The point is rather that the theoretical tradition that couches its problems in such terms has run into a dead end; other and potentially more fruitful ways of talking are available; and so it is reasonable to start talking in those ways to see how we get on. Thus Rorty could be seen as an advocate of what I shall be calling "theoretical diagnosis." (I should add that this is where agreement ends, for my specific diagnosis of sceptical problems has little if anything in common with Rorty's.) There is also in Rorty a prominent strain of pluralism that finds no counterpart in Hume. This is connected partly with Rorty's having taken the linguistic turn and partly with the shift of focus from metaphysical to moral-political-literary concerns which Rorty thinks takes place when we put the traditional epistemological enterprise behind us. New ways of talking, he argues, reflect and promote a new sense of where the fundamental problems lie. No problem is "deep" in the sense of "inherent in the human condition." Accordingly, abandoning the traditional epistemological project need not leave us with a permanent sense of intellectual dissatisfaction. So, to the extent that Rorty argues for the unnaturalness of sceptical doubts, he is no new Humean.

On the other hand, Rorty's writings, particularly his most recent, betray striking and recurrent echoes of Humean biperspectivalism. According to Rorty, we cope with the world with the aid of various "final vocabularies" which articulate and create different ways of living. Varied as they are, however, from the philosophical point of view all vocabularies share a common status. Because they are historical artifacts, not products of an unchanging human nature, philosophical reflection reveals them all as *just* vocabularies, none having a lien on the truth or a basis in reason. Of course, in our active, public lives, we cannot really think of them this way. But in our reflective, private moments we can. Thus Rorty is led to contrast the seriousness and commitment of public life with the rootlessness and detachment of the theorist, "liberal hope" with "*private irony*" (pp. 73ff). (Compare Rorty's theorist with Nagel's philosopher, who takes the view from *nowhere*.) In so far as irony threatens to break out of the study (or perhaps in Rorty's case the salon), it is undesirable. As he puts it, "In the ideal liberal society, the intellectuals would . . . be ironists, although the nonintellectuals would not" (p. 87). But Rorty seems undecided as to how far anyone can be an ironist in the public sphere. Though defining the ironist as one afflicted with "radical and continuing doubts about the final vocabulary she currently uses" (p. 73), he is very strongly committed to his particular version of liberalism, for which "cruelty is the worst thing." His ironist's doubts show themselves clearly only in such things as his willingness to acknowledge "the fragility and contingency" of his final vocabulary (p. 74): in other words, in reflective commentary on his final vocabulary rather than in its actual employment. This is the level at which the ironist contrasts with "the metaphysician" who, because of his attachment to the idea of "a single permanent reality" (p. 73), is constantly putting forward philosophical foundations for local prejudices. The parallels with Hume hardly need spelling out: irony/scepticism in private, commitment/belief in common life, etc. And note how Rorty's division of humanity into nonintellectuals, metaphysicians and ironists matches Hume's (less euphemistic) scheme of the vulgar, false philosophers and true philosophers, the true philosophers being of course sceptics. Though Rorty prefers "irony" to "scepticism," taking himself to have moved beyond all traditional epistemological options, the true irony may be that Rorty's ironist is everyone else's sceptic. Quotes from Richard Rorty, *Contingency,*

*Irony, Solidarity* (Cambridge: Cambridge University Press, 1989). Subsequent references given by *Contingency* and page number. For more on Rorty's equivocal relation to the epistemological tradition, see below, notes 51, 63, 64, 66 and 68.

39 *Claim* pp. 217ff.

40 "Disappointment," *Claim* p. 44; "relation," p. 45. Cf. Cavell on the bond between Wittgenstein and Heidegger which "implies a shared view of what I have called the truth of scepticism, or what I might call the moral of scepticism, namely, that the human creature's basis in the world as a whole, its relation to the world as such, is not that of knowing, anyway not what we think of as knowing" (p. 241).

41 *Significance* p. 39.

42 *Significance* p. 82.

43 *Claim*, p. 225.

44 John Skorupski, "The Intelligibility of Scepticism," paper read at the Sheffield Conference on the Origins of Analytic Philosophy 1988.

45 *Significance*, p. 168.

46 Crispin Wright, "Facts and Certainty," Proceedings of the British Academy (1985), cited henceforth as "Facts"; quotation pp. 429–30.

47 *Claim*, p. 241, my emphasis.

48 "Facts", p. 457.

49 "Facts", p. 461.

50 "Facts", p. 461.

51 Rorty welcomes revisionary solutions. Indeed, he thinks, plausibly, that conceptual revision is often the only way to get rid of persistent intellectual problems. Thus he writes: "Interesting philosophy is rarely the examination of the pros and cons of a thesis. Usually it is, implicitly or explicitly, a contest between an entrenched vocabulary which has become a nuisance and a half-formed new vocabulary which vaguely promises great things" (*Contingency*, p. 9). An example of such a contest, in his view, is that between the traditional "realist" or "correspondence" view of truth, which he takes to be deeply implicated in the problem of scepticism, and the "pragmatist" view that he favours and which, he thinks, pushes traditional epistemological problems aside. However, radical revision is more easily advocated than accomplished, and I sense in Rorty's position an essential tension very similar to that found in Wright's.

Rorty's ironist is supposedly led to "radical and continuing doubts about the final vocabulary she is currently using" through being "impressed by other vocabularies, vocabularies taken as final by people or books she has encountered" (*Contingency*, p. 73). This is reminiscent of *isosthenia*, the ancient Pyrrhonist's route to *epoche* by way of counterposing incompatible yet equally plausible views, and this kind of scepticism may well swing free of the doctrinal commitments that I believe underlie philosophical scepticism in its modern form. Equally, however, it is too thin to support the "radical and continuing doubts" that define the ironist. The fact is, being *aware* of alternative vocabularies does not, as a matter of course, equate to being *impressed* by alternative vocabularies, in the sense of finding them plausible replacements for one's own vocabulary. If irony depended entirely on the availability of equally impressive alternative vocabularies, irony itself would be far more occasional and contingent than Rorty allows. The ironist's doubts would not, in the normal run of things, be either radical or continuing. For example, Rorty himself is aware of anti-liberal political views but is certainly not impressed by them.

A step towards radical doubt is taken when Rorty's ironist draws a theoretical conclusion from her awareness of diversity. This awareness makes ironists "historicists and nominalists." Being "always aware that the terms in which they describe themselves are subject to change," they are "always aware of the contingency and fragility of their final vocabularies" (p. 74). Here Rorty is relying on a version of the ancient and fallacious argument from error: there is no direct move from allowing for the possibility of changing one's mind to *radical* doubts in respect of one's actual opinions. Accordingly, the recognition of contingency may or may not induce a sense of fragility.

So what really underlies the ironic outlook, as a permanent condition? I think the answer can only be an unrequited hankering after the discarded ideal of truth. Rorty's post-philosophical intellectual is ironic because he realizes that truth is not all he would like it to be. Irony depends essentially on a kind of *nostalgie de la verité*. It bears more than a passing resemblance to Cavell's "human disappointment with human knowledge."

52 *Significance*, p. 209.
53 Ibid., pp. 81–2.
54 *OC*, 346.
55 *OC*, 163, 167.
56 *OC*, 105.
57 *Sense and Certainty*, ch 8.
58 Meredith Williams, "Wittgenstein, Kant and the 'Metaphysics of Experience,'" *Kant-Studien* (1990), pp. 80–1. Cited below as "Metaphysics."
59 *Varieties*, pp. 19–20.
60 *OC*, 185.
61 "Metaphysics," p. 81.
62 *OC*, 204.
63 *OC*, 19.
64 John Dewey, *The Quest for Certainty: Gifford Lectures 1929* (New York: Capricorn, 1960), pp. 193–4.
65 Ibid., p. 196. Cf. Rorty on the importance, now that language has displaced ideas at the centre of epistemology, of seeing language "not as a *tertium quid* between Subject and Object, nor as a medium in which we try to form pictures of reality, but as part of the behaviour of human beings." We must recognize that "the activity of uttering sentences is one of the things people do in order to cope with their environment." We must not, however, let this "Deweyan notion of language as tool rather than picture" tempt us into thinking that "one can separate the tool . . . from its users" so as to "inquire as to its 'adequacy' to achieve our purposes." The crucial point is that "one cannot see language-as-a whole in relation to something else to which it applies, or for which it is a means to an end." To take this point to heart, Rorty thinks, is to acknowledge that philosophy as the attempt to explain how thought or language relates to the world – i.e. the sort of philosophy for which scepticism is an overriding concern

– is impossible. Notably, for both Rorty and Dewey, emphasizing the primacy of action goes hand in hand with a recasting of the notion of truth. But I think they mislocate the source of the problem. See chapter 6 below, where I argue that a correct diagnosis of scepticism obviates the need to recast the notion of truth. Richard Rorty, *Consequences of Pragmatism* (Minneapolis: University of Minnesota Press, 1982), pp. xviii–xix. Cited below as *Consequences*.

66 Rudolf Carnap, "Empiricism, Semantics and Ontology," in Carnap, *Meaning and Necessity* (Chicago: University of Chicago Press, 1958), p. 208. It is interesting that, although in the Introduction to *Consequences* Rorty is at pains to distance pragmatism from positivism, his views in *Contingency* often show a striking resemblance to Carnap's, "vocabularies" standing in for "linguistic frameworks." Like Carnap, Rorty makes a lot of the contrast between the routine rule-governed acceptance or rejection of individual sentences within a framework or vocabulary and the highly non-routine matter of replacing an entire framework or vocabulary with another. Also like Carnap, he finds the notion of correspondence truth particularly dubious at the framework level. Compare the quotation from Carnap in the text with Rorty's remark that "When the notion of 'description of the world' is moved from the level of criterion-governed sentences within language games to language games as wholes . . . the idea that the world decides which descriptions are true can no longer be given a clear sense" (*Contingency*, p. 5).

67 Carnap's claim that the question of the reality of the world, which he has apparently just formulated, cannot be formulated "in any theoretical language" calls to mind the sort of paradox we found in Cavell, that the sceptic cannot mean what he wants to mean. For an illuminating discussion of Carnap's way with scepticism, see Stroud, *Significance*, ch. V.

68 Rorty too differs from Carnap on this point. Though vocabulary shifts are not governed by criteria, neither do they result from arbitrary decisions. Thus: "The moral is not that objective criteria for choice of vocabulary are to be replaced with subjective criteria, reason with will or feeling. It is rather that the notions of criteria and choice (including that of 'arbitrary' choice) are no longer in point when it comes to changes from one language game to another" (*Contingency*, p. 6). This removal of choice from the arena of basic commitments is very much in the spirit of Hume's response to scepticism. Rorty could be thought of as marrying Carnap's linguistic relativism to Hume's anti-sceptical naturalism.

69 *OC*, 188.

70 *OC*, 200, 205.

71 *Significance*, pp. 273–4.

72 *Understanding*, p. 49.

73 *Varieties*, p. 10.

74 *Claim*, p. 223.

75 *Varieties*, p. 10.

76 *OC*, 250.

77 "Facts," p. 461.

78 *Significance*, p. 82.

79 *Significance*, p. 274.

80 In *Groundless Belief*, ch. 1.

81 *OC*, 53.
82 G. E. Moore, *Some Main Problems of Philosophy* (New York: Collier, 1962), p. 136. Discussed by Stroud, *Significance*, p. 106f.
83 *Significance*, p. 111.


## CHAPTER 2  THE PRIORITY OF EXPERIENCE

1 Peter Unger, *Ignorance: a Case for Scepticism* (Oxford: Oxford University Press, 1975).
2 On this I agree with Barry Stroud – see *Significance*, p. 13. I give a similar though less argued account of the task of epistemology in *Groundless Belief*, ch. 1.
3 *Significance*, p. 144.
4 A. J. Ayer, *The Problem of Knowledge* (Harmondsworth: Pelican, 1956), pp. 75–83.
5 *THN*, p. 195.
6 For more on this see *Groundless Belief*, ch. 4. But though subject to what strikes me as decisive criticism, the thought that belief in the existence of the external world can be defended by some kind of quasi-scientific inference dies hard. For a recent, Popperian variant, see John Watkins, *Science and Scepticism* (Princeton: Princeton University Press, 1984), pp. 258ff. I comment on Watkins in *Philosophy of Science* (1987).
7 *Possibility*, p. 550. I owe the formulation of the question "presupposition or by-product?" to Stroud.
8 See Diogenes Laertius, *Lives of the Philosophers*, tr. R. D. Hicks (London: Heinemann 1925) vol. 2, p. 501 (IX, 88). Also Sextus Empiricus, *Outlines*, vol. 1, pp. 164ff.
9 *OC*, 155.
10 For Wright's argument in full argument see "Facts", pp. 434–8.
11 Ch. 7.
12 *Sense and Certainty*, p. 8.
13 *OC*, 25–7.
14 *OC*, 52.
15 Descartes, *Meditations on First Philosophy: First Meditation*, in *The Philosophical Works of Descartes*, vol. 1, tr. Elizabeth Haldane and G. R. T. Ross (Cambridge: Cambridge University Press, 1972), quotation p. 145. Subsequent references to this edition given by *MFP*.
16 *Significance*, pp. 12–13.
17 H. H. Price, *Perception* (Oxford: Oxford University Press, 1932), p. 1.
18 *OC*, 250
19 *Significance*, p. 7.
20 *Significance*, p. 209.
21 *Significance*, p. 179.
22 Donald Davidson, "A Coherence Theory of Truth and Knowledge" in E. Lepore, ed., *Truth and Interpretation* (Blackwell: Oxford, 1986). Subsequent references given by "CTTK" and page number.
23 Ch. 7.

24 See e.g. "Has Austin Refuted the Sense-Datum Theory?" in K. T. Fann, ed., *Symposium on J. L. Austin* (New York: Humanities, 1969).
25 "Obstacle," *Significance*, p. 144; "truism," ibid., p. 209.
26 *Significance*, p. 141.
27 *Significance*, p. 140–41.
28 Wilfrid Sellars, "Empiricism and the Philosophy of Mind" in Sellars, ed., *Science, Perception and Reality* (London: Routledge, 1963), pp. 140ff.
29 *Perception*, p. 3.
30 *View*, p. 71.
31 *Significance*, pp. 109–10.
32 Stroud argues this way in *Significance*, pp. 21–2. Cf. Wright, "Facts," pp. 431–4.
33 *OC*, 250, 53.

## CHAPTER 3   EPISTEMOLOGICAL REALISM

1 *Understanding*, p. 32.
2 Ch. 6.
3 W. V. Quine, "Epistemology Naturalised" in *Ontological Relativity and Other Essays* (New York: Columbia University Press, 1969). On Quine's problematic attitude towards traditional epistemology, see Stroud, *Significance*, ch. VI.
4 *Possibility*, p. 551.
5 Ch. 5 below.
6 *Understanding*, p. 49.
7 Edmund Gettier, "Is Justified True Belief Knowledge?," *Analysis* (1963), reprinted in Paul K. Moser, ed., *Empirical Knowledge* (Totowa, NJ: Rowman and Littlefield, 1986).
8 Gilbert Harman, *Thought* (Princeton: Princeton University Press, 1973), p. 47.
9 *Thought*, ch. 11.
10 Alvin Goldman, "A Causal Theory of Knowing," *Journal of Philosophy* (1967), pp. 357–72.
11 Colin McGinn, "The Concept of Knowledge" in *Midwest Studies in Philosophy* IX (1984), quotation p. 547. Henceforth cited as "Concept."
12 "Concept," p. 549.
13 J. L. Austin, "Other Minds" in J. L. Austin, ed., *Philosophical Papers* (Oxford: Oxford University Press, 1961). Subsequent citations given by "OM" and page numbers.
14 *OC*, 506.
15 "Concept," p. 549.
16 This is the burden of *Understanding*.
17 *Understanding*, p. 47.
18 *Understanding*, p. 47.
19 *View*, p. 68.
20 *Understanding*, p. 32.
21 Descartes, *MFP*, p. 145; Hume, *THN*, p. xx.
22 I am grateful to Simon Blackburn for this useful phrase.

23 These quotations and the next *THN*, pp. xv–xvi.

24 *Novum Organum*, bk II in J. Spedding, R. Ellis, and D. Heath, eds, *The Works of Francis Bacon* (London: Longman, 1857–8), vol. IV. My example is slightly unfair to Bacon in that he did not intend to give instances of everything that would, in common parlance, be said to involve "heating." His aim was to collect instances which "agree in the same nature, though in substance the most unlike": *Novum Organum*, II, aphorism xi.

25 W. V. Quine, "Two Dogmas of Empiricism" in W. V. Quine, ed., *From a Logical Point of View* (New York: Harper, 1963).

26 H. P. Grice and P. F. Strawson, "In Defence of a Dogma," *Philosophical Review* (1956).

27 I must thank Alvin Goldman for pressing me on this point.

28 Myles Burnyeat ("Idealism and Greek Philosophy") thinks that Descartes's externalization of his own body is the key move in his invention of the problem of our knowledge of the external world. I see it as a consequence of his epistemological realism.

29 W. V. Quine, *Pursuit of Truth* (Cambridge Mass.: Harvard University Press, 1990), p. 80.

30 Ibid., p. 82.

31 However, it seems to me that the more a purely disquotational account of "true" can be shown to capture whatever we want out of the truth-predicate, the less reason there is for thinking that there must be some "truth-making" property that all true sentences share: the invitation to apply Occam's Razor ought to be irresistible.

32 Stephen Leeds, "Theories of Reference and Truth," *Erkenntnis* (1978).

33 Attempts to discuss the Gettier problem and traditional sceptical questions in the same breath often seem rather contrived. The epistemological analogue of Leeds's distinction explains why.

34 Keith Lehrer notes that the "definitional or formal" in his theory of knowledge, which "constitutes an analysis or explication of the concept of knowledge," "leaves open substantive issues." See Lehrer, "Knowledge Reconsidered" in Clay and Lehrer, eds, *Knowledge and Scepticism.*, quotation p. 132.

35 Laurence Bonjour, *The Structure of Empirical Knowledge* (Cambridge, Mass.: Harvard University Press, 1985), pp. 89ff. Subsequent citations given by *Structure* and page numbers.

36 The terminology of formal versus substantive foundationalism is also employed by Ernest Sosa: see "The Raft and the Pyramid," *Midwest Studies in Philosophy* V (1980), reprinted in Moser, *Empirical Knowledge*: citations given for this reprinting. However, I am uncertain whether my usage is the same as Sosa's. According to Sosa, "A type of *formal foundationalism* with respect to a normative or evaluative property 0 is the view that the conditions (actual and possible) within which 0 would apply can be specified in general, perhaps recursively. *Substantive foundationalism* is only a particular way of doing so" (p. 157, italics in original). From my point of view, everything depends on what is allowed to count as a "general" specification.

37 Though I have grave doubts about the notion of intrinsic credibility, having written about all this elsewhere (*Groundless Belief*, chs 2, 3, and 5) I will not

repeat myself. My interest here is in the foundationalist's conception of epistemological priority, which I see as his deepest theoretical commitment.

38 Letter to Mersenne (24 December, 1640), quoted from Anthony Kenny, ed., *Descartes: Philosophical Letters* (Minneapolis: University of Minnesota Press, 1981), p. 87.

39 *OC*, 250.

40 *OC*, 125.

41 Failure to appreciate this point is what vitiates Marie McGinn's intuitive reconstruction of the case for scepticism.

42 *OC*, 53.

43 For a succinct defence of contextualism, see David B. Annis in "A Contextualist Theory of Epistemic Justification," *American Philosophical Quarterly* (1978), reprinted in Moser, *Empirical Knowledge*. Annis sees Pierce, Dewey, and Popper as having been, historically, the key contextualists. He may be right, though I have doubts about how far these philosophers saw into the implications of contextualism. For example, I doubt whether Popper would be as suspicious as he is about justification if he were really a thoroughgoing contextualist.

44 Obviously, this kind of externalism is not the same as pure reliabilism, except in so far as the apparent theoretical simplicity of some forms of reliabilism is a sham. Consider, for example, Colin McGinn's suggestion (in "Concept") that knowing that p depends on the availability of a "way of telling" that p. This analysis does not guarantee any theoretical integrity in "ways of telling," and is therefore compatible with a contextual, hence anti-epistemological-realist, conception of knowledge.

45 For a useful discussion of the different grades of foundationalism, see Bonjour, *Structure*, pp. 26–30.

46 *OC*, 88.

47 *OC*, 163.

48 *OC*, 235.

49 *OC*, 341–3.

50 *OC*, 318, emphasis in original. Cf. the metaphor of the river bed at 95–8.

51 Ludwig Wittgenstein, *Philosophical Investigations* (Oxford: Blackwell, 1963), §289.

52 Nelson Goodman, *Ways of Worldmaking* (Indianapolis: Hackett, 1978), ch. 1.

53 *Significance*, p. 111.

54 Cf. David Lewis's discussion of Unger on certainty as an "absolute term." Lewis notes that while it is perfectly possible to create a context in which the standards of certainty are such that sceptical results seem to follow, "that does not show that there is anything whatever wrong with the claims to certainty that we make in more ordinary contexts"(p. 246). However, as will become clear in chapter 5, I am reluctant to follow Lewis in thinking of shifts in the range of relevant error-possibilities as being a simple matter of the raising and lowering of standards. See David K. Lewis, "Scorekeeping in a Language Game" in Lewis, ed., *Philosophical Papers* vol. 1 (Oxford: Oxford University Press, 1983), pp. 233–49. Henceforth cited as "Scorekeeping."

55 "Legacy", p. 756.

56 "Legacy", pp. 758ff.

57 "Legacy," pp. 762, 761.

## CHAPTER 4   EXAMPLES AND PARADIGMS

1 Haldane and Ross, *Descartes*, p. 101.
2 *MFP*, p. 145.
3 Sextus Empiricus, *Outlines*, vol. 1, 104.
4 *Significance*, p. 10.
5 *Claim*, chs, VI, VIII.
6 *Claim*, p. 132; adapted from Austin, "OM".
7 "OM," p. 52. For some recent criticism of Austin's approach see, in addition to Cavell, Stroud, *Significance*, ch. 2 and McGinn, *Sense and Certainty*, ch. 4. I am sympathetic to a great deal of what McGinn says, particularly to her central claim that "Austin's investigation of the conditions requisite for knowledge cannot yield a criticism of the sceptic's understanding of our epistemic concepts at all, for the sceptic can insist that he does not deviate from out ordinary understanding of the concepts of knowledge and justification" (p. 63). However, I have some difficulty squaring this with another, important point she argues for: that there is "an irreconcilable clash between Austin and the sceptic" (p. 61).
8 *MFP*, p. 145.
9 That this is how Austin means us to see things is evident from his comment on the doctrine that "we never directly perceive or sense material objects . . . , but only sense-data (or our own ideas, impression, sensa, sense-perceptions, percepts, etc.)." The traditional epistemologist is apt to see this doctrine as describing the position we find ourselves in after an initial encounter with sceptical considerations, or even as recording the final verdict on our epistemic position. But according to Austin, "it is a typically *scholastic* view, attributable, first, to an obsession with a few particular words, the uses of which are over-simplified . . . ;" and second, to an obsession with a few (and nearly always the same) half-studied "facts." The way to undermine such a doctrine is to make clear that "our ordinary words are much subtler in their uses, and mark many more distinctions, than philosophers have realised" and that "the facts of perception . . . are much more diverse and complicated than has been allowed for." Quotation from J. L. Austin, *Sense and Sensibilia* (Oxford: Oxford University Press, 1962), p. 3.
10 *OC*, 84.
11 *OC*, 1, 84, 100.
12 "OM," p. 55.
13 "OM," p. 56.
14 *Claim*, p. 161.
15 *Claim*, p. 161, emphasis in original.
16 *Claim*, p. 193.
17 John Skorupski, "The Intelligibility of Scepticism."
18 "Empiricism, Semantics and Ontology," pp. 206–8.
19 *Claim*, p. 220.
20 *Significance*, p. 261.
21 *OC*, 10.
22 "Are you suggesting . . . ," *Claim*, p. 206, "flamingly obvious," 211.

23  *OC*, 18.
24  *OC*, 84.
25  *OC*, 136, 151.
26  *OC*, 83, 302.
27  *OC*, 199, 205.
28  "Facts," section III.
29  "OM", p. 55
30  *Significance*, p. 10: "Whether, or in precisely what sense, the example [Descartes] considers can be treated as representative of our relation to the world around us is ... the key to understanding the problem of our knowledge of the external world.
31  Hilary Putnam, *Philosophical Papers* (Cambridge: Cambridge University Press, 1975) vol. 2, p. 141.
32  *Claim*, pp. 223ff.


## CHAPTER 5    SCEPTICISM AND REFLECTION

1  *Claim*, p. 140.
2  *Sense and Certainty*, p. 3.
3  *Sense and Certainty*, p. 152.
4  *OC*, 152.
5  *Sense and Certainty*, p. 152.
6  *OC*, 155, 467.
7  *OC*, 19.
8  Meredith Williams, who finds this view in Wittgenstein, connects the apparent difficulty of reflecting on the presuppositions of common sense with Wittgenstein's continuing commitment to his doctrine of "showing." I think she may be right; but I regard the need to invoke the idea of showing what cannot be said as another way of bringing out the paradoxical character of this line of criticism.
9  *Understanding*, p. 49.
10  See above p. 000.
11  *Significance*, p. 57f.
12  "Legacy"; *Significance*, ch. 2.
13  Fred Dretske, "Epistemic Operators," *Journal of Philosophy* (1970). Henceforth cited as "EO."
14  "EO," p. 1007.
15  "EO," p. 1017f: also Dretske, "Constrastive Statements," *Philosophical Review* (1972). But see "The Pragmatic Dimension of Knowledge," *Philosophical Studies* (1981), where Dretske argues that relevance and irrelevance also depend on what alternatives are objectively likely to be realized, and not just on what alternatives we happen to have in mind.
16  The previous note suggests how Dretske would handle the example of the spotters: they do know that a given plane is a type A if type X craft are, objectively speaking, very unlikely to be encountered. But a sceptic will note that Dretske advances the suggestion that objective probabilities determine relevance

in connection with a discussion of the *pragmatic* dimension of knowledge. The sceptic wants our verdict on knowledge after we have set all pragmatic concerns aside.

17 "EO", p. 1009.
18 All quotes "Legacy," p. 766.
19 "Legacy," pp. 767–8.
20 *Significance*, pp. 270–71.
21 "Legacy," pp. 760–1.
22 "Legacy," p. 760.
23 *Claim*, p. 140.
24 *Claim*, pp. 140–1.
25 *Claim*, p. 143.
26 *EHU*, p. 151.
27 *EHU*, p. 143.
28 *Sense and Certainty*, p. 3.
29 *EHU*, p. 151.
30 *Significance*, p. 41.
31 Clarke notes himself that his creatures "are not in a sceptical position" ("Legacy," p. 760). But all he means by this is that they are to be imagined as capable of knowledge of the world. He certainly intends the example to be a good analogy for how the traditional epistemologist conceives our radically sceptical predicament.
32 Here I am much indebted to Marie McGinn. See *Sense and Certainty*, ch. 2, especially p. 23f.
33 Clearly, the distinction between justified belief and justified believing complicates matters. But here we are investigating how practical and theoretical considerations influence one and the same dimension of justification: justification by way of evidential support for what is believed. Still, the issue of whether it is ever alright to *claim* things for which one has no evidence, even though it may be alright to believe them, is interesting and difficult, for there may be things that one is justified in believing only provided that they go unsaid. I take up the question of whether some knowledge is necessarily tacit in chapter 8 below, p. 350f.
34 Bernard Williams, *Descartes: The Project to Pure Enquiry* (Harmondsworth: Pelican, 1978), p. 33. Subsequent citations given by *Project* and page number.
35 *Project*, p. 36.
36 *Project*, p. 47.
37 *Project*, p. 46.
38 *Project*, p. 49.
39 Hume notes that Cartesian doubt may be taken two ways. Taken one way, it recommends "an universal doubt, not only of all our former opinions and principles, but also of our very faculties; of whose veracity . . . we must assure ourselves, by a chain of reasoning, deduced from some original principle, which cannot possibly be fallacious or deceitful." Taken the other, it suggests only that, in any inquiry, we "begin with clear and self-evident principles, . . . advance by timorous and sure steps, . . . review frequently our conclusions, . . . and examine accurately all their consequences" (*EHU*, pp. 149–50). Hume has sensed the

distinction between the demand for foundational epistemology and that for cautious disciplinary inquiry.

40 *Project*, p. 66.
41 *Project*, p. 64.
42 *Project*, p. 54.
43 *Project*, p. 57.
44 *Project*, p. 58.
45 *Project*, p. 55.
46 *Understanding*, p. 8.
47 *Understanding*, p. 9.

## CHAPTER 6   SCEPTICISM AND OBJECTIVITY

1 *Project*, p. 64.
2 *Project*, p. 64.
3 *Project*, p. 64.
4 *View*, p. 71.
5 *View*, p. 92.
6 *Significance*, p. 82.
7 Colin McGinn, "An A Priori Argument for Realism," *Journal of Philosophy* (1979), quotation p. 115.
8 Michael Dummett, *Truth and Other Enigmas* (Cambridge, Mass.: Harvard University Press, 1978), p. 146.
9 Hilary Putnam, "Realism and Reason" in *Meaning and the Moral Sciences* (London: Routledge, 1978), p. 125.
10 "CTTK," pp. 307–10.
11 Moritz Schlick, "The Foundation of Knowledge," *Erkenntnis* (1934) reprinted in A. J. Ayer, ed., *Logical Positivism* (New York: Free Press, 1959) pp. 209–27. Citations below as "Foundation."
12 Brand Blanshard, *The Nature of Thought* (London: Allen & Unwin, 1939), vol. 2, ch. 25. Henceforth cited as *Nature*.
13 Bonjour, *Structure*, p. 25.
14 "CTTK," p. 310.
15 "CTTK," pp. 310–12. Cf. my *Groundless Belief*, ch. 2.
16 *Nature*, p. 268.
17 *Nature*, p. 262.
18 Wilfrid Sellars, *Science and Metaphysics* (London: Routledge, 1968), chs 2–5; Richard Rorty, "The World Well Lost," *Journal of Philosophy* (1972); Hilary Putnam, *Reason, Truth and History* (Cambridge: Cambridge University Press, 1981), ch. 3. Rorty has recently claimed to have abandoned this view of truth: see "Pragmatism, Davidson and Truth" in Lepore, *Truth and Interpretation*.
19 Wilfrid Sellars, *Science and Metaphysics*, chs 4–5.
20 *Nature*, pp. 271, 269.
21 *Nature*, p. 270.
22 *Nature*, p. 271.

23 *Nature*, p. 262.
24 It is notable that, on occasion, Blanshard betrays hints of uncertainty as to whether such claims really answer the sceptic. He writes, "If the pursuit of thought's own ideal were merely an elaborate self-indulgence that brought us no nearer reality . . . the hope of knowledge would be vain. Of course, it may really be vain. If anyone cares to doubt whether the framework of human logic has any bearing on the nature of things, he may be silenced perhaps, but he cannot be conclusively answered" (*Nature*, p. 262). Since Blanshard uses "logic" in a broad sense which includes the criteria of coherence, this remark amounts to an admission that the problem of connecting coherence with truth, understood as the truth about "what is there anyway," is insoluble.
25 *Contingency*, p. 4.
26 True, Putnam was more interested in convergence when he was a realist: see *Meaning and the Moral Sciences*. But it is not clear that he was ever what he thinks of as a "metaphysical" realist.
27 *Structure*, p. 169f.
28 *View*, p. 77.
29 See *Consequences*, Introduction.
30 Michael Devitt, *Realism and Truth* (Oxford: Blackwell, 1984), p. 3. Henceforth cited as *Realism*.
31 *Realism*, p. 4.
32 *Realism*, p. 22.
33 Such a view is explained and defended in Paul Horwich, *Truth* (Oxford. Blackwell, 1990).
34 For a detailed defence of the virtues of a deflationary approach to truth, see Horwich, *Truth*. Also Arthur Fine, "The Natural Ontological Attitude" in J. Leplin, ed., *Scientific Realism* (Berkeley: University of California Press, 1984); and my own "Do We Epistemologists Need a Theory of Truth?," *Philosophical Topics* (1986).
35 "Afterthoughts, 1987" in A. Malichowski, ed., *Reading Rorty* (New York: Blackwell, 1990), pp. 134–8; quotation p. 135, emphasis in original.
36 Thus he writes: "Why on earth should we expect to be able to reduce truth to something clearer or more fundamental? . . . Putnam's comparison of various attempts to characterize truth to attempts to define 'good' in naturalistic terms seems to me . . . apt," "Afterthoughts, 1987," p. 136.
37 "CTTK," pp. 308–9.
38 Davidson makes his opposition to deflationary views of truth crystal clear in "The Structure and Content of Truth," *Journal of Philosophy* (1990), pp. 279–328. His main argument against disquotationalism is that to extend the applicability of "true" to other languages (or perhaps even just other speakers), disquotationalists must rely on the notion of translation which is far more obscure than and finally explicable only in terms of the notion of truth. For his reaction to my comment on the local usefulness of a device for semantic ascent as what carries over from language to language, see p. 296, n. 35.
39 Stephen Leeds, "Theories of Reference and Truth," *Erkenntnis* (1978), quotation p. 121.
40 Hilary Putnam, *Reason Truth and History*, p. 122.

41 This argument comes from Putnam, *Realism and Reason: Philosophical Papers Volume 3* (Cambridge: Cambridge University Press, 1983), pp. xiv–xv.

42 See "Why Reason Can't Be Naturalised," esp. pp. 234ff, in *Realism and Reason*.

43 Michael Friedman, "Truth and Confirmation," *Journal of Philosophy* (1979), pp. 361–82; quotations p. 379.

44 John Pollock, *Knowledge and Justification* (Princeton: Princeton University Press, 1974), p. 28.

45 I give in to this temptation in "Coherence, Justification and Truth," *Review of Metaphysics* (1980).

46 Arthur Fine, "And Not Anti-Realism Either," *Nous* (1984), p. 54.

47 *View*, p. 68.

48 *View*, pp. 70, 71, emphasis mine.

49 *View*, p. 69.

50 *Project*, p. 66.

51 *View*, p. 70.

52 Williams himself stresses the need to "detach the notion of the absolute conception . . . from the demand for certainty" (*Project*, p. 247). However, I see no difficulty here, since the demand for a certain kind of self-understanding and the demand for epistemological foundations, though closely related in Descartes's philosophy, are not essentially connected.

53 *View*, p. 77.

54 *View*, p. 77.

55 W. V. Quine, *Word and Object* (Cambridge Mass.: Press, 1960), p. 275.

56 W. V. Quine, "Epistemology Naturalised" in *Ontological Relativity and Other Essays* (New York: Columbia University Press, 1969), quotations pp. 74, 84. Henceforth cited as "EN".

57 "EN," p. 82.

58 W. V. Quine, "The Nature of Natural Knowledge" in Samuel Guttenplan, ed., *Mind and Language* (Oxford: Oxford University Press, 1975), pp. 67–81; quotation p. 67. Further citations given by "NNK."

59 "EN," p. 72.

60 "NNK," pp. 67–8.

61 "NNK," p. 68.

62 W. V. Quine, *The Roots of Reference* (La Salle Ill.: Open Court, 1974), p. 2

63 "EN," p. 82.

64 *Significance*, ch. VI. Stroud's discussion of Quine is extremely valuable and contains virtually every critical point worth making. My emphases, however, are somewhat different and reflect my disagreement with Stroud over whether scepticism is an intuitive problem.

65 W. V. Quine, "Reply to Stroud," in *Midwest Studies in Philosophy*, vol. VI (Minneapolis: University of Minnesota Press, 1981), p. 475.

66 "NNK," p. 68.

67 *Word and Object*, p. 22.

68 "EN," p. 87.

69 "EN," p. 87.

70 "EN," p. 89.

71 "EN," p. 85.

72 "EN," pp. 82–3.
73 W. V. Quine, "Natural Kinds" in *Ontological Relativity*.
74 "Natural Kinds," p. 127.
75 "Natural Kinds," pp. 126, 128.
76 "EN," pp. 75–6.
77 "EN," p. 84.
78 The need to respond to this objection was brought home to me by Arthur Fine.
79 These remarks are adapted from my paper "Realism and Scepticism" in John Haldane and Crispin Wright, eds, *Realism and Reason* (Oxford: Oxford University Press, 1991).

## CHAPTER 7  COHERENCE AND TRUTH

1 Davidson, "CTTK," pp. 309–10; Rorty, *Philosophy and the Mirror of Nature* (Princeton: Princeton University Press, 1978), p. 178
2 *Structure*: "... disregarded ...," p. 13; "if skeptics ...," p. 15; "to give an account ...," p. 9; "to provide ...," p. 158.
3 To give just a few illustrations, Ayer thought of basic propositions as those which are known to be true by direct comparison with the (experiential) facts; C. I. Lewis wrote of the need for "expressive" judgments; and the contemporary foundationalist, John Pollock, has followed Schlick in arguing that basic propositions essentially involve "a kind of mental pointing," so that the very way in which they are formulated guarantees a strong presumption in favor of their truth. See A. J. Ayer, *The Foundations of Empirical Knowledge* (London: Macmillan, 1940); C. I. Lewis, *An Analysis of Knowledge and Valuation* (LaSalle Ill.: Open Court, 1946), ch. 7; Schlick, "Foundation," p. 225; Pollock, *Knowledge and Justification* (Princeton: Princeton University Press, 1974), p. 74
4 "CTTK," p. 310.
5 "Foundation," p. 215.
6 "Foundation," p. 215.
7 "Foundation," p. 216.
8 "Foundation," p. 215.
9 "Foundation," p. 214.
10 *Structure*, p. 96.
11 *Structure*, p. 90.
12 F. H. Bradley, *Essays on Truth and Reality* (Oxford: Oxford University Press, 1914), p. 210.
13 Wilfrid Sellars, *Science, Perception and Reality* (London: Routledge, 1963), ch. 11, section 85.
14 *Structure*, p. 90. emphasis mine. There is, however, justice in Bonjour's claim that older coherence theorists tended to ignore the distinction between a coherence theory of justification and a coherence theory of truth. Bonjour differs sharply from e.g. Blanshard in thinking that we can have the former without the latter.
15 *Thought*, p. 159.
16 *Structure*, p. 98.
17 "CTTK," p. 308.

18 "CTTK," p. 314, emphasis mine.

19 *Structure*, p. 101.

20 *The Nature of Thought*, vol. 2, p. 227.

21 Lehrer notes himself that his definitions may be consistent with a "relevant alternatives" approach to justification: see "Knowledge Reconsidered," p. 139.

22 "Knowledge Reconsidered," p. 147.

23 Ibid.

24 Discussions with Richard Manning have helped me clarify my views of Lehrer's theory.

25 Sylvain Bromberger, "Why-Questions" in Robert G. Colodny, ed., *Mind and Cosmos* (Pittsburgh: University of Pittsburgh Press, 1966). pp. 86–111.

26 *Thought*, pp. 161ff.

27 *Structure*, p. 96.

28 *Structure*, p. 141.

29 For one important expression, see Wilfrid Sellars, "Empiricism and the Philosophy of Mind", section 32 in Sellars, *Science, Perception and Reality* (London: Routledge, 1963). The position is developed more clearly and in more detail by Bonjour (*Structure*, ch. 6), who gives Sellars a generous acknowledgement.

30 *Knowledge and Justification*, p. 28.

31 Ibid.

32 This and previous quote from *Structure*, p. 91.

33 Ibid.

34 Ibid., emphasis in original.

35 Ibid.

36 Ibid.

37 In "Coherence, Justification and Truth," *Review of Metaphysics* (1980), I appeal to an undeveloped form of contextualism to dismiss scepticism rather abruptly. Bonjour is right to take me to task for this.

38 Ibid., p. 103.

39 See Paul K. Moser, "Internalism and Coherentism: a Dilemma," *Analysis* (1988), pp. 161–3.

40 Bonjour has some tendency to make this equation (e.g. *Structure*, ch. 3). This may account in part for his lack of interest in the contextualist conception of justification.

41 *Structure*, p. 103.

42 Ibid., emphasis in original.

43 Ibid., emphasis in original.

44 *Structure*, p. 147.

45 *Structure*, pp. 30–3.

46 *Structure*, p. 105.

47 He writes, "the dialectical motive for the coherence theory depends heavily on the unacceptability of the externalist position. . . . It is thus crucially important that a coherentist view itself avoid slipping into a nonfoundationalist version of externalism" (*Structure*, p. 89).

48 *Thought*, p. 161.

49 Michael Dummett, *Frege: Philosophy of Language* (London: Duckworth, 1973), pp. 626–7. A similar line can be found in Anthony Quinton, *The Nature of Things* (London: Routledge, 1973), ch. 8.

50 Hilary Putnam argues against a purely criterial conception of rationality in *Reason, Truth and History* (Cambridge: Cambridge University Press, 1981), pp. 105–13. However, Putnam is inclined to connect the criterial conception with Logical Positivism and is, perhaps in consequence, more sympathetic to coherentist epistemologies than I am.

51 *Structure*, p. 141.

52 *Structure*, p. 187.

53 "Truth and Confirmation," p. 370.

54 "Truth and Confirmation," p. 369.

55 "Truth and Confirmation," p. 371.

56 W. V. Quine, *The Roots of Reference* (La Salle, Ill.: Open Court, 1974), p. 3; quoted by Friedman, "Truth and Confirmation," p. 372.

57 Ibid.

58 Quine, "Reply to Stroud," *Midwest Studies in Philosophy*, vol. VI (1981), p. 475.

59 Bertrand Russell, *An Inquiry into Meaning and Truth* Baltimore, MD: Penguin, 1965), p. 13. Quoted by Friedman, "Truth and Confirmation," p. 371.

60 "Truth and Confirmation," p. 378.

61 Ibid.

62 Ibid., pp. 378, 379.

63 "CTTK," p. 314.

64 Ibid.

65 "Afterthougts 1987," p. 136. Though in this brief addendum Davidson expresses regret at his use of "correspondence" and "coherence" to characterize his theories of truth and knowledge, he does not, so far as I can see, amend the substance of his argument. As I noted in the previous chapter, when it comes to truth, Davidson is a primitive property theorist; and, when it comes to justification, he is a radical holist. So although I understand that Davidson wants to stress aspects of his views that he regards as distinctive, I do not myself find his use of the terms "correspondence" and "coherence" especially inappropriate.

66 "Afterthoughts 1987," p. 135.

67 "CTTK," p. 314.

68 Ibid., p. 316.

69 "CTTK," p. 316.

70 "CTTK," pp. 317–8.

71 "CTTK," p. 316. According to Rorty, "Davidson weds the Kripkean claim that causation must have *something* to do with reference to the Strawsonian claim that you figure out what someone is talking about by figuring out what object most of his beliefs are true of. The wedding is accomplished by saying that Strawson is right if construed holistically. . . . The mediating element between Strawson and Kripke is the Quinean insight that knowledge *both* of causation *and* of reference is (equally) a matter of coherence with the field linguist's own beliefs," Rorty in Lepore, *Truth and Interpretation*, p. 340. This generous gloss is at best half right. First, it misses the methodological primacy of occasion sentences in radical translation. Second, it fails to ask the crucial question of whether the field linguist's procedure can provide a model for answering the sceptic, once we have agreed that a direct answer to scepticism must be given from a first-person rather than a third-person standpoint.

72 "CTTK," p. 316.
73 "CTTK," p. 310.
74 A useful discussion of the omniscient interpreter can be found in Bruce Vermaxen, "The Intelligibility of Massive Error," *Philosophical Quarterly* (1983). The omniscient interpreter makes a brief early appearance in "The Method of Truth in Metaphysics," in P. French, T. Uehling, and H. Wettstein, eds, *Midwest Studies in Philosophy*, 2, reprinted in *Inquiries*, pp. 199–214."Verific" might be better than "omniscient," for Davidson appeals only to the truth of the interpreter's beliefs and never to their justifiabiity.
75 "CTTK," p. 317.
76 Ibid.
77 "CTTK," p. 316.
78 See Peter Klein, "Radical Interpretation adn Global Scepticism" in Lepore, ed., *Truth and Interpretation*, pp. 368–86.
79 On this point, I am much indebted to Barry Stroud.

## CHAPTER 8   THE INSTABILITY OF KNOWLEDGE

1 Alvin Goldman, "A Causal Theory of Knowing," *Journal of Philosophy* (1967); D. M. Armstrong, *Belief, Truth and Knowledge* (Cambridge: Cambridge University Press, 1973); Robert Nozick, *Philosophical Explanations* (Oxford: Oxford University Press, 1981), cited below as *Explanations*; Colin McGinn, *Concept*; Fred Dretske, *Knowledge and the Flow of Information* (Cambridge Mass.: MIT Press, 1981), cited below as *Flow*.
2 E.g. Colin McGinn, *Concept*, p. 549.
3 *OC*, 308.
4 The same goes for dreaming. I may well know that I am not dreaming when I am not, even though, when I am dreaming, I am incapable of knowing whether I am or not (perhaps because dreaming is incompatible with knowing anything).
5 *Concept*, p. 543. McGinn has in mind Nozick's argument.
6 *Concept*, p. 543.
7 *Concept*, p. 543.
8 *Concept*, p. 544.
9 *EO*, p. 1014.
10 *EO*, p. 1015.
11 *EO*, p. 1014.
12 In Dretske's later work, the issue of nonclosure does not loom so large. In fact, I am not entirely sure that he still wants to deny closure, though he does treat scepticism in roughly the same way, and continues to use the zebra example to make the point.

Dretske defines knowledge in terms of information, in the communication engineer's sense of "information":

K knows that s is F = K's belief that s is F is caused (or causally sustained by) the information that s is F, and

> A signal r carries the information that s is F = The conditional probability
> of s's being F, given r (and k) is 1 (but given k alone less than 1),

where "k" stands for "whatever the receiver already knows (if anything) about
the possibilities that exist at the source" (*Flow*, pp. 86, 65). Here Dretske defines
knowledge in terms of what he calls "*de re* informational contents," so that the
definition of knowing given above concerns "knowing of something that it is F
where the something known to be F is fixed by perceptual (noncognitive)
factors" (*Flow*, p. 86). This takes us back to knowing the coffee is boiling without
knowing that it is coffee which is boiling. As we have seen, there is no threat to
closure here, only a need to keep scope distinctions in mind.

For a signal to carry certain information, various "channel conditions" must
hold. But that the channel conditions are met is not itself something that has to
be known. These conditions have to *be* stable, not *known* to be stable. And
although a signal will not carry the information it in fact carries unless
appropriate channel conditions are met, the signal itself does not carry the
information that they are met. But sceptical hypotheses, which present various
kinds of illusion or deception, concern violations of channel conditions. So
knowing a particular fact about the world does not automatically involve
knowing that various sceptical possibilities are not realised. This connects
Dretske's new conception of knowledge with his earlier thoughts about relevant
alternatives. Thus:

> The channel is that set of existing conditions that have no relevant alternative
> states, that in fact generate no (new) information. Whether the receiver is
> ignorant of these particular conditions or not is beside the point.

According to Dretske, these considerations explain "that seemingly
paradoxical fact that a person can know that s is moving (say), and know this
by sensory means (she can see that it is moving), without knowing that her
sensory system, the mechanism by means of which she tells that it is moving, is
in satisfactory working order". As he says, "One does not have to know that
one's eyes are not paralysed in order to see that something is moving" (all
quotes *Flow*, p. 123). However, that Dretske senses something paradoxical here –
and it is hard to see what the paradox could be, if not failure of closure –
suggests that he is still in the grip of the confusions explored above. For the
examples just given are cases in which I fail to know things that are presupposed
by my knowing that an object is moving, not by what I know.

13 Robert Nozick, *Explanations*, pp. 172–178.
14 As Nozick acknowledges: see *Explanations*, p. 689.
15 E.g. *Explanations*, p. 178: "Knowledge is a particular way of being connected to
   the world, having a specific real factual connection to the world: tracking it".
16 *Explanations*. p. 179.
17 *Explanations*, p. 185.
18 *Explanations*, p. 232.
19 *Explanations*, p. 232.

20 *Explanations*, p. 233.
21 *Explanations*, p. 233.
22 *Flow*, p. 115f.
23 *Structure*, p. 37ff.
24 *Structure*, p. 41.
25 *Structure*, p. 42.
26 Gilbert Harman, *Change in View* (M. I. T. Press: Cambridge MA. 1986), chs. 4–5.
27 Bernard Williams, *Ethics and the Limits of Philosophy* (Cambridge MA: Harvard University Press 1985), p. 167.

# Index